D1596038

RECOGNIZING STATES

RECOGNIZING STATES

International Society and the Establishment of New States Since 1776

MIKULAS FABRY

OXFORD

UNIVERSITY PRESS

UNIVERSITY PRESS

Great Clarendon Street, Oxford OX2 6DP

Oxford University Press is a department of the University of Oxford.
It furthers the University's objective of excellence in research, scholarship,
and education by publishing worldwide in

Oxford New York

Auckland Cape Town Dar es Salaam Hong Kong Karachi
Kuala Lumpur Madrid Melbourne Mexico City Nairobi
New Delhi Shanghai Taipei Toronto

With offices in

Argentina Austria Brazil Chile Czech Republic France Greece
Guatemala Hungary Italy Japan Poland Portugal Singapore
South Korea Switzerland Thailand Turkey Ukraine Vietnam

Oxford is a registered trade mark of Oxford University Press
in the UK and in certain other countries

Published in the United States
by Oxford University Press Inc., New York

British Library Cataloguing in Publication Data

Data available

Library of Congress Cataloging in Publication Data

Library of Congress Control Number: 2009938557

Typeset by SPI Publisher Services, Pondicherry, India
Printed in Great Britain
on acid-free paper by
the MPG Books Group, Bodmin and King's Lynn

ISBN 978-0-19-956444-6

3 5 7 9 10 8 6 4 2

For my parents

Contents

Acknowledgments

It is with pleasure and a deep sense of gratitude that I acknowledge the support of a number of people who, in one way or another, contributed to the completion of this book. My greatest intellectual debt is to Robert Jackson and Kal Holsti who oversaw the research of what was originally a doctoral dissertation written at the University of British Columbia. It was under Kal's initial supervision of my MA thesis that I first became interested in the subject of sovereign statehood in international relations. As I worked on that project, my attention gradually focused on the issues of acquisition and criteria of statehood. I had recalled witnessing the domestic debates on these issues before the dissolution of the country of my birth, Czechoslovakia, as well as following the international debates on recognition of new countries in the Balkans. Both episodes had left me with many unanswered questions, and Kal and Bob agreed that it would be worthwhile to probe them in a doctoral study. I was tremendously fortunate to have Bob supervise that study and Kal, despite his official retirement by then, serve as the "second-in-command."

Not only has their influence on my thinking about the questions animating this book as well as international relations more broadly been profound and is readily discernible in what follows, but both have also been serving as mentors and models of scholarly integrity and humility.

This study has also benefited greatly from early e-mail exchanges with Alan James and from discussions with Mark Zacher who pressed me to sharpen the structure and clarity of its arguments. I am grateful to Brian Job, David Long, Lee Seymour, Ian Townsend-Gault, and three reviewers for Oxford University Press who provided me with very helpful comments and suggestions on the various versions of the manuscript. I am also thankful for electronic and face-to-face conversations with David Armitage, Will Bain, Mlada Bukovansky, Molly Cochran, David Hendrickson, Jacques Hymans, Eddie Keene, Jean Laponce, Sam Laselva, John Owen, Sasha Pavkovic, Dick Price, Brad Roth, and David Schaefer, which were sources of learning and intellectual stimulation.

I have been fortunate to find myself in warm and hospitable environments during different phases of this project. I want to thank Brian Job for inviting me to join the University of British Columbia's Centre of International Relations and for supporting my activities there in numerous ways. Mark Zacher, its academic director, was, and has remained, a source of invaluable guidance and encouragement. For their support during my postdoctoral fellowship at Smith College, I thank my former colleagues in the department of government, especially Martha Ackelsberg, Don Baumer, Mlada Bukovansky, Pat Coby, Donna Divine, Howard Gold, Jacques Hymans, and Greg White. Finally, I was heartened by the cordial welcome I received from my department chair Bill Long and colleagues in the Sam Nunn School of International Affairs at the Georgia Institute of Technology, where I completed the book.

Over the course of research for this study, I received financial support from several sources. I would like to acknowledge with deep gratitude monetary assistance from the University of British Columbia's Faculty of Graduate Studies, the Killam Trust, the Social Sciences and Humanities Research Council of Canada, the Andrew W. Mellon Foundation, and Sibyl von der Schulenburg.

Parts of Chapter 6 appeared in *Global Society* (2002) and fragments from different chapters appeared in Aleksandar Pavkovic and Peter Radan (eds.), *On the Way to Statehood: Secession and Globalization* (2008). I thank the publishers of these publications, Taylor & Francis and Ashgate, for their permission to use them in this book.

Finally, I would like to thank my friends and family for their steadfast support. My brother Martin had the unique ability to cheer me up in any moment of adversity or frustration. My wife Kendra provided me with unwavering affection, patience, and support, including in the form of proofreading assistance. Above all, I would like to thank my parents, Tomas and Katarina. I could count on their unconditional love and help at all times and through any difficulty. It is to them that I dedicate this book.

M.F.
Atlanta, Georgia
October 2009

List of Tables

List of Abbreviations

CFE	Conventional Forces in Europe Treaty
CIS	Commonwealth of Independent States
CSCE	Conference for Security and Cooperation in Europe
EC	European Community
FRY	Federal Republic of Yugoslavia
FYROM	Former Yugoslav Republic of Macedonia
ICFY	International Conference for the Former Yugoslavia
IR	International Relations
JNA	Yugoslav People's Army
OAU	Organization of African Unity
PIC	Peace Implementation Council
SFRY	Socialist Federal Republic of Yugoslavia
UN	United Nations

Introduction

To recognize the independence of a new state, and so favor, possibly determine its admission into the family of nations, is the highest possible exercise of sovereign power, because it affects in any case the welfare of two nations and often the peace of the world.

(US Secretary of State William Seward in 1861[1])

We ought not to acknowledge the separate and independent existence of any [state], which is so doubtfully established, that the mere effect of that acknowledgment shall be to mix parties again in internal squabbles, if not in open hostilities.

(British Foreign Secretary George Canning in 1824[2])

On April 7, 1992, the United States and all twelve countries of the European Community (EC) extended recognition to the Republic of Bosnia and Herzegovina. While the EC communiqué did not provide reasons for the decision, the US statement did note that "the requisite criteria for recognition" had been met and that "the will of citizens of [Bosnia and Herzegovina] for sovereignty" had been expressed peacefully and democratically.[3] As many diplomats and observers had feared, the new state descended almost instantly into a ghastly war. That war involved principally Bosnia's citizens, and was fought over the purportedly decided matter of their will to constitute a sovereign state. By far the most serious armed confrontation in Europe since the end of World War II, the 1992–5 conflict ended with the arrival of international administration and the stationing of foreign troops throughout the republic. Ever since, their main task has been to protect the Bosnians from each other.

Given the progression of events, there appears little doubt that it was the EC and US recognition that precipitated the onset of the Bosnian war. This is not to say either that this act was the sole, or the most important, cause of this conflict or that without it there would have been no violence. However, the facts of the case are rather compelling to bear out the contention that recognition was the tipping event. There had been grave tensions in Bosnia since the passing of the controversial memorandum on sovereignty in the Sarajevo parliament in October 1991. Following the fiercely disputed referendum on independence in March 1992, these tensions had intensified, resulting in sporadic violent incidents. Nevertheless, the general hostilities erupted only on the heels of the coordinated EC and US decision.

How could a public pronouncement recognizing a new state have these weighty effects? What did this act mean and in what sense was it significant? Those engaged in the scholarly study of international law and politics do not provide ready answers. The prevalent contemporary view among international lawyers, who dominate academic study of the subject, discounts the significance of recognition.[4] The so-called declaratory theory holds that once a political community satisfies certain substantive criteria, often referred to as the classical or Montevideo criteria,[5] it becomes a state regardless of its recognition, or lack thereof, by other states. Recognition does not affect statehood as such or a state's international rights and obligations. It is a formality of very specific kind: a prerequisite for establishing diplomatic ties. Thus, to take the case of Bosnia, the act expressed willingness of countries around the world to engage in standard state-to-state dealings with the new country. Politically, the upgrade of relations with the world might have been of considerable symbolic value, but this did not have any bearing on Bosnia's already established standing as a sovereign state.

Some legal scholars dispute this account by arguing that foreign recognition is necessary for a state's sovereign status internationally – the subject has been debated in the international law literature for decades. Students of international relations (IR), on the other hand, commonly regard recognition as a somewhat arid, even tedious, topic that is better left outside of their academic departments. Despite its reputation as one of the most politicized and challenging phenomena in international law,[6] they have neither thought of it in broader theoretical terms nor inquired whether it may be an important institution in its own right.[7] The roots of this reluctance are likely to be found in the character of major questions guiding the dominant modes of IR theorizing. Generally speaking, discussions of interstate relations within and between classical realists, classical liberals, neorealists, neoliberal institutionalists, or historical sociologists take as a given, rather than problematize, the basic political–juridical attributes of modern statehood. For Machiavelli, Bodin, Hobbes, Locke, Spinoza, Montesquieu, Saint-Pierre, Rousseau, Hume, Kant, Bentham, Hegel, Austin, Weber, Morgenthau, Carr, Aron, Tilly, Waltz, Keohane, or Krasner, to mention some of the most eminent names linked to these schools of thought, states are self-constituted and self-contained bodies. They are assumed to exist because they have been able to perpetuate functioning government and domestic order. New states are no exception: they come into being because they have been capable of establishing structures of authority backed by a coercive apparatus of power. That power is what is ultimately able to fend off internal and external challenges to state authority. Foreign states can play a crucial role in maintaining a state's existence: for example, by way of alliances or collective security arrangements. They can be of critical import even in launching new states. Machiavelli's *The Prince* (1513), arguably the greatest book on state formation in the annals of political philosophy, contains a chapter on how to found a state by making use of the arms of others, including other principalities.[8] However, these eventualities are contingent to, not constitutive of, statehood.[9]

Scholars working in the international society or English School tradition agree on the subject of established states but are split as far as new states are concerned. Yet, this divergence has not really been explored or articulated. States are conceptualized by all to form an international society since they acknowledge "certain common interests and . . . some common values, they regard themselves as bound by certain rules in their dealings with one another, such as that they should respect one another's claims to independence, that they should honor agreements into which they enter, and that they should be subject to certain limitations in exercising force against one another."[10] For Grotius, Pufendorf, Wolff, Vattel, and everyone else, mutual recognition of independence lies at the core of international society.[11]

Differences emerge, though, on how new states acquire sovereignty. Writers such as Charles Manning and Alan James[12] continue the argument of early modern publicists, albeit without grounding it in natural law.[13] They contend that states exist ontologically prior to international society. States and their mutual recognition constitute a society of states but that society is not constitutive of its new members. These authors too hold that the modern state is a self-made and self-enclosed public authority. In the words of James, "the observation that a state is sovereign is one about the standing of the state in the eyes of its own constitutional law."[14] As such, "state sovereignty is a factual matter . . . it cannot, once obtained, be affected by anything which is said by outsiders."[15] Recognition is necessary for the establishment of diplomatic relations and, more generally, normal intercourse between states, but "recognition presupposes a state's existence; it does not create it."[16] "The recognition of a state indicates that the entity concerned possesses the characteristics of sovereign statehood, and hence exists as such, rather than helps to bring it into existence."[17]

Others implicitly dissent from this line of reasoning. Martin Wight introduces the concept of international legitimacy by which he means "collective judgment of international society about rightful membership of the family of nations; how sovereignty may be transferred; and how state succession is to be regulated, when large states break into smaller, or several states combine into one." He adds that "the branch of international law that is concerned with legitimacy . . . is the law concerning the recognition of states. This seeks to lay down principles to guide existing states in the matter of recognizing a new community as fulfilling the conditions of statehood and qualifying for membership of the society of nations."[18] If there is indeed such a thing as "rightful membership in the family of nations" and if other states may and do determine this membership or "transfer of sovereignty," then it cannot be said that sovereignty is merely a question for individual states themselves, or that new states are entirely self-constituted. The existing states have a definite constitutive and prescriptive role in the birth of new sovereign states.

In contrast to Manning and James, Wight's notion of international legitimacy implies that at some historical juncture – the moment the plurality of self-constituted states came to acknowledge each other's independence and to conduct their relations on a basis of shared law – the society of states came to exist ontologically prior to any new state. From that point in time on, political communities wishing to participate as formal equals in the workings of this society's law and institutions had to pass through external identification as "states."[19] The collectivity of states henceforth evolved "not as an aggregate of separate communities but itself a community: a community of communities tied together by its constitutive practices, including those defining the attributes of statehood."[20] In this community of communities, sovereign statehood itself developed into a status "defined by international law, not independent of it."[21] Wight's concept suggests that unlike Machiavelli's prince-founder, prospective sovereigns within the society of states cannot be solely "prophets armed." The creation of effective structures of power and domestic authority, as vital as that may be, is not enough. Seducing *Fortuna*, the higher force capable of improving one's odds of success in that effort, can accomplish only so much. Since sovereignty is "rationed and regulated by those who currently enjoy it,"[22] aspiring founders must entice existing states into formal acceptance. By suggesting that ideas and rules concerning rightful political authority are pervasive internationally, Wight's concept also presupposes that, contrary to postulates of realist theory, international relations take place within embedded normative structures.

Objectives and Approach of the Book

The purpose of this book is to offer an analytical and normative account of the practice of recognizing new states by building on the approach of the latter international society tradition. That the subject of new states is relevant at present can hardly be doubted. On top of long-standing cases, such as that of the Palestinians, the last twenty years have witnessed new or lingering demands for statehood in Central and Southeastern Europe, the former Soviet Union, the Horn of Africa, South and Southeast Asia, and the South Pacific, and some of them have turned into conflicts with major regional or international dimensions. The claims of some, like those of Bosnia and Herzegovina, Eritrea, Croatia, Moldova, Georgia and East Timor, have achieved general recognition; those of others, like Kosovo, Krajina, Bougainville, Abkhazia, Tamil Eelam, and Somaliland, have not.

The central question and point of contention in all these cases has been, who qualifies as a sovereign, independent state? Despite its seminal importance in contemporary world affairs, the issue of the norms or criteria of acknowledging new states has attracted little sustained attention even among international lawyers.[23] The declaratory theory has remained the dominant mode of conceiving recognition despite the fact that Bosnia and Herzegovina, Croatia, Azerbaijan, Georgia, or Moldova, similarly to a number of ex-colonies in the 1960s and the 1970s, have plainly not met the criteria postulated by the theory or to have been considered as states by international society prior to their recognition.

Furthermore, entities such as the "Republic of Somaliland" have met these criteria but are not deemed states in terms of international law. While, in light of recent cases, voices critical of this theory have been raised[24] – among them those holding the constitutive view – none have put forward an in-depth re-evaluation of the accrued thinking about recognition.

Indeed, one may wonder whether drawn-out legal debates that have tended to revolve around recognition theory have not come at the expense of concert-ed, systematic focus on recognition practice. There are certainly international lawyers who take this view. Ian Brownlie wrote more than twenty-five years ago that "there is no doubt room for a whole treatise on the harm caused to the business of legal investigation by theory. In the case of 'recognition' theory has not only failed to enhance the subject but has created a *tertium quid* which stands, like a bank of fog on a still day, between the observer and the contours of the ground which calls for investigation."[25] A book-long study of state recognition published recently opens with an observation that Brownlie's "desperation... has proven prescient. The fog has not lifted but in fact has thickened."[26] Moreover, it concludes by asserting that "the old doctrinal debate" between proponents of the declaratory and constitutive theories has become "less and less illuminating, if ever it illuminated much at all."[27] Brownlie explained the disconnect between theory and practice by suggesting that the theories "have assumed a 'theological' role as a body of thought with its own validity which tends to distract the student, and to play the role of master rather than servant."[28] The view that the legal theories, by serving as the exclusive prism through which the recognition practice is studied, have become detached from state conduct and acquired a life of their own, is also found in some older works. Writing more than four decades ago, William O'Brien and Ulf Goebel took it as a consequence of persistent intrusion into scholarly analyses of *a priori* notions about of what recognition ought to be. "International law authorities have rendered a most elusive subject even more complex by imposing their own unsubstantiated theories on a record of practice that is murky enough already and that often becomes further distorted by subjective analyses."[29] Both Brownlie and O'Brien along with Goebel called for practice to be the starting and focal point in academic analyses.[30]

This book is such a study of practice. While it takes full account of legal scholarship and has an obvious point of convergence with constitutive theorists in sharing the basic premise that if a new state entered automatically into the membership of family of nations then the function of recognition would be superfluous,[31] this inquiry does not delve into the doctrinal controversies be-tween the declaratory and constitutive schools. Considering that the practice of recognition is not purely formal,[32] I seek to make sense of it not by passing it through a filter of *a priori* theories but rather by understanding it on its own historical terms. Since international responses to claims of statehood cannot be divorced either from international law or international politics, this understand-ing lies not only in the analysis of legal rules but also the normative sources of those rules; and by taking account of not only legal concerns and consequences but also of political concerns and consequences. Statespersons who are responsible for recognizing particular states have always operated in the entire context of that international practice. Scholars who are interested in understanding the subject have little choice but to take a similar approach if they hope to provide an accurate and comprehensive picture of it. Thus, while the prime focus is on the norms or criteria for acknowledging new states, this inquiry also examines other considerations important to statespersons, such as timing, strategic use of, or conditions attached to, recognition decisions.

This book employs, as do most international society scholars, the classical interpretive approach that draws comprehensively on law, philosophy, and history.[33] Integrative and holistic in character, this approach rejects excessive compartmentalization of international relations into different subject areas as artificial. To see international politics, ethics, security, history, or law as essentially separate from each other is to be misled. From this perspective, the study can be seen as very sympathetic to recent calls for bringing the disciplines of international relations and international law[34] closer, as well as for paying increased attention to history in IR scholarship.[35]

An inquiry into any practice cannot do without at least some discussion of its past. In the case of recognition, history looms large. James Baker, the US secretary of state at the time of Bosnian recognition, could have spoken the words of his predecessor William Seward at the beginning of this chapter, and, despite their rhetorical flair, they would have rung true. Seward uttered them early into the US Civil War while trying to avert Franco-British recognition of the "Confederate States of America," which, he feared, would leave his government with no choice but to wage war against three enemies at the same time. The gulf of 130 years did not remove the possibility that an act of recognition may set off a large-scale armed conflict. Likewise, Douglas Hurd, the British foreign secretary in early 1992, could have evoked George Canning's assertion, uttered in response to the lobbying of British merchants for recognizing the nascent Latin American states in order to regularize mutual commercial relations, and the words would have been understood by all. International responses to claims of statehood have a long past, and dilemmas and controversies surrounding them disclose a remarkable degree of continuity and durability. Taken as a whole, however, the scholarly treatment of these responses is fragmented; this is particularly true of the period prior to the twentieth century. This book seeks a comprehensive grasp of state recognition by close contextual examination of most of its major episodes. It does so not out of faith that history stores readily discernible "lessons" for contending with, or "solutions" to, contemporary problems. Rather, the book hopes that we may learn something about the possibilities and limits of international politics and law from investigating past cases which shared at least some key aspects with the present ones. The expectation is that in thus understanding the practice as a whole, we will acquire an enhanced, critical appreciation of its current direction.

Recognizing New States: General Findings

What is the place of state recognition in world politics? Recognition is an indispensable precondition for a political community's status as a sovereign state in international relations and law. Although the determination to achieve it ordinarily arises from within a political community – by virtue of assertion of its constitutional independence – a state cannot be said to be independent simply on the basis of its domestic constitution. There is no guarantee that its assertion will be accepted and respected by existing states. Sovereignty, just like state borders,[36] has developed into both a national and international category: it simultaneously pertains to the state and to the society of states. Domestic constitutional law delineates the former, public international law the latter. The nexus linking the "inside" (or the internal aspect of sovereignty) with the "outside" (its external aspect) is recognition. State recognition is thus a constitutive, foundational practice of modern international society.

Sovereignty in international law is achieved when the already sovereign countries generally acknowledge a claimant to have international legal personality with sovereign rights and duties. This is to deny neither that unrecognized entities have existed throughout the modern states system nor that they have been commonly treated by the existing states as having some legal capacity. But it is to argue that they have not had sovereign status internationally and have thus not been full and equal members of the society of states.

Non-recognized existence has historically led to a range of adverse consequences. It has always been precarious and often lethal. One of the relatively milder upshots is the humiliation non-recognized entities have to bear by having their official name – official, that is, only in terms of their own constitutional law – commonly placed in quotation marks abroad. The use of quotation marks differentiates those who merely self-proclaimed to be sovereign, and thus from the perspective of foreign authorities feign statehood, from those who in the same eyes have actually been accepted as sovereign. A much more substantial effect is the inability to carry out normal diplomatic and economic relations, to join international organizations, and to sign international treaties and agreements. The most serious consequence of non-recognition, as will be seen, is that those who find themselves in this position are legally exposed to being forcibly displaced from the territory they claim and control by the state actually recognized as sovereign in that territory. In the case of recognized countries enjoying the full protection of international law, in contrast, successful external takeovers have been a rarity, and even then the enduring claim that these states' sovereignty was unjustly and illegally extinguished served in a few cases, such as Lithuania, Latvia, and Estonia in 1991, as a key justification for their later restoration.

The first thing to note about an act of state recognition is that it is no different in its structure from, say, an act of employing military force or an act of imposing economic sanctions or an act of expelling a foreign diplomat. Each is a single act with both legal and political aspects. Each is constrained by legal or quasi-legal norms that delineate permissible circumstances under which it can be undertaken, and molded by political, discretionary factors that decide its actual execution once those permissible circumstances have been deemed to be met. Although their actual decisions have been commonly affected by political factors such as national interests, pressures from domestic constituencies, or shared interstate interests, members of international society have nevertheless generally understood recognition of a new state to be an activity regulated by binding norms that are independent from, and logically precede, those factors. This has been the case even in situations where differences arose over which particular norms applied.

Second, recognition of new states, not unlike a whole array of other law-governed practices in a world without international government, has been characterized by decentralization. It is ultimately up to each state's executive branch to decide whether the circumstances postulated by the norms have been satisfied and to take into account pertinent political considerations. There have been multiple instances of joint and coordinated recognition or non-recognition, including decisions of international organizations such as the League of Nations and the United Nations binding on its members. Admission to the United Nations has certainly served as evidence of widespread recognition of particular entities as states. However, recognition as such remains a prerogative of each existing state.

The location of recognition authority at the state level could potentially lead to myriad disparate decisions, but, in reality, such messy outcomes have been relatively uncommon. The third general observation one can make is that state recognition has been a practice led and shaped by major powers, especially the great powers.[37] From the very beginning, claims of statehood have had a propensity to enmesh themselves with questions of wider international order, and questions of international order in turn have been a special preserve of the great powers.[38] Recognition by the great powers has normally preceded, and carried far more weight than, recognition by other states. Indeed, the latter have normally looked to the former for direction; where they did not, their expeditiousness was likely of little import.[39] In general, where the decisions of major powers would make up a "critical mass" – that is, no significant differences over acknowledgment of a particular state or group of states would arise among them – the smaller powers would follow with their recognition in a "snowball effect."[40] On the other hand, the bigger the incongruence among major powers over recognition norms either in general or in particular cases, the greater is the precariousness of recognition practice. The greatest volatility arose during great power wars, especially the Napoleonic Wars and World Wars I and II, paralleling the much broader volatility of the rule of international law. For all these reasons, this book, not unlike other studies of the subject, concentrates primarily on major powers.

Fourth, the practice has encompassed two analytically distinct categories of requests for recognition as a "new state." These categories reflect two sets of circumstances under which such requests have been put forward: following *externally* and *internally* effected changes to existing statehood. Entities formed as a direct consequence of the threat or use of force by an external power across international boundaries, usually referred to as "satellite" or "puppet" states, fall under the first category. The second and far more voluminous group consists of political communities established indigenously within those boundaries through secession from a state, state dissolution, merger of two or more states, or decolonization.

Fifth, for the last 200 years, recognition of new states has been tied to the idea of self-determination of peoples. In fact, recognition and self-determination have been, this study argues, two sides of the same coin. This differs markedly from the conventional view that self-determination, while having influenced the American and French Revolutions, had a substantial impact the practice of state recognition only following the end of World War I. State recognition can be said to have (*a*) emerged over two centuries ago as a full-fledged practice in response to the idea of self-determination of peoples and (*b*) altered with changes in its understanding that occurred since that time. The introduction now turns to this link in more detail.

Recognizing New States and Self-Determination of Peoples

Self-determination of peoples is a liberal idea of international justice that emerged in the second half of the eighteenth century. It was rooted in the proposition that a group of people sharing certain distinct social bonds vis-à-vis other groups of people has a right to establish, whether within or outside of the borders of the country in which it finds itself, alone or in union with other peoples, its own government. It was based on the classic liberal premise that adult human beings, as creatures capable of rational thought and action, are in the best position to know how to arrange their individual and collective lives.

The idea made its first institutionalized appearance in international relations in the early nineteenth century through the practice of recognizing *de facto* states. A *de facto* state, according to Canning, has "shown itself substantially capable of maintaining an independent existence, of carrying on a government of its own, of controlling its own military . . . forces, and of being responsible to other nations for the observance of international laws and the discharge of international duties."[41] Influenced by the Grotian natural law tradition – which held that each actually independent entity was naturally entitled to peaceful relations with all other independent entities – and tracing its historical genealogy to a small number of precedents, the practice of recognizing *de facto* states received a definite shape and a liberal normative grounding in the course of unilateral secessions in Latin America in the late 1810s and early 1820s. Crafted by British and American foreign policymakers, the practice was a product of their momentous political confrontation with the Holy Alliance and its solidarist conception of international society.[42] According to that conception, the states system rested on kinship among European kings whose right to rule stemmed from hereditary possession of thrones originally bestowed by God. The essence of that system was collective responsibility for dynastic and territorial integrity of all monarchies. The only acceptable method of transferring sovereignty or territory was by the freely given consent of the legitimate crown. Facts established otherwise could not nullify existing rights: illegitimate change was to remain unrecognized until the injured sovereign or fellow legitimate rulers intervening on his or her behalf could overturn it.

In contrast, the British and American founders of the *de facto* recognition doctrine espoused a pluralistic conception of international society with a fundamental division between the international and domestic spheres and foreign non-intervention into the latter. At its heart lay the belief that the state's right to rule derives from popular consent rather than divine will. Unless directly harmed, third parties had a general obligation to refrain from coercive interference into the domestic affairs of foreign countries because the right to determine their political destiny belonged to their peoples. As conscious believers in the respective legacies of the Glorious and American Revolutions, early-nineteenth-century British and American statespersons believed that this right to self-determination included a right to renounce the sovereignty and government under which one lived.

In international terms, that is, in terms of the relationship between a political community and international society, the right of self-determination was conceived of as a *negative* right. Negative rights are claims "to secured space in which subjects might pursue their own concerns without interference." In contrast, positive rights are claims "that the space be filled with something."[43] Whereas negative rights oblige those against whom they are held to refrain from intrusion (e.g., the right to free speech), positive rights establish for their holders entitlements to the provision of prerequisites for a meaningful life (e.g., the right to elementary education).[44] A negative right of self-determination required that outsiders desist from forcibly intervening in the self-determination process. It was, in Michael Walzer's words, "the right of a people 'to become free by their own efforts' if they can, and non-intervention [was] the principle guaranteeing that their success will not be impeded or their failure prevented by the intrusion of an alien power."[45]

Along with classical liberal thinkers such as Immanuel Kant and J. S. Mill, British and American foreign policymakers opposed coercive intervention that would turn wishes of foreign peoples into reality, no matter how much sympathy those claims might have engendered. They defended that opposition with a mixture of prudential, legal, and moral arguments. Nonetheless, as Walzer implies, the requirement that third parties abstain from intervening in the self-determination process also demanded that they respect the self-determined outcome. While in the case of a conflict over sovereignty, foreign states were obligated to respect the territorial integrity of the affected country, there was a limit to this obligation: the patent inability of the country to maintain its territorial integrity from within as demonstrated by the founding and continued empirical existence of a new independent state. The existing right was then invalidated by this self-determined fact.

A collectivity that had achieved sovereignty in observable fact was entitled to acknowledgment of this sovereignty in law due to its decisive normative meaning: the formation of a stable, effective state entity in which the population habitually obeyed the new rulers was taken as an authoritative expression of the will of the people to constitute an independent state. In the absence of international agreement as to what constitutes a valid method of verifying popular will, any foreign assessment thereof was necessarily presumptive:[46] it was grounded in the assumption that neither the *de facto* state's establishment nor its ongoing existence could come to pass without at least tacit approval by its inhabitants. It was this inference of popular consent – and its normative trumping of the idea of dynastic consent – that in British and American eyes converted the fact of new independent states into the right to independence and external recognition.

Gradually adopted by other states, this norm displaced dynastic legitimism. It was the defining consideration not only in response to unilateral secessions – in the Americas and Europe – but also to other types of internally generated changes to existing statehood, such as the merger of several states into a Kingdom of Italy (1859–61), the dissolution of Austria-Hungary (1918), or the decolonization of Iraq (1932). Moreover, it proved to be workable in a wide range of contexts, not excluding those where a coercive intervention took place to defend rights of third parties, as in the case of secessions of Belgium (1830/1) and Greece (1821–32).[47]

The American and British founders of the policy of recognition of *de facto* statehood were not only against the sort of interventionism defended by most continental monarchies, but also against the kind exhibited during the French revolutionary years. France's armed mission to foment or aid revolutions abroad after the collapse of the monarchy in 1792 metamorphosed into forcible annexation of foreign territories and carving of satellite entities wholly dependent on French power for their survival. The belief that the right to replace sovereignty was internal to the group asserting it led the American and British statesmen to reject annexation or partition of existing states by offensive *external* force just as they rejected foreign intervention to preclude new states from being erected by *internal* efforts. They were at least partly in accord with the other major powers, since at the Congress of Vienna (1815) all of them had supported delegitimization of unilateral conquests among sovereign states. The Vienna consensus proved extremely hard to uphold in the long run, particularly between 1856 and 1914: the more the concert of the great powers weakened, the harder it was to forestall such conquests. The Paris Peace Conference (1919) and the founding conference of the United Nations (UN) in San Francisco (1945) nevertheless went much further than the Congress of Vienna as the League of Nations Covenant abolished, and the UN Charter reaffirmed the demise of, the right of conquest as such. The obligation of non-recognition of forcible territorial changes across international boundaries, including those leading to proclamation of a new state – pronounced by the United States and the League of Nations in the Stimson Doctrine (1932) – became an indispensable part of this development.

However, while non-recognition of entities created in the aftermath of the external use of force became firmly entrenched in international law after 1945, the post-World War II period saw the abandonment of *de facto* statehood as the standard for recognition of indigenously founded new states. Since the 1950s, the determining factor in admission of new members into the society of states has been whether an entity has a prior right to independence, rather than whether it is independent. Actual conduct of states, if not always their rhetoric, suggests that the tenets that factual establishment of an independent state entitles one to foreign acknowledgment as well as its flipside – that falling short of it excludes one from such acknowledgment – have been largely discarded.

This change followed a shift in the understanding of self-determination from a negative to *positive* international right. According to this conception pioneered by US President Wilson in 1917/18, a people's right to determine their political future imposed an active obligation on international society to help bring it about. In marked contrast to the earlier negative right conception of self-determination, which prescribed no more than non-intervention in foreign self-determination endeavors of self-defined peoples and recognition of their successful conclusions, Wilson's progressive conception demanded that outsiders identify: (*a*) the peoples who qualify for the right of self-determination; (*b*) the correct procedure for assessing their will to be independent; and (*c*) the exact scope of positive international obligations owed to them. That presented arduous, if not insurmountable, operational difficulties which became apparent to some participants and observers even before the Paris Peace Conference convened in 1919. Three central questions had no obvious general answers and were contested in nearly all specific instances. Which peoples qualify for the right of self-determination? By what method is their will to be ascertained? How can existing states ensure the fulfillment of self-determination claims if claimant peoples are not actually in possession of what they claim? Conference participants, even Wilson, came to appreciate, however, that if the mere voicing of claims gave groups positive entitlement, and if outsiders would be bound to intervene to effect such claims, there would be no limit to state fragmentation and international disorder. The interwar period, and most gravely Nazi activities in the name of self-determination of ethnic Germans beyond Germany, reinforced this sentiment dramatically.

Yet, despite all the skepticism about self-determination as a positive claim against international society accumulated between 1919 and 1945, the Wilsonian conceptualization remained intellectually predominant. In fact, it only reached its apex in the period of universal decolonization that occurred in the decades following World War II. Reflecting the global normative consensus that developed in the course of the 1950s that colonial domination was no longer tolerable, international society defined, for the first time, specific peoples who were deemed to be entitled to state sovereignty—the populations who dwelt within the inherited boundaries of non-self-governing and trust territories. The key to their foreign recognition was not their attainment of *de facto* statehood but rather prior international acceptance of their asserted right to independence. This right required colonial powers to withdraw and third parties to facilitate the emergence of a new state in their place as soon as colonial peoples voiced, by virtually any means, their desire for independence. While in its most important political and legal documents decolonization was explicitly premised on the tenet that all peoples had a right to self-determination, it was again evident, just as in 1919, that self-determination could not be a universal positive right. The identification of the peoples eligible for independence inevitably entailed some corresponding notion of ineligibility. Whereas the grounds for limiting recognition of claims of statehood was evident in the past – the pool of peoples *capable* of establishing independence had always been smaller than the number of peoples *wishing* to have it – that grounds was not immediately evident now as the main self-determination texts left the "peoples" bearing the right undefined. The decolonization and post-colonial recognition practice clarified what the documents left obscure. The legitimate candidates for recognition have been restricted to colonial territories whose right to independence was blocked, violated, or not yet realized; to constituent units of dissolved states; and to seceding entities that received the consent of their parent states. Unilateral secession, which gave rise to recognition of *de facto* statehood, became illegitimate. As will be seen in Chapter 6, even the latest and still unsettled cases of recognition of Kosovo by roughly one-third of UN member states and of Abkhazia and South Ossetia by Russia, Nicaragua, and Venezuela have not changed this basic picture.

The development of self-determination as a positive international right, however, has not led to a disappearance of claims of statehood that stand outside of its confines. Groups that are deeply dissatisfied with their subordinate status within the recognized states in which they presently find themselves continue to make demands for independence – just as they had done since the late eighteenth century – in disregard of the fact that they may not have any positive entitlement to it. If the American Revolution, in Wight's words, opened the floodgates,[48] then those floodgates remain open. Whether existing states like it or not, demands for independence still generate various crises around the globe, including the aforementioned armed conflicts in the Balkans, the Caucasus, Eastern Africa, South and Southeast Asia, and the South Pacific.[49]

Is the contemporary practice of recognition of new states hence, in view of these facts, sustainable? This study concludes that it is not, for two major reasons. First, since self-determination cannot for obvious practical reasons be a universal positive right, its necessarily selective application is paradoxically bound to result in the denial of popular will. Those peoples who beyond any reasonable doubt have relinquished loyalty to a particular state are nevertheless obliged to remain part of that state – such as the various peoples of Bosnia, Georgia, and numerous ex-colonies. This includes peoples who have actually managed to form and for years maintain their own state-like body – such as the people of Somaliland. Second, unqualified insistence on the positive right of self-determination is bound to undermine the fundamental reason for sovereignty: self-government. States whose governments are not able to thwart secessions yet do not consent to loss of any of their territory are destined to endure permanently unsettled conflict (e.g. Georgia) or to require massive and long-lasting foreign involvement to keep them together (e.g. Bosnia). The latter will require some coercive intervention against breakaway parties and may well not do without international administrative arrangements that hark back to the paternalism of colonialism.

If post-colonial international society is to remain a community of sovereign states properly so-called – that is authorities that are supreme in relation to all other authorities in the same territorial jurisdiction, and that are independent of all foreign authorities[50] – then it is doubtful that there is any sustainable basis for recognizing states other than the one suggested by the nineteenth-century Anglo-American doctrine, namely *de facto* statehood. Our world may be different in countless ways from the one 200 years ago, but it is the same in at least one major respect: the persistent lack of agreement among parties affected by bids for independence as to who may become independent, or by which self-determination procedure. While not without its own limitations and problems, the practice of recognizing *de facto* statehood does have the decisive advantage of resting on a workable formula that seeks equilibrium between rights and interests of all parties concerned, that is, claimants of statehood, existing states against which such claims are made, and third parties in international society.

International Society Scholarship on Recognizing States

I have indicated which school of thought this book hopes to cultivate, but not yet on what scholarship it will elaborate. The international society scholarship that considers state recognition is relatively small. Martin Wight's work on international legitimacy, though very erudite and suggestive, was only a twenty-page paper,[51] which could understandably not deal with all the complexities behind the shifts in international recognition norms. James Mayall's volume on nationalism and international society devotes only a bit more space to the shifts – a major part of his book is devoted to the role of economic, as opposed to political, nationalism.[52]

Whereas a general picture of changes in international legitimacy can be constructed out of these and several other essay-length treatments,[53] detailed empirical studies of recognition as an institutionalized practice are scarce. Out of those, the period of decolonization has unquestionably received most attention. Robert Jackson's work examines the normative and other aspects behind recognition of former dependencies after 1945 and demonstrates that the key to establishing new countries in Africa, Asia, Oceania, and the Caribbean was the mounting illegitimacy of colonial rule and the rapidly growing belief that the right of self-determination must apply to every dependency.[54] The substantive coherence of prospective states, hitherto an essential factor in recognition, played virtually no role, with disastrous consequences for many of them. Still, Jackson shows that no matter how bad the internal conditions in these fragile states might have been, all of them, without exception, survived, not least thanks to their sovereign rights in international law. In a number of cases this was accomplished by non-recognition of secessionist would-be states, even if those had managed to become substantially effective realities.[55]

Other periods received less attention.[56] The beginnings of the idea of self-determination of peoples as a factor in recognition decisions during the nine-teenth century are particularly unexplored and shrouded in mystery. Wight's essay, for example, jumps from the founding of the United States virtually directly to the end of World War I. Though the international society tradition is, just as the larger IR discipline, routinely accused of Eurocentrism, its research has focused primarily on recognition and admission into international society of non-European states,[57] not those of Europe or the Americas.[58] Consider this brief comment on international legitimacy in Hedley Bull's most elaborate study of the society of states. Using Wight's definition of the term, he wrote:

> Before the American and French Revolutions...states were, for the most part, hereditary monarchies.... After the American and French Revolutions the prevailing principle of international legitimacy ceased to be dynastic and became national or popular: that is to say, it came to be generally held that questions of this sort should be settled not by reference to the rights of rulers, but by reference to the rights of the nation or the people. The dynastic marriage, as the means whereby acquisition of territory was made interna-tionally respectable, gave place to the plebiscite; the patrimonial principle to the principle of national self-determination. The actual course of events was no more determined by the national or popular doctrine of international legitimacy than in the earlier period it had been determined by the dynastical or monarchical one, but these doctrines did determine the kind of justifica-tions that could be offered for whatever was done.[59]

If the justifications given did not correspond to the actual reasons for recognition of numerous new states in Europe and the Americas, what did in fact determine their admission into the society of states? And if the actual reasons were indeed different from the stated ones, why did those in charge of foreign policy gradually go to greater and greater lengths to devise the latter? Can it not be that some established countries identified or came to identify with the new idea?

Structure of the Book

The early parts of this study attempt to answer precisely these questions. Chapter 1 considers the early practice of state recognition. It reveals that prior to 1815 international legitimacy revolved around the notion of state rights, which, given that most states were hereditary monarchies, was taken to imply dynastic rights. There was a general consensus that new states could be formed only with consent of their legitimate parent sovereign. The ability to take effective control of a territory could not by itself establish legitimate titles. Particular attention will be paid to acknowledgment of the United States and the verdicts made at the Congress of Vienna with respect to the restoration of monarchies that had been replaced by a network of French satellite states between 1792 and 1814. Chapter 2 is central to this inquiry. It examines the birth of the Anglo-American doctrine of *de facto* statehood, which came in response to claims of statehood emanating from Latin America. The *de facto* doctrine was a repudiation of the doctrine of dynastic rights and an embodiment of the classical liberal belief that people had a natural right to live under an independent government of their choosing. Chapter 3 charts the implantation of *de facto* statehood and the corresponding displacement of dynastic rights throughout nineteenth-century European practice. Chapter 4 explores Woodrow Wilson's reformulation of self-determination as a positive international right as well as its narrow impact on recognition of new European states after World War I. It also looks at the emergence of the Stimson Doctrine, which stipulated, *inter alia*, non-recognition of states created on the heels of cross-border use of force. Chapters 5 and 6 focus on the entrenchment of self-determination as a positive right after 1945: decolonization and its aftermath and the emergence of new European and Central Asian countries since the end of the Cold War. The conclusion summarizes the main findings of the study and argues in favor of the norm of *de facto* statehood.

Notes

1. Seward to Adams, April 10, 1861, *Papers Relating to the Foreign Relations of the United States* [hereinafter FRUS], Vol. 1 (1861) (Washington, DC: Government Printing Office, 1861), p. 79.
2. Speech to the House of Commons on Recognition of the Independence of South America, June 25, 1824, R. Therry (ed.), *The Speeches of the Honourable George Canning with a Memoir of His Life*, Vol. 5, 3rd ed. (London: James Ridgway and Sons, 1836), pp. 302–3.
3. Statement on United States Recognition of the Former Yugoslav Republics, April 7, 1992, *Public Papers of the Presidents of the United States: George Bush, 1992–1993*, Vol. 1 (Washington, DC: Government Printing Office, 1993), p. 521.
4. See Thomas Grant, *The Recognition of States: Law and Practice in Debate and Evolution* (Westport, CT: Praeger, 1999), p. 19.
5. These are taken to be state-defining criteria, an influential statement of which is found in the Montevideo Convention on the Rights and Duties of States of December 26, 1933. According to its Art. 1, "the state as a person of international law should possess the following qualifications: a) a permanent population; b) a defined territory; c) government; and d) capacity to enter into relations with the other states." For the text of the inter-American treaty, see *The American Journal of International Law*, 28, Official Documents Supplement (1934), pp. 75–8.

6. Colin Warbrick, "States and Recognition in International Law," in Malcolm D. Evans (ed.), *International Law*, 2nd ed. (Oxford: Oxford University Press, 2006), p. 248.

7. To the extent that IR scholars have written in recent years about state recognition, they commented primarily on its instrumentality and expediency – its contributions to stability or instability in various regions. See, among others, Richard Caplan, *Europe and the Recognition of New States in Yugoslavia* (Cambridge: Cambridge University Press, 2005); One study asked what the episode of Germany's unilateral recognition of Croatia reveals about the neoliberal theory of cooperation. See Beverly Crawford, "Explaining Defection from International Cooperation: Germany's Unilateral Recognition of Croatia," *World Politics*, 48 (1996), pp. 482–521. Recognition of governments has fared slightly better among IR scholars. See M. J. Peterson, *Recognition of Governments: Legal Doctrine and State Practice, 1815–1995* (New York: St. Martin's Press, 1997).

8. See Chapter VII "Of New Principalities That Are Acquired by Other's Arms and Fortune," in Niccolo Machiavelli, *The Prince*, transl. by Harvey C. Mansfield, 2nd ed. (Chicago, IL: The University of Chicago Press, 1998).

9. All of this applies as well to Hegel despite the fact that "recognition" as a social phenomenon and its constitutive effects are major themes in his work. When discussing international politics, Hegel discounts the importance of the political–juridical act of state recognition. According to him, recognition is necessary for the existence of legal contractual relationships between states because "contract presupposes that the parties entering it recognize each other as persons." But while recognition is clearly constitutive of states as international legal persons, international legal personality is separate from sovereign statehood as such. International law springs from relations among existing states – it does not define but merely presupposes statehood – and thus it cannot render legal criteria for recognition of new states. It follows that recognition is not constitutive of statehood: first, it can come only in the wake of already established statehood and, second, it is an arbitrary act on the part of a recognizing state. What is more, the importance of international law as a whole is rather limited. Because there is no higher authority above states, Hegel says, they remain ultimately in a state of nature, connected only by very minimal, imperfect and mostly formal social ties. See Georg F. W. Hegel, *Philosophy of Right*, transl. by T. M. Knox (Oxford: Clarendon Press, 1952), paras. 71, 330–40.

10. Hedley Bull, *The Anarchical Society: A Study of Order in World Politics*, 2nd ed. (New York: Columbia University Press, 1995), p. 13.

11. It should be noted that some authors who work within the burgeoning constructivist approach to international politics also agree that mutual recognition is a vital element in orderly relations among states. In the most meticulous exposition of this approach so far Alexander Wendt writes about "the role of mutual recognition of external sovereignty in mitigating the effects of international anarchy" and maintains that "in the particular culture of the Westphalian states system sovereignty is also a *right* constituted by mutual recognition, which confers on each state certain freedoms (for example, from intervention) and capacities (equal standing before international law)" (italics original). See Alexander Wendt, *Social Theory of International Politics* (Cambridge: Cambridge University Press, 1999), pp. 208, 182; However, constructivist studies of how new sovereign states become established and how that establishment relates to the states system have so far been rare. The volume treating these topics most thoroughly is Thomas J. Biersteker and Cynthia Weber (eds.), *State Sovereignty as Social Construct* (Cambridge: Cambridge University Press, 1996), especially chs. 1, 2, 8, and 9.

12. See C.A.W. Manning, "The Legal Framework in the World of Change," in Brian Porter (ed.), *The Aberystwyth Papers: International Politics 1919–1969* (London: Oxford University Press, 1972); Alan James, *Sovereign Statehood: Basis of International Society* (London: Allen & Unwin, 1986); James, "Diplomatic Relations and Contacts," in *The British Year Book of International Law 1991* (Oxford: Clarendon Press, 1992); James, "The Practice of Sovereign Statehood in Contemporary International Society," *Political Studies*, 47 (1999), pp. 457–73; and James, "States and Sovereignty," in Trevor Salmon (ed.), *Issues in International Relations* (London: Routledge, 2000).

13. Vattel's view is summarized in the following passage in book I, chapter I, paragraph 4 of his *Law of Nations* (1758): "Every nation which governs itself, under whatever form, and which does not depend on any other nation, is a *sovereign state*. Its rights are, in the natural order, the same as those of every other state. Such is the character of the moral persons who live together in a society established by nature and subject to the law of nations. To give a nation the right to a definite position in this great society, it need only be truly sovereign and independent; it must govern itself by its own authority and its own laws" (italics original). See Emmerich de Vattel, *The Law of Nations or The Principles of Natural Law: Applied to the Conduct and to the Affairs of Nations and of Sovereigns*, transl. by Charles G. Fenwick (Washington, DC: The Carnegie Institution, 1916), p. 11; Grotius, Pufendorf and Wolff also held that any entity that establishes effective independent self-government is automatically subject to, and under the protection of, natural law. They conceived of international society primarily in natural, not historical terms. Mutual recognition was for them in the first place a precept of natural and not – what at the time was still embryonic – customary international law.

14. James, "States and Sovereignty," p. 15.

15. James, *Sovereign Statehood*, pp. 152–3.

16. Ibid., p. 147. Compare this with Samuel Pufendorf's argument from 1672 that "a king owes his sovereignty and majesty to no one outside his realm..." If "a people which either first comes together to form a state or leaving a previous form of state" confers sovereignty on its ruler, the latter "need not obtain the consent or approval of other kings or states..." See book VII, chapter 3, paragraph 9 of his *De Jure Naturae et Gentium Libri Octo*, Vol. 2, transl. by C. H. and W. A. Oldfather (Oxford: Clarendon Press, 1934), pp. 1008–9.

17. James, "Diplomatic Relations and Contacts," p. 353.

18. Martin Wight, "International Legitimacy," in Martin Wight, *Systems of States*, ed. by Hedley Bull (Leicester: Leicester University Press, 1977), pp. 153, 158; The term "international legitimacy" is used throughout this study in the sense Wight defines it.

19. See Warbrick, "States and Recognition in International Law," p. 217, and Hedley Bull, "The European International Order," in Kai Alderson and Andrew Hurrell (eds.), *Hedley Bull on International Society* (London: Macmillan Press, 2000), p. 176.

20. Terry Nardin, "International Ethics and International Law," *Review of International Studies*, 18 (1992), p. 26; Hedley Bull put this idea thus: "A state's right to sovereignty... are not asserted against the international legal order, but conferred by it... A state's right to sovereignty or independence is not a 'natural right', analogous to the rights of individuals in Locke's state of nature: it is a right enjoyed to the extent that it is recognized to exist by other states." See Hedley Bull, "The State's Positive Role in World Affairs," in Alderson and Hurrell, *Hedley Bull on International Society*, p. 149.

21. Ibid., p. 23.

22. Robert Jackson, *The Global Covenant: Human Conduct in the World of States* (Oxford: Oxford University Press, 2000), p. 323.

23. Among political scientists, Stephen Krasner recently claimed, but did not substantiate, that "the basic rule of international legal sovereignty [is] that mutual recognition be extended among formally independent entities." He then aimed to show that this supposed rule had been extensively violated. See Stephen D. Krasner, *Sovereignty: Organized Hypocrisy* (Princeton, NJ: Princeton University Press, 1999), p. 8.

24. See, for example, Roland Rich, "Recognition of States: The Collapse of Yugoslavia and the Soviet Union," *European Journal of International Law*, 4 (1993), pp. 36–65; and Christian Hillgruber, "The Admission of New States to the International Community," *European Journal of International Law*, 9 (1998), pp. 491–509.

25. Ian Brownlie, "Recognition in Theory and Practice," in R. Macdonald and Douglas Johnston (eds.), *The Structure and Process of International Law: Essays in Legal Philosophy, Doctrine and Theory* (Dordrecht, The Netherlands: Martinus Nijhoff, 1983), p. 627. For a view that the discipline of international law as a whole has been dominated by doctrinal debates at the expense of empirical analysis and that this development should be reversed, see Bull, *The Anarchical Society*, p. 154, and Anthony Clark Arend, *Legal Rules and International Society* (New York: Oxford University Press, 1999), pp. 7–8, 189.

26. Grant, *The Recognition of States*, p. ix.

27. Ibid., p. 216. See also Robert Y. Jennings, "General Course on Principles of International Law," *Recueil des Cours: Collected Courses of the Hague Academy of International Law*, 121 (1967-II), p. 350, who called it "an arid controversy" more than forty years ago.

28. Brownlie, "Recognition in Theory and Practice," p. 634. For an analogous view, see Heather A. Wilson, *International Law and the Use of Force by National Liberation Movements* (Oxford: Clarendon Press, 1988), p. 105 (n. 44).

29. William V. O'Brien and Ulf H. Goebel, "United States Recognition Policy toward the New Nations," in William V. O'Brien (ed.), *The New Nations in International Law and Diplomacy* (New York: Frederick A. Prager, 1965), p. 98.

30. A very similar point was recently made by the editors of a survey of post-Cold War state succession and recognition. See "Conclusions," in Jan Klabbers, Martti Koskenniemi, Olivier Ribbelink, and Andreas Zimmermann (eds.), *State Practice regarding State Succession and Issues of Recognition: The Pilot Project of the Council of Europe* (The Hague: Kluwer Law International, 1999), p. 152. More focus on practice is also called for by Thomas Grant who criticizes the propensity of legal scholars to derive the meaning of statehood in international law from a mere glance at the text of the Montevideo Convention, a regional treaty from 1933. See Thomas D. Grant, "Defining Statehood: The Montevideo Convention and its Discontents," *Columbia Journal of Transnational Law*, 37 (1999), pp. 455–7.

31. See Lassa Oppenheim, *International Law*, Vol. 1, 2nd ed. (New York: Longmans, 1912), p. 117.

32. Ian Clark, *Legitimacy in International Society* (Oxford: Oxford University Press, 2005), pp. 26–7.

33. Hedley Bull, "International Theory: The Case for a Classical Approach," in Klaus Knorr and James N. Rosenau (eds.), *Contending Approaches to International Politics* (Princeton, NJ: Princeton University Press, 1969).

34. See, among others, Anne-Marie Slaughter, Andrew S. Tulumello, and Stepan Wood, "International Law and International Relations Theory: A New Generation

of Interdisciplinary Scholarship," *The American Journal of International Law*, 92 (1998), pp. 367–97; Arend, *Legal Rules and International Society*, Michael Byers (ed.), *The Role of Law in International Politics: Essays in International Relations and International Law* (Oxford: Oxford University Press, 2000); and Christian Reus-Smit (ed.), *The Politics of International Law* (Cambridge: Cambridge University Press, 2004).

35. See, for instance, Ole Wæver, "International Society – Theoretical Promises Unfulfilled?," *Cooperation and Conflict*, 27 (1992), pp. 112–13; Kai Alderson and Andrew Hurrell, "The Continuing Relevance of International Society," in Alderson and Hurrell (eds.), *Hedley Bull on International Society*, p. 67; João Marques de Almeida, "Challenging Realism by Returning to History: The British Committee's Contribution to IR 40 years On," *International Relations*, 17 (2003), p. 296; Geoffrey Roberts, "History, Theory and the Narrative Turn in IR," *Review of International Studies*, 32 (2006), p. 709; and Andrew Linklater and Hidemi Suganami, *The English School of International Relations: A Contemporary Reassessment* (Cambridge: Cambridge University Press, 2006), pp. 7, 80.

36. See Robert Jackson, "Boundaries and International Society," in B. A. Roberson (ed.), *International Society and the Development of International Relations Theory* (London: Pinter, 1998).

37. I use "great powers" in the traditional sense of systemic great powers. But "major powers" category includes also subsystemic powers, e.g. the United States in the Western Hemisphere in the nineteenth century.

38. See Bull, *The Anarchical Society*, ch. 9.

39. In 1991, Iceland was the first foreign country to establish diplomatic relations with the Baltic republics as well as to recognize Croatia, yet its actions barely registered at the time.

40. The terms are used in Rick Fawn and James Mayall, "Recognition, Self-Determination and Secession in Post-Cold War International Society," in Rick Fawn and Jeremy Larkins (eds.), *International Society after the Cold War: Anarchy and Order Reconsidered* (London: Macmillan Press, 1996), p. 209.

41. Canning to Lieven, September 26, 1826, *British and Foreign State Papers* [hereinafter BFSP], Vol. 40 (London: H.M. Stationery Office, 1863), p. 1216. *De facto* statehood is the same as "effective statehood" (a term employed mostly by international lawyers) and "empirical statehood" (a term used more by political scientists). See Robert Jackson and Carl Rosberg, "Why Africa's Weak States Persist: The Empirical and Juridical in Statehood," *World Politics*, 35 (1982), pp. 1–24.

42. According to Alderson and Hurell, in a solidarist conception of international society "the interests of the whole form the central focus rather than the independence of the states of which it is made up." The conception at least partially accepts the domestic analogy and attempts to go beyond "the provision of the necessary framework for the minimalist goal of continued coexistence." The norms of this society involve extensive schemes of cooperation to safeguard peace and security, to solve common problems and to sustain common values. Implementation of these norms is carried out "through the creation of a collective security system and through coercive intervention to promote common goals or uphold common values." In contrast, a pluralistic conception of international society is constructed around the goal of coexistence and reflects an ethic of difference. Its norms are built on the mutual recognition of states as independent and legally equal members of society. See Kai Alderson and Andrew Hurrell, "Bull's Conception of International Society," in Alderson and Hurrell, *Hedley Bull on International Society*, pp. 7–10.

43. See R. J. Vincent, *Human Rights and International Relations* (Cambridge: Cambridge University Press, 1986), p. 8.
44. Negative and positive rights protect two distinct concepts of liberty. Negative liberty is freedom from obstruction by other individuals and governments. Positive liberty is about the ability to realize one's conception of life. For a classic treatment see Isaiah Berlin, "Two Concepts of Liberty," in his *Four Essays on Liberty* (Oxford: Oxford University Press, 1969).
45. Michael Walzer, *Just and Unjust Wars*, 4th ed. (New York: Basic Books, 2006), p. 88.
46. See Brad R. Roth, *Governmental Legitimacy in International Law* (Oxford: Oxford University Press, 1999), pp. 38–9, 413–14.
47. This phase of the practice is best captured by Hersch Lauterpacht who in 1947 argued that although recognition was "declaratory of an existing fact, such declaration . . . [was] constitutive, as between the recognizing state and the community so recognized, of international rights and duties associated with full statehood." See H. Lauterpacht, *Recognition in International Law* (Cambridge: Cambridge University Press, 1947), p. 6.
48. Wight, "International Legitimacy," p. 160.
49. By one count, as of late 2006 there were twenty-six ongoing armed self-determination conflicts and another fifteen conflicts considered provisionally settled but at risk of reigniting. See David Quinn, "Self-Determination Movements and Their Outcomes," in J. Joseph Hewitt, Jonathan Wilkenfeld, and Ted Robert Gurr (eds.), *Peace and Conflict 2008* (Boulder, CO: Paradigm Publishers, 2008), pp. 33, 38.
50. See Robert Jackson, *Sovereignty* (Cambridge: Polity, 2007), p. 10.
51. His essay "International Legitimacy" was originally published, in a moderately longer form, in *International Relations*, 4 (1972), pp. 1–28.
52. James Mayall, *Nationalism and International Society* (Cambridge: Cambridge University Press, 1990).
53. See Oyvind Østerud, "The Narrow Gate: Entry to the Club of Sovereign States," *Review of International Studies*, 23 (1997), pp. 167–84.
54. See Robert Jackson, "Negative Sovereignty in Sub-Saharan Africa," *Review of International Studies*, 12 (1986), pp. 247–64; "Quasi-States, Dual Regimes, and Neoclassical Theory: International Jurisprudence and the Third World," *International Organization*, 41 (1987), pp. 519–49; and "The Weight of Ideas in Decolonization: Normative Change in International Relations," in Judith Goldstein and Robert Keohane (eds.), *Ideas and Foreign Policy: Beliefs, Institutions and Political Change* (Ithaca, NY: Cornell University Press, 1993).
55. See Jackson and Rosberg, "Why Africa's Weak States Persist"; Robert Jackson, *Quasi-States: Sovereignty, International Relations and the Third World* (Cambridge: Cambridge University Press, 1990); and Jackson, "Juridical Statehood in Sub-Saharan Africa," *Journal of International Affairs*, 46 (1992), pp. 1–16.
56. This applies also to the post-Cold war period. One essay that analyzes contemporary developments in the practice is Fawn and Mayall, "Recognition, Self-Determination and Secession in Post-Cold War International Society."
57. The two terms are not interchangeable. While all cases of state recognition are also admissions into international society, the reverse is not true. Political communities such as the Ottoman Empire, Japan, China, Siam, Persia, or Ethiopia were never considered, and therefore never recognized, as "new states" – they were regarded by the Euro-Atlantic world to be old countries. Their admission into the society of states was signified by their upgrade into equal sovereign status in positive international law. Their previous lack thereof had made them stand *outside* the society of states. In

contrast, recognition of a new state, the subject of this book, is acknowledgment of a changed juridical situation *within* the society of states and positive international law. In other words, some "old" state or states must have previously had sovereign status over the new state's territory.

58. In addition to Jackson's work, see Hedley Bull and Adam Watson (eds.), *The Expansion of International Society* (Oxford: Clarendon Press, 1984); Gerrit W. Gong, *The Standard of "Civilization" and International Society* (Oxford: Clarendon Press, 1984); and Yongjin Zhang, "China's Entry into International Society," *Review of International Studies*, 17 (1991), pp. 3–16. Bull and Watson's volume, despite its general title, does not contain any contributions on the new European countries of the nineteenth century or those recognized in 1918/19, though Watson does have a chapter on "New States in the Americas." Nineteenth-century Europe is also missing from Peter Lyon's, "New States and International Order," in Alan James (ed.), *The Bases of International Order: Essays in Honour of C. A. W. Manning* (London: Oxford University Press, 1973). One recent exception in this relative neglect is Yannis Stivachtis, *The Enlargement of International Society: Culture Versus Anarchy and Greece's Entry into International Society* (Basingstoke, UK: Macmillan, 1998).

59. Bull, *The Anarchical Society*, p. 33.

1

State Recognition Prior to 1815

To ascertain the precise historic origin of complex international practices is notoriously difficult. This is because incidence of sharply conspicuous "clean slates" is quite rare in world politics. Even shifts that are in retrospect judged as tectonic usually materialize only following a long gestation period. Major disruptive events do happen, but international change is typically cumulative and institutional: more often than not it consists of incremental and protracted institutionalization of new ways of doing things and gradual abandonment of old ones.[1] The displacement of political authority of the Holy Roman Empire and the papacy by that of the sovereign states – the great transformation from the medieval to modern world – was this type of change. While Martin Wight finds some evidence of modernity as early as the Council of Constance (1414–18), F. H. Hinsley argues that we can only talk about a fully formed system of independent states since the beginning of the eighteenth century.[2] The current debate about the significance of the Treaties of Westphalia (1648),[3] conventionally understood as ushering in sovereignty as a new mode of political and legal organization, illustrates the hazards of operating with images of total and absolute historical breaks. Supposing that Westphalia was more than an important milestone in the evolution of modern statehood and state system ignores, for example, that until 1806 countries of Europe and the German principalities forming the Holy Roman Empire considered the ultimate constitutional authority to be vested in the Empire, not the individual principalities with differentiated and unequal authority.

Mindful of possible pitfalls of being too categorical about the exact date of origin of institutions, two points can be made about the early phase of recognition of new states. It could emerge as a full-fledged and discrete practice only once European countries came to regard themselves as forming a larger association of formally like entities and once positive law of this association gained a distinct foothold over natural law as its defining institution. Historically, the first condition preceded the second. In 1758, Emmerich de Vattel wrote in *The Law of Nations* that

> Europe forms a political system in which the nations inhabiting this part of the world are bound together by their relations and various interests into a single body. It is no longer, as in former times, a confused heap of detached parts, each of which had but little concern for the lot of others, and rarely troubled itself over what did not immediately affect it. The constant attention of sovereigns to all that goes on, the custom of resident ministers, the

continual negotiations that take place, make of modern Europe a sort of republic, whose members – each independent, but all bound together by a common interest – unite for the maintenance of order and the preservation of [state] liberty. This is what has given rise to the well-known principle of the balance of power, by which is meant an arrangement of affairs so that no state shall be in a position to have absolute mastery and dominate over others.[4]

But Vattel's principal focus still remained natural law, even though he gave more due to state practice and customary and treaty law than earlier writers on the law of nations such as Grotius, Pufendorf, and Wolff.

In contrast, the first writings on recognition of new states can be traced to the German jurists Jacob Moser (1778), Johann von Steck (1783), and Georg-Friedrich von Martens (1789), who clearly were legal positivists and whose analytical concern was predominantly state practice.[5] Why did these works begin to appear when they did? Charles Alexandrowicz gives this explanation:

The need for sorting out state practice in the field of recognition and for ascertaining certain principles presented itself during the period of the gradual decline of dynastic legitimism. With the occurrence of frequent changes in membership of the family of nations and with the appearance of new forms of government and the corresponding conflicts between the new state and mother state ... third powers started looking for legal guidance and recognition came to claim a separate chapter in the treatises of international law which it did not enjoy in the works of the great classical writers of the late naturalist and earlier positivist period.[6]

Dynastic legitimacy – the prevalent, though not exclusive, way of justifying both domestic government and numerous international rights – and its key element, unchecked monarchical authority, began to crack in the second half of the eighteenth century under the growing impact of political liberalism. Liberal thinkers such as Locke, Montesquieu, Spinoza, Voltaire, Rousseau, Kant, and their intellectual followers deemed the people, not the divinely invested monarch, to be the source of political authority. Because human beings were thought to possess the faculties of reason and judgment, they were also capable of determining the political direction of their countries. This made the office of absolute monarch at best obsolescent and at worst oppressive. Government was to be based, according to liberals, on the will of those subject to it and not, as theorists of royal authority such as Jean Bodin or Robert Filmer would have it, on the benevolent will of kings. States could have no other foundation, Locke's *Second Treatise of Government* asserted, "but the consent of the people."[7]

Perhaps the most thorough faith in individual reason is found in Immanuel Kant's political theory. Kant's starting point was the observation that while causal laws may affect our body, they do not affect our minds and inner selves. We are not cogs in the wheels of natural or social forces: to be free means that we can reason and make choices. Kant argued that without volition of one's course of life it is impossible to speak of morality at all. The essence of human beings is their capacity for self-determination: they are autonomous beings and, as such, can select from a multitude of beliefs and courses of action. They can act rightly or wrongly, properly or improperly but, at all times, they must be allowed to choose.[8]

The worst that one can do to human beings is to deny them their free choice. Kant forcefully rejected all paternalism in politics. Under "a paternal government" the subjects are obliged to "behave purely passively and to rely upon the judgment of the head of state as to how they ought to be happy, and upon his kindness in willing their happiness at all." A government of the benevolent ruler who treats his subjects "as immature children who cannot distinguish what is truly useful or harmful to themselves . . . is the greatest conceivable despotism." "The only conceivable government" for Kant was one in which "everyone in the state . . . regards himself as authorized to protect the right of the commonwealth by laws of the general will, but not to submit it to his personal use at his own absolute pleasure."[9] "A state, unlike the ground on which it is based, is not a possession," he wrote in *Perpetual Peace* (1795). "It is a society of men, which no one other than itself can command or dispose of."[10] Still, while Locke, Kant, and other liberal philosophers made clear that the state was to be based on popular consent rather than dynastic inheritance, they left the question of how this consent can be given – by what institutional method and by which group of people – largely unexplored.

As with the exact emergence of the modern society of states or sovereignty as an international institution, the first appearance of liberal constitutional ideas in interstate relations is not a settled matter. As early as 1774, Russia and the Ottoman Empire, conventionally regarded as among the most oppressive countries of the time, agreed in Art. 3 of the Treaty of Kutchuk-Kainardji that "all the Tartar peoples . . . shall without any exception, be acknowledged by the two Empires as free nations, and entirely independent of every foreign power, governed by their own sovereign, . . . elected and raised to the throne by all the Tartar peoples." The ruler of the Crimean Tartars was to "govern them according to their own ancient laws and usages" and the St. Petersburg and Constantinople governments pledged to "acknowledge and consider the said Tartar nation, in its political and civil state, upon the same footing as the other powers who are governed by themselves."[11] However, Tartar independence was short-lived[12] and this meant that, as with the earlier French defeat of the movement for Corsica's independence in the late 1760s, international society did not face a great challenge to its rules and norms of membership.

The American Revolution and the French Revolutionary Wars, especially their Napoleonic phase, did pose such a test. Therefore, this chapter focuses on the recognition of the United States and the Congress of Vienna, which followed the defeat of France. It shows that while US independence was justified in novel terms, its admission into international society was accommodated by prevailing norms. Besides France, all states acknowledged the United States only after it was evident that Britain chose to forfeit its sovereignty over the secessionist republic. Though state recognition was not a well-defined practice at the time – one had to reach for precedents all the way back to the acknowledgment of the Dutch

Republic, Switzerland, and Portugal in the mid-seventeenth century[13] – there was a distinct sense it would be against the existing state rights to acknowledge sovereignty of a country's territory prior to that country's renunciation thereof. In contrast, the network of new satellite states, which were part and parcel of the French "system of conquest,"[14] posed a fundamental challenge to the rules of membership in the family of nations. Conquest as such was legal, but its unrestricted character between 1792 and 1814 threatened the very survival of the society of states as it disrupted the independence of most continental states. The Vienna settlement rejected the legitimacy of all satellite states created in the wake of France's external use of force and, with a few exceptions, restored the pre-revolutionary states with their old dynasties.

Recognizing the United States of America

On July 4, 1776 the representatives of thirteen British colonies in the Second Continental Congress proclaimed independence of the United States. Their move represented a culmination in the long-standing, intensifying political and in 1775/6 also military conflict with the British government. The *US Declaration of Independence* stated that (*a*) all men are created equal and are endowed with certain inalienable rights; (*b*) governments are instituted to uphold and further these rights, and derive their just powers from the consent of the governed; (*c*) when a form of government becomes destructive of these ends, it is the right of the people to alter or abolish it, and to institute new government; and (*d*) while, crucially, "governments long established should not be changed for light and transient causes," it may in "the course of human events [become] necessary for one people to dissolve the political bonds which have connected them with another, and to assume among the powers of the earth, the separate and equal station to which the laws of nature and nature's God entitle them."[15]

After listing "repeated injuries and usurpations" committed by King George III, the declaration proclaimed that the thirteen colonies "are, and of right ought to be free and independent states," "are absolved from all allegiance to the British crown," and "all political connection between them and the State of Great Britain, is and ought to be totally dissolved." It concluded then by stating that as "free and independent states, they have full power to levy war, conclude peace, contract alliances, establish commerce, and to do all other acts and things which independent states may of right do."

The phrase "may of right do" implied that the United States considered itself bound by the law of nations, and the entire sentence that its relations with Great Britain would henceforth be governed by this law and not municipal law of the British empire.[16] But the British authorities spoke of the newly proclaimed entity as its "colonies in a state of rebellion," categorizing it as such already in August 1775. They were by now fully engaged in an armed campaign to re-establish imperial rule.

No foreign country accepted the US claims. None looked upon the situation as anything other than a civil war. But whereas public endorsements for the American cause were not forthcoming, there were countries that might welcome the prospect of US independence, or at least a prolonged war of independence against the British, chiefly France. The government of Louis XVI long resented the hegemonic position of Great Britain overseas and its unduly strong influence on the continent, both of which came mainly at France's expense. The humiliation was dated to the 1763 Treaty of Paris, which, even as it ended the Seven Years War, stripped France of almost all its possessions in the Western Hemisphere. The French government was eager to see Britain weakened, its territory overseas reduced, and the balance of power restored. A close ally of France in this endeavor was the fellow Bourbon kingdom of Spain, which, though less than France, had also suffered territorial losses at the hands of Britain in the eighteenth century.

Americans tried from the very beginning to exploit the anti-British sentiments. American foreign relations got their first institutional expression in November 1775 when the Second Continental Congress established a Committee of Secret Correspondence (in April 1777 renamed "Committee for Foreign Affairs"), the purpose of which was to gain support abroad for the American cause. As early as March 1776 it sent an agent to France to arrange purchase of military supplies and to find out under what conditions "if the colonies should be forced to form themselves into an independent state, France would . . . acknowledge them as such, receive their ambassadors, enter into any treaty or alliance with them for commerce or defense, or both."[17] In September, the Congress proceeded to appoint three commissioners to the court of France to negotiate these issues. In addition, they were directed by the Congress to approach ambassadors of other countries residing in France "to obtain from them a recognition of our independency and sovereignty, and to conclude treaties of peace, amity, and commerce between their princes or states and us."[18] These instructions make apparent that the Americans understood from the very beginning that they needed to ask foreign states for acknowledgment, and that they saw it as the precondition of their relations with the outside world as a sovereign state.

The anti-British sentiment in France and Spain, potent as it was, did not translate itself into any automatic recognition of the United States. While the French government officials communicated with the American commissioners and decided to provide them with secret military assistance indirectly through a private company, and Spanish ports remained opened to American merchant ships and privateers, they were reluctant to do more. Comte de Vergennes, the French minister of foreign affairs, argued in a March 1776 paper submitted to and approved by Louis XVI that French recognition would be premature while the Americans had been mere insurgents and not in effective possession of territory:

> It would not be in keeping with the dignity of the king, nor in his interest, to make a pact with the insurgents. . . . This pact, in fact, would only be worthwhile insofar as they make themselves independent and do not find it in their interest to break it, as the system does not change into an administration

both mobile and necessarily unstable.... Such an arrangement can only be solidly based in mutual interest, and it seems that it will only be time to decide this question when the liberty of English America has acquired a positive consistency.

His initial conclusion was ambivalent. He thought that "it is perhaps problematical whether [the Bourbon monarchies] should desire the subjection or the independence of the English colonies" and was concerned that "they find themselves threatened in either hypothesis." France and Spain were threatened both by the prospect of a quick defeat of the insurgents – this would perpetuate Britain's colonial and maritime supremacy – and by helping the Americans, thus being exposed to the wrath of the colonial power. The most advantageous course of action was to encourage "the continuation of the war," which would tie down British resources, but at the same time "persuade the English ministry that the intentions of France and Spain are pacific, so that it does not fear to embark upon the operations of a brisk and expensive campaign" and then turn against the two kingdoms.[19]

In April, a report by Joseph de Rayneval, the first secretary to Vergennes, signaled a clear, though not yet public, support for independence. While Rayneval agreed with his superior on the proposed course of action, he argued that France should support the independence of the colonies. He believed that "in whatever manner Great Britain maintains her supremacy in America, there will always be considerable advantages for her in it, while by losing it she would suffer an inestimable injury which will also be permanent."[20] He did not think France could avoid an armed confrontation with Britain and advocated open support for the colonies when it was apparent that they had been able to succeed on the battlefield and when France was ready to "strike decisive blows" to the British forces. Rayneval also considered Spanish worries that an independent United States may endanger dynastic legitimacy, particularly in Spain's American dominions. Interestingly, he dismissed these concerns. The menace was understood in terms of a potential expansion that would spread revolutionary universalistic ideology, but Rayneval believed, together with many contemporaries, that republican systems of government are inherently peaceful and primarily inward-oriented:

It will be said the independence of the English colonies will set the stage for a revolution in the New World; scarcely will they be at peace and assured of their liberty, when they will be seized with the spirit of conquest; whence could result the invasion of our colonies and of the rich possessions of Spain in South America. But two considerations seem capable to reassure those who have such fears: (1) the war in which the colonies are now engaged will exhaust and impoverish them too much for them to be able to think soon of taking up arms to attack their neighbors; (2) there is good reason to think that if the colonies achieve their aim, they will give a republican form to their new government; now it is generally held, from experience, that republics rarely have the spirit of conquest,... that they know the pleasures and advantages of commerce and that they have need of industry, and consequently of peace to procure for themselves the conveniences of life....

Rayneval completed the discussion of this theme by reassuring Vergeness that "even supposing that the colonies will encroach upon the Spanish possessions, nothing is less proved than that this revolution would be prejudicial to France."[21]

The US commissioners in France spent the year 1777 seeking to obtain French and Spanish recognition and treaties of friendship and commerce.[22] Concurrently, the French government contemplated what further steps – beyond the official non-recognition of the United States and limited material aid – to take. No prospects of advantage vis-à-vis the British could prod Spain to acknowledge the United States: despite its animosity toward Britain, the Spanish government had consistently believed that the Americans were rebels against a lawful monarch. In contrast, by the end of the year France had become firmly convinced that the only viable policy was to support US independence. Besides the fact that assistance to North America became known to Britain and raised tensions with its government to a critical level and, just as Rayneval had predicted, war seemed unavoidable, the Americans were able to secure several major military victories. The battle of Germantown in early October and, even more crucially, the defeat of General Burgoyne's army at Saratoga later that month proved to be of signal importance.

French diplomatic documents reveal that following the battle of Saratoga the royal government reached the judgment that the Americans had shown the ability to set up and defend their state. Conrad Gerard, Vergennes' undersecretary, communicated to the US commissioners that "the king, henceforth persuaded that the United States were resolved to maintain their independence, had decided to cooperate efficaciously in maintaining it and in making it firmly established."[23] He told them that Louis XVI had an "essential interest in weakening his natural enemy, and that this sensible and permanent interest would henceforth render the cause of the Americans common to France."

France recognized the United States on February 6, 1778, when Gerard was directed to sign two treaties with the US commissioners. The purpose of the treaty of alliance (the other was treaty of amity and commerce) was "to maintain effectually the liberty, sovereignty and independence" of the United States. In the case of war between France and Britain the parties agreed that neither shall "lay down their arms until the independence of the United States shall have been formally or tacitly assured by the treaty or treaties that shall terminate the war."[24]

Can one trust French explanations that the news of the victory at Saratoga had been decisive in France's decision to recognize the United States? Some historians doubt it and put forward other factors: the completion of France's rearmament, the deterioration of Franco-British relations, or the threat of possible US–British reconciliation.[25] According to this view, Saratoga offered an opportune moment for France to trigger a war with Britain. However, even if this belief is partially true – and there is no reason to think that the three above factors were necessarily absent – there are at least two reasons why the significance of Saratoga should not be discounted. First, France had time and again insisted that it would recognize the United States only when it saw evidence of effective statehood. While one could, of course, doubt whether the North American states were, to quote Gerard, "truly in possession of their independence," it is much more difficult to argue that Saratoga was used as pure window-dressing. France had to justify its actions not only to its archenemy, Britain, but also to its closest friend, Spain. The other member of the Bourbon Family Compact hoped the war in North America would weaken Britain, not establish a new state that could undermine the rights of existing monarchies. It refused to entertain recognition of the United States. Yet French justifications given to Britain and Spain were at the core very similar. In January 1778, Louis XVI wrote to his uncle Charles III of Spain that "the recent destruction of Burgoyne's army and the imperiled state of [British commander-in-chief] Howe have recently made a total change in the relations of the parties. America is triumphant . . . the impossibility of [her] being subdued by arms being now demonstrated."[26]

In March, the French ambassador in London submitted to the British a *pro memoria*, informing them that France and the United States had signed the treaty of amity and commerce as the United States had been in full possession of independence proclaimed by their declaration of July 4, 1776.[27] In its reply, Britain did not seek to rebut this proposition. Instead, George III classified France's conduct as "an aggression on the honor of his crown and the essential interests of his kingdom, . . . subversive of the law of nations, and injurious to the rights of every sovereign power in Europe."[28] France responded by appealing to the "incontestable principle of public law" that the fact of the effective possession of US independence was enough to justify the king to sign treaties with the United States without examining the legality of that independence. Neither the law of nations nor treaties, morality, or policy imposed upon Louis XVI the obligation to become the guardian of the fidelity of British subjects to their sovereign: it was sufficient that the colonies had established their independence, not merely by a solemn declaration, but also in fact, and had maintained it against all the efforts of the parent country. The French response continued that this was the position of the United States when the king began to negotiate with US representatives and that France was free to consider them as an independent country or as subjects of Great Britain. The king had chosen the first alternative because his safety, the interests of his people, and the secret projects of the court in London obliged him to do so. France was bound neither to assist Britain against the colonies nor to repulse them when they presented themselves to Louis XVI as an independent people. It had a right to consider them as such primarily because their former sovereign had shown by long efforts the impossibility of reducing them to obedience.[29]

Clearly, the two sides operated with what they understood to be existing international legal principles: that of dynastic rights and effective possession. Neither party denied the validity of either principle as such; the quarrel was rather which one applied to the American case of secession from a sovereign crown. Though the records of the debate in the British House of Commons reveal that the French argument actually found sympathy among opposition members,[30] no country sided with France. The prevalent international standard was dynastic legitimacy, which allowed a territorial or jurisdictional change only with consent of the affected monarch. France did refer to past instances when Britain had allegedly strayed from this norm[31] – expressly citing Queen Elizabeth I's recognition of the Netherlands without prior Spanish recognition in the 1580s.[32] But Britain disputed the accuracy of this reading of its history and retorted that "the king never acknowledged the independence of a people who has shaken off the yoke of their lawful prince."[33] It took the acknowledgement of its revolted subjects, irrespective of whether they were actually independent, as a *casus belli* and opened hostilities against France.

Louis XVI's court had to face the onset of war without having continental allies. Over-anxious Spain declined to join the Franco–US coalition. France's main diplomatic objective was to persuade Spain to declare war on Britain, especially after it had become obvious that the original coalition would not be able to bring a swift defeat of its adversary. France succeeded when it offered to fight until Spain recovered its former territories and reduced British presence in the Americas. In the secret Convention of Aranjuez of April 1779, Spain promised France to declare war on Britain. It is revealing to observe how the parties handled the issue of US independence. In Art. 4 the French king proposed, "in strict execution of the engagements contracted by him with the United States of America," that Spain recognize US independence and not lay down arms until Great Britain does the same. Spain refused to commit itself and reserved the right to make recognition a matter of bilateral bargaining with the Americans.[34]

Americans were intent on seeking recognition directly from various countries. Besides France, they focused primarily, though by no means exclusively, on Spain, Russia, and the Dutch Republic. Spain was the country closest to France and shared with it the hostility against Britain. Russia under Catherine II became a leading continental power. On the other hand, the Dutch Republic was a financial powerhouse and at least nominally shared with the Americans the republican system of government. The envoys to these states spent approximately two years each in their appointed capitals, yet with the exception of the emissary to the Netherlands (John Adams) they achieved very little.

Spain's negative attitude toward the Americans did not change by American efforts in Madrid. Spain declared war on Britain in June 1779, but its government declined to refer to the United States as "ally," instead preferring the term "co-belligerent." An ally could have been only an internationally legitimate country and as far as Spain was concerned, the United States did not meet this criterion. John Jay, the commissioner to Madrid, admitted in frustration that Spain's war objectives "did not include ours" and its conduct as a whole was "not very civil to our independence."[35]

Russia did not support American claims of independence, but while Catherine the Great did not endorse either the legality or justice of the North American uprising, it equally refused George III's solicitation of direct military help and alliance.[36] For the Americans, nevertheless, Russia's importance lay in the February 1780 proclamation of its armed neutrality, which was later joined by most neutral states of Europe in a coalition known as the League of Armed

Neutrality. Its purpose was to resist efforts to suppress trade of neutrals with the belligerent powers. Because it was Britain that had seized most neutral ships and their cargo, the policy effectively had an anti-British slant and an unintended consequence of aiding the Americans. Armed neutrality isolated Britain: it was alone in protesting against it.

The Congress wanted to accede to the League of Armed Neutrality. The invitation to join, however, was not extended. Besides being a warring party, the United States was not acknowledged as an independent state by any of its signatories. The Continental Congress appointed Francis Dana as the minister to Russia in December 1780 to achieve support for US sovereignty and the adherence to armed neutrality. However, Dana never even presented his credentials to the Russian government. Russia and Austria were at the time involved in attempts to mediate an end to the war between Britain and its Bourbon adversaries, and Dana was persuaded by Vergennes, Franklin, and Marquis de Verac, the French minister in St. Petersburg, that it was unlikely that Russia would compromise its function as an impartial mediator by recognizing US independence when that independence had itself been the crux of contention.[37] Although, following a major American victory at Yorktown, Dana received instructions from Secretary for Foreign Affairs Robert Livingston not to fail "to make use of this intelligence which must fix our independence not only beyond all doubt, but even beyond all controversy," he agreed not to reveal his public character in Russia, but "to appear only as a private citizen of the United States."[38]

The Dutch Republic would be the only additional country to recognize the United States before Britain, but the process of reaching this decision was even more protracted than in the case of France and came around the time when the British cabinet itself admitted that US independence was the only plausible outcome of the war. The Congress was confident that the Dutch tradition of republican government would make recognition relatively unproblematic, but in the late 1770s and early 1780s that republicanism was not, at least as far as the central government in The Hague was concerned, easily discernible. Previously elective, the office of the stadtholder became permanently hereditary in 1747. William V of the House of Orange-Nassau, the stadtholder of the day, was actually a close relative of George III and pro-British. The Americans began their dealings in the Dutch Republic by seeking a large loan from private lenders. John Adams, later the second American president, obtained a commission from the Congress to borrow money, but after he had arrived in The Hague in August 1780 he was told that a loan would be difficult to negotiate until the States General (the country's parliament) recognized American independence.[39]

The situation seemed to offer more promise toward the end of 1780 as relations between Britain and the Dutch Republic sharply deteriorated. The British began seizing "contraband" Dutch ships bound for France, and in response the Hague government opted to join the League of Armed Neutrality. Citing that this violated bilateral treaty commitments toward Britain and accusing the Dutch of planning to conclude a treaty with the United States, the British cabinet declared war on the republic in December. Still, facing the same enemy did not mean, as in the case of Spain, that the Dutch were willing to acknowledge US independence. The central government feared a prolonged conflict with Britain and in March 1781 it accepted the Russian offer to extend its mediation to the British–Dutch war. The mediation could hardly have proceeded if, in the midst of it, the Dutch would have acknowledged the Americans. Unlike his colleague Dana, however, Adams pressed immediately and publicly for recognition and diplomatic relations, arguing that his country was "in possession of sovereignty by right and in fact."[40] The grand pensionary of Holland (an equivalent of the prime minister), however, replied that even though the United States and the Dutch Republic faced the same foe, the recognition of US independence was "a matter somewhat delicate for the republic."[41] Adams' memoranda and pleadings failed.[42] Perturbed by his inability to obtain a much-needed loan, achieve Dutch recognition, and conclude a treaty of amity and commerce, the future US president suffered an apparent nervous breakdown.[43]

Adams' mission was saved by the intense struggle on the Dutch political scene and the help from French diplomacy. The government of the pro-British stadtholder was fiercely opposed by the Patriots, a liberal party advocating the return to the true republican roots of the country. The Patriots were pro-American and enjoyed widespread, if uneven, support in the constitutionally strong Dutch provincial assemblies. This was a considerable advantage for the Americans because recognition of the new state would have to be endorsed by all seven provinces before it could be approved by the central government. To prevent possible reconciliation between Britain and the Dutch Republic, French ambassador in The Hague, Duc de la Vayguyon, and Patriot representatives tried to influence provincial assemblies into voting for recognition. The Patriots, supported by the pro-American trade sector, organized a petition campaign across the country to rally public opinion and put pressure on the provincial deputies.[44]

The campaign had a galvanizing effect as Dutch recognition took less than two months to complete. One province after another voted in support of the United States and the stadtholder, according to Adams's dispatch to Livingston, declared that he had "no hopes of resisting the torrent, and therefore that he shall not attempt it."[45] After all the provinces had given their approval, the States General passed, on April 19, 1782, a resolution admitting Adams as minister plenipotentiary and thus acknowledging the United States as a sovereign state.[46]

As significant as the acknowledgments by France and the Dutch Republic were, they did not by themselves make the United States an internationally legitimate actor. This came only once Britain concluded a provisional peace treaty with its "colonies in a state of rebellion" in November 1782: In its very first article the king acknowledged the United States as a sovereign, independent country, and relinquished all claims to it "for himself, his heirs and successors."[47]

How did this decision come about? There were several reasons, the most important being Britain's inability to defeat the Americans by force of arms.

One might have had misgivings about the French contention that the Americans had possessed effective control of their territory in early 1778, but three and half years later, only very few doubted it. After the spectacular US victory at Yorktown in October 1781 the British, fighting simultaneously against three European powers, proved unable to mount a counteroffensive.

However, one should also not underestimate the opposition to the war that developed within the British parliament. While few advocated US independence as a solution to the war until late into its course, there were always those who accepted that at least some American claims were just. Edmund Burke, a Whig member of parliament, belonged to the former group. He had criticized his government policy toward the American colonies since the 1760s and argued that its elements, primarily the lack of political representation by people in the colonies, actually violated the spirit of the British constitution. Once the war commenced, Burke thought that the Americans opted for secession from the crown only as a last resort and that to let them go would be better than to wage war against them. Such war was inevitably designed to subdue, and forced submission was denial of freedom for the subjugated as well as those doing the subjugation.[48]

Though Burke's views were initially highly unpopular and he was denounced as a traitor, following the loss at Yorktown, views like his appeared with growing frequency. In February 1782, the ministry of Lord North lost its parliamentary majority and the House of Commons passed a motion that declared enemies of their country all those "who should advise, or in any way attempt to prosecute an offensive war in America for the purpose of reducing the colonies to obedience by force."[49] The foreign and colonial secretaries in the new government, Charles James Fox and Lord Shelburne (from July 1782 the prime minister), both agreed that American independence had to be conceded. Their peace envoys in Paris were openly discussing the acceptance of US independence already in mid-April, at the time of Dutch recognition and before the US–Dutch treaty of amity and commerce of October 1782.[50] Given that Lord Stormont, the previous foreign secretary, remarked to Austria's ambassador as late as October 1781 that "the king of England would recognize the independence of the colonies when the French were masters of the Tower of London,"[51] the decisive shift in the British position occurred rather speedily.

Once the United States obtained acknowledgment of its parent country, first in the preliminary treaty of peace and then in the definitive treaty of peace signed in Paris in September 1783, other states did not see formal barriers to recognizing the new state and establishing diplomatic, trade, and other relations. Sweden signed a treaty of amity and commerce with the Americans in April 1783, Prussia in 1785. Russia indicated that it would not object to establish diplomatic relations with the United States after the signature of the definitive peace treaty.[52]

To sum up so far, the United States became widely recognized and thus admitted into international society only after it had become acknowledged as independent by its parent country. To treat it as a sovereign state before this acknowledgment was considered by most states to be a hostile act violating the rights of the British crown. Such act was expected to engender the gravest of consequences, including a declaration of war by the injured state, and recognition was therefore regarded as a matter of utmost sensitivity. France did not agree that its recognition of the United States constituted such a violation and instead explained its decision in terms of the principle of effective possession.[53] Still, it is important to emphasize that from the very beginning states considered it essential to defend recognition of a new state in terms of their shared normative standards. Rather than treating recognition as merely an instrument by which to pursue their interests, they felt impelled to appeal to common moral and legal rules. Even France, which did not deny political expediency in its public exchanges with Britain, did not want to act, and appear to be acting, arbitrarily. As much as France desired to weaken British power and prestige, its government nonetheless believed it could not have gone ahead with US recognition had the Americans not been capable of pushing the British forces out from most of their territory.

The American case revealed other important things in regard to state recognition. It demonstrated the fate awaiting unrecognized entities: before its acknowledgment and despite the assertions of the *Declaration of Independence*, the United States could not sign international treaties, have diplomatic relations, form formal military alliances, raise foreign loans, join international organizations, or benefit from regularized trade and commerce. Its survival depended almost solely on its internal strength. It could not successfully claim protection of state rights as they were interpreted at the time; though, as the cases of Poland or Genoa later demonstrated, these rights would not always be a perfect shield for the recognized states either.

The US case also demonstrated the centrality of great powers in recognition of states, just as in other areas of international decision-making. Though the Americans sought acknowledgment by all sovereign countries, including such small polities as Ragusa (Dubrovnik) or Tuscany, they concentrated their efforts on the major powers. These powers carried most weight in international society and smaller states tended to follow their initiative and example. Their role became even more evident just before and at the Congress of Vienna.

There is little evidence beyond the lone case of the Dutch Republic that liberal sympathies played a role in the recognition of the United States. Rather, the American leaders were successful in channeling the anti-British resentment of France and, more generally, playing the game of European balance-of-power politics for their own purposes. There can be little doubt that French recognition and the ensuing military, commercial, and financial relations with the United States, as well as *de facto* alliances with Spain and the Dutch Republic, contributed mightily to the successful establishment of the United States as an effective state. It would prove a supreme irony of history that in the attempt to help consolidate US independence, the French *ancién regime* sowed the seeds of its own destruction. But while Louis XVI might have been executed in January 1793 as an implacable feudal reactionary, nothing changes the fact that he was in effect a founding father of the first country created explicitly on the basis of the consent of the governed.

The French Revolution and the Congress of Vienna

From the perspective of the last ninety years, the founding of the United States may appear as a critical event in international relations, but it was not perceived as such by the governments of the late 1770s and early 1780s. Even when there was awareness that the US constitutional system was grounded in different principles than those dominating in Europe and that this may carry an external revolutionary potential, the new state was not seen as having the ability to achieve great power standing and to influence events far beyond North America. Modern international society had never consisted exclusively of hereditary monarchies before 1776. Even if it had been uniformly European and Christian, it contained a certain diversity of constitutional arrangements. Hereditary monarchies had lived side by side with several republics (the Dutch Republic, Genoa, Venice, Ragusa, and Switzerland), elective monarchies (Poland and the Holy Roman Empire), and ecclesiastical principalities.[54] As long as the differences among members remained relatively limited, there had been willingness to accommodate them.

In contrast, the French revolution and its post-1792 period in which France found itself in war with virtually entire Europe was understood as a mortal threat to the order based predominantly on rule of legitimate royal houses and during its Napoleonic phase even to the system of sovereign states as such. By passing the *Declaration of Man and of the Citizen* the revolutionaries upset the traditional notions of legitimate statehood on the continent.[55] Beginning in 1792, they would not only propagate the ideas of popular sovereignty within France but also seek to export them abroad. France's expansion disrupted the territorial integrity of many existing states and dramatically changed the map of Europe. With Napoleon's defeat no new entity created under France's auspices was allowed to survive and the *status quo ante bellum* was essentially restored.

Self-determination first came up as an international issue in 1790/1 when the French troops occupied Avignon and Comtat Venaissin, two jurisdictions of the States of the Holy See. French revolutionaries went further than the leaders of the American war of independence as they formally renounced conquest in a National Assembly decree.[56] When a delegation of representatives from these territories demanded annexation to France, the National Assembly refused and demanded a plebiscite in which people would have a choice of either joining France or remaining a part of the Holy See. The vote appeared to be relatively free, the majority of people and communes voted in favor of merger with France, and the assembly then incorporated both territories.[57]

This episode was not an instance of creating a new state, but it is relevant to this discussion as it was the first case ever in which people were directly consulted on the question: in what country do you wish to live? Still, for all its innovative and revolutionary qualities this free exercise was not repeated elsewhere in the period between 1791 and 1815. Indeed, France's activities abroad gradually appeared too much like old-fashioned territorial expansionism. Its revolutionary government annexed one territory after another – Savoy, Nice, Monaco, the Austrian Netherlands (Belgium), Rhineland, and the Bishopric of Basle – without first soliciting the wishes of their populations.[58] Their former sovereigns would then be forced to accede to these annexations in bilateral treaties.

Foreign policy of the French revolution exhibited two contradictory currents. On the one hand, it espoused the principle of self-determination, which demanded that a people choose its own government. The National Assembly repudiated intervention into the affairs of other countries as well as wars of conquest. These policies would have, by themselves, had minimal impact on international society, as they discouraged unwarranted interference abroad. However, on the other hand, there were voices among the French revolutionaries arguing that as the principle of self-determination is not valid just for their country but for the entire world, France has an obligation, even mission, to support peoples who want to get rid of despotic monarchies. They were to become free by way of French intervention and assistance. The measures of the French authorities were to protect the peoples in question and were to be only temporary – until such time as they gave themselves a constitution based on the general will and were able to govern themselves in freedom.

Once the revolution had radicalized with the abolition of monarchy in 1792, the second current took over French foreign relations.[59] France conferred on itself the right to decide how, when, and by what means would other peoples become free – under which leaders, under what constitution, and in what jurisdiction.[60] This policy culminated during the reign of Napoleon Bonaparte who went so far as to put at the helm of foreign governments members of his own family. France changed the constitutions of several countries, in a number of cases repeatedly, and it also helped create or created a number of brand new entities. The defeated countries whose territories had been carved up or those powers that, for whatever reason, had to cease their struggle against Napoleon were often forced to recognize these entities as a condition of peace in a series of bilateral treaties.[61] Napoleon's domination of Europe introduced a new phenomenon of satellite or puppet states: entities whose founding and any continued empirical existence are a direct result of a prior threat or use of force by a foreign power (see Table 1.1).

If the new polities managed to survive during Napoleon's reign – some of them were annexed by France and some eliminated in the course of victories by the anti-French coalition – they were not allowed to outlive Napoleon's demise in 1814. Nearly all states with sovereign status in 1792 were reinstated. Paradoxically, Napoleon was defeated and the old regimes restored partly on the strength of popular resistance to France in Spain, Italy, Germany, and the Low Countries. The theoretically implausible notion of self-determination of peoples in a French

Table 1.1 Satellite states of revolutionary France, 1792–1814

The Rauracian Republic (1792–3)
The Batavian Republic (1795–1806)
The Transpadan Republic (1796–8)
The Lombardian Republic (1797–8)[a]
The Ligurian Republic (1797–1805)
The Anconitan Republic (1797–8)[b]
The Helvetic Republic (1798–1803)
The Lemanic Republic (1798–1803)
The Piedmontese Republic (1798–9)[c]
The Roman Republic (1798–9)
The Cisalpine Republic (1798–9, 1800–2)
The Parthenopean Republic (January–June 1799)
The Kingdom of Ertruria (1800–8)[d]
The Republic of Valais (1802–10)
The Kingdom of Italy (1805–13)
The Confederation of the Rhine (1806–13)
The Kingdom of Holland (1806–10)
The Kingdom of Westphalia (1807–14)
The Grand Duchy of Warsaw (1807–14)[e]
The Illyrian Republic (1809–13)

[a] The Lombardian Republic soon changed its name to the Cispadan Republic and in 1798 it united with the Transpadan Republic to form the Cisalpine Republic. The Cisalpine Republic was later renamed the Italian Republic (1802–5).
[b] Merged with the Roman Republic.
[c] Later restored and renamed the Subalpine Republic (1800–2).
[d] Nominally part of Spain.
[e] Nominally part of Saxony.

empire proved to be a practical oxymoron as well: while many absolute monarchs were deeply unpopular and their removal elicited in a number of places initial exhilaration for France, Napoleonic rule over continental Europe became eventually detested nearly everywhere.

The post-war settlement was constructed in a series of treaties, first among the countries of the anti-French coalition and then between the coalition and France. Its purpose, stated most succinctly in the Treaty of Reichenbach, the first agreement leading to the creation of the last coalition, was to "re-establish the independence of the states oppressed by France."[62] Beyond that, the territorial settlement, according to the later Treaty of Chaumont, was to establish a "just equilibrium of power." That "European system" was to contain: Germany composed of sovereign princes united by a confederative bond; Switzerland in its former limits; Italy divided into independent states with intermediaries between the Austrian possessions in Italy and France; Spain in its former limits and governed by Bourbon Ferdinand VII; and independent Holland under the sovereignty of the House of Orange-Nassau, with an increased territory and with the establishment of suitable frontiers.[63]

That the goal of the anti-Napoleonic coalition was the return to pre-revolutionary Europe is evident from the First Treaty of Paris, a peace agreement signed in May 1814 with the already restored Bourbon government of France.[64] Besides publicly repeating stipulations from Chaumont, it returned France, with small modifications, to the borders from the beginning of 1792. France renounced sovereignty over the tiny principality of Monaco, which was restored "on the same footing on which it stood before the 1st of January, 1792." The effects of treaties signed between Napoleon and Austria, Portugal and Prussia, some of which had contained recognition of French satellite states, were annulled in additional articles. Whereas the treaty did not settle all outstanding issues – one of its articles provided for a general congress to be held in Vienna to complete the settlement – its preamble did not leave much doubt about what kind of government the allies preferred. Because it specified that, unlike under the previous regime, France offered "the assurance of security and stability to Europe" under "the paternal government of her kings," one may infer that monarchical rule, at least in major states (and France never ceased to be deemed one of them despite its military defeat), was considered to be a prerequisite for the endurance of the European system of states. The survival was thought to depend, most crucially, on the sanctity of treaties, the respect for independence of other countries, the balance of power and moderation in foreign policy – and the regimes of post-1792 France were seen as undermining all these values. Part of this equation was the great power agreement, if only informal one, to disallow future unilateral conquests.[65]

The General Act of the Congress of Vienna was to be the most significant and comprehensive document of the post-war settlement.[66] The act faithfully followed the objectives of the Treaty of Chaumont. Whereas the Holy Roman Empire was not resurrected, a similar German Confederation was created in its place. The major difference between the two entities was that the latter had no constitutional head and instead of hierarchical authority relations, postulated equality of its members. Its object was no more than "the maintenance of the external and internal safety of Germany, and independence and inviolability of the confederated states." All pretensions from the pre-revolutionary period that the Dutch state was a republic in more than just the name were cast aside when the House of Orange-Nassau was endorsed as the hereditary ruler of the kingdom of the Netherlands. A protocol of the allied countries then in June 1814 specified that Holland should be united with Belgium (prior to 1792 a province of Austria). According to its first article "the Union was decided by virtue of the political principles adopted by [the allied powers] for the establishment of a state of equilibrium in Europe; they put those principles into execution by virtue of their right of conquest of Belgium."[67] In Italy, the Congress of Vienna reinstated the kings of the Kingdoms of the Two Sicilies and Sardinia[68] and the dukes of Central Italy – all rulers of states that, in empirical terms, had at least temporarily disappeared from the Italian peninsula during the Napoleonic expansion.

However, not all states that had existed before 1792 reappeared in 1815. The territories of the republics of Venice, Ragusa, and Genoa were incorporated into Austria and Sardinia. Most notably, the Congress of Vienna confirmed the partition of the elective monarchy of Poland among Austria, Russia, and Prussia that had in 1795 extinguished Polish sovereignty. Genoa and Poland were also the most controversial cases because of the strength of popular resistance to the loss of their sovereign status and because the British argued for their restoration along with the rest of the conquered states (the Republic of Genoa actually reconstituted itself in 1814 after liberation by the Royal Navy).[69] These decisions were justified, as was the enlargement of the former Dutch Republic, by reference to the principle of balance of power. The stipulations that the king of Sardinia "shall receive an increase of territory from the State of Genoa" as well as Austrian territorial enlargements in northern Italy are included among provisions of the secret attachment to the First Treaty of Paris outlining "a system of real and permanent balance of power in Europe" that were to be "derived" at the congress in Vienna.

But, as prevalent as dynastic legitimacy and balance-of-power thinking were in Vienna, the congress could not altogether disregard the new idea of popular sovereignty. The French Revolutionary Wars made the European leaders aware of it far more than the war of American independence and in some cases continental monarchs themselves had to appeal to it when mobilizing the resistance against Napoleon. In the Constitutional Charter promulgated after Napoleon's abdication, Louis XVIII declared that "although all authority in France resides in the person of the king," changes to the traditional notions would have to be made in light of "ever increasing progress of enlightenment . . . during the past half century." He admitted that "the wish of our subjects for a constitutional charter was the expression of a real need" and professed that the most durable constitution is where "the wisdom of the king freely coincides with the wish of the people."[70] In fact, the entire document resembles more the 1791 constitution, adopted during the early moderate phase of the French revolution, than the political organization of the kingdom prior to 1789.[71]

That this kind of thinking was present just before and at the Congress of Vienna is evident, again, most prominently in the Polish case. In the above-mentioned Prussian–Russian treaty, for example, the reference to the balance-of-power was accompanied by the insistence that "the national spirit . . . has been taken into consideration" in the Polish settlement. The preamble of the complementary Austro–Russian treaty stated that the parties are "desirous of coming to an amicable understanding upon the measures most proper to adopt for consolidating the welfare of the Polish people."[72] The general act, then, resolved that "the Poles, who are respective subjects of Russia, Austria and Prussia, shall obtain a representation and national institutions, regulated according to the degree of political consideration, that each of the governments to which they belong shall judge expedient and proper to grant them." Russia, which got the largest part of the former country, created a separate Polish jurisdiction, the Kingdom of

Poland. The kingdom was to enjoy "a distinct administration" and have, among others, a Pole in the office of the royal governor and a distinct Polish army.

These provisions fell woefully short of Polish aspirations of independence, but seen from the perspective of history of international legitimacy, they did signal a novel development. However weak and insufficient they may appear, the references to "national spirit" or "national institutions" and the intimation that political arrangements should serve "the welfare of a people" – and not just dynastic interests – represent probably the first formal acknowledgment of the new idea in a multilateral forum. However small a step, the Polish provisions reveal that legitimate statehood at the Congress of Vienna was not entirely about royal hereditary property, even if it was mostly about that.

Elements of the new idea are apparent in other components of the Vienna settlement as well. The preamble of the agreement confirming Swiss independence proclaimed that the powers "obtained every information relative to the interests of the different cantons" and took "into consideration the claims submitted to them by the Helvetic legation." Included in this was also the Bishopric of Basle, a former ecclesiastical principality and then, from 1792 to 1793, an "independent" Rauracian Republic, which was attached to canton Bern.[73] As for the ecclesiastical states of Avignon and Comtat Venaissin, both of which voted in the 1791 referendum to unite with France, the First Treaty of Paris expressly affirmed them to be parts of France. This occurred despite strong protests from the Holy See and even though the congress restored to it other territories lost to the French empire or its satellite states. Avignon and Comtat Venaissin continued to be part of France even after signing of the Second Treaty of Paris, which, following the unsuccessful attempt by Napoleon to lead France once again, returned France to the borders of 1790.

Conclusion

As the formation of the United States and the proceedings of the Congress of Vienna reveal, there was a general consensus that new states could be formed only with the free consent of their legitimate parent sovereign, regardless of how a new state might actually justify its own establishment. Where this free consent was not given, as was judged in regards to the political communities created under the aegis of French expansion, their claims to existence were rebuffed. International legitimacy in the pre-1815 period clearly centered on the notion of state rights in customary international law, which, given that most states were hereditary monarchies, was taken to imply dynastic rights. The insistence on these rights despite changes in effective statehood (i.e., appearance and disappearance of *de facto* states) shows that the ability to take effective control of a territory, whether from within or without, could not, by itself, establish legitimate titles.

As for the new idea, the French Revolutionary Wars showed it could be just as easily abused by power politics as the principles of the eighteenth-century international society. The balance-of-power principle had been defended as a guarantee of independence of "historic" states, yet at the Congress of Vienna it was used to justify cases, even if only very few, of state elimination. Similarly, the idea of self-determination was used to justify the exact opposite of its original purpose. Its claim was that a people have the moral right to decide their political destiny, yet the radical revolutionaries and then Napoleon used it to defend the creation of satellite states and, more broadly, an imperial-like policy of unrestrained interference into the affairs of others.

Notes

1. See K. J. Holsti, *Taming the Sovereigns: Institutional Change in International Politics* (Cambridge: Cambridge University Press, 2004), ch. 1.
2. See Martin Wight, "The Origins of Our States-System: Chronological Limits," in Bull, *Systems of States*; and F.H. Hinsley, *Power and the Pursuit of Peace: Theory and Practice in the History of Relations between States* (Cambridge: Cambridge University Press, 1963), ch. 8.
3. See, among others, Stephen Krasner, "Westphalia and All That," in Judith Goldstein and Robert Keohane (eds.), *Ideas and Foreign Policy: Beliefs, Institutions and Political Change* (Ithaca, New York: Cornell University Press, 1993); Andreas Osiander, "Sovereignty, International Relations, and the Westphalian Myth," *International Organization*, 55 (2001), pp. 251–87; Benno Teschke, *The Myth of 1648: Class, Geopolitics, and the Making of Modern International Relations* (London: Verso, 2003); and Sasson Sofer, "The Prominence of Historical Demarcations: Wesphalia and the New World Order," *Diplomacy & Statecraft*, 20 (2009), pp. 1–19.
4. Vattel, *The Law of Nations*, book III, chapter III, paragraph 47, p. 251.
5. C.H. Alexandrowicz, "The Theory of Recognition *In Fieri*," in *The British Year Book of International Law 1958* (London: Oxford University Press, 1959), pp. 180–7.
6. Ibid., p. 196.
7. John Locke, "Second Treatise of Government," in John Locke, *Two Treatises of Government*, ed. by Peter Laslett (Cambridge: Cambridge University Press, 1988), p. 384.
8. See Isaiah Berlin, "Kant as an Unfamiliar Source of Nationalism," in Isaiah Berlin, *The Sense of Reality: Studies in Ideas and Their History*, ed. by Henry Hardy (London: Pimlico, 1996).
9. Immanuel Kant, "On the Common Saying: 'This May be True in Theory, but it Does not Apply in Practice,'" in Immanuel Kant, *Political Writings*, ed. by Hans Reiss and transl. by H.B. Nisbet, 2nd enlarged ed. (Cambridge: Cambridge University Press, 1991), p. 74.
10. Immanuel Kant, "Perpetual Peace: A Philosophical Sketch," in ibid., p. 94.
11. Treaty of Kutchuk-Kainardji, July 21, 1774, M. S. Anderson (ed.), *Documents of Modern History: The Great Powers and the Near East 1774–1923* (London: Edward Arnold, 1970), pp. 9–14.

12. The Tartars were unable to form a durable government or gain wider international recognition. Their khanate was in fact gripped by constant disorder and factional struggles ever since it had declared independence from the Ottoman Empire in 1772. The Porte interfered in Tartar affairs and, according to Russia, "was beginning to exercise sovereign power over the Tartar lands." With the explanation that "this act destroys our former obligations regarding the liberty and independence of the Tartar peoples," Russia annexed the Tartar-inhabited Crimea in 1783. See Catherine II's Manifesto, April 19, 1783, ibid., pp. 14–15; Russia occupied the peninsula in the war that ended in 1774 and if the Tartars themselves could not now govern it, the Turks were to be prevented from acquiring it.

13. See James Kent, *Commentary on International Law*, ed. by J. T. Abdy, 2nd ed. (Cambridge: Deighton, Bell & Co., 1878), p. 85 (n. 3) and Jochen A. Frowein, "Transfer or Recognition of Sovereignty – Some Early Problems in Connection with Dependent Territories," *The American Journal of International Law*, 65 (1971), pp. 568–71.

14. See Preamble, Definitive Treaty of Peace between Great Britain, Austria, Prussia, and Russia, and France, November 20, 1815, Edward Hertslet (ed.), *The Map of Europe by Treaty* [hereafter MET], Vol. 1 (London: Harrison and Sons, 1875), p. 343.

15. Declaration of Independence, July 4, 1776, Thomas Jefferson, *Selected Writings*, ed. by Harvey C. Mansfield (Wheeling, Illinois: Harlan Davidson, 1979), pp. 7–11; The only previous modern declaration of independence, the 1581 Dutch Act of Abjuration, presupposed paternal government. See Edict of the States General of the United Netherlands by which they Declare that the King of Spain has Forfeited the Sovereignty and Government of the Afore-Said Netherlands, July 26, 1581, E. H. Kossmann and A. F. Mellink (eds.) *Texts Concerning the Revolt of the Netherlands* (London: Cambridge University Press, 1974), pp. 217, 224.

16. Edward Dumbauld, "Independence under International Law," *American Journal of International Law*, 70 (1976), pp. 425–6.

17. Committee of Secret Correspondence: Instructions to Silas Deane, March 3, 1776, Mary A. Giunta (ed.), *Documents on the Emerging Nation: US Foreign Relations 1775–1789* (Wilmington, DE: Scholarly Resources, 1998), p. 6.

18. Additional Instructions to Benjamin Franklin, Silas Deane, and Arthur Lee, October 16, 1776, Francis Wharton (ed.), *Revolutionary Diplomatic Correspondence of the United States*, Vol. 2 (Washington, DC: Government Printing Office, 1889), p. 172.

19. Comte de Vergennes: Considerations on the Affairs of the English Colonies in America, March 12, 1776, Giunta, *Documents of the Emerging Nation*, pp. 18–24. The paper was drawn up before the *US Declaration of Independence*, but almost a year after the battles of Concord and Lexington, that is when Britain's authority was already under significant challenge in the thirteen colonies.

20. Joseph Matthias Gerard de Rayneval: Reflections on the Situation in America, April 1777, Giunta, *Documents of the Emerging Nation*, pp. 24–9.

21. Retrospectively, this is a remarkable statement. Historians have well established that the enormous costs of the French participation in the US war of independence contributed significantly to the subsequent near-bankruptcy of the French treasury and the downfall of *ancién regime* in 1789. No less remarkable is that French minister of finance Turgot actually predicted the collapse of public finances should his country assist the Americans and thus, in all probability, invite an all-out war with Britain. He believed that a British victory over the rebels would in fact be good for France as it would force Britain to commit large military resources for policing its defiant colonies. For these reasons

he strenuously opposed Vergeness and Rayneval. The latter two won the dispute and Turgot was ousted from his office in May 1776, but the episode shows that there was absolutely nothing pre-ordained about the French policy toward the insurgent British colonies, and that state interests are matter of argument and debate rather than being naturally given or otherwise predetermined.

22. The appeals of the commissioners to the French and Spanish governments are notable for being formulated in the language of contemporary world of states and for the absence of vocabulary of the *US Declaration of Independence.* The three wrote to Vergennes in January 1777 that "North America is . . . ready to guarantee in the firmest manner to [France and Spain] all their present possessions in the West Indies, as well as those that they shall acquire from the enemy in a war that may be consequential of assistance [to North America]. The interest of the three nations is the same." Despite the negative attitudes of America's founders toward interstate conquest as such, there was a pledge of acceptance of French and Spanish conquests from Britain. In March, the commissioners reported to the Committee of Secret Correspondence that they had explained "the utility to France that must result from our success in establishing the independence of America." See American Commissioners to Comte de Vergennes, January 5, 1777, and American Commissioners to Committee of Secret Correspondence, March 12, 1777, Giunta, *Documents of the Emerging Nation,* pp. 32, 38.

23. Conrad Alexandre Gerard: Report of Conference with the American Commissioners, January 9, 1778, Giunta, *Documents of the Emerging Nation,* pp. 52–8.

24. Treaty of Alliance Eventual and Defensive, February 6, 1778, Jonathan Dull, *A Diplomatic History of the Revolution* (New Haven, CT: Yale University Press, 1985), pp. 165–9.

25. Dull, *A Diplomatic History of the Revolution,* pp. 91–5.

26. Louis XVI to the King of Spain, January 8, 1778, Wharton, *Revolutionary Diplomatic Correspondence,* Vol. 2, p. 467.

27. Declaration of the French Ambassador to the Court of London, March 13, 1778, *Annual Register for the Year 1778* (London: J. Dodsley, 1778), p. 291.

28. Message from George III to both Houses of Parliament, March 17, 1778, ibid., p. 290.

29. Observations of the Versailles Court in relation to the British Justificatory Memoir, 1779, Wilhelm G. Grewe (ed.), *Sources Relating to the History of the Law of Nations,* Band 2, Vol. 2 (Berlin: Walter de Gruyter, 1988), pp. 448–50; importantly, French intra-governmental communications contain a similar explanation. See Vergeness to Gerard, March 29, 1778, Wharton, *Revolutionary Diplomatic Correspondence,* Vol. 2, pp. 523–6.

30. According to these records, a number of deputies urged immediate British recognition of the United States because the latter established independence "too firm to be shaken by our utmost efforts." See *Annual Register for the Year 1778,* p. 163.

31. A Manifesto displaying the Motives and Conduct of his Most Christian Majesty towards England, 1779, *Annual Register for the Year 1779,* p. 393.

32. See Henry Wheaton, *History of the Law of Nations in Europe and America from the Earliest Times to the Treaty of Washington, 1842* (New York: Gould, Banks & Co., 1845), pp. 292–3.

33. The Justifying Memorial of the King of Great Britain in Answer to the Exposition of the Court of France, 1779, *Annual Register for the Year 1779,* p. 409.

34. Convention of Aranjuez, April 12, 1779, Wharton, *Revolutionary Diplomatic Correspondence,* Vol. 1, pp. 356–7.

35. Quoted in Richard B. Morris, *The Peacemakers: The Great Powers and American Independence* (New York: Harper & Row, 1965), p. 223.

36. Nikolai N. Bolkhovitinov, *Russia and the American Revolution*, transl. and ed. by C. Jay Smith (Tallhassee, FL: The Diplomatic Press, 1976), p. 11.

37. Indeed, in the mediation proposals during 1780 and 1781 the thirteen US states were referred to only as "American colonies" by Russia and Austria. The mediation project, however, faltered because the Americans maintained they would not negotiate a peace treaty before being acknowledged as independent by Britain, and Britain, in turn, insisting it could never consent to such a demand. See ibid., ch. 3.

38. Livingston to Dana, October 22, 1781 and Dana to Vergennes, March 31, 1781, Wharton, *Revolutionary Diplomatic Correspondence*, Vol. 4, pp. 802, 343.

39. James H. Hutson, *John Adams and the Diplomacy of the American Revolution* (Lexington, KY: The University Press of Kentucky, 1980), p. 78.

40. J. Adams's Memorial to the States-General, Wharton, April 19, 1781, *Revolutionary Diplomatic Correspondence*, Vol. 4, p. 375.

41. J. Adams to the President of Congress, May 3, 1781, Wharton, *Revolutionary Diplomatic Correspondence*, Vol. 4, p. 398.

42. Hutson, *John Adams and the Diplomacy of the American Revolution*, p. 92.

43. Ibid., p. 98.

44. Ibid., p. 107.

45. J. Adams to Franklin, March 26, 1782, Wharton, *Revolutionary Diplomatic Correspondence*, Vol. 5, p. 275.

46. Jan Nordholt, *The Dutch Republic and American Independence*, transl. by Herbert H. Rowen (Chapel Hill, NC: The University of North Carolina Press, 1982), pp. 214–15. For the text of all the resolutions, see J. Adams to Livingston, April 19, 1782, *Revolutionary Diplomatic Correspondence*, Vol. 5, pp. 315–19. Neither provincial nor States General resolutions contain any reference to international recognition norms, but they were passed in the aftermath of Yorktown as the House of Commons prohibited British offensive operations in North America and the new British government reconciled itself to American independence and was negotiating the terms of peace with US envoys in Paris. In any case, the Dutch recognition of the United States, while not meeting with approval beyond France, gave rise to no international controversy.

47. The Preliminary Terms of Peace between Britain and the United States, November 30, 1782, Dull, *A Diplomatic History of the American Revolution*, pp. 170–4.

48. Letter to the Sheriffs of Bristol, April 3, 1777, David P. Fidler and Jennifer M. Welsh (eds.), *Empire and Community: Edmund Burke's Writings and Speeches on International Relations* (Boulder, CO: Westview Press, 1999), pp. 155, 165.

49. Lord North to King, March 4, 1782, Sir John Fortescue (ed.), *The Correspondence of King George the Third*, Vol. 5 (London: Macmillan and Co., 1928), p. 376.

50. Richard Oswald's Journal, April 18, 1782, Mary A. Giunta (ed.), *The Emerging Nation: A Documentary History of the Foreign Relations of the United States under the Articles of Confederation, 1780–1789. Volume One: Recognition of Independence* (Washington, DC: National Historical and Records Commission, 1996), p. 349. See also the Minute of Cabinet, attached to Lord Shelburne to the King, April 26, 1782, Fortescue, *The Correspondence of King George the Third*, p. 488.

51. Quoted in H.M. Scott, *British Foreign Policy in the Age of the American Revolution* (Oxford: Clarendon Press, 1990), p. 314.

52. Memorandum of a Conversation between Ivan A. Osterman and Francis Dana, April 23, 1783, Nina N. Bashkina et al. (eds.), *The United States and Russia: The Beginning of Relations, 1765–1815* (Washington, DC: Government Printing Office, 1980), pp. 181–3.
53. The early writings on recognition referred to earlier in this chapter reflected this split. From the legitimist perspective, Steck observed that the declaration of independence was not enough for an entity to be sovereign, even if it managed to establish itself as *de facto* independent. The parent country had to renounce its sovereignty first and until it did so, no third power could recognize the independence of the new state. Premature recognition, in his view, amounted to a violation of the parent country's right against unsolicited foreign intervention. For Martens, on the other hand, a third party ought to acknowledge a new *de facto* state as sovereign irrespective of whether the parent country relinquished its sovereignty first. See Alexandrowicz, "The Theory of Recognition *In Fieri*", pp. 182–3, 185–6; While France's conduct was by and large consistent with Martens' view, the French court did not accept it had a duty to recognize the United States.
54. See, for example, Saint-Pierre's proposed list of nineteen major and several smaller states that were to constitute the federation of peace in "Abstract and Judgment of Saint-Pierre's Project for Perpetual Peace (1756)", in Stanley Hoffmann and David Fidler (eds.), *Rousseau on International Relations* (Oxford: Clarendon Press, 1991), p. 72.
55. In its Art. 3 "the representatives of the French people, organized as a National Assembly" proclaimed that "the source of all sovereignty resides essentially in the nation; no group, no individual may exercise authority not emanating expressly therefrom." See Declaration of the Rights of Man and Citizen, August 27, 1789, John Hall Stewart (ed.), *A Documentary Survey of the French Revolution* (New York: Macmillan, 1951), p. 114.
56. This decree of May 22, 1790 was then integrated into Title VI of the 1791 constitution, which says that "the French nation renounces the undertaking of any war with a view of making conquests, and it will never use force against liberty of any people." See The Constitution of 1791, September 3, 1791, Hall, *A Documentary Survey of the French Revolution*, pp. 230–65.
57. Jean Laponce, "National Self-Determination and Referendums: The Case for Territorial Revisionism", *Nationalism and Ethnic Politics*, 7 (2001), pp. 38–9.
58. In the case of Belgium, for example, the key concern seemed to be that its independence could be harmful to France. While it was proper that Belgium should have liberty, its sovereignty might have worked to Britain's advantage, so Belgium's "freedom" was to take the shape of union with France. See David Armstrong, *Revolution and World Order: The Revolutionary State in International Society* (Oxford: Clarendon Press, 1993), pp. 286–7; Belgium was probably the first case of manipulated referendum on the status of a territory and showed the potential for various abuses of this procedure. General Dumoriez, the officer in charge of the French forces, later confessed that "the plebiscite in Belgium was nothing other than a bitter comedy. Suppression and looting succeeded the conquest and a strong countermovement against France broke out at the end of 1792. Thirty commissioners, dispatched from Paris, were charged with ensuring that the people voted for integration with the French Republic. The voting usually took place in churches, which were surrounded by soldiers." See Wilhelm G. Grewe, *The Epochs of International Law*, transl. and rev. by Michael Byers (Berlin: Walter de Gruyter, 2000), p. 421 (n. 20).

59. In November 1792, the National Assembly adopted a solemn resolution promising protection and fraternity to all peoples rising up for the sake of freedom and ordered the generals of the republic to support these peoples and defend all citizens who were persecuted because of their desire for freedom. See Declaration for Assistance and Fraternity to Foreign Peoples, November 19, 1792, Frank Malloy Anderson (ed.), *The Constitutions and Other Select Documents Illustrative of the History of France, 1789–1901* (Minneapolis: The H.W. Wilson Company, 1904), pp. 129–30. This disposition is in marked contrast to the views of American independence leaders who, while firmly believing that the consent of the governed is a universal principle, never indicated that the United States has a duty to assist other peoples in struggles against their governments.

60. In December 1792, a decree of the National Assembly instructed the generals of the republic to declare the old constitutions and laws null and void in any territory they may occupy, proclaim the principle of sovereignty of the people, and call the citizens together for the purpose of establishing a liberal authority. See Decree for Proclaiming Liberty and Sovereignty of All Peoples, December 15, 1792, ibid., pp. 130–3.

61. For example, Austria was forced to recognize the Cisalpine Republic in Art. 8 of the Treaty of Campo Formio (1797) and the Helvetic and Batavian Republics in Art. 18 of the Treaty of Pressburg (1805). Britain signed the Treaty of Amiens (1802) not only with France, but also the Batavian Republic, thus conveying the latter's recognition. Russia and Prussia concluded separate Treaties of Tilsit (1807) with France. Each acknowledged the Duchy of Warsaw (Russia, Art. 5; Prussia, Art. 15) and the Confederation of Rhine (Russia, Art. 15, Prussia, Art. 4). See Fred Israel (ed.), *Major Peace Treaties of Modern History, 1648–1967*, Vol. 1 (New York: Chelsea House Publishers, 1967), pp. 436–77.

62. See Art. 1 of the Convention between Great Britain and Prussia, June 14, 1813, Clive Parry (ed.), *Consolidated Treaty Series*, Vol. 63 (Dobbs Ferry, NY: Oceana Publications, 1969), pp. 273–9.

63. See preamble as well as Art. 1 of Secret Codicil, Treaty of Union, Concert and Subsidy between Austria, Great Britain, Prussia, and Russia, March 1, 1814, ibid., pp. 83–95.

64. Definitive Treaty of Peace between Great Britain, Austria, Portugal, Prussia, Russia, Spain, Sweden, and France, May 30, 1814, MET, Vol. 1, pp. 1–28.

65. See Matthew M. McMahon, *Conquest and Modern International Law: The Legal Limitations on the Acquisition of Territory by Conquest* (Washington, DC: Catholic University of America Press, 1940), p. 46.

66. Its annexes contain seventeen other bilateral and multilateral agreements completed during the congress negotiations from September 1814 to June 1815. See General Treaty between Great Britain, Austria, France, Portugal, Prussia, Russia, Spain, and Sweden, June 9, 1815, MET, Vol. 1, pp. 208–77.

67. Protocol of Conference between Great Britain, Austria, Russia, and Prussia, June 14, 1814, MET, Vol. 1, pp. 40–1.

68. Treaty between Austria, Great Britain, Russia, Prussia, France, and Sardinia, May 20, 1815, ibid., pp. 155–69. This treaty was attached as Annex 13 to the general act.

69. The British delegation argued for the restoration of Poland and Genoa, but, being alone in this effort, it did not succeed during conference bargaining. This failure elicited strong rebukes in the House of Commons. See Extracts from a Speech of Sir James Mackintosh on the Transfer of Genoa, April 27, 1815, Charles K. Webster (ed.), *British Diplomacy 1813–1815: Select Documents Dealing with the Reconstruction of Europe* (London: G. Bell and Sons, 1921), pp. 404–9.

70. Constitutional Charter, June 4, 1814, Anderson, *The Constitutions and Other Select Documents Illustrative of the History of France,* p. 457.
71. The founding treaty of the Quadruple Alliance, concluded shortly after the Congress of Vienna, acknowledged the Constitutional Charter. Its preamble explicitly noted that "the repose of Europe is essentially interwoven with the confirmation of the order of things founded on the maintenance of the royal authority and the Constitutional Charter" in France, thus modifying the statement made in the preamble of the First Treaty of Paris. See Treaty of Alliance and Friendship between Great Britain, Austria, Prussia, and Russia, November 20, 1815, MET, Vol. 1, p. 372.
72. Treaty between Austria and Russia relative to Poland, May 3, 1815, ibid., pp. 94–104.
73. Declaration of the Eight Powers on the Affairs of the Helvetic Confederacy, March 20, 1815, ibid., pp. 64–9.

2

———

New States in Latin America

The influence of 1789 and its aftermath on post-1815 Europe was rather incremental. The one region where the ideas and events emanating from France had brought nearly instant changes to the existing distribution of sovereignty – and this, because of its relatively minor role in international relations subsequently in the nineteenth century, has not been widely appreciated among students of world politics – was Central and South America.[1] Between 1810 and 1830 this vast area witnessed the birth of twelve new countries.[2] In contrast to most states restored in 1815, none was an absolute kingdom, yet they all eventually gained foreign recognition. With the sole exception of monarchy in Brazil they were all defined constitutionally as democratic republics; still, by the mid-1830s all the obstacles blocking their formal co-optation into international society had been cleared. In terms of qualitative change of membership of the society of states, the New World triumphed where twenty-five years of the French revolutionary period in the Old World fell short. Dynastic legitimacy got its first sustained blow not in Europe, but in Latin America.

The aim of this chapter is to chart and disentangle this development. How could Latin Americans achieve acknowledgment so soon after the restorative Congress of Vienna? The answer lies in the decisive repudiation by two powers, Britain and the United States, of the post-Vienna conception of dynastic legitimacy. That conception not only defined state rights as rights held *outward* against other states with rights held *inward* against state subjects, as was the case prior to 1789; it also propounded active interventionism to guard the monarchies' dynastic and territorial integrity against internal upheaval. In the wake of the French Revolutionary Wars, it saw external stability as hinging on the nature of internal rule: domestic revolution in one country today was thought to open doors for international conflict tomorrow. In contrast, Britain and the United States argued that state rights can be held exclusively in relation to other states and that coercive intervention into matters essentially within a state's domestic jurisdiction was inadmissible. They linked this view of foreign relations to the liberal representative character of their respective domestic political systems.[3] Despite their rivalry, the two countries shared the belief that their domestic system of government demanded respect for the choice of government made abroad.

The British and American response to the Latin American struggles for independence was a reflection of this basic approach to international relations.

The two powers rejected the amorphous category of "revolutionary usurpation" that confounded the distinction between international and civil conflict. There was an elementary difference between Napoleon, who directed force against other states, and the Latin American insurgencies, which concerned the relations between the ruler and the ruled. The latter, as internal conflicts, called for neutrality of third parties and the British and American governments remained neutral despite formidable domestic sympathies for, and in the US case even pressures to take active side of, the rebels. Spain and Portugal were deemed to have a right to demand respect for the sovereignty and territorial integrity of their overseas possessions. But that right – and the corresponding British and American duty to uphold it – was not absolute. It could not but cease with the actual loss by Spain and Portugal of their possessions and the parallel emergence of new polities. Their settled existence was taken as conclusive evidence of the will of their respective peoples to constitute them. As such, it was the source of entitlement to admission to international society. The rise of new *de facto* entities did also have an all-important practical dimension: somebody had to be held responsible for performance of international legal duties toward third parties that had prior relations with Spanish and Portuguese America. However, the need for such accountability did not resolve who should be accountable. In the absence of some notion of who is the rightful authority there was no *a priori* reason why the Americans and British should prefer the infant *de facto* states over reinstatement of Spanish and Portuguese rule by third party force.

The policy of recognizing *de facto* statehood thus could not emerge without a non-interventionist conception of international society among major powers. Holy Alliance interventions to recover Iberian rule could have done away with independence of at least a few new entities, and both Britain and the United States worked to forestall the rumored Russian and French expeditions on behalf of the Spanish crown. If tolerated, forcible takeover of one new entity by another would have had an identical effect. Deprecating interstate conquest no less than foreign intervention, the British and American policymakers endorsed the application of the principle *uti possidetis juris*, which was designed to shield from external force the sovereignty and territorial integrity of all entities that had attained *de facto* independence. In the international realm, the original interdict of Roman property law *uti possidetis, ita possidetis* – or "as you possess, so you may possess" – was to prescribe that unless nascent states agreed otherwise, they inherited borders they had previously had as non-sovereign jurisdictions. Though it was initially applied only to interstate relations within Latin America, the rule has had, as Chapters 5 and 6 will show, a prominent place in the recognition of new states in the last fifty years, undergoing a thorough makeover in the process. In Latin America of the 1820s and 1830s, *uti possidetis juris* functioned as an auxiliary to the *de facto* principle; since the mid-1950s, it has served to keep this principle at bay.

Spanish American Revolutions

The origins of Latin American movements for independence can be traced back to events on the Iberian peninsula between 1808 and 1810. Spain's military defeat by Napoleon, the forced abdication of the king, and the ensuing installation of Napoleon's brother Joseph Bonaparte as the king in Madrid in 1808 threw open the question of Spanish America's political loyalty. In Spain itself, or, to be more precise, in the part that Napoleon failed to conquer, a government with liberal majority but loyal to king Ferdinand VII, called *junta central*, was established in Seville. Its main objective was to fight the Bonapartist invasion and transform the country into a constitutional monarchy. Spain's American territories accepted it as the legitimate Spanish government, but when the *junta central* collapsed in 1810 following Napoleon's further advances and Ferdinand's internment in France, they refused to do the same for its replacement, the regency centered in Cadiz.

Believing that Spain was about to pass under complete foreign domination, and replicating the pattern from Spain following the deposition of its king, the liberal-dominated groups in Hispanic America founded their own provisional *juntas*. These acts were not tantamount to assertions of independence from the crown; on the contrary, the *juntas* were proclaimed in Ferdinand's name. Their formation was justified by a tenet in Spanish medieval law, according to which in the absence of the monarch, government reverted directly to the people.[4] However, because the provisional governments repudiated the existing overseas authorities composed of peninsular officials as illegitimate, they invited conflict over who was the rightful government of the crown in the American territories. Most of Spanish America became, as a result, embroiled in civil war. The liberal character of the regency was soon to appeal to some factions – loyalists from Spanish American provinces would send their delegates to the recently assembled Cortes (parliament) – but it never managed to command widespread allegiance outside the metropole. The nature of the dispute changed fundamentally with the Bourbon restoration in 1814. Besides returning to absolute government – by rescinding the constitution, dissolving the Cortes, reinstating the Inquisition and the feudal tribute – Ferdinand reacted harshly against *juntas* for defying Iberian authorities. The counterreaction of Spanish American territories culminated in a series of proclamations of independence from the parent country.[5]

The liberal and democratic character of Spanish American independence documents as well as the first constitutions is readily apparent. Indeed, it is striking just how much they mirrored, both in substance and structure, French and American revolutionary texts. Venezuela's proclamation of independence, made under "the authority held from the virtuous inhabitants of Venezuela," in several passages appears to have been directly inspired by the founding document of the United States.[6] The Declaration of Independence of the United Provinces of the Rio de la Plata was anchored in "the unanimous will of the people," Peru's in "the general will," and Guatemala's in "the general wish of the people of

Guatemala." Chile's proclamation stated that the citizens had in "the first act of a free people" irrevocably consented to Chile being "a free, independent and sovereign state." The deputies of Bolivia's parliament heralded independence "in the name and absolute authority of their worthy electors."[7]

On the whole, the outside world did not at first react to the hostilities in the New World with much concern. The wars did not make it, for example, on the diplomatic agenda in Vienna. The disquiet grew in 1817/18, after the Spanish side had begun to incur major losses by having been either territorially marginalized or completely uprooted from several of its possessions. Some powers, notably the United States and Britain, were compelled to formulate a response because they were being approached by agents of the newly proclaimed states asking for recognition and because their existing trade with Central and South America was continually menaced and frequently disrupted by fighting. It is at this point that we can detect the earliest signs of a major controversy that pitted these two countries against the continental members of the Quintuple Alliance.[8]

The first formal British position on the conflict was formulated in 1812 when Foreign Secretary Castlereagh offered his services as mediator.[9] Castlereagh's proposal professed both a "desire to see the whole of the Spanish monarchy united in common obedience to their lawful sovereign" and an opinion that Spain's transatlantic provinces "will no longer submit to be treated as mere colonies." The suggested remedy for the "impatience and hatred of the colonial system" was to lift Spanish America from its subordinate position in the empire to "an equal share in the national representation."

Britain refused to admit the envoy of the "United Provinces of Venezuela" when he arrived in London to ask for recognition of his country and establish diplomatic relations in 1811. But at the same time, Britain made it clear that the future of Spanish American provinces depended on the nature of Spanish rule and its acceptability or non-acceptability to their inhabitants. This would be a permanent theme of British statements on the conflict in the Americas. However, despite the fact that the regency in Cadiz was a liberal government – its constitution adopted in the same year (1812) is in fact considered to be the most progressive document of the entire French revolutionary period – it declined Britain's mediation proposal.

As it became clear that Spain would not easily recover its overseas control, Britain reiterated its mediation offer in 1817, on roughly the same terms as in 1812. A Foreign Office memorandum circulated to the European powers as well as to Spain claimed that "were Spain now, however late, to change her policy and avowedly to adopt towards her South American subjects a more liberal system of government, a reasonable hope might still be entertained that the Spanish colonies would return to their allegiance."[10] The Spanish reaction to the British advice was again negative. Spain's ambassador in London pronounced the "liberal system" in the American dominions to be impossible and illusory. In its place, he pleaded for a joint endeavor to quell the American revolutions. The alternative to an alliance along the lines of the last coalition against Napoleon was a domino-like collapse of dynasticism:

Wherever usurpation sets up her throne, wherever the sacred principle of legitimacy is profaned, it becomes necessary to stifle the evil in its very bud. The interest is general, the cause is common, and the means ought to be uniform, expeditious and decisive.... This interest greatly increases by the reflection that America will be metamorphosed...on the theatre of organized subversion, usurpation and domination, and under the auspices of that hateful family, who have carried the destruction of legitimate thrones and of public welfare through all the recesses of Europe.

Nothing but a confederacy of the great powers, a sincere and strong manifestation of their intentions and a determination to exert their power, should it become necessary, will put down the empire of the factious, stimulate the loyal and consolidate the political edifice constructed by means of so many sacrifices, and on whose duration depends the happiness of the human race.[11]

Not being able to launch conciliation bilaterally, both Britain and Spain were anxious to draw other great powers into the discussions. Spain solicited backing particularly from France, the fellow Bourbon kingdom, and Austria and Russia, the two key legitimist powers. Spain was willing to make concessions, but should the territories have rejected the offer, it demanded from its allies guarantees of direct assistance in subduing them. Russia and France began to draft a mediation scheme along these lines, but Britain took strong exception to any proposal involving economic sanctions or armed force by third parties and at the Congress of Aix-la-Chapelle (1818) derailed its adoption.[12] The foreign secretary countered the Spanish call for an intervention of the Quintuple Alliance by contending that the Alliance was "not entitled to arbitrate or to judge between His Catholic Majesty and his subjects, and as a consequence, not competent to enforce any such judgment directly or indirectly." Mediation and facilitation were admissible; threats and coercion were not.[13]

This stance fitted into a pattern of unyielding British opposition to the developing continental doctrine of general interference into the domestic affairs of states.[14] In a seminal state paper and other important documents that provided intellectual guidance to successive generations of nineteenth-century British foreign policymakers, Castlereagh contended that the purpose of the anti-Napoleonic alliance was to liberate Europe from French conquests, not to set up a "union for the government of the world, or for the superintendence of the internal affairs of other states."[15] He rejected the idea of "an 'Alliance Solidaire' by which each state shall be bound to support...succession, government and possession within all other states from violence and attack"[16] on prudential, legal, and moral grounds. The prudential objection was the unpredictable consequences of such an extension in permissible use of force on international order. The legal one was that such a "federative system" was never codified in international law, either prior to 1789 or in 1814/15. The sovereignty-based international legal system, in fact, precluded internal legality from being an object of authoritative judgments by outsiders: "How can foreign states safely be left to judge of what is legal in another state?"[17]

The moral objection was that coercion on behalf of incumbent power might well be coercion on behalf of abusive power. Internal legitimacy of states was to rest not on external collective force "to be prostituted to the support of established power," but on "the justice and wisdom of their respective systems."[18] By explicitly repudiating the "exploded doctrine of divine right and of passive obedience," which England renounced when "the House of Stuart forfeited the throne"[19] in the Glorious Revolution of 1688/9, Castlereagh implied that the governed had a pre-constitutional right to replace their government, by revolutionary means if they judge necessary. Third party non-interference with the process of replacement was part and parcel of that right. "By what right," he asked the Russian ambassador when discussing a possible scenario in Spanish America in late 1817, could Britain "force a population, which had freed itself because its government was oppressive, to place itself once more under the domination of the same government?"[20] He insisted that "no country having a representative system of government could act" upon the Holy Alliance doctrine of coercive intervention.[21] States had a right to interfere only where the "internal transactions" of another state seriously endangered their own immediate security or essential interests; they did not have a general license for crusading against revolutionary movements everywhere.[22]

US Recognition of Spanish American Republics

Recognition was first raised not in Europe, but in the United States. There was an obvious *prima facie* affinity between the United States and Spanish America. The latter was engaged, just as the former some forty years previously, in a separatist conflict against its parent country. Moreover, the justification for its struggle was couched in very similar terms. But while the highest levels of the US government were well disposed to, and the American public opinion was decidedly with, Spanish American patriots, there was nothing predestined about how the United States would act.

In fact, when the conflict erupted the United States, like Britain, announced its neutrality. Venezuela's emissary to the administration of James Madison in Washington had no more luck with his plea for recognition than his compatriot dispatched to London. Between 1815 and 1818 the government enacted a series of neutrality measures that barred American citizens from enlisting in foreign armies and fighting against a country with which the United States was at peace – an evident step against those who in their zeal for the Spanish American cause would commit hostile acts against Spain.[23]

With the wave of independence proclamations and royalist losses the requests for acknowledgment by the United States began to mount. After having been approached by the envoy of the "United Provinces of the Rio de la Plata" in 1817, President James Monroe asked his Secretary of State John Quincy Adams to clarify the conditions under which US recognition of Spanish American states would be permissible. Adams, who would play a central role in shaping the policy toward Latin America, rejoined:

> There is a stage in such contests when the parties struggling for independence have, as I conceive, *a right to demand* its acknowledgment by neutral parties, and when the acknowledgment may be granted without departure from the obligations of neutrality. It is the stage when independence is established *as a matter of fact* so as to leave the chance of the opposite party to recover their dominion utterly desperate. The neutral nation must, of course, judge for itself when this period has arrived; and as the belligerent nation has the same right to judge for itself, it is very likely to judge differently from the neutral and to make it a cause or pretext for war, as Great Britain did expressly against France in our revolution, and substantially against Holland.
>
> If war thus results in point of fact from the measure of recognizing a contested independence, the moral right or wrong of the war depends upon the justice, and sincerity, and prudence with which the recognizing nation took the step. I am satisfied that the cause of the South Americans, so far as it consists in the assertion of independence against Spain, is just. *But the justice of a cause, however it may enlist individual feelings in its favor, is not sufficient to justify third parties in siding with it. The fact and the right combined can alone authorize a neutral to acknowledge a new and disputed sovereignty. The neutral may, indeed, infer the right from the fact, but not the fact from the right.*[24] (italics added)

With his political views firmly rooted in the ideas of the *US Declaration of Independence*, Adams operated with the premise that "lawful government was a compact and not a grant." He contrasted the American conception of unalienable right, reflected by the former, with the Holy Alliance conception of unalienable allegiance, which sprang from the latter. The understanding of government as a divine grant deemed any rebellion unlawful by definition; that of government as a social compact considered those subject to it to have a natural right to withdraw their consent from any regime destructive of their inherent rights, and to institute, by extra-constitutional methods if necessary, a new regime.[25] There was no question that the Spanish American "assertion of natural right"[26] included the right to secede; after all, the *US Declaration of Independence* opened with a general maxim that "the laws of nature and nature's God entitle" a people to "throw off" their oppressive government and "to assume among the powers of the earth the separate and equal station."

Still, acknowledging the right of Spanish Americans to revolution and independence if they deemed Ferdinand VII to have violated their rights did not put an end to the obligations of the United States toward Spain. The law of nations, according to Adams, imposed a duty on third parties to continue to respect Spain's sovereignty and territorial integrity in the Americas. The duty, however, depended on Spanish America not ceasing being in Spanish hands. The displacement of the parent country by a *de facto* state extinguished that obligation; it gave rise to a new right to independence, of which a right to foreign recognition formed an integral part. As long as Spain "could entertain a reasonable hope of maintaining the war and of recovering her authority, the acknowledgment of the colonies as independent states would have been a wrong to her;" but if it "was manifestly disabled from maintaining the contest," it would have had "no right to, upon the strength of this principle, to maintain the pretension, . . . and by unreasonably withholding her acknowledgment, to deprive the independents of their right to demand the acknowledgment of others."[27] A collectivity that had achieved actual sovereignty was entitled to its legal acknowledgment owing to the conclusive normative force of that fact: The formation of a stable, effective state entity in which the population habitually obeyed the new rulers was taken as an authoritative expression of the will of its people to constitute an independent state as neither the *de facto* state's founding nor its continued existence could come to pass in without at least tacit approval by its inhabitants. In the absence of commonly agreed international procedures for verifying popular will, the *de facto* state was taken to embody, in Thomas Jefferson's words, "the will of the nation substantially declared."[28] It was this presumption of popular consent that converted the fact of new states into their right to independence and external recognition.

The Monroe administration delayed the recognition of the Rio de la Plata because the government in Buenos Aires, which declared itself the successor to the colonial government of the multi-jurisdictional Viceroyalty of the Rio de la Plata, was not in control of all the territory it claimed. The administration had no reason to act otherwise in relation to the other revolted colonies since their situation did not appear settled either. The reports of three government missions to South America to ascertain substantive conditions there were inconclusive.[29] What became apparent was that victories over royalist troops did not translate into internal political stability.[30] Even Buenos Aires, the only jurisdiction with no Spanish presence in 1818, experienced a number of irregular changes of government.

The continued neutrality of the United States, however, came under sustained attack in Congress. The Holy Alliance could not assume neutrality with respect to Spanish America because it favored the royalist side, and the faction led by Speaker of the House of Representatives Henry Clay rejected the neutral stance because it championed the patriot side. Buoyed by the pro-insurgent public opinion, Clay repeatedly urged the administration to participate actively in achieving Spanish American independence by all means short of direct military action. In his opinion, it was both a moral duty and interest of America to "give additional tone, and hope, and confidence to the friends of liberty throughout the world."[31] The advent of sister republics in the Americas was poised to make the cause of liberty and the position of the United States vis-à-vis the European alliance more secure.

Adams countered the criticism by contending that belief in the righteousness of a cause of foreign independence did not justify discarding the principle of non-intervention. His defense of the principle had both prudential and moral facets. Adams worried that foreign independence struggles, just as other kinds of internal conflict, conceal at least some ignoble human qualities and that intervention in them could lead to perilous entanglements abroad and risks to society at home.[32] But apart from prudential concerns, Adams believed that while the inalienable rights cited in America's founding document were universal, securing them was the responsibility of particular political communities. Each people formed a distinct "moral person" and each member of a people was "personally responsible for his society."[33] This meant not only that the primary responsibility of a country's statespersons was to their polity, but also that authoritative judgments of secessionist causes belonged to those waging the contest rather than outsiders. "By what *right* we could take sides?," Adams asked the critics of his Latin American policy of neutrality and non-intervention. "Who in this case of civil war constituted us the *judges* which of the parties has the righteous cause?"[34] (italics original). His conclusion was that attainment of independence cannot but rest on the shoulders of the people who wish it. President Monroe expressed this point more bluntly: if the revolting territories did not beat Spain on their own accord, they did not deserve to be free.[35]

By the end of 1821 the Clay–Adams intervention versus neutrality debate was largely overtaken by events. Mexico, Colombia, Chile, Guatemala, and Buenos Aires had all but evicted the colonial authorities from their territories and Peru, the last bastion of Spanish power in South America, launched its war of independence.[36] As well, the US position became less isolated internationally: it became plain that the British policy toward Latin America rested on the same basic foundations. Though the Monroe administration did not synchronize its policy with London – there were soundings from both sides but the mutual mistrust generated by the wars of 1776–83 and 1812–14 was still palpable – it must have been comforted by the fact that Britain had parted ways with its continental allies on non-intervention in the New (and Old) World. The chances that recognition would drag the United States into a dangerous confrontation with the Holy Alliance hence diminished considerably.

In the March 22, 1822 message to the Congress, President Monroe proposed recognition of those "provinces" that manifestly attained effective independence (Buenos Aires, Chile, Colombia, and Mexico). This, he stressed, did not change his country's standing vis-à-vis the belligerents: it would "observe, in all respects, as heretofore, should the war be continued, the most perfect neutrality between them."[37] The subsequent protest of the Spanish ambassador in Washington provided an occasion for perhaps the best synopsis of the American views of recognition as well as self-determination. In his rejoinder Secretary Adams stated:

> In every question relating to the independence of a nation, two principles are involved; one of *right*, and the other of *fact*; the former exclusively depending upon the determination of the nation itself, and the latter resulting from the successful execution of that determination.... The United States, far from consulting the dictates of a policy questionable in its morality, yielded to an obligation of duty of the highest order by recognizing as independent states nations which, after deliberately asserting their right to that character, have

maintained and established it against all the resistance which had been or could be brought to oppose it.... This recognition ... is the mere acknowledgment of existing facts, with the view to the regular establishment, with the nations newly formed, of those relations, political commercial, which it is the moral obligation of civilized and Christian nations to entertain reciprocally with one another.[38] (italics original)

British Recognition of Spanish American Republics

The European powers reacted to the Spanish collapse overseas and the United States recognition, an act that explicitly trampled on the norms of dynastic legitimacy, with an ever-increasing gulf between the attitudes of Britain and the rest. Though Austrian, Russian, and French diplomats were on occasion critical of Spain and even suggested that some concessions vis-à-vis the Americas may be in Spanish self-interest, they nevertheless held that South American recognition could not proceed without prior acknowledgment from Madrid. Upon learning of Monroe's proposal of recognition, Austria's Chancellor Metternich disputed the American assertion that *de facto* statehood could be assumed to incarnate genuine political will:

> If the political systems upon which these declarations are founded should be generally approved in Europe, it is evident that henceforth the most illegal and the most audacious enterprises will be judged only by their material success, that any revolt would be sanctioned by the mere fact that the results existed *de facto*, and finally that there would no longer prevail among men any other right than that of force or any other bonds than those imposed by victorious usurpation of a particular moment – bonds which might be dissolved the following moment.

He summarized the Holy Alliance position on recognition as follows:

> As long as there shall exist a Spanish government under a legitimate sovereign, and as long as that government shall not have legally renounced its authority over its former colonies, the courts of Europe ought to suspend any measure which would consecrate as an integral part of international law what up to the present time has been only the fruit of insurrection and civil war.... Whatever may happen, we shall never undertake to deprive the crown of Spain of one of its most precious possessions, nor to sanction by a formal and premature recognition, revolutions to which only a fully demonstrated necessity would some day make us acquiesce.[39]

For Metternich fact could not invalidate right, even if this was slightly qualified by a vague allusion to a potential necessity of acquiescence. Britain, on the other hand, was gradually moving to a position similar to that of the United States. Castlereagh's reply to Spain's complaint about the American decision was that "the state which can neither by its councils nor by its arms effectually assert its own rights over its dependencies, so as to enforce obedience and thus make itself responsible for maintaining their relations with other powers, must sooner or later be prepared to see those relations establish themselves, from the overruling necessity of the case, under some other form."[40]

A decisive British move came in November 1822, just before another congress of the five principal powers in Verona. New Foreign Secretary George Canning admitted for the first time, albeit only to his cabinet colleagues, a possibility that Britain would recognize Spanish American states without the parent country's prior consent: "No man will say that there is a reasonable hope of [Spain] recovering [its colonial] jurisdiction. No man will say that under such circumstances our recognition can be indefinitely postponed. The question is, therefore, one entirely of time and degree." Listing several "late colonies" that achieved effective statehood, just like Monroe did earlier that year, Canning explained the shift by the inability or unwillingness of the Madrid government to prevent and redress the harassment and confiscations of British commercial ships.[41] He insisted that "the general proposition of non-interference in the revolutions of independent nations is necessarily limited by the condition that other nations are not to be directly sufferers by their disorganization." Having complained then about the specific harm done by not reining in, or even tacitly countenancing, attacks on British vessels, he asked whether Britain had any other option but to rely on the constitutive effect of recognition: "What recourse do we have but to take away all pretext for the enforcement of these absurd and obsolete pretensions against us, by conferring on the colonies, so far as our recognition can do it, an independent, instead of a colonial character, thus cutting short all disputes as to Spain's colonial jurisdiction?"[42]

The stance that sovereignty entails international responsibilities and not just rights was communicated then to the allies at the Congress of Verona. Though some powers of the Holy Alliance, notably France, were inclined to see Britain's wish to bring an end to its maritime woes as valid, all of them objected adamantly to any scenario entailing recognition without prior Spanish approval as violating international law and legitimacy.[43] The Duke of Wellington, the head of the British delegation at the congress and the former commander of his country's Iberian expedition against Napoleon, even reported to his superior that behind the scenes the continental representatives expressed regret that Britain behaved as if it had been "the protector of Jacobins and insurgents in all parts of the world."[44]

The congress terminated without any agreement. Still, Britain did not forsake the multilateral "Concert of Europe" approach and opt for a unilateral recognition. It continued to search for reconciliation between the parent country and Spanish America. In 1822, Castlereagh undertook initial explorations of conflict resolution on the basis of independence of new states, and Canning continued in that track. Spanish America was to be offered Spain's recognition. The carrot presented to Spain was the potential transformation of the new republics into monarchies headed by princes from the Spanish royal family.[45] Like his predecessor, Canning preferred Britain's kind of constitutional monarchy to a republic,[46] and wished to see it as an element of the final settlement. But as much as he might have wanted this outcome, he unreservedly opposed its imposition by coercive means. The foreign secretary encouraged the continental allies to persuade Spain to negotiate accession of Bourbon princes with the new states, but if he had to decide between independence of *de facto* republics and an armed campaign to impose monarchy, he chose the former without hesitation. This attitude in fact mirrored that of the Monroe administration: it verbally encouraged republican-ism south of its borders, but it was by no means disinclined to recognize monarchies (as it did Mexico, an empire from 1822 to 1823, and Brazil).[47]

The clearest indication of this disposition was Canning's reaction to wide-spread reports in the fall of 1823 that France, which intervened on behalf of the Holy Alliance in Spain to restore absolutism earlier that year, was also preparing a naval campaign against Spanish America. In a series of conversations with French ambassador in London Prince de Polignac, the minutes of which were abridged into the so-called *Polignac Memorandum*, Canning conveyed the opinion that

> whenever the mother country shall have clearly lost the means of enforcing the submission of the colonies, neither justice, nor humanity nor the interests either of Europe or of America would, in the opinion of His Majesty's government, allow that the struggle . . . should be taken up afresh by other hands; but would rather *prescribe* the recognition of such of those states as, after establishing the fact of their independence, shall have formed also governments apparently of sufficient consistency to contract and maintain external political relations. (italics added)

The foreign secretary put France and later other allies on notice that Britain could not look with indifference either to transfer of any colonies to any foreign power or at intervention of any power on behalf of Spain.[48] A very similar warning – in its fundamentals if not in all of its concerns and scope – was uttered in President Monroe's address to the Congress in December 1823; this more famous statement became known as the Monroe Doctrine.[49] Though unconnected,[50] both pronounce-ments were interpreted in South America as an affirmation of a non-interventionist "American system."[51]

Britain made known its choice to recognize new republics in December 1824 by making public its intention to negotiate treaties of commerce and amity with three countries that unquestionably separated themselves from Spain. The measure was decided after the January 1824 offer of British mediation had been rejected by Madrid – Ferdinand was consistently against independence of Spanish America in any form.[52] Mexico, Colombia, and Buenos Aires were recognized on the grounds that they had attained effective statehood[53] and there was a pressing need to have regulated relations with them, so that they could be held them accountable for treatment of British subjects on their land and off their coasts. In a dispatch communicated to the government of Spain as well as to all major European powers, Canning wrote of "the utter hopelessness of the success of any attempt to bring those provinces again under subjection to the mother country." Because Peru still had some royalist resistance, and because Britain had no precise information about the situation on the small Chilean archipelago of Chiloe, which had hitherto been under royalist control, their recognition was delayed.

The most inflamed reaction to the British announcement was predictably that of Spain. In the lengthy protest note, Foreign Minister Francisco de Zea Bermudez accused Britain of abandoning the moral and legal precept that "rebellion does not constitute a right" and of "disowning the legitimate rights of the King of Spain and the Indies." What will become of the society of states, he asked, if Britain, having engaged in exemplary resistance against Napoleon's usurpations, "now takes up the cause of a handful of rebels?" Zea Bermudez promised that Ferdinand VII would "never abandon the rights of his crown" and "never cease to employ the force of arms against his rebellious subjects, conformable to the principles of the rights of nations, inherent in the existence of all thrones."

Yet, in contrast to the British response to France's recognition of the United States in 1778, Zea Bermudez did not dwell purely on the subject of dynastic rights. He also assailed Canning's assertion that the countries Britain wanted to recognize had been effective states. The minister was adamant that the "pretended" states of Mexico, Colombia, and Buenos Aires had been in the grip of civil war, anarchy, and disorder. "Are these consolidated governments? Are these the governments which present sufficient stability and security to induce Great Britain to treat with them?"[54] These comments suggest that the question of fact was not deemed meaningless even by as ultra-legitimist a power as Spain.[55]

Canning began his rebuttal by stating that Spain was in "a denial of the facts" concerning the three countries. Without elaborating further, he concentrated in the remainder of his reply on the issue of right. Having been accused of violating international law, he asked rhetorically: "Has it ever been admitted as an axiom, or ever been observed by any nation or government, as a practical maxim, that no circumstances, and no time should entitle a *de facto* government to recognition?" He replied negatively and gave two examples from Spanish history itself – the Dutch Republic and Portugal – the former, ironically, listed in France's response of 1779 to the British charge of premature recognition of the United States. The parent country recognized their separation decades after the fact, but third parties did not in the meantime wait for "the slow conviction of Spain" and established direct relations with the two *de facto* entities.

Then Canning turned to the situation Britain had faced in the Western Hemisphere. He stressed that "the separation of the Spanish colonies has been neither our work, nor our wish." But it was "the duty of the British government" to tend to "the plain and legitimate interest of the nation whose welfare is committed to its charge" and to remedy adverse repercussions of that separation. And he clinched the discussion of international right with the following point:

> All political communities are responsible to other political communities for their conduct: that is, they are bound to perform the ordinary international duties, and to afford redress for any violation of the rights of others by their citizens or subjects.

Now, either the parent country must have continued responsible for acts over which it could no longer exercise the shadow of a control, or the inhabitants of those countries, whose independent political existence was, in fact, established, but to whom the acknowledgment of that independence was denied, must have been placed in a situation in which they were either wholly irresponsible for all their actions, or were to be visited, for such of those actions as might furnish ground of complaint to other nations, with the punishment due to pirates and outlaws.

If the former of these alternatives, the total irresponsibility of unrecognized states, be too absurd to be maintained, and if the latter, the treatment of their inhabitants as pirates and outlaws, be too monstrous to be applied, for an indefinite length of time, to a large portion of the habitable globe, no other choice remained for Great Britain, or for any country having intercourse with Spanish American provinces, but to recognize in due time their political existence as states, and thus bring them within the pale of those rights and duties, which civilized nations are bound mutually to respect and are entitled reciprocally to claim from each other.[56]

The response makes it plain that Britain had not regarded the Spanish American insurrections in any way comparable to Napoleon's usurpations. The British lay more emphasis on the international responsibility argument in their defense of recognition of Hispanic America than did the Americans in theirs,[57] but that does not mean that they would have disagreed with the American proposition that *de facto* states deserve recognition since they represent "the will of the nation substantially declared." Castlereagh's rejection of the Holy Alliance doctrine of coercive intervention, after all, reflected partly the conviction that those living under an abusive government had a right to remove it. If one admitted that such a government could be justifiably ousted, then it was only logical for that person to accept the ouster itself. Indeed, it is hard not to conclude that Canning's international responsibility argument was grounded in, and depended directly on, the primary justice argument. For if the only concern was that there is a government responsible to third parties, then there was no *prima facie* reason why that government could not be that of Spain, restored by a Franco–Russian military expedition.

How did other powers react to the British recognition? The United States was the sole country that endorsed it. Austria, Russia, France, and Prussia all protested against it, albeit, it must be added, not with overt hostility. Prussia judged the British decision to be "contrary to the rights of sovereigns and to the principles of legitimacy – principles which had been established as the rule of conduct for the great European alliance."[58] Conveying worries about the future of dynastic legitimacy, Austria not only described Britain's announcement as "the final blow to the interests of Spain in the New World," but also expressed apprehension that it "tended to encourage the revolutionary spirit, which it had been so difficult to restrain in Europe."[59] Russia echoed Prussia's concern about infringements on "the rights of sovereignty"[60] and France reiterated Austria's apprehension about signals sent by "a successful resistance to legitimate authority."[61]

Although they diverged from Britain on what the facts were or what their weight was in relation to dynastic rights, even the most legitimist regimes now made references to facts. Russia disputed that Mexico had been an effective state and that royalist troops had been defeated conclusively. Whereas in early 1822 Metternich criticized the resort to factual arguments concerning the actual state of American territories in the Spanish protest against US recognition,[62] in late 1823 he conceded that "the re-establishment of the royal authority over those possessions appeared to be almost hopeless" and said to the possibly baffled British ambassador in Vienna that "if after all Spain could not be brought to adopt a line of conduct consistent with the situation in which the course of events had placed her with respect to the Spanish colonies, it would remain for each power to take the line which might be most conducive to its own interests."[63] The seemingly schizophrenic position of, on the one hand, the fear that "great calamities would be brought upon Europe by the establishment of . . . vast republics in the New World" and, on the other, the political impossibility to forever disregard *de facto* independence of the new states when some European countries (not Austria) had prior relations with them, may provide clues as to why the Austrian reaction to the British decision was overall so tepid.

In the end, Prussia, France, the Netherlands, Denmark, Portugal, and Sweden did not put off recognition of Spanish American republics until Spain did so. In the case of France, the change occurred after the July Revolution of 1830. The court of the "bourgeois king" Louis Philippe quickly formalized ties with most Spanish American republics and was actually the first to have acknowledged Bolivia.[64] Spain also began extending recognition after the demise of domestic absolutism. In 1836, three years after the death of Ferdinand VII, the restored Cortes approved unanimously the report of its special committee examining the issue of signing treaties with the new states.[65] After a consensus during the chamber debate that these countries had been *de facto* independent, the report blamed for previous non-recognition the pre-1833 absolutism:

> At various epochs the Cortes has expressed its opinion concerning the necessity and advantage of recognizing the independence of our former continental possessions in America; but the vicissitudes of which we have been the witnesses and victims have always found in the absolute government an obstacle to prevent that opinion from producing results as effective as the nation desired.[66]

Recognizing Brazil

On the surface, the process of international emancipation of Portuguese America differed from that of Spanish America. Brazil's independence was acknowledged by European states after Portugal's recognition, as the doctrine of dynastic legitimacy required. In addition, Brazil was the only claimant of statehood in the hemisphere to conserve monarchy. Even if its liberal constitution did not have contemporary equivalents on the European continent, in the eyes of legitimist powers Brazil belonged to a class distinct from its republican neighbors. Though reproaching it for defying the parent country, they regarded Brazil far more favorably than other claimants in the Americas. Still, in terms of principles of recognition espoused, on the one hand, by Britain and the United States and, on the other, by the Holy Alliance Portuguese and Spanish America were not distinct. A closer look at the recognition of Brazil can help us appreciate them more fully.

By 1808, Portugal had been, just like its neighbor, overrun by Napoleon. The royal Braganza family was able, however, to avoid the fate of Ferdinand: with British assistance it managed to escape to its possession of Brazil. The court remained there even after the restoration of 1814/15 and returned to Lisbon only in 1821. A year after King John VI and his entourage left Rio de Janeiro, the Brazilian parliament, unhappy with the attachment to the country which wanted to treat Brazil as a dependency despite its elevation to the status of a separate kingdom in 1815, in a quick succession of unilateral moves proclaimed independence from Portugal and then elected John's son Peter, previously appointed as the kingdom's prince regent, as Emperor of Brazil. The justification of independence resembled that of the United States or Spanish America in that it presented a long catalogue of abuses by the metropole, the impossibility of their expiation with time, and the popular consent for independence. Emphasizing that government must be founded on "popular power," Peter in his manifesto to the world announced that independence had been acceded to on the basis of "the general will of the Brazilian people."[67] In 1824, then, the parliament in Rio de Janeiro adopted a constitution that was, according to Adam Watson, "a model of liberalism and balance of powers, based on British and American as well as Brazilian practice."[68]

Immediately after the proclamation of independence, Brazil sent its envoys abroad to ask for recognition. To the legitimist powers Peter claimed that he had been forced into independence; that without it the preservation of the House of Braganza in Brazil was threatened, as the dominant liberal faction in the parliament was prepared to make Brazil a sovereign republic or even to break it up into several republics. But his attempt faltered: the diplomats assembled at the congress in Verona refused to admit the Brazilian representative who arrived to address them officially as a delegate of a new state. The United States was also initially reluctant to treat Brazil as a sovereign state as armed clashes erupted between the followers of Peter and those with allegiance to his father and Portugal.

But as the year 1823 progressed, the relatively mild contest waned. Those who wished for independence prevailed decisively. The Monroe administration opted to recognize Brazil soon thereafter and established diplomatic relations with it on the same ground as with other Latin American states. To the Portuguese protest that this constituted an unfriendly act, John Quincy Adams replied that his country was always neutral in the conflict between Brazil and Portugal and that it merely recognized a state existing in fact:

Faithful to the principle that every independent people have the right to form, and to organize their government as to them shall see best, in the pursuit of their own happiness, and without encroaching upon the rights of others, they have recognized the Brazilian government, as existing in fact, and exercise all the authorities essential to the maintenance of the usual relations between the United States and other foreign independent powers.[69]

The British principles also did not deviate from those enunciated in regards to Spanish America. In February 1823, Canning wrote that because independence of Brazil appeared "a consummation little liable to failure," its recognition was only a question of time. He did not expect future implosion that would disrupt it because "the apparent acquiescence of the Brazilian people in the new order of things alleviates in a great measure the apprehension of internal commotion and civil war."[70] Just as in the case of Spain and Spanish America, Britain professed preference for mutual reconciliation to any premature recognition and offered mediation to Portugal and Brazil, informing about it its continental allies. In contrast to Spain, Portugal agreed. Britain was joined in the task by Austria, interested in the Brazilian settlement because of Peter's marriage to a Habsburg princess. Britain's goal was to preserve Brazil's monarchy as well to prevent the tension with Portugal from escalating into a full-fledged war. Austria wanted the same, but in addition it sought to ensure respect for dynastic right. Despite agreement with Britain on "the utter impossibility of reuniting Brazil to Portugal as a colony,"[71] Austria was not disposed to recognize Brazil should the mediation have failed due to Portuguese obstinacy.[72]

Metternich also wanted to scale back Brazil's emerging liberal institutions. He chastised Brazil not only for its "frontal attack on the principle of legitimacy," but also for its new constitution.[73] The basic law contained "perilous" ideas, "above all the dogma of the sovereignty of the people," which was "extremely dangerous everywhere." When notified by Brazilian agents that nothing could be done about the constitution lest the monarchy might crumble, Metternich was compelled to moderate his design. In an April 1825 policy statement, he had to admit that "independence is demanded by Brazil. This step is popular in that country and it is possible that the last security of the dynasty of Braganza is to be found in the support of Brazilian independence."[74] Thereafter, he pushed first and foremost for a speedy reconciliation with Portugal.

Portugal signed a treaty of recognition with Brazil in August 1825.[75] For Britain this meant that it did not have to face the quandary it confronted with respect to Spanish America. While several months earlier Canning had questioned whether it was "true dignity to insist upon pretensions which there are not the means of maintaining"[76] and had resolved not to "hold out against an indefinite and unreasonable refusal of Portugal to comply with the necessity of her situation and come to some arrangement with Brazil,"[77] his fears of prolonged intransigence were dispelled. Following Portugal, Britain, Austria, and other countries proceeded with their own acknowledgment.

It is noteworthy that Britain's move was preceded by an appeal that Brazil terminates and renounces the slave trade. This was one of the first instances that a recognition claimant was asked to pledge or perform something that went beyond the requirement that a new state be legitimately founded (irrespective of whether one took as the standard of legitimacy dynastic right or settled fact).[78] Britain was the leading advocate of the abolition of the slave trade but could make a case that it was acting in the international as opposed to national interest: this important "standard of civilization" of the time was agreed to in a convention signed during the Congress of Vienna by all maritime powers present except Portugal.[79]

Uti Possidetis Juris

Uti possidetis did not have its international premiere in Latin America. The United States, for instance, offered it as the basis of a settlement with Britain during its war of independence. Still, it was not until the rise of multiple new states in Latin America that the principle developed into a rule applicable to new entities simultaneously acceding to independence.

The advent of a dozen new states within a decade brought with it a number of jurisdictional problems. The principal one was that independent states of Spanish America had to supplant the stratified, overlapping, and at times mercurial organization of Spanish administration overseas. Spain distinguished between colonial jurisdictions of higher type (viceroyalties) and lower type (captaincies-general, *presidencias, audiencias,* and provinces). In all but one case, political identities and loyalties of inhabitants had been attached to smaller, juridically lower units and it was those units that declared independence. Nevertheless, the independence movement in viceroyal capitals would in a number of instances claim them on the ground that they had been part of a former viceroyalty. The authorities in Buenos Aires, the former metropolis of the Viceroyalty of the Rio de la Plata and the capital of the newly heralded "United Provinces of the Rio de la Plata," controlled only what would eventually become Argentina, but also claimed the jurisdictions of Charcas (later Bolivia), Paraguay, and the Banda Oriental (later Uruguay). The government in Lima, the former capital of the Viceroyalty of Peru, controlled no more than what later became the Peruvian Republic, but that did not stop it from claiming Charcas, since in 1810, in a measure not accepted by Buenos Aires, the Spanish crown transferred the *audiencia* from the Rio de la Plata to Peru. Asserting that Quito (later Ecuador), as an *audiencia* of the former Viceroyalty of New Granada, was rightfully part of New Granada's "successor state," the Colombian Republic, Simon Bolivar, Colombia's president, had occupied it even before the representatives of this jurisdiction had an opportunity to decide on their allegiance.[80]

These and other actual and potential conflicting claims promised, if unchecked and acted upon, unremitting disorder. To forestall this scenario, the leaders of the newly formed republics gradually agreed to accept all political communities that managed to establish themselves *de facto* within the administrative divisions drawn by the Spanish crown, without regard for their previous standing in the hierarchy of Spanish colonial law.[81] In other words, where major colonial lines did not prove to be politically feasible – that is, loyalties had not existed at the level of viceroyalties – lesser administrative boundaries delineated by Spain were followed.[82] *Uti possidetis juris* did not determine which units were eligible for sovereign status, but it did determine that once they established themselves as *de facto* states, they were to inherit whatever borders they had under colonial law and were not entitled to territory beyond them.[83] *Uti possidetis juris* was thus expressly tied and subordinated to the *de facto* principle.[84] In the case of South America the "borders at the time of independence" were taken to be the divisions of 1810, in the case of Central America those of 1821.[85]

The insistence on *uti possidetis juris* manifested itself in several places around the time of Latin American independence. The most important example from the perspective of this inquiry is the establishment of Uruguay on the territory of the former province of the Banda Oriental. As most of the Spanish-speaking continent, the province became embroiled in 1810 in revolutionary activity. By 1816, it became obvious that the Banda Oriental established independence against Spain and Buenos Aires, both of which claimed it. However, in 1816, the Portuguese troops stationed in neighboring Brazil invaded and occupied the Banda Oriental. This was not their first time on the territory's soil: in 1812, having been unable to suppress the revolutionary movement in the restless province, the royal governor in Montevideo invited the Portuguese army. With the involvement of British diplomats the Portuguese subsequently left. In 1816, the presence of the Portuguese was not requested, though. They cited the need to restore order so as to thwart the disrupting effects of anarchy on Brazil.

Spain protested and demanded withdrawal. Portugal refused but agreed that its presence would be provisional, provided that Spain compensated it for cross-border damages suffered by Brazil. It also accepted mediation by European powers. The mediation failed to solve the lingering crisis and the conflict was eventually transformed into one between Brazil and the Rio de la Plata. After 1822, Brazil claimed the province on account of effectively occupying it at the time of independence,[86] whereas the newly formed United Provinces of the Rio de la Plata demanded the Banda Oriental as belonging to the former viceroyalty. All of Spanish America opposed the Brazilian claim as tantamount to forcible takeover and the inhabitants themselves fought the occupying troops.[87] Brazil also had no support among European states. Unilateral conquest between crowns was disapproved no less by the continental powers than by Britain and the United States.

As both states were soliciting international recognition,[88] a war between them broke out over the province in 1825. Soon thereafter they invited Britain to mediate between them. Foreign Secretary Canning in his instructions to intermediary Lord Ponsonby outlined two possible outcomes: the province was to be either ceded to Buenos Aires or erected into an independent state.[89] Canning categorically rejected the claim that the Banda Oriental belonged to Brazil since

Brazil had occupied it at the time of independence, suggesting that, if made good upon, it would amount to "absolute conquest." He implored Brazil to accept what the Spanish American republics had already embraced, *uti possidetis juris*:

> Unless by a general tacit agreement the *states* of the New World be admitted to stand towards each other in respect to geographical *rights* and limits exactly as they stood when colonies, questions of the utmost perplexity will infallibly arise out of rival and conflicting pretensions, and the whole continent of America, whether Spanish or Portuguese, will ultimately be laid open to the designs of any enterprising adventurer who may think fit to carve out for themselves new dominions.[90] (italics added)

After several months of what amounted to an early exemplar of shuttle diplomacy, Ponsonby expressed his preference for Canning's second option. He came to believe that the hostilities between the countries could be terminated most effectively by placing a barrier between them. But besides the strategic consideration, there was one more significant factor to take into account:

> The Orientalists are as little disposed to permit Buenos Aires to have the supremacy over them as they are to submit to the sovereignty of His Imperial Majesty, the Emperor. They fight against the Brazilians, but it is to rescue themselves and their country from a galling thralldom, not to place it under the authority of Buenos Aires; and if the Emperor shall ever be driven from the Banda Oriental, the Orientalists will soon be just as ready to fight against Buenos Aires for their independence as they are to do so now against Brazil.[91]

Thereafter Britain sought to persuade the Buenos Aires government that independence for the province east of the river Uruguay was the best option for the future internal peace of the Rio de la Plata as well as for the regional stability. In the end, it accepted the British proposal. Brazil did too, after having been warned by the British of the urgings upon Bolivar to organize an expedition of Spanish American republics against Brazil[92] and pleadings not to endanger the sole remaining monarchy in the Western Hemisphere.[93]

Conclusion

The recognition of new states in Latin America disclosed a distinct turn away from the notion of dynastic rights. This shift, which required both extended argumentation and assertion of power, was primarily the work of the United States and Great Britain. For all the suspicion precluding close Anglo-American cooperation, both countries shared a basic approach to the claims of independence emanating from Central and South America. This approach can be summarized as follows:

1. There is a fundamental difference between external and internal challenges to the sovereignty and territorial integrity of an existing state. The former

involving relations between states are quintessential international questions; the latter, involving relations between the government and its people, are not.

2. The question of the change of sovereignty title from inside an existing state has two distinct dimensions – one concerns the existing state in which the change is about to take, or is taking, place and the other concerns third parties.

3. Looking from inside the existing state, renunciation of sovereignty by a segment of its population comes in the form of an assertion that the parent government violated its constitutional or natural rights. Looking from outside the existing state, this decision to secede is part and parcel of a natural right to determine one's government.

4. From an external perspective, the execution of the decision to change one's sovereignty pertains to those who made it. Just as third parties cannot judge authoritatively the merits of the decision, so they cannot intervene coercively to bring it about.

5. If independence is declared from within the existing foreign state and this declaration is contested by the parent government, the proper posture for third parties is one of non-intervention and neutrality with respect to either side of the contest.

6. While an existing state has a right to demand respect from third parties for its territorial integrity, its internal replacement by a *de facto* independent state effectively extinguishes that right. As "the will of the nation substantially declared," the d*e facto* state alters the moral as well as practical situation for third parties.

7. The *de facto* state has a right to independence vis-à-vis international society. As such, it has a right to obtain foreign recognition and third parties have a corresponding obligation to extend it. A third party can postpone recognition, but neither arbitrarily nor indefinitely: there must be compelling reasons for a delay.

8. A recognized state has an automatic obligation to abide by customary international law in its relations with the recognizing states.

9. Borders of a recognized state should coincide with its *de facto* limits. Excluded are claims of territories not actually controlled by that state or territories taken by force from other (*de facto*) states.

10. It is reasonable of states responding to a request for recognition to ask a *de facto* state – that is an entity which otherwise qualifies for recognition – for the commitment to fulfill extra conditions which are of general interest to international society.

Though recognition of *de facto* states was essentially the product of the United States and Britain, its practice was gradually adopted by other powers. While in the US case, only France and the Dutch Republic *preceded* British recognition, Austria and Russia were the only major powers that *waited for* Spanish recognition to follow with their own acknowledgment of Spanish American republics.

De facto statehood became the undisputed standard of recognition in the Americas as well as by American states[94] and a mighty challenge to Europe's legitimist powers. How the *de facto* principle planted seeds in Europe of the nineteenth century is the theme of Chapter 3.

Notes

1. One recent exception is Benedict Anderson, *Imagined Communities: Reflections on the Origins and Spread of Nationalism*, rev. ed. (London: Verso, 1991), ch. 4.
2. They were, in alphabetical order: Argentina, Bolivia, Brazil, Colombia, Chile, Ecuador, Guatemala, Mexico, Paraguay, Peru, Uruguay, and Venezuela.
3. During the French Revolutionary Wars Britain began to undergo a series of constitutional reforms designed to weaken the authority of the crown, which proved very strong around the time of the US War of Independence, and to strengthen the representative character of its government.
4. See, for example, Act of the Supreme Junta of New Granada, relative to the Relations between the Provinces and the Kingdom of Spain, July 26, 1810, BFSP, Vol. 1, part 2, pp. 1237–42.
5. The only country in which the local *junta* did so before Ferdinand's return to the throne was Venezuela.
6. See Declaration of Independence of the Confederated Provinces of Venezuela, July 5, 1811, BFSP, Vol. 1, part 2, pp. 1108–13. On the influence of the *US Declaration of Independence*, see also David Armitage, *The Declaration of Independence: A Global History* (Cambridge, MA: Harvard University Press, 2007), pp. 118–22.
7. In addition, the famous sentence in Art. 3 of the 1789 Declaration of the Rights of Man and the Citizen – "sovereignty resides essentially in the nation" – can be found, either verbatim or slightly altered, in the early constitutional documents of Venezuela, the United Provinces of the Rio de la Plata, Chile, Colombia, Peru, Mexico, Bolivia, and Uruguay. References to "the rights of the man and the citizen" were inserted into the constitutions of Guatemala and the Dominican Republic. All of these constitutions then entrenched popular representation as one of the main principles of their government. See BFSP, Vols. 6 (1816–19), 8 (1820/1), 9 (1821/2), 10 (1822/3), 11 (1823/4), 13 (1825/6), and 14 (1826/7).
8. The Quadruple Alliance of 1815 became quintuple by admission of France at the Congress of Aix-la-Chapelle in 1818.
9. Castlereagh to Wellesley, April 1, 1812, and Instructions to the Commissioners of Mediation to Spanish America, April 2, 1812, Charles K. Webster (ed.), *Britain and the Independence of Latin America*, Vol. 2 (London: Oxford University Press, 1938), pp. 309–16 and 317–21.
10. Foreign Office "Confidential Memorandum," August 20, 1817, Webster, *Britain and the Independence of Latin America*, Vol. 2, p. 354.
11. San Carlos to Castlereagh, December 10, 1817, Webster, *Britain and the Independence of Latin America*, Vol. 2, pp. 360–3.
12. See William S. Robertson, *France and Latin American Independence* (New York: Octagon Books, 1967), pp. 153–4.
13. Castlereagh to Bathurst, November 2, 1818, Webster, *Britain and the Independence of Latin America*, Vol. 2, p. 64.

14. Though it was frequently confused at the time, and still is, the Quadruple Alliance (from 1818 Quintuple Alliance) was not the same thing as the Holy Alliance. Each was founded by a different document. The purpose of the former was to implement and uphold the Vienna settlement. The latter, not signed by Britain, was a vague agreement to support Christian principles in domestic and foreign policy. In the minds of proponents of dynastic legitimacy, the two documents grew inseparable, but Britain consistently opposed this view. Moreover, its leaders argued the settlement was to protect the parties only against external threats. For the treaty that set up the Quadruple Alliance, see note 71 of Chapter 1 and for the treaty that established the Holy Alliance see Treaty between Austria, Prussia, and Russia, September 18, 1815, MET, Vol. 1, pp. 317–19.

15. State Paper of May 5, 1820, Harold Temperley and Lillian M. Penson (eds.), *Foundations of British Foreign Policy: From Pitt (1792) to Salisbury (1902)* (New York: Barnes & Noble, 1966), p. 54.

16. Memorandum on the Treaties of 1814 and 1815 submitted by the British Plenipotentiaries at the Conference of Aix-la-Chapelle, October 1818, in Charles K. Webster, *The Congress of Vienna, 1814–1815* (New York: Barnes & Noble, 1969), p. 192.

17. Ibid., p. 191.

18. Ibid., p. 192.

19. Castlereagh to Stewart, December 17, 1820, Sabine Freitag and Peter Wende (eds.), *British Envoys to Germany, 1816–1866*, Vol. 1 (Cambridge: Cambridge University Press, 2000), p. 509.

20. Quoted in Charles K. Webster, *The Foreign Policy of Castlereagh, 1815–1822: Britain and the European Alliance* (London: G. Bell and Sons, 1925), p. 415.

21. State Paper of May 5, 1820, Temperley and Penson, *Foundations of British Foreign Policy*, p. 61.

22. Circular Dispatch to British Missions at Foreign Courts, January 19, 1821, MET, Vol. 1, pp. 664–6. Castlereagh responded in this document directly to the Protocol of Troppau in which Austria, Russia, and Prussia arrogated for themselves "an indisputable right in contemplating common measures of safety against states in which the government has been overthrown by rebellion, and which, if only as an example, must consequently be treated as hostile to all lawful constitutions and governments." See Circular Dispatch of the Courts of Austria, Russia, and Prussia, December 8, 1820, Mack Walker (ed.), *Metternich's Europe* (New York: Walker and Company, 1968), p. 128.

23. William S. Robertson, "The Recognition of the Hispanic American Nations by the United States," *The Hispanic American Historical Review*, 1 (1918), pp. 243–4.

24. Adams to Monroe, August 24, 1818, Worthington Ford (ed.), *Writings of John Quincy Adams*, Vol. 6 (New York: Macmillan, 1916), pp. 442–3.

25. See Adams to Anderson, May 27, 1823, William R. Manning (ed.), *Diplomatic Correspondence of the United States Concerning the Independence of the Latin American Nations*, Vol. 1 (New York: Oxford University Press, 1925), p. 198–9.

26. Ibid., p. 198.

27. Ibid., pp. 194–5.

28. Jefferson asserted that "it accords with our principles to acknowledge any government to be rightful which is formed by the will of the nation substantially declared" in a letter to the US ambassador in France seeking instructions on how to deal with the government that deposed the monarchy. See Jefferson to Morris, November 7, 1792, Francis Wharton (ed.), *A Digest of the International Law of the United States*, Vol. 1

(Washington, DC: Government Printing Office, 1887), p. 521; This is how Grotian thinkers such as Pufendorf and Vattel, as noted in the introduction, thought about rightful authority. According to Julius Goebel, however, there is no evidence that Jefferson drew on them directly. See his *The Recognition Policy of the United States* (New York: Longmans, Green & Co., 1915), p. 98; It is also important to note that foreign policymakers, whether legitimists, or *de factoists*, did not differentiate between rules guiding recognition of states and recognition of governments. Adams thus only applied to recognition of states the *de facto* criteria that Jefferson articulated with respect to recognition of governments.

29. See Arthur P. Whitaker, *The United States and the Independence of Latin America, 1800–30* (Baltimore: The John Hopkins Press, 1941), pp. 248–50.
30. See Frederic L. Paxson, *The Independence of the South American Republics: A Study in Recognition and Foreign Policy*, 2nd ed. (Philadelphia: Ferris & Leach, 1916), p. 136.
31. Toast and Response at Public Dinner, May 19, 1821, James F. Hopkins (ed.), *The Papers of Henry Clay*, Vol. 3 (Lexington: University of Kentucky Press, 1963), p. 80.
32. In a landmark speech, which was a direct response to Clay's public campaign, Adams said:

> Wherever the standard of freedom and independence has been or shall be unfurled, there will [America's] heart, her benedictions and her prayers be. But she goes not abroad, in search of monsters to destroy. She is the well-wisher to the freedom and independence of all. She is the champion and vindicator only of her own.... She well knows that by once enlisting under other banners than her own, were they even the banners of foreign independence, she would involve herself beyond the power of extrication, in all the wars of interest and intrigue, of individual avarice, envy, and ambition, which assume the colors and usurp the standard of freedom. The fundamental maxims of her policy would insensibly change from *liberty* to *force*.... She might become the dictatress of the world. She would be no longer the ruler of her own spirit. (italics original)

See Address of July 4, 1821, Walter LaFeber (ed.), *John Quincy Adams and American Continental Empire* (Chicago: Quadrangle Books, 1965), p. 45.

33. Quoted in Greg Russell, "John Quincy Adams and the Ethics of America's National Interest," *Review of International Studies*, 19 (1993), p. 30.
34. Adams to Everett, December 29, 1817, in Ford, *Writings of John Quincy Adams*, Vol. 6, p. 281.
35. Monroe to Jackson, December 21, 1818, quoted in Whitaker, *The United States and the Independence of Latin America*, p. 211; This was hardly an unrepresentative or isolated view. Classical liberal thinkers such Immanuel Kant and John Stuart Mill argued that genuine self-determination could be achieved only by one's arduous efforts and admitted intervention only on behalf of established *de facto* states. In addition to the already cited passages of Kant in Chapter 1, this is also suggested in Preliminary Article no. 5 of his *Perpetual Peace* which prohibits foreign intervention into an ongoing separatist conflict: "As long as this internal conflict is not yet decided, the interference of external powers would be a violation of the rights of an independent people who is merely struggling with its internal ills." See Kant, "Perpetual Peace," p. 96; Mill argued that "the only test possessing any real value, of a people's having become fit for popular institutions, is that they, or a sufficient portion of them to prevail in the contest, are willing to brave labour and danger for their liberation.... If they have not sufficient love of liberty to be able to wrest it from merely domestic oppressors, the liberty which is bestowed on them by other hands than their own will have nothing real, nothing

permanent. No people ever was or remained free, but because it was determined to be so . . ." See his "A Few Words on Non-Intervention," Gertrude Himmelfarb (ed.), *John Stuart Mill: Essays on Politics and Culture* (Garden City, NY: Doubleday and Company, 1962), pp. 410–11.

36. The Republic of Colombia, formed in 1819, eventually comprised three former parts of Spanish America: the Captaincy-General of Venezuela, the *Audiencia* of Quito (later Ecuador), and what in 1811 became the United Provinces of New Granada (today Colombia and Panama). In 1830, this "Great Colombia," as it was called, dissolved. The United Provinces of Central America was proclaimed on the territory of the former Captaincy-General of Guatemala in 1821, and was, therefore, habitually referred to as "Guatemala." Soon after its establishment it merged with Mexico. In 1823, it cut, without resistance, its constitutional ties to Mexico. In 1824, Chiapas, one of the component jurisdictions of the United Provinces of Central America, voted in a plebiscite to join Mexico. In 1838–41, the federation broke up into its remaining constituent units: El Salvador, Honduras, Costa Rica, Nicaragua, and Guatemala. As with the three successors of Great Colombia, all of them attained mutual and international recognition. The permissibility of recognition of new states created through mutual agreement or at least non-opposition was in principle not disputed, though this did not do away with the requirement that the new states be effectively independent.

37. Monroe to the United States House of Representatives, March 8, 1822, Manning, *Diplomatic Correspondence*, Vol. 1, pp. 146–8.

38. Adams to Andagua, April 6, 1822, ibid., pp. 156–7.

39. Metternich to Lebzeltern, June 5, 1822, quoted in William S. Robertson, "Metternich's Attitude toward Revolutions in Latin America," *The Hispanic American Historical Review*, 21 (1941), pp. 540–1.

40. Londonderry to Onis, June 28, 1822, Webster, *Britain and the Independence of Latin America*, Vol. 2, p. 388.

41. The British trade with the colonies had been regulated by a bilateral treaty with Spain from 1810. It suffered at the hands of pirates and various Spanish naval units trying to disrupt the commerce of the insurgent territories.

42. Canning's Memorandum for the Cabinet, November 15, 1822, Webster, *Britain and the Independence of Latin America*, Vol. 2, pp. 393–8.

43. See documents relating to the Congress of Verona – the British memorandum, Austrian, Russian, Prussian, and French replies as well as relevant excerpts from the conference minutes – in Webster, *Britain and the Independence of Latin America*, Vol. 2, pp. 76–83.

44. Wellington to Canning, November 26, 1822, Webster, *Britain and the Independence of Latin America*, Vol. 2, p. 78.

45. Some Latin American leaders, Simon Bolivar among them, were open to consider monarchical government in their countries. This stemmed from their dissatisfaction with the internal instability of the new republics and/or admiration for the British model of government.

46. British leaders of the period generally believed that democratic republics born out of revolution were potential threats to the stable international order. In this they did not differ from the statesmen of the Holy Alliance. In light of the experience of 1792–1815 and in contrast to the diplomacy surrounding US independence, the internal system of government of prospective states was a key issue for the European great powers.

47. Goebel, *The Recognition Policy of the United States*, p. 139.

48. Canning to Polignac, September 22, 1823, Webster, *Britain and the Independence of Latin America*, Vol. 2, pp. 114–15.
49. The president's address, *inter alia*, declared:

> With the existing colonies or dependencies of any European power we have not interfered and shall not interfere. But with the governments who have declared their independence and maintained it, and whose independence we have, on great consideration and on just principles, acknowledged, we could not view any interposition for the purpose of oppressing them, or controlling in any other manner their destiny, by any European power in any other light than as the manifestation of an unfriendly disposition toward the United States.

Monroe also stated unambiguously that for the United States "the government *de facto* was the legitimate government." See Message of President Monroe, at the commencement of the first session of the Eighteenth Congress of the United States, December 2, 1823, Manning, *Diplomatic Correspondence*, Vol. 1, p. 217.
50. Canning offered Adams a joint declaration, but mutual suspicions in the end scuttled the scheme. However, it is apparent from the exchanges between the two powers that they agreed upon the fundamental features of interstate relations in the Americas. See Dexter Perkins, *A History of the Monroe Doctrine* (Boston: Little, Brown and Company, 1955), pp. 36–7.
51. See William S. Robertson, "South America and the Monroe Doctrine, 1824–1828," *Political Science Quarterly*, 30 (1915), pp. 82–105.
52. Canning warned his allies in the *Polignac Memorandum* that the British government had had no desire to act precipitously "so long as there was any reasonable chance of an accommodation with the mother country by which such a recognition might come first from Spain," but it could not wait indefinitely for, or make its own recognition of new states dependent on, this result. See Memorandum of a Conference between the Prince de Polignac and Mr. Canning, Begun Thursday October 9 and Concluded Sunday, October 12, 1823, Webster, *Britain and the Independence of Latin America*, Vol. 2, pp. 115–20.
53. Before making its decision, the British government sent commissioners to each party interested in obtaining UK recognition. Their goal was to determine: (*a*) whether the party renounced irrevocably all political connections with Spain; (*b*) whether it had the power as well as the will to maintain the independence which it has established; and (*c*) whether "the frame of its government was such as to afford a reasonable security for the continuance of its internal peace and for the good faith with which it would be enabled to maintain whatever relations it might contract with other powers." See, for instance, Canning to Parish, August 23, 1824, ibid., Vol. 1, p. 114; Several polities requesting recognition were also asked whether they abolished the slave trade. In contrast to the first three questions, the aim of this query was not to ascertain presence of effective statehood but rather incorporation of an international standard into the domestic legislation. See, for instance, Queries submitted to the Minister of Foreign Affairs of the State of Chile, May 15, 1824, ibid., Vol. 1, p. 354.
54. Zea Bermudez to the British Chargé d'Affaires at Madrid, January 21, 1825, Herbert A. Smith (ed.), *Great Britain and the Law of Nations*, Vol. 1 (London: P. S. King & Son, 1932), pp. 152–60.
55. Spain had resorted to the factual arguments also in the protest against President Monroe's announcement of recognition in 1822. The Spanish ambassador in Washington had accused the United States of not waiting for the outcome of the

purportedly still ongoing contest between the mother country and would-be republics. He had also denied in some detail that the latter had formed *de facto* states. See Anduaga to Adams, March 9, 1822, Manning, *Diplomatic Correspondence*, Vol. 3, p. 2010.

56. Canning to Los Rios, March 25, 1825, Smith, *Great Britain and the Law of Nations*, Vol. 1, pp. 162–70.

57. That this was also an American concern is obvious not only from the already quoted reply to the Spanish protest against Monroe's message of recognition, but also from the (abortive) American proposal to Britain in 1819 to coordinate their recognition decisions:

> [T]hese newly formed states should be regularly recognized not only because the right to such recognition cannot with justice be long denied to them, but that they may be held to observe on their part to ordinary rules of the law of nations, in their intercourse with the civilized world. We particularly believe that the only effectual means of repressing the excessive irregularities and piratical depredations of armed vessels under their flags and bearing their commissions, will be to require of them the observance of the principles, sanctioned by the practice of maritime nations. It is not to be expected that they will feel themselves bound by the ordinary duties of sovereign states, while they are denied the enjoyment of all their rights.

See Adams to Rush, January 1, 1819, Manning, *Diplomatic Correspondence*, Vol. 1, p. 87.

58. Maltzahn to Canning, March 4, 1825, Manning, *Diplomatic Correspondence*, Vol. 3, p. 1541.

59. Wellesley to Canning, January 17, 1825, Webster, *Britain and the Independence of Latin America*, Vol. 2, p 35.

60. Lieven to Canning, March 2, 1825, Manning, *Diplomatic Correspondence*, Vol. 3, pp. 1538–40.

61. Granville to Canning, February 20, 1825, Webster, *Britain and the Independence of Latin America*, Vol. 2, p. 167.

62. Metternich to Vincent, March 6, 1822, quoted in Robertson, "Metternich's Attitude toward Revolutions in Latin America," p. 542.

63. Wellesley to Canning, December 20, 1823, Webster, *Britain and the Independence of Latin America*, Vol. 2, p. 20. Once Metternich saw the complete futility of Spanish attempts to defeat the secessions, he seemed to prefer Madrid's negotiations with them about the establishment of Bourbon monarchies in Spanish America, even at the price of their independence. See Robertson, "Metternich's Attitude toward Revolutions in Latin America," p. 547.

64. Robertson, *France and Latin American Independence*, p. 553; Legitimist Charles X, however, recognized the independence of Haiti, which cast off French rule in 1804, in 1825.

65. William S. Robertson, "The Recognition of the Spanish Colonies by the Motherland," *The Hispanic American Historical Review*, 1 (1918), pp. 80–1.

66. Quoted in ibid., p. 77.

67. Succinct, and True Exposition of the Facts, that Led the Prince, now Emperor, and the Brazilian People to Declare Brazil a Free, and Independent Nation, August 6, 1822, Manning, *Diplomatic Correspondence*, Vol. 2, pp. 780–4.

68. Adam Watson, "New States in the Americas," in Bull and Watson, *The Expansion of International Society*, p. 129.

69. Adams to Pereira, June 9, 1824, Manning, *Diplomatic Correspondence*, Vol. 1, pp. 222–3; "Government" means "state" in this instance. In the English usage of the time the term

"government" referred to both the state and the governing regime, so one has to be sensitive to context in order to discern the correct of the two meanings.

70. Canning also showed understanding, for Brazil's move to secede and alter its official name: "It was no wonder that [Peter] was forced to proclaim independence in view of the attacks upon him by the Portuguese Cortes. The titles Empire and Emperor are only incident to this independence, but they were in fact concession to the 'democratical' party in Brazil, which was strong enough to overthrow the monarchy altogether if defied." See Canning to Stuart, March 14, 1825, Webster, *Britain and the Independence of Latin America*, Vol. 1, p. 267.

71. Wellesley to Canning, September 4, 1823, Webster, *Britain and the Independence of Latin America*, Vol. 2, p. 15.

72. By October 1824 all the principal European powers, except Britain and France, had pledged not to acknowledge Brazil unless Portugal did so. See Alan K. Manchester, "The Recognition of Brazilian Independence," *The Hispanic American Historical Review*, 31 (1951), p. 89 (n. 33).

73. Quoted in Robertson, "Metternich's Attitude toward Revolutions in Latin America," p. 551.

74. Metternich to Eszterhazy, April 19, 1825, quoted in Robertson, "Metternich's Attitude toward Revolutions in Latin America," p. 555.

75. See Treaty between His Most Faithful Majesty and His Imperial Majesty, concerning the Recognition of the Empire of Brazil, August 29, 1825, BFSP, Vol. 12, pp. 675–6.

76. Canning to Stuart, March 14, 1825, Webster, *Britain and the Independence of Latin America*, Vol. 1, p. 267.

77. Canning to Chamberlain, January 12, 1825, ibid., p. 253.

78. For its part, the United States demanded from Brazil as well as Spanish American republics to be placed upon the footing of the most favored nation in trade. Equal commercial terms among established states were not a norm at the time, but the United States was of the opinion that new states ought not to discriminate, in commercial terms they offer, among prospective recognizing countries. See Adams to Monroe, August 24, 1818, Ford, *Writings of John Quincy Adams*, Vol. 6, p. 443.

79. See Canning to Chamberlain, February 15, 1823, Webster, *Britain and the Independence of Latin America*, Vol. 1, pp. 220–1.

80. Jaime E. Rodriguez, *The Independence of Spanish America* (Cambridge: Cambridge University Press, 1998), pp. 223–6.

81. See Santiago Torres Bernárdez, "The *Uti Possidetis Juris* Principle in Historical Perspective," in Konrad Ginther et al., *Völkerrecht zwischen Normativen Anspruch und Politischer Realität* (Berlin: Duncker & Humblot, 1994), pp. 417, 424.

82. See Lyon, "New States and International Order," p. 32.

83. For a detailed description of how the advent of *uti possidetis juris* in Latin America undermined the right of conquest, see Sharon Korman, *The Right of Conquest: The Acquisition of Territory by Force in International Law and Practice* (Oxford: Clarendon Press, 1996), pp. 234–8.

84. See Suzanne Lalonde, *Determining Boundaries in a Conflicted World: The Role of Uti Possidetis* (Montreal: McGill-Queen's University Press, 2002), p. 237; the case of the Dominican Republic serves to illustrate this point. The Dominican Republic declared independence from Spain in December 1821. In the course of establishing itself as a *de facto* state, however, it was attacked and conquered by its neighbor Haiti in February 1822. There was subsequently no suggestion internationally that the Dominican Republic, not yet a *de facto* state, had had a right to exist or a right to have its colonial

boundaries normatively protected. When the Dominicans overthrew Haitian rule in 1844, they were recognized, just as those entities that had cast off Spanish rule, as a new state on the *de facto* basis.

85. *Uti possidetis juris* did not avert boundary disputes or even wars in Latin America. However, the overwhelming majority of them did not arise out of non-acceptance or violation of *uti possidetis*, but out of difficulties with determining the actual location of the borders of 1810 and 1821. The colonial cartographic documents and maps were often sketchy and imprecise and this left a fertile ground for competing boundary claims. But while there have been plenty of such disputes, major forcible territorial changes have been very rare.

86. Brazil professed *uti possidetis de facto*, the inheritance of all territory actually possessed at the time of independence, as the principle to be applied to Latin America. This did not find any support abroad and was, in fact, strenuously opposed by the South American republics.

87. See the document of August 25, 1825, reasserting the independence of Banda Oriental and declaring the Brazilian annexation null and void in Albert P. Blaustein, Jay Sigler, and Benjamin R. Beede (eds.), *Independence Documents of the World*, Vol. 2 (Dobbs Ferry, NY: Oceana Publications, 1977), p. 744.

88. As indicated in the earlier discussion of US recognition of Spanish America, the United States refused to acknowledge the Rio de la Plata with the territory it claimed. As early as 1819 Adams indicated that his eventual recognition "will be a mere acknowledgment of the fact of independence...without deciding upon the extent of their territory, or upon their claims of sovereignty, in any part of the Provinces of La Plata, where it is not established or uncontested." See Adams to Rush, January 1, 1819, Manning, *Diplomatic Correspondence*, Vol. 1, pp. 87–8. When it came, the US acknowledgment only applied to the territory the Rio de la Plata had actually controlled, the "province of Buenos Aires." See Adams to Rodney, May 17, 1823, ibid., p. 187 and John B. Moore (ed.), *A Digest of International Law*, Vol. 1 (Washington: Government Printing Office, 1906), pp. 90–1. Britain acted in the same fashion. See Canning to Parish, December 26, 1824, in Webster, *Britain and the Independence of Latin America*, Vol. 1, pp. 119–20. In fact, the two powers normally referred to the new country simply as "Buenos Aires."

89. Canning to Ponsonby, February 28, 1826, Webster, *Britain and the Independence of Latin America*, Vol. 1, p. 138.

90. Canning to Ponsonby, March 18, 1826, ibid., pp. 139–44. For an official view of the United States supporting the principle of *uti possidetis juris* in the Americas, see Moore, *Digest of International Law*, Vol. 1, p. 303.

91. Ponsonby to Canning, October 20, 1826, p. 159.

92. Canning to Ponsonby, March 18, 1826, p. 142.

93. See "Preface," in Webster, *Britain and the Independence of Latin America*, Vol. 1, p. 70.

94. The United States adhered to the standard even when it could have been used against its own territorial integrity during the secessionist attempt of the "Confederate States of America" in 1861–5. While it insisted that "it is the right of this government to ask all foreign powers that the latter shall take no steps which may tend to encourage the revolutionary movement of the seceding states," the Union leadership admitted "that a nation may, and even ought, to recognize a new state which has absolutely and beyond question effected its independence, and permanently established its sovereignty; and that a recognition in such a case affords no just cause of offence to the government of the country from which the new state has so detached itself." See Black to US Ministers

Abroad, February 28, 1861, Wharton, *A Digest of the International Law of the United States*, Vol. 1, pp. 540, and Seward to Adams, April 10, 1861, FRUS, Vol. 1 (1861), pp. 76–7; Appealing to the *de facto* principle, the United States recognized also Haiti and Liberia. Prior to the Civil War, fears of revolt by slaveholding Southern states prevented successive US administrations to recognize the two black republics. The case of Haiti in particular is a good example of vital domestic interests overriding the otherwise consistently applied recognition criteria as well as the advocacy by prominent figures such as John Quincy Adams. In 1861, Abraham Lincoln repudiated that stance by proclaiming to the Congress that "if any good reason exists why we should persevere longer in withholding our recognition of the independence and sovereignty of Haiti and Liberia, I am unable to discern it." See his Annual Message to Congress, December 3, 1861, Roy P. Basler (ed.), *Collected Works of Abraham Lincoln*, Vol. 5 (New Brunswick, NJ: Rutgers University Press, 1953), p. 39; On recognition of Haiti and Liberia see Charles H. Wesley, "The Struggle for the Recognition of Haiti and Liberia as Independent Republics," *The Journal of Negro History* 2 (1917), pp. 369–83, and Tim Matthewson, "Jefferson and the Non-Recognition of Haiti," *Proceedings of the American Philosophical Society* 140 (1996), pp. 22–48.

3

New States in Nineteenth-Century Europe

The settlement of 1815 had two main purposes: (*a*) to restore the European monarchies that had been conquered by France and (*b*) to inaugurate close cooperation among the most powerful of them so as to uphold international order and prevent another major war. The second objective proved full of challenges since the Quintuple Alliance in its role of the guardian of the post-Napoleonic system found itself, as Chapter 2 suggested, in the midst of a profound philosophical split on the scope of its responsibility. The principal reason for this divergence was the British, and after July 1830 also French, dismissal of the idea that maintenance of international order requires the alliance to concern itself with internal as well as external affairs of states.

Despite these rifts, the essential contours of recognition of new states in nineteenth-century Europe were consistent with the American and British policy toward Latin America. Whether for normative reasons or reasons of pragmatic necessity, members of the society of states moved toward recognizing indigenously established *de facto* states. This view became evermore entrenched with the demise of the Holy Alliance in the mid-1850s. By the 1870s, dynastic legitimacy had been in visible retreat: it played only a marginal role in the recognition of a united Germany in 1871 and none at all in that of the Balkan states in 1878. In Quincy Wright's words, "the political right of revolution, the legal right to recognition, and the policy of recognizing *de facto* governments, suggested by the Declaration of Independence and Monroe Doctrine, were increasingly recognized by all states during the nineteenth century."[1]

This development was in no small measure due to changing domestic politics of European states themselves. Between the 1820s and the late 1870s the number of absolutist regimes markedly dropped and that of at least nominally constitutional monarchies correspondingly climbed. However shaky or reversible the course of this transformation, countries that espoused political and constitutional liberalism at home found it impossible to be consistently indifferent to its principles abroad. Besides Great Britain, this was true above all of France, which, as a great power, was heavily engaged in the formulation of European policies.[2] As it underwent substantial reforms and federalization in 1866–7, the same also applied to Austria. As for Russia, it remained both a stalwart defender of dynastic rights in western and central Europe and domestically absolutist; in the southeastern corner of the continent, on the other hand, it turned into the strongest foreign exponent of the claims of Orthodox peoples for national emancipation.

The mapping of state recognition in nineteenth-century Europe in this chapter can be conveniently divided along geographical lines. The first part covers new states founded in the area of the Vienna settlement. Belgium's independence as well as unification of Italy and Germany entailed direct revisions of the covenants from 1814 to 1815 or of subsequent agreements that amended them. The second covers countries in the southeastern corner of Europe – Greece, Serbia, Monte-negro, and Romania – formed out of the decomposing Ottoman Empire. That empire was neither present in Vienna nor was it fully integrated into the interna-tional legal system prior to 1856.

Foreign acknowledgment of these states shared common attributes. As in Latin America, the question of their recognition did not arise before evidence of substantial *de facto* establishment. Outsiders got involved only when the contests began to have detrimental external effects – whether on security of third parties, the authority of interstate treaties, maritime trade of neutrals, or a combination thereof. Because the great powers shared a collective function of custodians of the European order, they also played the vanguard in all recognition decisions. While they continued to place a premium on collaborative practices, the attachment to the Concert of Europe "rules of the game" weakened in the second half of the nineteenth century, especially in regards to the repudiation of unilateral con-quest. This became particularly apparent in the German unification. There, first Austria and Prussia, and then Prussia alone, were successful in using and fostering disunity among the other powers to prevent opposition to their forcible acquisi-tions of several neighboring states.

The border delimitation of the new European states, just as those of Central and South America, was informed first and foremost by the *de facto* territorial principle. The great powers recognized both those countries that had had previ-ous juridical status and those that had not. In the latter case the new boundaries enclosed essentially the area of *de facto* independence. Other factors such as integrity of lines of communication, frontier defensibility, or economic necessity could have warranted adjustment of those boundaries, but their importance was secondary and the scope of the modifications relatively minor.

THE AREA OF THE VIENNA SETTLEMENT

Recognizing Belgium

The Vienna settlement incorporated Belgium, prior to 1790 an Austrian realm, into the United Kingdom of the Netherlands. For a variety of reasons, the unity of the Belgian and Dutch provinces came under severe strain in the 1820s. The linguistic, economic, administrative, educational, and religious policies of King William II of Orange engendered a growing Belgian opposition to his rule. While not overtly oppressive, Dutch rule made the Belgians feel like second-class citizens.[3] A revolt against the king broke out in August 1830. As William failed to address satisfactorily the Belgian grievances, a provisional government, formed in Brussels, declared independence in October invoking "the will of the inhabitants."[4] All the laws of the provisional legislative body began with the heading, "In the Name of the Belgian People," and the title of the new head of state was to be "King of the Belgians," thus invoking the "King of the French" given to Louis XVI by the National Assembly in 1790. The Belgian revolution was rapidly triumphant – barely a month after the proclamation of independence the volunteer militias managed to evict royal troops from the entire country except Antwerp.

Having incurred rapid losses, William appealed for military intervention to the great powers as guarantors of the 1814–15 treaty provisions concerning the Low Countries. The powers showed immediate concern about the Belgian events as large-scale changes, which the revolt augured, necessarily affected the strategic situation in Europe. The crucial position of the territory – captured shortly after the fall of the French monarchy in 1792 – in the system of balance of power that the Vienna settlement sought to establish had been explicitly acknowledged in the First Treaty of Paris and its frontiers with France were thereafter fortified so as to protect the Low Countries, the Rhineland, and even the British Isles from a French attack. Those fortresses were now in insurgent hands. The Holy Alliance, in addition, saw in the separatist uprising yet another assault on dynastic legitimacy.

With the exception of Russia, which initiated mobilization of its army, the great powers were reluctant to heed the Dutch request. Britain and the new "King of the French" Louis Philippe,[5] who took power in the wake of the revolt against the absolute king just a month before the uprising in Belgium, professed belief in non-intervention in internal affairs of foreign countries. Austria worried about mounting a major campaign far away from home and Prussia about bearing the brunt of any fighting. Perceiving the lack of enthusiasm to aid William II and facing large-scale revolt in Russian Poland in November 1830, Russian Tsar Nicholas I decided against proceeding alone. But in words virtually identical to those of Ferdinand VII pleading with the allies to understand what was at stake in the battle against the Spanish territories in the Americas, he warned: "It is not Belgium which I understand to be battling here, it is revolution, which, from closer and closer, and quicker than anyone would believe, threatens even us, if we are seen trembling before it."[6]

Given the potentially grave implications of the events in the Low Countries, the great powers nonetheless decided to coordinate their response when asked by the Dutch king to mediate the conflict. The chosen method was a diplomatic conference in London, the first objective of which was to arrange for an armistice. When by mid-December both parties had officially accepted it, the conference moved to deliberate larger political questions "with a view to remedy the derangement which the troubles that have taken place in Belgium have caused in the system established in treaties of 1814 and 1815."[7]

The swift collapse of Dutch rule and its replacement by provisional Belgian authorities combined with the immense strategic value of the region compelled the great powers to think about a change of Belgium's international standing. That the old arrangement had not met the expectations and, therefore, could not continue was quite clear from Protocol No. 7 of the London Conference. It left no doubt that a realistic solution could not but encompass two sovereign entities.[8] However, if the great powers were clear on independence of Belgium, they were also unambiguous on its obligations as a successor state to the kingdom established in 1814–15:

> United to Holland, and forming an integral part of the Kingdom of the Netherlands, Belgium had to fulfill its part of the European duties of that kingdom, and of the obligations which the treaties had caused it to contract towards other powers. Its separation from Holland cannot liberate it from that part of its duties and obligations. The conference will consequently proceed to discuss and concert new arrangements, as may be proper for combining the future independence of Belgium with the stipulation of treaties, with the interests and security of other powers, and with the preservation of the balance of power in Europe.

Recognition of Belgium, like that of South America, thus entered the diplomatic agenda only with the strong prospect of its *de facto* independence. The British government had harbored misgivings about the Dutch king for months, but it was not before the separation was judged to be an "irreversible fact" that Foreign Secretary Palmerston talked publicly about the inevitability of two independent states.[9] His position was to reject right at the outset armed coercion, as did his predecessors in relation to Latin America: "Any attempt to again join those countries together under any modification of union would probably be as repugnant to the wishes of the Dutch, as it would be to the wishes of the Belgians, and to any attempt to re-establish such a union by force, Her Majesty's government never could consent." He suggested that it would be contrary to Britain's principles to "interfere otherwise than by [its] counsel in the arrangements which the Belgians may make for the constitution of their internal government, except in so far as any proposed arrangement might affect the interests of neighboring powers or the general security of Europe." The French government expressed similar views.[10]

The mandate of Russia's representative in London was to see the kingdom's "integrity under the domination of the House of Orange, and with complete security for the fortresses which must protect its independence."[11] Russia might have wanted to safeguard the legitimist cause, but it did not find much support for keeping the Netherlands united, even in Austria. As early as mid-October, Metternich presciently reported to his emperor that the cause of the Netherlands was completely lost.[12] Given the fear in the Holy Alliance that the king of the French might recommence "Jacobin" foreign policy, the main objective of Austria was to settle the conflict in a way that would avert France's annexation of Belgium.

In Protocols Nos. 11 and 12 of January 20 and 27, 1831, the great powers outlined terms of separation and state succession and combined them in eighteen articles titled *Bases destined to establish the independence and future existence of*

Belgium.[13] With few exceptions where contiguity and existing communication lines demanded minor alterations so as to ensure viable countries, the territories of Holland and Belgium were to conform to those of the Dutch Republic in 1790 and Belgium in 1815, respectively. *Uti possidetis juris* is not mentioned expressly anywhere in the conference records, but seeing that the contesting parties were not able to agree on a territorial settlement, the powers clearly favored the extant juridical lines. To preclude a possible disruption of the European balance of power by way of invasion, Belgium was to be perpetually neutral on the model of Switzerland from 1814 to 1815. Its neutrality and territorial integrity were to be underwritten by the five powers.[14]

At first, the Dutch side protested the decisions of the conference. Its objection to Protocol No. 7, on the one hand, expressed disappointment at the "extreme promptitude" of concluding that the union could not be maintained and stressed that a parliamentary committee looked into reforming laws so as to "satisfy the expectations of an immense majority of the inhabitants"; and, on the other, deemed it to violate the treaties from 1814 to 1815, undermine respect for "conservative principles" and ignore "the danger which at present more than ever results from every deviation from the legally established rule."[15] Upon the adoption of the *Bases of Separation* by the conference, the Dutch king raised his objections to being placed "on the same footing as that of the revolutionary government which has established itself in Belgium," to the very authority of the conference, as a mediating body, to separate a part of his territory, and to the bases themselves for being "derogatory of his sovereignty" and "subversive of the rights of nations."[16] Though not rejecting the *Bases of Separation* outright, the Belgian government did not approve the document either: it was unsatisfied with the territorial settlement as well as with requirement of automatic succession to the treaty obligations of the erstwhile kingdom.

Having run up against discontent and criticism from both parties, the five powers believed it necessary to defend their authority and conduct. Their quarrel concerning Spanish America did not recur because they were all in agreement that if internal affairs of a state have immediate and serious repercussions externally, they appropriately become international concerns. Recalling first their role in establishing the Kingdom of Netherlands in 1814–15, they contended in Protocol No. 19 that the union between Holland and Belgium was, in fact, broken, and continued:

> It did not belong to the powers to judge of the causes which severed the ties which they had formed. But when they beheld these ties broken, it belonged to them again to accomplish the object which they proposed to themselves in forming them. It belonged to them to secure, by means of new combinations, that tranquility of Europe, of which the union of Belgium with Holland had constituted one of the bases. To this duty the powers were imperiously called. They had the right, and events rendered it their duty, to prevent the Belgian provinces, become independent, from disturbing the general security and the balance of power of Europe.

To Belgium's objections that it had not signed the treaties to which the Netherlands was a party and was, therefore, not bound by them, the conference retorted that "each nation has its particular rights, but Europe has also her rights; it is social order that has given them to her." Belgian infringements of the agreements signed by the Netherlands would have brought on "confusion and war." Only heeding them conformed to the "interest and repose of the great community of European states." And the five powers added a more general point about external consequences of succession of one state by another: "The events which give birth to a new state in Europe, give it no more right to alter the general system into which it enters, than the changes that may have arisen in the conditions of an ancient state, authorize it to believe itself absolved from its anterior engagements."[17]

Belgium also could not "make conquests" from Holland or from other states whose integrity had been previously confirmed in international law. The powers announced that they could not "recognize a right in another state which they refuse to themselves, and it is upon this mutual renunciation of all idea of conquest that the general peace and the European system at this time rest."[18] Responding to the new Belgian constitution that had stipulated the borders of sovereign Belgium to be those of the 1790 Austrian Netherlands rather than those of (smaller) Belgium of 1815,[19] the powers asserted – reminding one of the earlier British stance in regard to Brazil's extravagant claim of the Banda Oriental – that "no state can arrogate to itself the right of alone fixing its own limits, of comprehending within such pretended limits the territory of its neighbors, and of maintaining that whoever should endeavor to prevent such encroachments, would be interfering in its internal affairs."[20]

Despite its initial protests, the court at The Hague reversed its decision and hastily accepted the *Bases of Separation*. The Belgian government's reluctance continued, but later accepted the slightly altered proposal of treaty of separation with the five powers known as the Twenty-Four Articles – not least because of the threat of the allies to isolate and suspend all relations with it.[21] Taking exception to its provisions on the division of debt, navigation of rivers, and delimitation of borders, the Dutch government withheld its consent from signing treaties either with the allies or Belgium. Following Belgium's signature of the treaty with the five powers, it went so far as to claim that by accepting the *Bases of Separation* it had not agreed to two distinct sovereign states but only to two substantially autonomous units under the same crown. However, the powers stood their ground and after much time and effort – including two conference-backed counter-interventions by France in 1831 and 1832 to evict the invading Dutch troops from the territory assigned to Belgium[22] – the Netherlands accepted the Twenty-Four Articles and signed a treaty on separation with the powers as well as Belgium in 1839.[23]

The success of insurgent Belgians was another bitter pill to swallow for the legitimist powers; however, there were several mitigating factors. Belgium was a monarchy, even if it constitutionally resembled France, Britain, or Brazil more than any devotee of the Holy Alliance. Its geopolitically sensitive position remained protected against possible French designs should France have wished to repeat in the future any of its past revolutionary exploits. Moreover, the London conference was a case of successful great power cooperation that kept wider international structures intact. In the eyes of conservative diplomats this limited the revolution's impact.

Italian Unification

While reducing somewhat the number of entities within them, the Vienna settlement left Italy and Germany divided. The politics in the former was dominated by Austria, which both obtained large swaths of northern Italy in 1815 and had close family ties to, and alliances with, the dynasties ruling central and southern Italy. The public life in the latter was characterized by the rivalry for primacy between two strongest powers within the German Confederation, Austria, and Prussia. In the following decades, dissatisfaction with the settlement grew.

Although the Italian and German national movements, split as they were into myriad factions, emerged as notable social forces not long after the defeat of Napoleon, their first lasting impact on the Vienna system came during the revolutionary years of 1848–9. Sardinia and Prussia, the largest Italian and German powers respectively, then adopted liberal constitutions and intervened militarily on behalf of Italians and Germans beyond their borders. These efforts did not succeed. Sardinia, succored by volunteers from the entire peninsula, intervened to assist the uprisings in the Austrian kingdom of Lombardy-Venetia,[24] but after initial gains was twice defeated by the Austrian army. Endorsed by the confederal diet in Frankfurt, Prussia invaded the ethnically German-populated duchies of Schleswig, Holstein, and Lauenburg – all parts of the Kingdom of Denmark and the latter two also members of the German Confederation – after local Germans had declared their opposition to the plans of the Danish government to end their separate legal status and absorb them into Denmark proper. It signed an armistice and withdrew in the wake of condemnation and warnings from Britain, Russia, and France.

Successive British ministries expressed broad sympathies with both Italian and German movements for greater unity. Though intent on maintaining the policy of non-intervention, they also made it clear that if the wishes of the Italians and Germans to change their political structures were to be accomplished without undue disorder and disruption to the European balance of power, they would meet with British approbation.[25] Whatever route Italian and German unifications might have taken[26] – and for Britain the question was not whether but how it should advance – the British government insisted that they were, no less than Belgium's international status, a European matter, and thus required assent of the signatories of the General Act of the Congress of Vienna.

Austria, the chief benefactor of the Houses of Habsburg and Bourbon on the Italian peninsula, was the stoutest opponent of Italian unification. By 1848 it had been patently obvious that Italy could be unified only at the expense of these dynasties, all absolutist and to varying degrees repressive. Indeed, had it not been for Austria's patronage, including, on occasion, direct armed involvement, most would have likely not survived the multiple attempts at their overthrow as long they had. In contrast, Austria was not in principle opposed to the unification of Germany. There was scarcely anybody content with the day-to-day functioning of the cumbersome arrangements made at the Congress of Vienna in relation to Germany. However, despite this widespread dissatisfaction, there was no consensus on how to modify them. Because Austria and Prussia could not overcome their intra-German rivalry and agree on necessary reforms, the *status quo* was hard to alter.

As a defender of dynastic legitimacy, Russia supported the Austrian position in Italy and indicated that it would endorse a consensual monarchical solution to the German problem. Because the Prussian assault on the duchies went counter this principle by violating the rights of the Danish king, Russia strongly objected to it. What is more, the dependence on the ethnic argument as opposed to accord among established jurisdictions threw into doubt possessions of many European countries; in the case of Russia as well as Prussia, this being most significantly the sizeable lands populated by the Poles.

France's initial positions on Italy and Germany after Louis Napoleon's assumption of presidency in December 1848 were similar to those of Britain. Despite worries that a nephew of Napoleon Bonaparte might revive the aggressive foreign policy of his uncle for revisionist ends, France repeatedly professed the need for a collective Concert of Europe approach toward both. Though he preached political liberalism at home and abroad – Louis Napoleon was the first head of state or government on the continent elected by universal suffrage and argued for some time that the European stability could not be achieved until the "nationalities problem" was solved – his government intervened on the invitation of the papacy and in consultation with Catholic powers to suppress Mazzini's radical "Roman Republic" and restore the Holy See's sovereignty over the Papal States in April 1849.[27] Regarding the question of the Elbe Duchies, France followed the Anglo-Russian line.

The international situation and France's political standing, however, changed dramatically in the wake of the Crimean War. Russia was noticeably weakened in that conflict and in the Treaty of Paris (1856) had to accept stringent restrictions on its naval presence in the Black Sea. Britain, France, and Sardinia – which joined the Ottoman Empire against Russia – came out of it strengthened and re-invigorated. Austria, instead of supporting its most vital conservative ally chose to diminish Russia's influence in southeastern Europe and stayed neutral in the war. Russia's defeat and its alienation from Austria in effect marked the passing of the Holy Alliance.

In these circumstances of sudden Austrian weakness, Sardinia, forced by Austria in 1849 to replace its king but not to drop its constitution, became bent on ejecting Austria from Italy. By fighting in the Crimean War, Sardinia could bring the Italian affairs to the attention of the great powers at the subsequent peace congress and two years later it found a willing partner in Napoleon III with whom it formed a defensive alliance.²⁸ Napoleon and Sardinian Prime Minister Camille di Cavour skillfully provoked Austria into rashly snubbing a great power mediation of the Austro–Sardinian disarmament row by issuing a unilateral ultimatum to, and then declaring war on, Sardinia.²⁹

That the European system had by 1859 changed in dramatic ways since the Congress of Vienna was evident when Sardinia, restored in 1814–15 as an absolute monarchy, proclaimed in its declaration of war that it was taking up arms not only in the defense of the Sardinian throne, but also for liberty, honor, and rights of the whole Italian nation, and ended it with the cry *Viva l'Italia*.³⁰ Thanks to the participation of troops of Napoleon III, whose stated goal was to help a people who "groan beneath foreign oppression,"³¹ Austria was quickly defeated and had to cede Lombardy to Sardinia.

Rather than resolving the Italian question, the war further complicated it. France and Sardinia did not necessarily share the same ultimate objectives. Since 1848 Napoleon consistently advocated a voluntary Italian confederation headed by the pope and modeled after the German Confederation and in both the preliminary peace Treaty of Villafranca and the final Treaty of Zurich Austria concurred to join France in encouraging its creation. In return, France accepted in Art. 19 of the Treaty of Zurich that:

> As the territorial delimitations of the independent states of Italy, who took no part in the late war, can be changed only with the sanction of the powers who presided at their formation and recognized their existence, the rights of the Grand Duke of Tuscany, of the Duke of Modena, and of the Duke of Parma, are expressly reserved for the consideration of high contracting parties.³²

The problem facing France was that revolts in central Italy, which accompanied the war, left the rulers of these principalities in Viennese exile and the papacy fighting to save control of its dominions. Provisional authorities in all the duchies as well as the papal state of Romagna called on Sardinia to send its troops and administrators. Following hurriedly organized legislative elections, the assemblies voted overwhelmingly for unification with Sardinia, thus rebuffing the plans for confederation.

While both France and Austria came to an informal understanding at Villafranca that a European congress similar to the one on Belgium was to be summoned to settle the affairs of Italy – with other powers wishing for the same – a mutually acceptable procedure for one could not be found. Austria wanted the congress to consecrate the existing rights and treaties. This would include return of the deposed dukes to central Italy, by great-power sanctioned military imposition, if necessary. But British Foreign Secretary Lord Malmesbury as early as May 1859 stated that in Britain's long-held view "no country has a right authoritatively to interfere in the internal affairs of a foreign state, or, with a sound policy, long withhold its acknowledgment of any new form of government which may be adopted and established, without territorial usurpation or absorption, by the spontaneous wish of the people."³³ France in principle sided with Britain. Russia and Prussia's "liberal–conservative" government favored Austria's legal argument, but they had no appetite for a military intervention in, and policing of, the recalcitrant duchies.

In the absence of accord on what the projected congress should achieve or how it should proceed in its deliberations, reactions of the great powers to concrete events on the ground became decisive. The British government had a history of criticizing authoritarian and unpopular regimes in Italy that seemed to subsist only due to sponsorship from Vienna and once these were removed, Britain opposed foreign reinstatement of the *émigré* rulers. Lord John Russell, the new foreign secretary and veteran of previous Whig ministries, which included the office of the prime minister during the years 1848–9, wrote to his foreign counterparts that "the people of any country are the best judges of the institutions under which they live" and on this basis "the people of Italy ought to be free to choose how they would be governed, provided they did not injure their neighbors."[34] According to him, the reasons for transfers of sovereignty in Italy were no less compelling than they were in the post-1815 precedents – South America, Greece, or Belgium.[35]

As one by one central Italian assemblies voted against the return of the former rulers and in favor of annexation to Sardinia, the British government repeatedly declared that the United Kingdom would respect their decision. Russell's justification echoed that of Castlereagh forty years earlier. In Russell's view, the "doctrines of 1688," supported by a succession of British statespersons, laid down that "all power held by sovereigns may be forfeited by misconduct, and each nation is the judge of its own government."[36] Since the people of the duchies had overthrown their rulers and declared themselves in favor of unity with Sardinia, Sardinia's claim of authority over them was lawful and its occupation of central Italy could not have been seen as a forcible foreign intervention or a conquest. If Austria had reversionary rights in the duchies, those rights fell "with the parent trunk."[37]

Unsurprisingly, Austria denounced the events taking place in central Italy and the propitious British reactions to them. Its rationalization of the war on Sardinia depicted the empire as a conservative power for whom "religion, morality and historical right are sacred" and warned that "the pretension of forming new states according to the limits of nationalities is the most dangerous of utopian schemes."[38] As continued ducal rule was being renounced in the assemblies, the Austrian government denied that "a people have the right of expelling or of electing their sovereigns."[39] It also refused to accept non-intervention when its vital interests, as in the peninsula, were at stake.

This repudiation turned out to be aimed at the principle. In practice, the recently defeated Austria was too weak to intervene and reinstate the pre-1859 rulers and it had no allies to do so either. Though France was initially unhappy about the extent and speed of changes in Italy – the informal concord between Napoleon III and Cavour did not provide for Sardinia's occupation of the duchies and the Romagna – Britain convinced it that not to accept them would be to go against France's own purported reason for waging the 1859 war: to free Italy from foreign domination. Russia did not admit British or French principles, but as the changes in Italy did not seem to it to upset the "general interests of Europe," it declared merely an indirect interest in the matter.[40] Prussia voiced concern about the breach of dynastic principles, but it betrayed no sign of favoring intervention either.[41]

In this relatively munificent international environment, central Italy held plebiscites on unification with Sardinia and in the ballots based on universal suffrage confirmed the earlier decisions of the assemblies. The official annexation decrees anchored the act in "the result of universal voting," which showed "the general wish of the population" for unity with Sardinia.[42] The expatriate dukes and the pope formally protested against the decrees by denouncing both the "pretended idea" that sovereignty can be transferred or extinguished by popular vote and what they alleged had been fraudulent balloting.[43] The protests portrayed annexations as a product of "sacrilegious usurpation," and all declared them to be a flagrant violation of the law of nations and thus "null and void." However, given the actual dearth of opposition to Sardinia in the duchies, it was these protests, and not Sardinia's decrees, that rang null.

The whole process of unification was to a large extent replicated – and the differences between the United Kingdom and the waning forces of dynastic legitimacy were further sharpened – in the last bastions of *ancién regime* in Italy, the Kingdom of the Two Sicilies, and the rest of the Papal States. Two months after the voluntary annexations of the duchies, Giuseppe Garibaldi, a former military commander of Mazzini's "Roman Republic" and recently decommissioned Sardinian general, assembled an expedition of armed volunteers from Sardinia to Sicily. Sardinia's government claimed it tried to stop the private militia but could not. Garibaldi's goal was to instigate revolutions that would overthrow the legitimist governments so that free southern Italy could express its wish for unification with Sardinia. He had at his disposal only around 1,000 mostly non-professional fighters, but his legion was nevertheless able to spur large-scale uprisings both in Sicily and, after landing on the mainland, in Naples.

Though both Britain and France warned Sardinia not to invade and conquer the Bourbon kingdom by force, the British government was not willing to interfere in a homegrown insurgency against what it referred to as "a misgovernment which has scarcely a parallel in Europe."[44] The Neapolitan government alternately requested Britain's assistance and complained about its views, but in vain. The Neapolitan foreign minister was told that if the royal cause was losing ground, it was because of bad government.[45] The people of Sicily and then Naples could have come together and defend their king against Garibaldi's small force, British officials repeatedly noted, but instead of trying to repel him as an alien invader, they welcomed him as their native liberator.[46]

With Garibaldi's troops nearing Naples in September 1860, Sardinia crossed into the neighboring Church provinces of Umbria and the Marches, where non-Italian mercenaries in the service of papal spiritual authority fought a Garibaldi-inspired uprising. As it spoke of the "duty in the face of Europe . . . not to allow the Italian movement to lose itself in anarchy and disorder," the government explained that its objective was to "reestablish order" by counter-intervening against what it construed as a foreign intervention and by giving the population "full scope for the manifestation of their sentiments."[47] While Austria strongly berated the step, Britain endorsed it on the very basis of Sardinia's rationale.[48]

As Sardinia's troops also entered the Kingdom of the Two Sicilies – its soil, save a tiny coastal area, was free of Bourbon rule but with no firm substitute authority – Britain found itself impelled to further explicate its stance to the fellow great powers. Foreign Secretary Russell argued that while states normally have the unrestricted power to put down rebellions in their territories, "there occur, from time to time, cases in which the ordinary rules established by the law of nations cannot be observed without promoting the continuance of wars . . . threatening a wide extension, and dangerous to the general balance of power." Italy was, according to him, one such exceptional case. The Sardinian king Victor Emmanuel until the intervention respected the territories of the pope and the Neapolitan king, but could not ignore the fact that "the governments of Naples and of Rome were so tyrannical, so corrupt, so demoralizing, so odious to their subjects that their fall might at any time have been expected." Russell declared that the British government "cannot share in the regret which is felt in some parts of Europe at the fall of these governments."[49]

Other powers condemned Sardinia's actions. On the mild side, Prussia argued that although, as a German power, it assigned "the principle of nationalities a very great importance," this principle was not absolute and could not override the obligatory respect "due to the principle of right."[50] Shedding its earlier blasé attitude toward the changes in central Italy, Russia now denounced Sardinia's "infractions of right" which "tended to shake the very basis on which reposes the authority of established governments" and withdrew its chargé d'affaires from Turin.[51] France also removed its ambassador as it objected to the invasion of the Papal States (France had troops in Rome protecting the pope continuously since 1849). But the most embittered reaction came from the besieged king of Naples. His government declared in a memorandum to all the cabinets of Europe that allowing the kingdom's ruin was "the clearest proof that the law of nations and public right no longer exist."[52] The death of international law came about as a result of total loss of respect "for that brotherly claim which should bind monarchs together, in consequence of the divine mandate which they have in common, and of similarity of their interests."[53] Immediate individual interests, whether in the form of material desire for aggrandizement or in the form of "political indifferentism," rather than the collective interest and solidarity carried the day; yet, acting without regard for the "great association of princes" could not eventually yield anything but "the successive demolition of all thrones."

Great Britain rejected all these arguments. In his counter-memorandum to the remnant Neapolitan government Russell wrote, "no force of treaties, no ancient right, no armaments by sea and land, can protect the throne of a sovereign whose counselors rely for safety on arbitrary and cruel punishments rather than on the affections of the people."[54] Treaty arrangements needed to be confirmed by "national feeling and opinion";[55] it was not a duty of foreign powers to "compel by force the obedience of subjects to sovereigns who have not succeeded in securing affection towards their person or respect for their authority."[56]

Once Sardinia took control of southern Italy, its administrators oversaw plebiscites akin to those in the former duchies and the Romagna.[57] Unlike central Italy, which had been appended to the Kingdom of Sardinia, southern Italy was adjoined to the "Italian State."[58] Though in contrast to the conservative powers, Britain did not object to the institution of popular referendum *per se*, it, interestingly, shared their skepticism about the way the Italian plebiscites had been conducted. To Russell the votes in southern Italy appeared to have little validity as they followed upon "acts of popular insurrection, or successful invasion, or upon treaties, and do not in themselves imply any independent exercise of the will of the nation in whose names they are given."[59] A different situation would arise, he informed Prime Minister Cavour, if "the deliberate act" of the representative of the several Italian states, chosen in the upcoming election for the newly constituted national legislative assembly, decided to "constitute those states into one state, in the form of a constitutional monarchy." And the foreign secretary crucially added:

> When the formation of this state shall be announced to Her Majesty, it is hoped that the government of the king will be ready to show that the new monarchy has been erected in pursuance of the deliberate wishes of the people of Italy; and that it has all the attributes of a government prepared to maintain order within, and the relations of peace and amity without. The obligations of the various states of Europe towards each other; the validity of the treaties which fix the territorial circumscription of each state; and the duty of acting in a friendly manner towards all neighbors with whom it is not at war – these are the general ties which bind the nations of Europe together, and which prevent the suspicion, distrust and discord that might otherwise deprive peace of all that makes it happy and secure . . . After the troubles of the last few years Europe has a right to expect that the Italian kingdom shall not be a new source of dissension and alarm.

Once Cavour addressed Russell's concerns and supplied him with information about the constitutional measures passed in the new parliament, Britain, "acting on the principle of respecting the independence of the nations of Europe," was the first to recognize the Kingdom of Italy in March 1861.[60] France ensued in June of that year[61] and Russia in mid-1862 when it returned its diplomatic envoy to Turin.[62] Archenemy Austria formally accepted Italy's existence in 1866 following the war against the alliance of Prussia and Italy.

German Unification

If anything, Germany's road to unification should have been easier than that of Italy as no great power opposed it in principle. There were, however, two major areas of disagreement: what kind of union should be sought and how, by what means, could it be constructed so as to be domestically and internationally acceptable. These dissensions – whether a new Germany should be liberal or conservative, what territories should it include, what political and legal structures should replace those of the confederation, and by what procedures – existed both among the Germans and the great powers. There was not much the latter agreed on beyond the insistence that a new Germany had to be sanctioned by the signatories of the General Act of the Congress of Vienna.

The first indication of a direction in which the process of German unification might go was the rekindled crisis over the Elbe duchies in 1863. That year the Danish king, under tremendous public pressure, adopted a new constitution that in the name of national consolidation terminated, as in 1848, Schleswig's separate juridical identity within the Danish monarchy. The act disturbed the *status quo* agreed upon a decade earlier in the Treaty of London (1852), the final agreement settling the Prusso–Danish war of 1848–9.[63] All the great powers censured the measure as a breach of Denmark's promise not to tamper unilaterally with Schleswig's legal identity. The situation escalated after Prussia warned that if Denmark refused to revoke its constitution as it applied to the duchy, the German powers would hold themselves released from their obligations to observe the Treaty of London and the confederal diet threatened to detach Schleswig, Holstein, and Lauenburg from Denmark altogether.

The difficulty was that, according to the treaty of 1852, the maintenance of Danish territorial integrity as "connected with the general interests of the balance of power in Europe" was appraised to be "of high importance to the preservation of peace." Britain, Russia, and France found themselves in a delicate position. Though the London treaty did not bind them directly as guarantors of Denmark's integrity, they wanted to preserve Danish territory intact, but this very objective could very well involve them in a war against Prussia and other German states.

Both Britain and Russia urged negotiations and warned Prussia and its allies to desist from using force. Foreign Secretary Russell warned against a "war of conquest undertaken by Germany" and Prime Minister Palmerston announced in the House of Commons that should there be parties bent on violently overthrowing Danish integrity or rights "it would not be Denmark alone with which they would have to contend."[64] Still, Palmerston and Russell faced opposition from Queen Victoria and many in their own cabinet who argued either that Denmark itself behaved unreasonably or that a war on its behalf was not worth fighting, or both. Russia and France were not enthusiastic about the option of war either.[65]

Sensing a lack of resolve to oppose them, Prussian King William I and Prime Minister Otto von Bismarck recruited Austria jointly to occupy the duchies so as to make the Danes repeal the Schleswig law. They disregarded the promise of the Danish king to do so as soon as the dissolved parliament is elected even at a price of engaging in hostilities with the Danish army as they crossed into Schleswig. The British cabinet was unable to overcome paralysis of indecision. It was willing to accept, together with Russia and France, the occupation of Schleswig as long as Prussia and Austria pledged their adherence to the 1852 treaty, but could not agree on any measures to be undertaken should this pledge be violated. The contemplated three-power naval demonstration in the Baltic as a deterrent against Prussia never materialized. Split over how to proceed, the cabinet invited the signatories of the treaty to a conference in London.[66]

The London conference managed to arrange a temporary cease-fire in May so the substance of the dispute could thus be discussed. Prussia and Austria, the latter only recently legitimist in Italy but now loath to fall behind in its intra-German competition with Berlin, declared that they no longer respected their prewar engagements vis-à-vis Denmark and demanded a new arrangement. In the wake of this avowal, the British cabinet decided that given that there was no willingness on the part of either France or Russia to use force in the defense of the 1852 treaty and Britain would not do it with Sweden alone, a new settlement should be considered.[67] All the powers accepted that Schleswig should be partitioned between Denmark and Germany,[68] but divisions over how to determine the line proved insurmountable; in the case of Britain, even within the delegation itself. A plebiscite proposal did not succeed: Prussia wanted to restrict it to the duchy, but Danish plenipotentiaries argued that Schleswig was an integral part of the Danish monarchy and that, therefore, the whole of Denmark should determine its fate.[69]

Prussia and Austria along with Denmark were incapable of resolving the impasse and neither were other participants at the conference. Britain suggested mediation by a party not present in London, but while Russia, France, and Sweden accepted the proposal, Austria and Prussia accepted it only conditionally, and Denmark rejected it. The conference ended in failure and Denmark was left on its own. The hostilities resumed and in a matter of weeks the government in Copenhagen was compelled to plea for an armistice and give up the three duchies in their entirety including the ethnically Danish northern Schleswig.

Though Britain found itself unable to actively oppose Denmark's diminution, many in its government were aghast at the way Prussia and Austria had seized the duchies. In Belgium or Italy, international treaty provisions were modified internally, by way of self-determination. Even Sardinia's intervention in, and occupation of, central and southern Italy came only after its *ancien régimes* had been brought to their knees from within. But the case of the Elbe duchies was different. What terminated their Danish status was a forcible external takeover, not an internally affected secession carried out by the population dissatisfied with being part of Denmark. Foreign Secretary Russell condemned the Convention of Gatstein (1865), which divided the principalities between the two countries, in these scathing terms:

> It might have been expected that . . . if an order of rights had been overthrown, another title drawn the assent of the people would have been set up, and that title might have been received with respect and maintained with a prospect of permanence.
>
> But all rights, old and new, whether founded on the solemn compact of sovereigns or on the clear expression of popular will, have been set at naught by the Convention of Gatstein, and the dominion of force is the sole power acknowledge and regarded.

> Violence and conquest are the bases upon which alone the partitioning powers found their agreement.
>
> Her Majesty's government deeply laments the disregard thus shown to the principles of public right, and the legitimate claims of a people to be heard as to the disposal of their own destiny.[70]

Unwittingly, Russell implied that the recognition policy rooted in facts could well take an unintended – and unsavory – direction. From Castlereagh on, British foreign policymakers consistently favored acknowledgment of entities that succeeded in erecting themselves on the ground. The *de facto* polities they endorsed had been presumed to spring from the "clear expression of popular will." Other countries, big and small and not excluding those professing dynastic legitimacy, then sooner or later acquiesced in their existence. But the drive for a new Germany suddenly seemed to introduce a quite different mode of state-making. It also relied on effectively established facts, but these *faits accomplis* would not be the result of internal self-determination but external conquest.[71] These would be exceedingly difficult to overturn when there was no binding obligation to assist the victimized parties, and when the Concert of Europe appeared to be only a feeble version of its former self and those who created the facts themselves hailed from the ranks of great powers. And what is more, precisely because of the power and importance of those who brought them about, the facts would not withstand denial of recognition for too long.

The unification of Germany, in fact, proceeded in a manner similar to the capture of Schleswig-Holstein. As Prussia got involved in a dispute with Austria over its intent to annex the Elbe duchies (the Gatstein agreement did not settle their final status but merely outlined their administration) in early 1866, none of the other great powers found sufficient reasons to resist Prussia's use of force. Britain did not want to partake in a conflict over the division of spoils, if it had decided not to fight against the acquisition of those spoils in the first place; Napoleon III assumed that two countries are of more or less equal military strength and that France could only benefit from their mutual attrition; and Russia, albeit sympathetic to Austria, was not in a position to act alone. The three powers did not resist Prussia's unilateral declaration that it deemed the pro-Austrian German Confederation dissolved; or the forcible incorporation (and thus unilateral extinction of international status) of the Kingdom of Hanover, the Electorate of Hesse-Casel, the Duchy of Nassau, and the Free Town of Frankfurt, Austria's allies among smaller northern German states, upon the quick Austrian defeat in July 1866; or the formation of a Prussia-dominated, Austria-excluding North German Confederation in 1867. Britain remonstrated that "the Confederation owing its existence to the general assent of Europe and having been accepted as a substantive European institution by all the states of Germany, it is not in the power of a single state ... to dissolve the Confederacy without the concurrence of the other non-German powers, who were parties to its institution."[72] Russian foreign minister Gorchakov wrote a statement to be presented commonly with Britain and France that Prussia could not arrogate to itself the right of forming a new confederation on a basis that might affect the balance of power in Europe.[73] But all these efforts were to no avail. Prussia could be stopped only by force and none of the three powers was disposed to entertain that option.

France decided to confront Prussia as the Berlin court had appeared to want to extend its influence beyond Germany by accepting the candidature of a member of its Hohenhollzern dynasty for the vacant Spanish throne in 1870. Britain and Russia supported Napoleon's demands for the retraction of the candidature, but not what they perceived as a gratuitous ultimatum, once the demand was met, to vow in writing never to accept the Spanish throne. Interpreting the rejection of the ultimatum as a slight to French honor and a threat to its "territorial security" as well as "the general balance of power in Europe," France declared war on Prussia in July 1870.[74] Seen as assaulting the whole of Germany, though, France found itself fighting not only North Germany but also the south German states.

Britain and Russia declared, together with other European countries, their neutrality in the conflict. Britain concentrated its diplomatic efforts to obtain formal pledges from the belligerents they would not violate the internationally guaranteed neutral status of Belgium and Luxembourg.[75] As the French army suffered an ignominious defeat and Bismarck made an announcement that North Germany wanted to annex the captured border provinces of Alsace and Lorraine as a defensive buffer zone so as to avert a future French aggression, Britain and Russia persistently turned down the desperate French pleas for direct aid. They also did not object to the agreement of the southern monarchies to join North Germany in November 1870 and the subsequent proclamation of a united "German Empire" in occupied Versailles on January 18, 1871. The other great powers, Italy and the Ottoman Empire in fact recognized the "German Empire" – with no objections raised – mere six days after its proclamation at a London conference dealing with the revision of certain clauses of the 1856 Treaty of Paris.[76]

Some British officials were disturbed by the forced cession of Alsace-Loraine, vocally opposed by its inhabitants as well as its political representatives in the French parliament, no less than by that of the Elbe duchies. Echoing Rousseau's and Burke's revulsion at the custom of transferring inhabitants from sovereignty to sovereignty without any say on their part, Prime Minister William Gladstone asked his foreign minister Lord Granville whether "there was not anything better than simply handing them over as chattels,"[77] "without any voice from collective Europe."[78] The two sounded Russia's views, but Gorchakov's response was that "the mere opinion of the neutral powers without any intention to support it by arms would be disregarded and would have no influence on the military operations against Paris."[79] The British government ultimately adopted this opinion as its own.

OTTOMAN EUROPE

The struggles for national emancipation in the European part of the Ottoman Empire had their origins in the early years of the nineteenth century. Under the influence of the ideas of the early French revolution and the German national movement – a combination simultaneously accentuating political liberalism and ethnonational bonds – their prominence steadily increased. Along with other factors, their rise suggested substantial weaknesses of the once-mighty empire. But if the Ottoman state was in decline, it did still spread from the Danubian basin in the west to Persia in the east, and from the Caucasus in the north to northwestern Africa in the south. Given its location as a gateway to Europe, Asia, and Africa, the fate of the moribund empire could not but touch on various interests of the great powers. Because these interests were time and again in competition with each other, it was apparent that unbridled pursuit of advantages at the expense of other great powers could precipitate a major clash among them. While the Ottoman Empire had not been present at the Congress of Vienna or had not been even treated on the same legal basis of sovereign equality as nominally Christian states of the Euroatlantic world,[80] the five power alliance did regard its vast lands as a component of the European balance of power system.

Recognizing Greece

The first independent state established on Ottoman territory was Greece. Its formation and recognition, at least as for concerns and propensities of the great powers, shared many similarities with Latin America and Belgium. The outbreak of the Greek revolt in 1821 and the declaration of independence a year later elicited no involvement on their part – the Congresses of Laibach (1821) and Verona (1822) rejected Greek pleas for aid and recognition addressed to them – despite sympathies of British and continental public opinion for the Greek cause and Russia's decades-long role as the protector of the empire's Christian subjects.[81] Consistent with its policy of non-intervention, Britain avowed strict neutrality in the internal contest while it was going on and was not affecting the outside world. The Holy Alliance, including Russia, on the other hand, saw the struggle for independence as revolutionary and potentially harmful beyond its confines even though it never extended the concept of dynastic legitimacy to the Ottoman Empire.

The Greek leadership tried also to appeal to the great powers individually. While around the same time the envoys of Brazil's Peter I sought acknowledgment by the United States as a sister liberal democracy, by the United Kingdom as a fellow constitutional monarchy, and by the Holy Alliance as a monarchy headed by a heir of a legitimate king, the provisional government of Count Capodistrias tried to impress Britain with its liberal constitutionalism, Russia with the bonds of Orthodoxy, and both Britain and Austria, suspicious of Russia's intentions vis-à-vis the Ottoman Empire, with Greece's potential to serve as a barrier against Russian expansionism. All were promised that Greece would eventually constitute a monarchy and that the Greek crown would go to a member of a distinguished European royal family.

The unfavorable situation for the Greeks changed only after the sultan – unable to prevail over the insurgents for four years – received naval and infantry aid from his vassal, the Egyptian *pasha*, and the contest began to inflict serious harm on the trade and shipping in the Mediterranean. Despite numerous differences and rivalries among them on issues concerning the Balkans and the Near East, Britain, France, and Russia, the three key actors in the Mediterranean, were able to launch intermittent consultations in the form of ambassadorial meetings and arrive at a common position. In the 1827 Treaty of London they demanded an armistice and offered their mediation to the Porte to end the conflict on the basis of an autonomous Greece. The three powers – endorsed by Prussia though not Austria – defended their involvement by the need to put an end to the struggle which "daily causes fresh impediments to the commerce of the states of Europe and gives opportunity for acts of piracy . . . [exposing] the subjects of high contracting parties to grievous losses"; by Britain and France having been asked by the Greeks to mediate; and by humanitarian motives to stop the increasingly vicious violence.[82] The first, and the most important, rationale was thus identical to the British argument for involvement in Spanish America, later accepted even by the reluctant conservative powers.

The Greeks accepted the mediation on the basis of autonomy, but the Ottoman side refused it as a foreign interference contrary to Muslim law.[83] The treaty provided for coordination of measures aimed at cessation of fighting even if one or both parties rejected its terms and the three governments jointly decided to compel the end of injury-causing hostilities on the sea. The enforcement of this agreement led first to the naval confrontation at Navarino in October 1827, which destroyed the combined Turko–Egyptian fleet, and then to the dispatch of French troops to the island of Morea, invaded by the Egyptians in 1825. The allied interference, not intended to bring Greek independence closer, however, had precisely that effect. The weakened Ottoman forces, short of the vital ally who withdrew in humiliation, were now even less capable of prevailing against the inchoate Greek authority. Furthermore, even Austria's Metternich, previously cold to the "revolution," joined his allies to demand Greek autonomy or independence as a means of restoring order in southeastern Europe.[84]

Even as Russia declared war on the Ottoman Empire in April 1828 over a matter unrelated to the Greek question, the three powers continued their meetings to flesh out the general propositions of the Treaty of London. In a crucial Boundary Protocol of Poros of December 1828, endorsed by Austria, they suggested Greece's territory should include: (*a*) the territories, both insular and mainland, held exclusively by the Greeks; (*b*) those parts of the continent "which have taken the most active and persevering share in the insurrection, and in which the Christian population generally, in consequence of its numbers, and of the comparative extent of its possessions, has the best claims to the independence contemplated by the treaty"; and (c) a single island and a few continental localities not in possession of the Greek government but deemed indispensable for securing Greece's maritime and land frontiers.[85] Significantly, the relatively large regions of Thessaly and Epirus, which the provisional Greek government demanded, were to be excluded from Greece since only a few of their districts had taken any share in the insurrection, several regional chieftains had actually fought on the sultan's side, and the Greek population had lived peacefully alongside the local Turks. We can thus again discern the decisive influence of the *de facto* principle in determination of new international borders: the basis of the new entity's boundaries was to be the territory on which a people freed themselves from their former master. In the Americas or Belgium the peoples defined themselves by pre-existing juridical lines; in contrast to this civic notion of nationhood, the Greeks, who did not have prior to this moment bounded juridical existence, were defined ethnically.[86] Still, the *de facto* principle was the guiding rule of determining borders in all these instances.

The deliberations on the future of Greece culminated in February 1830 in three further protocols, the most important of which proposed that Greece should be an independent state under their guarantee and a monarchy whose ruler should not hail, as it would be a year later in the case of Belgium, from the house of any attending great power.[87] In the end, this was found to be a more practicable arrangement than a tributary autonomy, and the Porte accepted it. The new state, for its part, was requested to institute full religious equality. Because a perfect line for separating the intermingled Greeks and Muslim Turks, as Annex A to the Boundary Protocol of Poros had noted, could not be found and because there were other non-Orthodox minorities with established privileges, Greece was asked to guarantee equal treatment of all its subjects so as to spare the country "from the calamities which the rivalries of the religions therein professed might excite."[88] Like the condition placed on Brazil to end the slave trade, religious equality had no obvious connection to *de facto* statehood, which Greece had already appeared to achieve. It seemed, however, to be considered a "standard of civilization" that, besides being worthy in and of itself, was thought necessary for Greece's internal peace, and thus avoiding future need for foreign involvement.

The final legal articulation of Greek statehood was the 1832 convention between the three powers and Bavaria. The pact was reached after two years of internal turmoil during which the Greek factions had been unable to agree on the head of state and most pleaded with the three powers to take up the task. In the convention the three powers "duly authorized for this purpose by the Greek nation" offered the crown of the new kingdom to Prince Otto of Bavaria and his successors and promised to promote his acceptance by other powers.[89] The Kingdom of Greece was acknowledged by Austria and Prussia in 1833 and within four years by remaining European countries.[90]

Recognizing Romania, Serbia, and Montenegro

The importance of movements for national emancipation grew steadily following the Greek war of independence. Between the 1820s and 1870s there were instances of struggle against the Ottoman Empire among the Serbs, Romanians, and Montenegrins. By the 1870s the movements were a mass phenomenon, reaching even the previously illiterate rural population. The more popular they were, the more difficult it was for the Ottoman authorities to maintain their European subjects' allegiance. The first instinct of the great powers was to preserve the empire as intact as possible, but, at the same time, they understood its intensifying weaknesses and the long-term practical difficulties with the *status quo*. The solution of choice, where possible, was autonomy under national government, at first also proposed in regard to Greece and long existing in Montenegro. The Serbs and Romanians had these arrangements confirmed in the 1829 Treaty of Adrianople and then the 1856 Treaty of Paris, which ended the Crimean War.

But the most daunting challenge for the great powers became the so-called "Great Eastern Crisis" of 1875–8. The crisis began with the anti-Ottoman insurrection in the province of Bosnia and Herzegovina in July 1875. While it initially took the form of peasant uprising against onerous taxation and involved Muslim farm laborers no less than Christian ones, the revolt promptly acquired overtones of a national struggle of Bosnian Croats and Serbs for freedom from Ottoman rule.

The response to Bosnia was at first muted. As with Greece, none of the great powers wanted to interfere in the conflict. Their initial position, however, did not prove tenable for long because the anti-Ottoman agitation spread throughout Serbia, Montenegro, and the Bulgarian provinces and, as such, threatened to upset the very fragile order in southeastern Europe. The violence sent across the Austro-Hungarian border thousands of Serb and Croat refugees. Even more seriously from the point of Austria-Hungary,[91] both Serbia and Montenegro threatened to join the Bosnian Serb struggle. The Habsburg Empire objected to Serbia's potential territorial expansion into Bosnia. Given that southern parts of Austria and Hungary contained a significant Serb population, the governments in Budapest and Vienna feared that a stronger Serbia would pose an implacable irredentist danger. Austria-Hungary thus initiated consultations on Bosnia with other powers.

Whereas it clearly did not intend to put into question the territorial or constitutional *status quo*, the note drawn by Austro-Hungarian Foreign Minister Andrassy on behalf of Austria-Hungary, Germany, and Russia proposed a series of political and economic reforms to be undertaken by the Sultan. The great powers ascribed the violence to the plight of "Bosnian Christians . . . [who] feel oppressed under the yoke of a real servitude" and the failure of the Porte to carry out reforms designed to bring "amelioration of the lot of Christians" promised in the 1856 Treaty of Paris. The powers justified their involvement in the Bosnian crisis in the following terms:

The state of anarchy which prevails in the provinces to the northwest of Turkey not only involves difficulties for the Sublime Porte, but also conceals grave danger to the general tranquility; and the different European states cannot see with indifference the continuation and aggravation of a state of affairs which already weighs heavily on commerce and industry, and which, by daily shaking more and more the public confidence in the preservation of peace, tends to compromise the interests of all parties.

We, therefore, believe that we are fulfilling an imperative duty in calling the serious attention of the guaranteeing powers[92] to the necessity of counseling the Sublime Porte to complete its undertakings by such measures as appear indispensable for the re-establishment of order and tranquility in the provinces now ravaged by scourges of civil war.[93]

While the Porte declared its willingness to institute reforms, it contended it could not do so while the rebellion continued. The rebels, on the other hand, demanded great power involvement – they did not trust the Ottoman promises without external guarantees. The violence continued unabated and spread to other parts of European Turkey, most seriously to Bulgaria.

There was, however, no agreement among the guaranteeing powers on what to do. The principal division was between Britain and Russia. Since the 1820s, the British policy was to help preserve the Ottoman state as a bulwark against feared Russian designs on Europe and Asia – designs that in the mid-1870s were seen as potentially perilous to the critically important British possessions like India or the Suez Canal. Prime Minister Benjamin Disraeli was a staunch defender of this policy. But others within the Tory government such as Foreign Secretary Derby, not to mention the Liberal opposition of Gladstone, were far less comfortable with such a resolute pro-Turkish stand: The political culture of a well-established constitutional state and the importance of public opinion allowed them even less than in the previous cases of Greece or Italy to disregard gross abuses of authority. Gladstone argued, as he would in other contexts of the Eastern crisis, that the Balkan conflicts could not be properly classified as an unadulterated civil war because they arose out of "the alleged non-fulfillment of engagements taken by the Sultan in 1855–6 to his own subjects, which we, apart from our interests, are under obligation, in common with the rest of Europe, to promote the fulfillment of."[94]

Besides having a convulsing effect in Britain, the Balkan events also stirred Russia's public and government. As mentioned earlier, Russia had long had close ties to the Christian peoples of the Ottoman Empire. These ties further intensified under the influence of Panslavism, a popular movement which had developed in Russia in the 1860s and which sought to aid the national aspirations of fellow Slavic peoples.[95] Panslavism had its champions in the Russian government, but it would be a mistake to suppose that it was the sole or even the main factor driving Russian foreign relations. Most of those formulating Russian policy understood that an unrestrained quest for the removal of the Ottoman Empire from Europe would generate strong hostility among the other great powers and would likely lead to an encirclement of the country similar to that of 1853. Russia's attitude toward southeastern Europe thus, as in the case of Britain, manifested different proclivities: on the one hand, the desire to help the Christian peoples of European Turkey generated by fellow-feeling of Russian society and, on the other, the wish to operate within the cooperative framework of the 1856 Treaty of Paris.

Tsar Alexander II tried to dissuade Serbia and Montenegro, as did all other European powers, from joining the fight against the Ottoman Empire. His admonitions failed. Faced with the ever-widening armed struggle, the Russian and Austro-Hungarian emperors and their foreign ministers, Gorchakov and Andrassy, met in Reichstadt to contemplate further actions. Though the accounts of the meeting later somewhat varied, it is still instructive to read what they contained. The confidential discussions considered two scenarios: a Turkish victory and a Turkish defeat. As for the first possibility, there was agreement between the two accounts of the meeting: "there was to be no question of any territorial modification, either on one side or on the other." There was only a presumption that long-autonomous Montenegro would become independent and Serbia would not;[96] otherwise the two governments merely held that "efforts were to be made to prevent the war from becoming a struggle for extermination" and that the Balkan peoples ought to obtain "the liberties and the reforms which have been requested of the Porte and promised by it." In the eventuality of Turkish defeat, it was agreed that Bulgaria might form an auton- omous state and that Serbia and Montenegro should be allowed to expand territorially. There are differences in the two versions with respect to the concrete limits of this aggrandizement – Bosnia was to be divided among Vienna, Belgrade, and Cetinje – but Andrassy made clear that Serbia must overall remain small or else it would present "a danger to the provinces of the monarchy."[97]

The Reichstadt talks point to several conclusions. Easily defeated anti-Ottoman uprisings were unlikely to steer the great powers away from the territorial *status quo* policy in European Turkey. Conversely, the successful use of force or incidents of exceptionally brutal retribution on the part of the Porte could persuade them that the Balkan peoples should receive an improved international status and/or more territory. The Bulgarians had, for instance, never been mentioned as a candidate for autonomy in any international forum before the atrocities of 1876. Still, the agreement was to remain secret – "particularly to the Serbians and Montenegrins" – presumably to discourage them from an unreasonable escalation of the conflict.

Since the outbreak of the Serbo-Montengrin hostilities against the Porte the main British objective had been to guard against unilateral Russian military interference in the conflict. This became difficult as the civil war turned increas- ingly ferocious and the Serb troops incurred heavy losses. At the end of October 1876 Russia issued an ultimatum to the Ottomans demanding an immediate armistice because "the carnage has latterly assumed proportions which wound the feelings of humanity."[98] Great Britain proposed a conference of six guarantee- ing powers in Constantinople, but Tsar Alexander II warned that "should [a general agreement on the conditions of peace] not be achieved, and should I see that we cannot obtain real guarantees for carrying out what we have a right to demand of the Porte, I am firmly determined to act alone."[99]

At the same time, Gorchakov went on the diplomatic offensive and in two dispatches[100] he criticized the British for their unrelenting suspicion of Russia. He reiterated that Russia did not seek territorial expansion and preferred the maintenance of the *status quo*. Then he asked: "Is it our fault if the Turks ... [have rendered] their sway intolerable to their Christian subjects? Has not the English policy contributed to the abuse by exciting the suspicions of the Porte against Russia through her own rivalry, and in assisting her to make force the sole basis of her power?" Gorchakov's questions as well as his comments were surely to resonate with most Liberals and at least some liberal Tory critics of Disraeli:

> English public opinion itself has been aroused; and much more so, and more naturally, the national and Christian sentiment of Russia.... What prevents England from ... joining us for the protection of the Christians and sharing with us their gratitude and sympathy? The Eastern Question is not only a Russian question: it involves the repose of Europe, peace and general prosperity, humanity and Christian civilization.

In his second dispatch, Gorchakov suggested that the non-intervention stipulation of the Treaty of Paris ought to give way to the active enforcement of the Ottoman guarantees, found in the very same convention, toward its Christian peoples. This attitude was earlier insinuated in the Berlin Memorandum[101] and, as seen, was explicitly demanded by Gladstone. The Constantinople conference, which began in December 1876, was able to achieve a truce between the Porte and Serbia, but otherwise it was seen as a failure since the Ottomans rejected the great power recommendations for reform.[102]

As it became apparent that the Ottomans were reluctant to introduce substantial reforms, Andrassy met secretly with Russia's ambassador in Vienna, Eugene Novikov, to consider what might occur in the wake of a fissure between Russia and the Ottoman Empire. In the secret Treaty of Budapest resulting from these negotiations, the Habsburg monarchy promised benevolent neutrality in the case of Russia's military confrontation with Turkey in exchange for Russia's promise to back any post-war arrangement of Austria-Hungary's occupation of Bosnia and Herzegovina.[103] The most interesting aspect of the agreement is that while it did not, in contrast to Reichstadt, advocate the division of Bosnia, neither did it favor a national autonomous administration for the territory, as in the case of Bulgaria. Autonomy was conceived of, as in the proposal for Greece from 1826–30, as the first institutional response to a political community demonstrating a desire for self-government, and Bosnia did not appear to constitute such a community. On the contrary, Bosnia was mired in a conflict that had its roots, as the Andrassy Note had observed, in "the sentiments of enmity and rancor which animate the Christian and Mohammedan inhabitants against each other."

Following the Treaty of Budapest, Russia attempted to negotiate a common position on the enforcement of Ottoman reforms with the other powers. Russia's activities did not bear fruit primarily because of Britain's reluctance to act forcefully against a country whose preservation it considered vital to its interests. Still, it is noteworthy that at yet another meeting of the guaranteeing powers, all continued to emphasize strongly the necessity of internal improvements in the empire. The protocol of their gathering in London in fact contained this stern warning:

> If their [i.e., those of the guaranteeing powers] hopes should once more be disappointed, and if the condition of the Christian subjects of the sultan should not be improved in a manner to prevent the return of the complications which periodically disturb the peace of the East, they think it right to declare that such a state of affairs would be incompatible with their interests and those of Europe in general. In such case they reserve to themselves to consider in common as to the means which they may deem best fitted to secure the well-being of the Christian populations, and the interests of the general peace.[104]

The Ottoman government rejected the London protocol just as it had the proposals of the Constantinople conference by invoking the Treaty of Paris' article on non-intervention.

Russia was firmly resolved to go to war in the case of Turkish intransigence, even if that meant fighting alone and with almost certain disapproval of Britain: "there remains no alternative but to allow the state of things to continue which the Powers have declared incompatible with their interests and those of the Europe in general, or else seek to obtain by coercion what the unanimous efforts of the Cabinets have not succeeded in obtaining from the Porte by persuasion."[105] As expected, the British rejected this justification for the use of force. But while Disraeli demanded a vehement response and was able to persuade his cabinet to send the Royal Navy to the Besika Bay and then to strengthen the British garrison in Malta, it was Derby's position that proved to have more support in the government. Derby did not wish to interfere in the conflict and was able to convince his colleagues that Britain should declare its neutrality. The cabinet declined to join the Turkish side and urged the virtually isolated prime minister to re-examine a partition of the Ottoman Empire as the only way to preserve it as a solid, if diminished, state.[106]

Austria-Hungary promised Russia its benevolent neutrality already in the secret Treaty of Budapest. The additional convention to that treaty operated on that premise as well. The convention's opening article declared that the two countries had "as their ultimate aim the amelioration of the lot of Christians," but that they also wished "to eliminate any project of annexation of a magnitude that might compromise peace or the European equilibrium, which is neither in their intentions nor in the interests of the two Empires."[107] To achieve the latter point, the parties agreed that "in case of a territorial modification or of a dissolution of the Ottoman Empire, the establishment of a great compact Slavic or other state is excluded; in compensation, Bulgaria, Albania, and the rest of Rumelia might be constituted into independent states."[108]

Russia's war effort thus continued unhindered. In fact, it got a boost from the Balkan principalities. The government in Bucharest declared war on the Porte in May 1877 and Romanian independence in June. Romanian Prince Charles understood what the Reichstadt agreement was supposed to keep concealed from him: that a serious – and only a serious – demonstration of the will for independence could possibly lead to recognition by the great powers. Just before the declaration of war Charles wrote that "only on the battlefield could the independence of the country be sealed."[109] In December, Romania and Montenegro (which never signed an armistice with the Porte) were joined by Serbia.[110]

Russia and the Balkan principalities were able to break the Ottoman resistance and in January 1878 the Porte, facing the prospect of the Russian army marching on Constantinople, pleaded for a truce. In the January 1878 Adrianople agreement on the preliminary bases of peace the Ottoman Empire recognized the independence of Serbia, Romania, and Montenegro. It also accepted the demand of the Constantinople conference that Bulgaria ought to be "an autonomous tributary principality with a national Christian government" and that Bosnia and Herzegovina should have its own administration.[111] In March the preliminary treaty of peace was signed in San Stefano.[112]

The reaction of Great Britain, Austria-Hungary, and Germany to the Treaty of San Stefano was unanimously one of shock and reproof. Russia, it appeared to them, was bent upon prosecuting alone not only the war against the Turks but also the post-war settlement. But there were several major problems with such a solution. First, any modifications to the 1856 Treaty of Paris – and San Stefano certainly brought about substantial changes – had to be ratified, according to that treaty, by all the guaranteeing powers collectively. Second, the creation of a large Bulgarian state violated the letter of Russia's protocol with Austria-Hungary that no large state would be created in the Balkans. And finally, what in effect seemed to be Russia's single-handed remaking of the map of southeastern Europe signaled to the other great powers extension of political influence that contravened the principle of the balance of power.

The other great powers began demanding that they have a say in the settlement immediately following the armistice. Russia maintained that its treaties with Turkey could be open to the guaranteeing powers' revision only to the extent that they involved "European interests." In contrast, Britain and Austria-Hungary maintained vociferously that the six powers must validate all the provisions of San Stefano. It must be underscored, however, that whatever Britain's objections to the preliminary treaty, its government came to understand that major changes in the Balkans were necessary and unavoidable. Salisbury admitted that the policy of reforming the Ottoman government, defended as late as the Constantinople conference, failed:

> [The preservation of the Ottoman Empire] could only be brought about by rendering the different populations so far contended with their positions as to inspire them with a spirit of patriotism, and make them ready to defend the Ottoman Empire as loyal subjects of the sultan.

This policy was frustrated by the unfortunate resistance of the Ottoman government itself, and, under the altered circumstances of the present time, the same result cannot be attained to the same extent by the present means. Large changes may, and no doubt, will be requisite in the treaties by which southeastern Europe has hitherto been ruled. But good government, assured peace, and freedom, for populations to whom those blessings have been strange, are still the objects which this country earnestly desires to secure.

After pressure from all sides, Russia finally acknowledged that all clauses of preliminary peace with Turkey could be subject to negotiations. It accepted an invitation to a congress of the guaranteeing powers in Berlin, the sole purpose of which would be collective consideration, and where necessary overhaul, of the Treaty of San Stefano.

Unlike the creation of a large autonomous Bulgaria, the Adrianople and San Stefano recognition of Serbia, Montenegro and Romania was not disputed at the congress. All three principalities had prior juridical existence and during the 1877–8 war they freed themselves from all remaining vestiges of Ottoman rule. The congress protocols are not as clear on the principles informing the delimitation of borders of the three new states as those pertaining to Greece. Some extrapolation is nevertheless possible. Each country obtained additional land, but the territorial modifications were quite moderate – they were more boundary than territorial changes. Mutual rivalries and the premium given to the balance of power militated against any radical alteration of the *status quo ante bellum* beyond the general consensus that contraction of the Ottoman Empire in Europe was unavoidable.[113] The logic of both ran against sanctioning sweeping territorial changes in the case of the three new states no less than in the case of Bulgaria, which was not to include the Ottoman province of Eastern Rumelia, and Bosnia and Herzegovina, which was to be administered by Austria-Hungary but remain under Turkish sovereignty.[114]

Designated merely as "rectification of frontier" in the preliminary treaties,[115] the San Stefano increases given to Montenegro and Serbia were actually reduced at Berlin. The guaranteeing powers evoked three sets of concerns as rationalization for the modifications that were made. One was frontier defensibility of the new states and their neighbors. This consideration had precedents in the cases of Belgium or Greece and was particularly discernible in the deliberations on the respective frontiers of Serbia and Montenegro with the Ottoman Empire.[116] Another concern was economic: landlocked Montenegro obtained several kilometers of the Adriatic coast and the commercial port of Antivari.[117] And lastly, there was also a consideration of ethnic loyalty: as Russia insisted on retrocession of southern Bessarabia, a region it had to relinquish in 1856 as a war indemnity, the great powers decided to compensate Romania by assigning it the coastal district of southern Dobrudja of roughly equal size populated by ethnic Romanians.[118]

The Congress of Berlin confirmed the principle of treaty succession that had been established after a controversy at the London conference on Belgium[119] and made the recognition of the new states conditional on their formal commitment to religious liberty and equality similar to the one extracted from the Greeks five decades earlier. In contrast to the Greek Protocol No. 3 of February 3, 1830, which also alluded to international security concerns, the demand for religious liberty at Berlin was based solely on the "standard of civilization" argument. During the debate on Serbia's recognition, French plenipotentiary Waddington, backed by his colleagues, declared that "Serbia, which demands to enter into the European family upon the same footing as the other states, should in the first place acknowledge the principles which form the basis of social organization in all the states of Europe, and accept them as a necessary condition of the favor she solicits."[120] All the new independent states (and Bulgaria) had to accept provisions respecting civil and political rights of all regardless of their confession.[121] If the Balkan peoples had been treated as second-class citizens because of their religion, then they had to guarantee that they would not do the same with those who were distinct from the majority population of their new states.

Conclusion

As in Spanish and Portuguese America before, political communities that were capable of establishing themselves as *de facto* states in nineteenth-century Europe obtained international recognition. In the process, the recognizing powers sharpened, and where tackling novel phenomena extended, the conditions for admission into international society. The European practice established that the automatic duty to observe customary international law includes the principle that the new state is bound by all the international treaties it was bound by prior to its accession to sovereignty. It also expanded the extra conditions falling under the "standard of civilization" rubric: where Brazil had to commit itself to terminate the slave trade, the Balkan states had to pledge protection of their religious minorities.

Despite their intense rivalries and frequent disputes, the great powers showed the ability to work closely together and reach common positions, particularly regarding Belgium and the Balkans. Even where joint decisions proved impossible, as in the case of Italy, Britain applied criteria that were virtually indistinguishable from the collective criteria framed during the London conference on Belgium. The only worrying case in this respect was Germany. The Belgian protocols, as seen, confirmed the understanding from the Congress of Vienna not to permit unilateral externally affected changes of the territorial *status quo*, but the acquiescence to Prussia's conquests seriously, if not fatally, undermined it.[122] Germany's unification was by no means simply a product of Prussian force – there were numerous German states that joined first the North German Confederation and then the German Empire voluntarily – but it nevertheless suggested a novel moment in state recognition. The weakening of the Concert of Europe carried with it a disquieting potential.

Notes

1. Quincy Wright, "Recognition and Self-Determination," *American Society of International Law Proceedings*, 48 (1954), p. 27.
2. Whatever its standing in the Americas, the United States asserted voluntary non-involvement in intra-European politics in the Monroe Doctrine and did not play a vanguard role in nineteenth-century recognition practice on the continent. While espousing the *de facto* principle, it followed rather than led the decisions of European powers.
3. On Dutch royal rule and Belgian grievances, see J. S. Fishman, *Diplomacy and Revolution: The London Conference of 1830 and the Belgian Revolt* (Amsterdam: CHEV, 1988), pp. 21–6.
4. Le Beau to Verstolk, May 9, 1831, *The House of Commons Parliamentary Papers 1801–1900* [hereafter HCPP], Vol. 42 (1833) (Cambridge: Chadwyck-Healey Microform Publishing Services, 1980), p. 600.
5. One of the first moves of the king from the Orleans dynasty was to revert to the royal title from the early French Revolution.
6. Quoted in Fishman, *Diplomacy and Revolution*, p. 61.
7. Protocol No. 7, December 20, 1830, HCPP, Vol. 42 (1833), p. 298.
8. In it the representatives of Britain, France, Russian, Austria, and Prussia agreed that

> In forming...the Union of Belgium with Holland, the powers who signed these treaties...had in view to found a just balance in Europe, and to secure the maintenance of the general peace. The events of the last four months have unhappily demonstrated that the perfect and complete amalgamation which the powers wished to effect between the two countries had not been effected; that it would henceforth be impossible to effect it; that, therefore, the very object of the union of Belgium and Holland is destroyed; and that it now becomes indispensable to have recourse to other arrangements to accomplish the intentions which the union in question was designed to carry into execution.

See ibid.
9. Palmerston to Ponsonby, December 1, 1830, BFSP, Vol. 19, pp. 783–6. See also Fishman, *Diplomacy and Revolution*, pp. 29–30, 54–5.
10. See Fishman, *Diplomacy and Revolution*, pp. 56–7.
11. Nesselrode to Matusiewicz, October 31, 1830, quoted in Fishman, ibid., p. 62. See also J. A. Betley, *Belgium and Poland in International Relations 1830–31* (The Hague: Mouton & Co., 1960), p. 49.
12. Metternich to Emperor Francis, October 11, 1830, quoted in Fishman, *Diplomacy and Revolution*, p. 58. Interestingly, just as he had been incensed over the conduct of Ferdinand VII toward his overseas possessions, Metternich complained of the Dutch king's policies in Belgium.
13. Protocol No. 11, January 20, 1831, and Protocol No. 12, January 27, 1831, HCPP, Vol. 42 (1833), pp. 306–8, 308–14. The Bases form Annex A to Protocol 12.
14. This formal guarantee made the previously indispensable physical defenses redundant and they were slated for dismantlement. See Protocol of a Conference between Great Britain, Austria, Prussia, and Russia, relative to the Demolition of Dutch Fortresses, April 17, 1831, MET, Vol. 2, p. 856.
15. Falck to Palmerston, December 22, 1830, HCPP, Vol. 42 (1833), pp. 571–3.

16. Falck and de Zuylen to the Conference, January 25, 1831, HCPP, Vol. 42 (1833), pp. 315–7.
17. Protocol No. 19, February 19, 1831, HCPP, Vol. 42 (1833), p. 318.
18. Instructions addressed to Lord Ponsonby and M. Bresson, January 9, 1831, Annex B to Protocol No. 10, HCPP, Vol. 42 (1833), p. 305.
19. Most notably, the constitution included the Grand Duchy of Luxembourg, detached from the Netherlands in 1815 and a member of the German Confederation. The powers refused to even contemplate assigning Luxembourg to Belgium. According to their reasoning, Belgium's juridical existence was first laid down internationally only in the treaties of 1814–15. Before 1790, the argument went, it had been merely a possession of Austria.
20. Answer to the Plenipotentiaries of Austria, Great Britain, Prussia, and Russia to the Communication of the Plenipotentiary of France, March 17, 1831, Annex B to Protocol No. 20, HCPP, Vol. 42 (1833), p. 332.
21. Treaty between Great Britain, Austria, France, Prussia and Russia, and Belgium, relative to the Separation of Belgium from Holland, November 15, 1831, MET, Vol. 2, pp. 858–71.
22. The French land operations were supplemented by the Royal Navy's blockade of Dutch ports.
23. Treaty between Great Britain, Austria, France, Prussia, and Russia, on the one part, and the Netherlands, on the other, April 19, 1839, and Treaty of Separation between Belgium and the Netherlands, April 19, 1839, MET, Vol. 2, pp. 979–93, 994–5.
24. The uprising in Venetia took form of proclamation of an independent "Venetian Republic."
25. To prevent future disorder, in 1849 Prime Minister Palmerston urged the Austrian government – to no avail – that it was in Austria's interest to voluntarily abandon its Italian possessions. See Paul W. Schroeder, "Austria as an Obstacle to Italian Unification and Freedom, 1814–1861," *Austrian History Newsletter*, 3 (1962), p. 15.
26. As in Brazil, British politicians made it plain that they favored moderate monarchical groups. They frowned upon militant republican secret societies – such as *Giovane Italia* (Young Italy) led by Giuseppe Mazzini – as these aspired to overthrow the entire Vienna-based international order.
27. This ostensibly odd act can be explained by a combination of domestic and international factors. Though Louis Napoleon was elected by universal suffrage, he came to office at the end of a very tumultuous year that had transformed France from a monarchy to a republic. To consolidate his rule, Louis Napoleon sought to appeal to conservative and Catholic voters and their parties. In addition, the alternative to France's involvement was intervention led by arch-conservative Austria. By his participation, Louis Napoleon hoped to convince the papacy to return to the liberal constitution the pope introduced and then rescinded in 1848. In fact, he envisaged an Italian confederation that would satisfy Italian wishes for closer national unity. See William E. Echard, "Louis Napoleon and the French Decision to Intervene At Rome in 1849: A New Appraisal," *Canadian Journal of History*, 9 (1974), pp. 263–74.
28. In 1852, France became an empire and Louis Napoleon assumed the title Napoleon III, Emperor of the French.
29. Austria's impetuousness left it isolated. The German states were not obligated to come to its aid in an offensive strike under the terms of the confederal constitution, and stayed neutral, Britain denounced Austria's resort to arms, and Russia wished revenge on Austria for its recent abandonment of Russia and in March 1859 signed a secret treaty with France promising benevolent neutrality in the case of Franco–Austrian war.

30. Sardinian Proclamation of War with Austria, April 29, 1859, MET, Vol. 2, pp. 1365–6.
31. Proclamation of War by France against Austria, May 3, 1859, MET, Vol. 2, p. 1368.
32. Treaty of Peace between Austria and France, November 10, 1859, MET, Vol. 2, pp. 1380–411.
33. Malmesbury to Her Majesty's Ambassador in Paris, May 5, 1859, MET, Vol. 2, pp. 1372–3.
34. Russell to Odo Russell, July 28, 1859, BFSP, Vol. 49, p. 123; and Russell to Earl Cowley, October 31, 1859, BFSP, Vol. 49, p. 249.
35. Russell to Cowley, November 26, 1859, BFSP, Vol. 49, pp. 310–11.
36. Russell to the Queen, January 11, 1860, Arthur Benson and Viscount Esher (ed.), *The Letters of Queen Victoria*, Vol. 3 (London: John Murray, 1907), p. 489.
37. Russell to the Queen, January 12, 1860, G.P. Gooch (ed.), *The Later Correspondence of Lord John Russell, 1840–1878*, Vol. 2 (London: Longmans, 1925), pp. 254–5.
38. Circular addressed to the Austrian Representatives at Foreign Courts, April 29, 1859, A. N. Makarov and Ernst Schmitz (eds.), *Digest of the Diplomatic Correspondence of the European States 1856–1871*, Vol. 1 (Berlin: Carl Heymanns Verlag, 1932), p. 87.
39. Loftus to Russell, September 15, 1859, BFSP, Vol. 49, p. 217.
40. Crampton to Russell, July 29, 1859, BFSP, Vol. 49, p. 142.
41. Bloomfield to Russell, February 4, 1860, BFSP, Vol. 50, p. 541.
42. Decree of the King of Sardinia, uniting Tuscany to the Kingdom of Sardinia, March 22, 1860, MET, Vol. 2, p. 1417. See also Decree of the King of Sardinia, constituting the Provinces of Emilia a part of the Kingdom of Sardinia, March 18, 1860, ibid., p. 1416.
43. See Protest of the Duke of Modena against the Annexation of the Duchy of Modena to the Kingdom of Sardinia, March 22, 1860; Protest of the Pope against the Annexation of Romagna to Sardinia, March 24, 1860; Protest of the Grand Duke of Tuscany against the Annexation of the Grand Duchy of Tuscany to the Kingdom of Sardinia, March 24, 1860; and Protest of the Duchess of Parma against the Annexation of the Duchy of Parma to the Kingdom of Sardinia, March 28, 1860, MET, Vol. 2, pp. 1418–21, 1422–3, 1424–8, 1432–4.
44. Russell to Elliot, January 16, 1860, BFSP, Vol. 51, p. 1356. The most repressive in Italy, their regimes had been frequent targets of internal revolutions in the period between 1815 and 1859.
45. Cowley to Russell, July 18, 1860, HCPP, Vol. 67 (1861), p. 142.
46. Russell to Cowley, September 7, 1860, ibid., p. 161.
47. Memorandum relative to the Entry of the Sardinian Troops into the Roman States, enclosed in D'Azeglio to Russell, September 21, 1860, HCPP, Vol. 67 (1861), pp. 193–5.
48. Russell to Fane, September 21, 1860, ibid., p. 182.
49. Russell to Crampton, October 4, 1860, ibid., p. 200.
50. Schleinitz to Brassier de St. Simon, October 13, 1860, ibid., p. 222.
51. Gorchakov to Gagarin, September 28, 1860, ibid., pp. 245–6.
52. Memorandum, enclosed in Ludolf to Russell, October 20, 1861, ibid., p. 217.
53. Casella to Ludolf, November 12, 1860, ibid., p. 281–3.
54. Memorandum, enclosed in Russell to Ludolf, October 24, 1860, ibid., p. 230. In another defense of British conduct toward Italy, Russell once again invoked the Glorious Revolution when he asked "what wonder...that in 1860 the Neapolitan mistrust and resentment should throw the Bourbons, as in 1688 England had thrown off the Stuarts?" See Russell to Hudson, October 27, 1860, John Earl Russell, *Recollections and Suggestions, 1813–1873* (Boston, MA: Roberts Brothers, 1875), p. 232.

55. Russell to Cowley, October 29, 1860, ibid., pp. 236.
56. Russell to Fortunato, November 29, 1860, ibid., pp. 287.
57. The difference was that there was no reference to Sardinia. Whereas in the first wave of plebiscites, the electorate voted yes or no on whether they wish to be merged with Sardinia, in the second the sentence was, "The people wish Italy united and indivisible with Victor Emmanuel, the constitutional king, and his legitimate descendants." See Decree, enclosed in Elliot to Russell, October 16, 1860, ibid., pp. 224–5.
58. Decrees of the King of Sardinia, uniting the Neapolitan Provinces, Sicilian Provinces, Provinces of Umbria and Provinces of the Marches to the Italian State, December 17, 1860, MET, Vol. 2, pp. 1458–61.
59. Russell to Hudson, January 21, 1861, HCPP, Vol. 67 (1861), p. 343.
60. Russell to D'Azeglio, March 31, 1861, ibid., p. 356.
61. Lauterpacht, *Recognition in International Law*, p. 24 (n. 2).
62. Barbara Jelavich, *A Century of Russian Foreign Policy, 1814–1914* (Philadelphia, PA: Lippincott, 1964), p. 143.
63. Treaty between Great Britain, Austria, France, Prussia, Russia, and Sweden and Norway, on the one part, and Denmark on the other part, relative to the Succession of the Crown of Denmark, May 8, 1852, MET, Vol. 2, pp. 1151–5.
64. Quoted in Werner Mosse, *The European Powers and the German Question, 1848–71* (Cambridge: Cambridge University Press, 1958), pp. 161, 152.
65. Russia was more distrustful of France, which espoused the Polish cause in the anti-Russian uprising of 1863, than of Prussia, which itself had a sizeable Polish population. At the end of the day, Russia needed to have good relations more with Prussia than Denmark. Napoleon III, on the other hand, felt a tension between tending to France's national interest, which could have hardly included forcible enlargement of Prussia or Germany that trampled on European treaties, and his prior championing of the cause of nationalities, which would presumably not lead him to openly oppose a prominent national cause.
66. Even before the conference began, Prussia and Austria extended hostilities to Denmark proper.
67. Russell to Brunnow, May 14, 1864, quoted in Mosse, *The European Powers and the German Question*, p. 194.
68. The northern part of Schleswig was predominantly ethnically Danish, the southern one ethnically German.
69. Mosse, *The European Powers and the German Question*, p. 201.
70. British Circular relative to the Annexation of the Danish Duchies to Prussia, September 14, 1865, MET, Vol. 3, pp. 1645–6.
71. Prime Minister Palmerston wrote to his foreign secretary in the aftermath of the Convention of Gatstein that "if the duchies had forced themselves from Denmark by their own exertions, they would have acquired a right to dispose of themselves." See Palmerston to Russell, September 19, 1865, Gooch, *The Later Correspondence of Lord John Russell*, Vol. 2, p. 316.
72. Clarendon to Buchanan, June 21, 1866, quoted in Mosse, *The European Powers and the German Question*, p. 238.
73. Buchanan to Clarendon, July 4, 1866, quoted in ibid., p. 239.
74. French Announcement to the Prussian Government of the Causes of War with Prussia, July 19, 1870, MET, Vol. 3, p. 1880.
75. In 1867 Luxembourg, a part of the German Confederation until its end in 1866, was made perpetually neutral similar to Belgium.

76. See Protocol No. 2, January 24, 1871, BFSP, Vol. 61, p. 1199.
77. Gladstone to Granville, September 26, 1870, quoted in Mosse, *The European Powers and the German Question*, p. 338.
78. Gladstone to Granville, September 30, 1870, quoted in ibid., p. 338.
79. Buchanan to Granville, October 17, 1870, HCPP, Vol. 71 (1871), p. 184. To the French appeal that Britain and Russia lead the neutral states in a joint declaration to Prussia that any cession of French soil was contrary to justice, humanity, and the interest of Europe, Granville replied that his country was "not inclined to take steps unless there was reason to believe that they would be acceptable and effective," and that "the adherence to the conditions of not yielding an inch of territory or a stone of fortresses was an obstacle to peace." See Granville to Lyons, November 4, ibid., p. 216.
80. In his influential history of international law, published in 1845, Henry Wheaton wrote:

> In respect to the mutual intercourse between the Christian and the Mohammedan powers, the former have been sometimes content to take the law from the Mohammedan, and in others to modify the international law of Christendom in its application to them. Instances of the first may be found in the cases...where the milder usages established among Christian nations have not yet been adopted by the Mohammedan powers. On some other points, they are considered as entitled to a very relaxed application of the peculiar principles established by long usage among the states of Europe.

See Wheaton, *History of the Law of Nations in Europe and in America*, p. 555.
81. This role was acknowledged in Art. 7 of the 1774 Treaty of Kutchuk-Kainarjdi. See Anderson, *Documents of Modern History*, p. 10.
82. Treaty between Great Britain, France, and Russia, July 6, 1827, MET, Vol. 1, pp. 769–74; this was an almost exact copy of the Anglo–Russian Protocol signed the previous year.
83. Stivachtis, *The Enlargement of International Society*, p. 149.
84. Ibid., p. 152.
85. Protocol of December 12, 1828, HCPP, Vol. 32 (1830), pp. 661–81; In Annex A to the protocol the three envoys summarized their objectives concerning the delimitation of Greece in the following terms:

> The representatives have made it their business to seek a line which, traversing the continent of Greece, should offer a natural frontier, clearly defined, easy of defense, containing a reasonable portion of the Greek population which was really in the state of insurrection against the Porte; lastly, traced in such a manner as to afford the least possible risk of any subjects of dispute arising between its inhabitants and those of adjoining Turkish provinces.

Annex A then goes on to say that the three representatives had to bear in mind that the Greek population was generally so intermingled with the Turkish one that perfect line for separating the two did not exist.
86. As part of the peace settlement between Russia and the Porte at Adrianople in September 1829, the latter accepted both the 1827 treaty and the March 1829 protocol, which contained the territorial outlines of the December 1828 protocol. See Art. 10, Treaty of Peace between Russia and Turkey, September 14, 1829, MET, Vol. 2, pp. 820–1.

87. Protocol No. 1 of the Conference held at the Foreign Office, London, February 3, 1830, Thomas Erskine Holland (ed.), *The European Concert in the Eastern Question: A Collection of Treaties and Other Public Acts* (Oxford: Clarendon Press, 1885), pp. 28–32.

88. Protocol No. 3 of the Conference held at the Foreign Office, London, February 3, 1830, ibid., p. 33.

89. Convention between the Courts of Great Britain, France, and Russia on the one part, and the Court of Bavaria on the other part, relative to the Sovereignty of Greece, May, 7, 1832, ibid., pp. 33–8.

90. Stivachtis, *The Enlargement of International Society*, p. 180; The United States also acknowledged Greece in 1833. Its secretary of state announced that "it has been the principle and the invariable practice of the United States to recognize that as the legal government of another nation, which by its establishment in the actual exercise of political power might be supposed to have received the expressed or implied assent of the people." He then based America's recognition of Greece on the assurance received from Russia, Britain, and France that they had been duly authorized to make the 1832 arrangements by the people of Greece. See Livingston to Vaughan, Serurier and Krudener, April 30, 1833, Moore, *Digest of International Law*, Vol. 1, p. 112.

91. Austria transformed in 1867 from a unitary state to a dual federation of Austria-Hungary.

92. The designation "guaranteeing powers" refers to the provisions of the Treaty of Paris. In Art. 7, Russia, France, Great Britain, Sardinia, and Prussia declared the Ottoman Empire "admitted to participate in the advantages of the public law and system (concert) of Europe" and committed themselves to "respect the independence and the territorial integrity of the Ottoman Empire; guarantee in common the strict observance of that engagement; and . . . consider any act tending to its violation as a question of general interest." Article 9 stipulated that the powers had no right to "interfere, either collectively or separately, in the relations of His Majesty the Sultan with his subjects, nor in the internal administration of his Empire." At the same time, however, the Ottoman Empire vowed to treat its subjects "without distinction of religion or of race" and expressed its "generous intentions towards the Christian population." See General Treaty of Peace between Great Britain, Austria, France, Prussia, Russia, Sardinia, and Turkey, March 30, 1856, MET, Vol. 3, pp. 1254–5.

93. Andrassy to Beust, December 30, 1875, HCPP, Vol. 84 (1876), pp. 222, 225; The note was endorsed by the cabinet of Benjamin Disraeli in January 1876.

94. Quoted in Richard Seton-Watson, *Disraeli, Gladstone and the Eastern Question* (London: Frank Cass, 1971), p. 35.

95. In practice this support was given primarily to the Orthodox peoples in the Ottoman lands: Catholic Poles in Russia were, for example, excluded as "rebellious traitors" and the Romanians and Greeks, though not Slavs, were often supported because they belonged, as did the Russians, to the Orthodox Church. See Misha Glenny, *The Balkans 1804–1999: Nationalism, War and the Great Powers* (London: Granta Books, 1999), p. 129.

96. Montenegro was up to that point the closest Balkan ally of Russia.

97. The Austrian version is Resume of the Secret Conferences of Reichstadt, July 8, 1876, Alfred Pribram (ed.), *The Secret Treaties of Austria-Hungary*, Vol. 2 (Cambridge, MA: Harvard University Press, 1921), pp. 189–90. For the description of the Russian account of what transpired in Reichstadt, see A. L. Macfie, *The Eastern Question 1774–1923*, rev. ed. (London: Longman, 1996), p. 109.

98. Russian Ultimatum to the Porte, October 31, 1876, Snezana Trifunovska (ed.), *Yugoslavia Through Documents from Its Creation to Its Dissolution* (Dordrecht, The Netherlands: Martinus Nijhoff, 1994), p. 75.

99. Speech of the Emperor of Russia on the State of Affairs in Turkey, November 10, 1876, MET, Vol. 4, p. 2518.

100. Gorchakov to Shuvalov, November 3, 1876 and Gorchakov to Shuvalov, November 19, 1876, MET, Vol. 4, pp. 2513–5 and 2520–5.

101. This was a communication sent to the Ottomans by Germany, Russia, and Austria in May 1876, five months after the Andrassy Note. In it they observed that the Bosnian strife had been extended to Bulgaria and again implored the Porte to implement the reforms it had pledged to the guaranteeing powers. The three imperial courts indicated that in the event of Turkey's refusal, "it would become necessary to supplement their diplomatic action by the sanction of an agreement with a view to such efficacious measures as might appear to be demanded in the interests of general peace, to check the evil and prevent its development." The French and Italian governments embraced the memorandum, but the British cabinet rejected it because of its threat. See Enclosure 2, Odo Russell to Derby, May 13, 1876, HCPP, Vol. 84 (1876), pp. 416–17.

102. Bulgaria was to be a small autonomous state with a native ruler, temporarily policed by the peacekeeping troops from neutral Belgium; Serbia and Montenegro were permitted small territorial gains without any change in their legal status; and Bosnia and Herzegovina were to form a single province headed by a governor appointed by the Sultan.

103. Treaty of Budapest, January 15, 1877, Pribram, *The Secret Treaties of Austria-Hungary*, pp. 191–9; Remarkably, the government in Vienna sought to occupy Bosnia despite repeated objections from the Hungarian government and Andrassy (himself a Hungarian). They worried, in retrospect quite justifiably, that the intake of large numbers of Serbs and Croats into the Empire would destabilize Hungary which had already had significant Serb and Croat populations. The occupation of Bosnia was advocated primarily by the military: its goal was to be better protection of the empire's unstable southern flank.

104. Protocol between Great Britain, Austria-Hungary, France, Germany, Italy, and Russia, March 31, 1877, Trifunovska, *Yugoslavia Through Documents*, pp. 83–4.

105. Gorchakov to Shuvalov, April 19, 1877, MET, Vol. 4, p. 2587.

106. Stanley Weintraub, *Disraeli: A Biography* (New York: Truman Talley Books/Dutton, 1993), p. 575.

107. Additional Convention, March 18, 1877, Pribram, *The Secret Treaties of Austria-Hungary*, pp. 199–203.

108. Germany too declared its neutrality in the conflict. Its Emperor William I expressed his outrage at the Turkish protest against the London protocol "which makes the impression that an unjustly accused civilized state is defending itself, whereas an uncivilized state has by centuries of oppression driven its Christian subjects to revolt." Quoted in Seton-Watson, *Disraeli, Gladstone and the Eastern Question*, p. 172; Bismarck also supported neutrality, though, in contrast to his sovereign, he was inspired more by *realpolitik* than any particular enthusiasm for improving the lot of the Christians. His main objective from Schleswig-Holstein had been to prevent a rise of anti-German coalition and he did not regard the Ottoman lands as either actual or potential ground for Germany's sphere of influence. The best option in his mind was for Germany to see "gravitation" of other great powers' rivalries there so that they would be "deterred as far as possible from

coalitions against us by their relations with each other." At the same time, however, Bismarck did not want these rivalries, as already indicated, to precipitate a major war. He saw the solution to the Eastern question in "the negotiating of a peace which would satisfy both [Britain and Russia] at the expense of Turkey." See quoted in Macfie, *The Eastern Question*, pp. 111–12.

109. Quoted in Barbara Jelavich, "Diplomatic Problems of an Autonomous State: Romanian Decisions on War and Independence," *Southeastern Europe*, 5 (1978), p. 33.

110. In a manifesto that served simultaneously as a declaration of resumption of war and a declaration of independence Serbian Prince Milan repeated the point: "Nations cannot attain true freedom until they have purchased it by their own exertions, and, if necessary, by their blood." See Manifesto of the Prince of Serbia, Proclaiming a Renewal of the War with Turkey, December 13, 1877, MET, Vol. 4, p. 2649.

111. Preliminary Bases of Peace between Russia and Turkey, January 31, 1878, ibid., pp. 2658–60.

112. Preliminary Treaty of Peace between Russia and Turkey, March 3, 1878, ibid., pp. 2672–94.

113. W. N. Medlicott, *The Congress of Berlin and After: A Diplomatic History of the Near Eastern Settlement 1878–1880* (Hamden, CT: Archon Books, 1963), pp. 133–4. The reluctance to engage in large-scale territorial changes was obvious from the rejection of the Greek conference pleadings for Thessaly and Epirus.

114. Bosnia and Herzegovina were to be administered by Austria-Hungary on international peace and order grounds. As the Ottoman Empire was deemed to be a weak state, Austria-Hungary, which was affected most directly by the Bosnian events – it suffered incursions of insurgents as well as inflows of 200,000 refugees – was to administer the province in its stead. Provincial autonomy was explicitly ruled out as a viable status because of the animosity between Christian and Muslim inhabitants of Bosnia and Herzegovina. Other possible solutions were not officially discussed in Berlin. See Protocol No. 8 of the Congress of Berlin, June 28, 1878, HCPP, Vol. 83 (1878), pp. 504–7.

115. See Art. 1 of the Treaty of San Stefano (Montenegro) and Art. 3 of the Bases of Adrianople (Serbia).

116. See the decision of Protocol No. 12 of July 4, 1878 regarding the Montengrin–Ottoman frontier (pp. 573–4) and the decision of Protocol No. 15 of July 8, 1878, concerning the Serbo–Ottoman frontier (pp. 623–4) in HCPP, Vol. 83 (1878); on the decisions regarding the Serbo-Ottoman border, see also Medlicott, *The Congress of Berlin and After*, pp. 94–5, 117–8.

117. In exchange, Montenegro had to pledge not to have any ships of war, so as not to upset the naval balance in the Adriatic.

118. Protocol No. 10, July 1, 1878, HCPP, Vol. 83 (1878), pp. 546–7; the ethnic loyalty factor also played a role in the objections to a large Bulgaria, as that entity would have contained a large, and presumably antagonistic, Greek population. See Protocol No. 2, June 17, 1878, ibid., p. 416.

119. In his capacity as the president of the congress, Bismarck declared that it was "a matter of general right that a province separated from a state should not be able to emancipate itself from treaties by which it had been hitherto bound." See Protocol No. 8, ibid., p. 513.

120. Ibid.; Waddington made a similar statement with respect to Romania. See Protocol No. 10, ibid., p. 545.

121. Several great powers waited to give the official notes of recognition to the Romanian government until early 1880. At issue was Art. 7 of the 1866 Romanian constitution which allowed only the naturalization of Christians and thus discriminated against the large number of the country's Jews. Coordinating among themselves, France, Britain, and Germany pressured Romania to modify the constitution so as to bring it in accordance with the Treaty of Berlin. The Romanian parliament did so in late 1879. The country was then notified of recognition in 1880. See Beatrice Marinescu, "Great Britain and the Recognition of Romania's State Independence," *Revue Roumaine d'Histoire*, 15 (1976), and W. N. Medlicott, "The Recognition of Romanian Independence, 1878–80," Part I and II *The Slavonic and East European Review*, 11 (1933), pp. 354–72, 572–89.

122. Sharon Korman lists in her study of conquest only one instance of unilateral annexation in Europe between 1815 and 1865 – Austria's incorporation of the Free City of Cracow in 1846. See Korman, *The Right of Conquest*, pp. 80–2.

4

New States Between 1918 and 1945

The advent of new states in the aftermath of World War I is usually regarded as an integral part of the intellectual revolution in international affairs inspired and spearheaded by American President Woodrow Wilson in 1916–18. Specifically, their emergence is closely associated with his concept of self-determination of peoples. The idea had a prominent place in several famous addresses to the US Congress that outlined Wilson's vision of the post-war order. Richard Holbrooke's view in the foreword to a recent best seller on the Paris Peace Conference that Wilson introduced a "groundbreaking" concept[1] is typical.

Wilson's idea of self-determination as unveiled in his wartime speeches and the public eminence to which he elevated the term were without doubt groundbreaking. The US president substituted the nineteenth-century conception of self-determination as a negative international right for a conception of self-determination as a positive international right. Whereas the negative conception demanded of states respect for foreign self-determination endeavors by not interfering with them, the positive one imposed on states a duty to help bring these endeavors to the desired conclusion. However, it became quickly apparent that there were great difficulties in applying Wilson's conception. Third parties had to decide which peoples qualified for the right of self-determination, how to ascertain their will for independence, and what precise obligations they actually owed them. None of these decisions had to be made in the nineteenth century: the right to self-determination applied to any self-defined people and outsiders were required to do no more than to recognize the *de facto* attainment of what was presumed to be their will. Were the groups entitled to self-determination now to be identified merely by some public assertion that they possessed such a right or did they in addition have to satisfy objective criteria such as ethnicity? What procedure was to verify the will of the people to be independent once the bearers of the right to self-determination had been defined and territorially demarcated? And after the groups to whom the right belonged had been identified and their will ascertained, what was to be the role of third parties if those groups were not actually in possession of what they claimed? These questions had no apparent general answers and were contested in nearly all specific cases.

A careful examination of state recognition between the years 1918 and 1922 reveals that the United States and other Allied powers, in the end, built on, rather than broke from, the previous practice. Their leaders, even Wilson, came to realize that if the mere voicing of claims gave groups a positive entitlement to statehood, there would be no limit to international chaos and instability. Foreign acknowledgment was accorded exclusively to the political communities that had already attained *de facto* independence, even if none of them could establish independence when they did without the military defeat of the German, Austro-Hungarian, and Russian Empires. This was true both of the new states that were admitted to partake in the peace conference (Poland, Czechoslovakia, and Yugoslavia) and those formerly belonging to the Russian Empire that were not (Finland,[2] Lithuania, Latvia, Estonia, Armenia, and Georgia). As in the past, the decisive moment for all entities coveting admission into international society was recognition or non-recognition by the great powers of the day. In continuity with the nineteenth century, recognition of some new states went hand in hand with the requirement that they pledge fulfillment of various conditions that went beyond the primary norm of *de facto* statehood.

The process of recognition of the three countries participating at the Paris Peace Conference, however, disclosed a discontinuity with previous practice in one major respect: the delineation of borders of new states. Border-making at Paris did not adhere to the nineteenth-century principle that limits of new states should basically enclose the territories held *de facto*, or, put differently, the territories whose inhabitants exhibited unforced acquiescence to the new authorities. That principle could not have, and had not, been absolute: Europe's, and in particular Ottoman Europe's, complex demographic makeup – people of different *ethnos* and political allegiances living intermingled or inhabiting non-contiguous areas – guaranteed that some would find themselves in newborn states against their will. And there had been additional, secondary factors of viability of new states that occasionally needed to be taken into account in boundary construction as well.

In contrast to nineteenth-century Europe and Latin America, there was no consensus at Paris on the general principles of drawing borders of new states. When they did not conflict with each other, the claims based on the Wilsonian conception of self-determination had to compete frequently with supplementary demands of territory which were to render defensible and historical frontiers, economic viability, integrity of major communication arteries, and access to the sea. The victorious powers, including the United States, accepted that both kinds of claims could be valid, but operating with different expectations of the post-war international order, they could not agree on how to prioritize them either in principle or in practice. The paradoxical outcome was that in both absolute and relative terms far many more people who opposed being included into Czechoslovakia, Poland, or Yugoslavia ended up being part of them than had been the case with Greece, Belgium, Serbia, Montenegro, or Romania. Given the enormous hopes put into Wilson's idea of self-determination, however, this result was also harder to digest for those disadvantaged by the decisions of the conference. The boundary settlement gave rise to powerful resentment and revisionism.

The Paris Peace Conference left one more lasting and truly innovative legacy for state recognition. The collective commitment to respect and to preserve the territorial integrity and existing political independence of all League of Nations members in Art. 10 of the League's Covenant made wars of conquest, such as those that had preceded German unification, invalid as a means of creating new states. The clause became a normative foundation of several post-war treaties and of the so-called Stimson Doctrine by which first the United States and then the League members refused to recognize the "State of Manchukuo," an entity claiming sovereignty on Chinese territories forcibly wrested by Japan. Whereas the Stimson Doctrine as a rule of non-recognition faltered among the League members in the years immediately prior to World War II, it came back to life in late 1939. The following chapters will show that the rule has endured to this day.

Woodrow Wilson and Self-Determination as a Positive International Right

The subject of new states during the war was first brought up by the Central Powers rather than the Entente. In November 1916, Germany and Austria-Hungary, vying for Polish support in their war effort, proclaimed an independent "Kingdom of Poland" on Russia's territory populated by ethnic Poles. The re-establishment of independence had never ceased to be the aspiration of many Poles after the final division of their country in 1795, and the issue periodically made its way onto the international agenda as a result of recurring Polish revolts against foreign rule. Given that the "kingdom" was proclaimed on territories occupied by two imperial armies and by Kaiser Wilhelm II and Emperor Franz Joseph I rather than by the Poles themselves, there was little doubt abroad that it was intended to be a satellite of the Central Powers. The proclamation appeared to be part of a concerted propaganda strategy of "liberation" from the Russian Empire – the German-led push toward secession of various dissatisfied nationalities in Russia's western periphery, and thus toward enfeeblement of a powerful enemy. But not wanting to fall behind in wooing the large (and with the stalemate in fighting potentially decisive) Polish constituency, the Russian, and then other Entente governments promised Polish independence too.

The first influential formulation of the post-war order, Woodrow Wilson's "Peace without Victory" address in January 1917, did not mention self-determination by name, but expressed his belief that

> no peace can last, or ought to last, which does not recognize and accept the principle that governments derive all their just powers from the consent of the governed, and that no right anywhere exists to hand peoples about from sovereignty to sovereignty as if they were property.... Any peace which does not recognize and accept this principle will inevitably be upset. It will not rest upon the affections or the convictions of mankind.[3]

In another public speech later that year, Wilson reiterated his point in more audacious and absolute terms when he warned, "no people must be forced under sovereignty under which it does not wish to live."[4]

Wilson elaborated on his ideas for the future in a series of crucial speeches in early 1918, at which point the United States was already engrossed in the fighting and its participation began to look like the decisive moment of the war. In his "Four Points" address, Wilson declared that "national aspirations must be respected; peoples may now be dominated and governed only by their consent. 'Self-determination' is not a mere phrase. It is an imperative principle of action, which statesmen will henceforth ignore at their peril." Only domestically legitimate states could be the building blocks of an internationally legitimate order, Wilson believed, and international legitimacy was a necessary condition for peace.[5] As for the post-war settlement, he proposed:

> First, that each part of the final settlement must be based upon the essential justice of that particular case and upon such adjustments as are most likely to bring a peace that will be permanent;
>
> Second, that peoples and provinces must not be bartered about from sovereignty to sovereignty as if they were mere chattels or pawns in a game, even the great game, now forever discredited, of the balance of power; but that
>
> Third, every territorial settlement involved in this war must be in the interest and for the benefit of the populations concerned, and not as a part of any near adjustment or compromise of claims among rival states; and
>
> Fourth, all well-defined national aspirations shall be accorded the utmost satisfaction that can be accorded to them without introducing new or perpetuating old elements of discord and antagonism that would be likely in time to break the peace of Europe and consequently the world.[6]

An obvious source of Wilson's beliefs was the *US Declaration of Independence*. Its principle of "the consent of the governed" was proclaimed universally applicable and pertained to the state no less than to the governing regime. As suggested in Chapters 2 and 3, key figures in the Anglo–American practice of state recognition in the nineteenth century also shared the belief in the consent of the governed. But Monroe, Adams, Canning, Palmerston, and Russell did not think – just as Jefferson or Madison before them had not thought – that the natural moral right of peoples to change sovereignty under which they live imposed duties on other peoples to bring this change about. Adams expressed this sentiment succinctly when he said that his country – he could well have spoken for Britain too – "is the well-wisher to the freedom and independence of all. She is the champion and vindicator only of her own." The actual right of independent existence – and its corollary, the right to be recognized as a sovereign state – had to be earned. Self-determination was expressed by the self's striving for, and the consent of the governed externally gauged through the self's attainment of, independent statehood.

President Wilson's words, in contrast, went much further. They did not demand respect for self-attained outcomes but for "wishes" and "aspirations." This, as Wilson's own reference to "an imperative principle of action" suggests, could not have come about without outside participation in realizing those wishes. His assertion that no people could be forced under sovereignty under which it did not wish to live was not a rallying cry for peoples to liberate themselves but a description of the condition that third parties were positively obliged to help bring about. Unlike Jefferson or Adams, Wilson conveyed the impression that he wanted the United States to be an active benefactor of statehood for others; as he put it on one occasion, to liberate "men who never could have liberated themselves."[7] Only the clarity of verbally articulated claims seemed to matter in deciding whose cause to pursue:[8] in none of his famous speeches did Wilson allude to active effort at launching one's own state as a prerequisite. When he suggested in the "Peace without Victory" address that the Monroe Doctrine should be accepted as "the doctrine of the world: that no nation should seek to extend its polity over any other nation or people, but that every people should be left free to determine its own polity, its own way of development – unhindered, unthreatened, unafraid, the little along with the great and powerful," he did not appear to realize that his predecessor spoke of peoples who had already succeeded in constituting themselves as *de facto* states. Nor did Wilson's language suggest that he saw any wisdom in heeding Adams' warning that, by acting on aspirations rather than settled facts, the United States might involve itself "beyond the power of extrication, in all the wars of interest and intrigue, of individual avarice, envy, and ambition, which assume the colors and usurp the standard of freedom."

However, for all his exalted oratory, there was little indication that Wilson grappled with challenges that his idea of self-determination might pose. How did one externally determine the peoples whose will was to count and how was this will to be ascertained? What precisely was the responsibility of outsiders if some claims clashed? What was their obligation if some peoples were nevertheless kept under sovereignty under which they did not wish to live? If the Irish people had a right to self-determination and clearly wanted independence from British rule, as the delegation of Irish dignitaries announced to Wilson in October 1918, was it, then, the responsibility of the peace conference to dislodge Britain from Ireland?[9] Wilson also discussed few specific claims. The legendary "Fourteen Points" address called for an independent Poland, an objective already formally endorsed by all key belligerents. Beyond this, the program talked only about "autonomous development" for the peoples of Austria-Hungary as well as the non-Turkish peoples of the Ottoman Empire, and about border adjustments in Italy and the Balkans consonant with the lines of nationality.[10] The combined effect of Wilson's public utterances was rather curious. On the one hand, the universalistic and sweeping tone as well as extensive public exposure of his pronouncements on self-determination raised fervent expectations of recognition among peoples worldwide;[11] and, on the other, a country like Austria-Hungary welcomed the Fourteen Points as the guarantee of its survival.

The major allies of the United States in Europe, Britain, Russia, France, and Italy, officially espoused self-determination too. Even prior to the "Fourteen Points" address, for example, Prime Minister David Lloyd George referred to "self-determination or, as our earlier phrase goes, government by consent of the governed," when, in a speech outlining the British war aims, he said:

> The days of the Treaty of Vienna are long past. We can no longer submit the
> future of European civilization to the arbitrary decisions of a few negotiators
> striving to secure by chicanery or persuasion the interests of this or that
> dynasty or nation ... government with the consent of the governed must be
> the basis of any territorial settlement in this war.[12]

However, major European allies had never thought of the principle as expansively
as Wilson did. As early as autumn 1916, a British Foreign Office memorandum
asserted that "the principle of nationality ... should be one of the governing
factors in the considerations of territorial arrangements after the war," stressing
at the same time that "we should not push the principle of nationality so far as
unduly to strengthen any state which is likely to be a cause of danger to European
peace in the future."[13] This was fairly consistent with British thinking on the
border settlement at the Congress of Berlin. France, with its northeast completely
devastated by the war, held the same opinion. Its main objective was to enervate
Germany so as to prevent yet another invasion of France, even if it meant
trampling on self-determination of the German people. Italy wanted the Austro-Hungarian territories promised in the secret Treaty of London (1915),[14]
several of which contained non-Italian majorities. Post-Tsarist Russia was in
fact the first Allied country to pronounce itself officially on self-determination
when it announced, in April 1917, that "its object is to establish a durable peace
on a basis of the rights of nations to decide their destiny,"[15] but the Bolshevik
coup d'état in November of that year effectively removed Russia from the Entente
and the war. All in all, it was not at all obvious how the Americans and their allies
would react to the concrete claims of statehood put forward.

Recognizing Poland, Czechoslovakia, and Yugoslavia

Besides the Polish claim, which had a lengthy history, the best formulated were
perceived to be the demands of the Czechs and Slovaks whose representatives
decided during the war that they would seek the establishment of a joint state;
and the Slovenes, Croats, and Serbs of Austria-Hungary whose leaders proposed
the creation of a South Slav state and in 1917 formally received Serbia's pledge to
join it. The question for the Allies was to what extent to encourage them. On the
one hand, their thinking was motivated by the exigencies of war. They wanted to
bring a speedy defeat of Austria-Hungary and its military disengagement from
Germany, and they had themselves experienced the Central Powers' active nour-
ishment of separatism among the discontented nationalities of the Russian
Empire. On the other hand, it was not clear how to evaluate the demands that
(*a*) had been voiced for the most part by private individuals in the Entente exile;
(*b*) were not established on the ground; and (*c*) had no evident international
history prior to 1914. In this respect, the Entente countries thus found themselves

in a situation similar to what France had confronted in North America since 1775. France's bitter enmity with Britain dictated instrumental thinking with respect to the mounting prospects of independence of Britain's thirteen colonies, but their recognition, as argued in Chapter 1, was not a simple matter of expediency. France found it necessary to justify the act in terms of rules and norms of the society of states. Although US Secretary of State Robert Lansing advised President Wilson in May 1918 that a policy toward the nations of Austria-Hungary "should be considered always from the standpoint of winning the war," he at the same time did not want America to do anything "dishonorable or immoral."[16] The "legal objections" to potential acts of recognition, however expedient those acts might have appeared, had to be taken fully into account.[17]

A change in fortunes of the Czechoslovak and Yugoslav movements was signaled with the formation of military units out of Czech and Slovak deserters and prisoners of war held in Italy, France, and Russia,[18] and with Serbia's active promotion of the Yugoslav cause. By setting up an army, the Czechoslovaks showed willingness both to fight for the Entente cause and to liberate the lands inhabited by their people. As they engaged in military operations, the Czechoslovak legions, especially those in Siberia, gained respect and admiration in the Entente countries. Conversely, Serbia was the beneficiary of widespread Entente sympathies as one of the most afflicted victims of Austro–German aggression. If the Slavs of southern Austria-Hungary wished to unite with Serbia, that project was unlikely to be opposed by the allies.

The boldness of President Wilson's speeches notwithstanding, the US administration proceeded with caution, just as its major allies did. To the communiqué of the Rome Congress of Oppressed Races of Austria-Hungary in April 1918 demanding a public announcement of their right to "constitute themselves independent states recognized by Entente,"[19] Secretary of State Lansing merely replied, consistently with the Fourteen Points, that "the nationalistic aspirations of the Czecho-Slovaks and Yugo-Slavs for freedom have the earnest sympathy of this government."[20] In June, the Czechoslovak National Council approached the French government and proposed, among other things, "recognition by the government of the republic of the existence of a Czecho-Slovak state."[21] But France's response was only that it acknowledged "the National Council as the supreme organization of the Czecho-Slovak movement in the Entente countries," though the reply did add that the government would "support in all earnestness the aspirations to independence for which its soldiers are fighting in the ranks of the allies."[22]

Although by the summer of 1918 he personally came to believe that Austria-Hungary should "disappear," Lansing too came out, in his counsel to Wilson, against giving "full recognition to the Czecho-Slovaks as a sovereign nation."[23] In his *Memorandum on the Recognition of the Czecho-Slovaks as a Nationality*, the secretary of state conceded the immediate wartime advantages of, and considerable enthusiasm of the American public for, all-out recognition of Czechoslovakia as an independent state. Still, he cautioned that it was necessary "to go very slowly before we take a step which commits this government to the recognition of an independent state based upon the principle that a people who have been oppressed and their native land held in subjection by superior force are entitled to be free and to possess the land." In what appeared as an evocation of Kant's categorical imperative, Lansing warned, "we must so far as we can avoid committing ourselves to a policy or a principle which can not be uniformly applied when a readjustment of nationalities takes place as it undoubtedly will." The secretary's recommendation was to fall back on the practice set in the past. He wanted to acknowledge the factually more accurate status of belligerency of the Czechoslovaks first – as the United States and Britain had done with respect to the Latin Americans or Britain had done with respect to the Greeks[24] – and then put the onus on the outcome of their struggle:

> I am . . . opposed to recognizing the national independence of the Czecho-Slovaks or to accept them as a sovereign state. The better and safer course seems to me to recognize their belligerency as they are prosecuting open war against Austria-Hungary and her allies. *If they succeed in their revolt and are associated with the United States and Entente in a military victory, they will have established by force of arms their sovereign right to self-rule and independence.*
>
> I believe much the same policy should be followed in the case of Yugoslavs when they are able to maintain their rebellion against Austria-Hungary. Until there is this open manifestation of independent power we should be extremely cautious of our policy in dealing with them.[25] (italics added)

The United States thus came to share France's course in recognition policy. In fact, by the time of Lansing's memorandum, Italy and Britain too acknowledged the Czechoslovak legions as a co-belligerent army, and the Czechoslovak National Council as the supreme authority of the two peoples. It is worth noting that despite Wilson's imprint on European public consciousness, throughout the spring and summer of 1918 the representatives of prospective states perceived American officials as rather timid. Serbia's ambassador in Washington complained that the coy and nebulous endorsement of the Yugoslav and Czechoslovak movements, subsequently adopted by the Supreme Allied Council as well, had actually played into the Austrian hands.[26] The Czechoslovak leader Tomas Masaryk, already having official ties to several European capitals, had to implore in Washington: "I dispose of three armies . . . I am, as a wit said, the master of Siberia and half Russia, and yet I am in the United States formally a private man."[27]

Secretary Lansing responded to the ambassador's letter in June by clarifying that "the position of the United States government is that all branches of the Slav race should be completely freed from German and Austrian rule."[28] This public admission came not only when it was already clear that the Habsburg government would not forsake Germany for a separate peace with the Entente, but also when the military units composed of those peoples were already engaged in hostilities against the two powers. This aspect was highlighted in the US recognition of Czechoslovak belligerency solicited by Masaryk:

> The Czecho-Slovak peoples having taken up arms against the German and Austro-Hungarian Empires, and having placed organized armies in the field

which are waging war against those Empires under officers of their nationality and in accordance with rules and practices of civilized nations; and

The Czecho-Slovaks having, in prosecution of their independent purposes in the present war, confided supreme political authority to the Czecho-Slovak National Council,

The Government of the United States recognizes that a state of belligerency exists between the Czecho-Slovaks thus organized and the German and Austro-Hungarian Empires.

It also recognizes the Czecho-Slovak National Council as a *de facto* belligerent government clothed with proper authority to direct the military and political affairs of the Czecho-Slovaks.

The Government of the United States further declares that it is prepared to enter formally into relations with the *de facto* government thus recognized for the purpose of prosecuting the war against the common enemies, the empires of Germany and Austria-Hungary.[29]

The gulf between Wilson's sweeping language on self-determination with its emphasis on "wishes" and the declaration's circumspection and accent on "facts" is glaring. However, the US president approved the announcement and complimented its author, the secretary of state: "you have successfully stated both the actual facts and the new legal relationship we assume."[30] Together with similar statements of other major allies, the American acknowledgment of Czechoslovak belligerency has all too often been taken as an act of recognition of Czechoslovak independence, but this is erroneous. These declarations, as the historian Harold Temperley writes, "all struck a futurist note, recognizing only the efforts of armies and the existence of an embryonic government striving to achieve independence."[31]

In the end, the biggest boost for the independence movements did not come from these provisional and reversible acts[32] or whatever other verbal statements of support they had received from the Entente powers,[33] but from the extraordinarily rapid breakdown of Austria-Hungary's public institutions and armed forces, which was set in motion in the early fall of 1918. New administrative councils pledging allegiance to the future states sprang up in several places, and the war-strained government was unable to thwart them. The Czech, Yugoslav, and Polish deputies of the Austrian parliament demonstratively quit Vienna and traveled to Prague, Zagreb, Cracow, and other cities to assist in the organization of their nascent national authorities. In response, the German Austrian deputies called for an ethnically German Austrian state. In Hungary, the government, fearing a loss of territory as a defeated state, declared the federal arrangement of 1867 with Austria dead. On November 11, Austro-Hungarian Emperor Karl, who failed to stem the tide of disintegration by proclaiming federalization of Austria, abdicated. A day later, German Austria was declared a republic. This entity was to be, consistently with some pan-German schemes of 1848–71, "a constituent part of the German Republic."[34] On November 16, the Hungarian government proclaimed a republic too.[35] As one historian puts it, "long before the peace conference met, the Habsburg Empire had ceased to exist, and nothing but force could have reconstructed it."[36] Astoundingly, Austria-Hungary, a great power for close to four centuries, had in its dying days no domestic defenders.

The immediate post-war months were a period of considerable fluidity in Central and Eastern Europe, but Czechoslovakia, Poland, and Yugoslavia managed to establish their authority relatively quickly after the armistice with the rump Habsburg government on November 3. The Allied powers indicated that the process of their recognition would be completed only at the peace conference in Paris, due to begin in January 1919, with the final delimitation of their frontiers.[37] Thus, the real task for the impending conference was not devise a standard that would determine who can qualify as a sovereign state. That norm – the *de facto* state[38] – was undisputed, and the vanquished powers accepted the legitimacy of Polish, Czechoslovak, and Yugoslav statehood prior to the peace conference no less than the victorious ones.[39] The real issue as far as the new states were concerned was to determine their international boundaries.

Not long after the armistice was concluded, it was apparent that this would not be a simple undertaking. As in late 1918 and early 1919 the Polish, Czechoslovak, and Yugoslav governments began to extend their writ over the areas they had regarded as rightfully theirs, it became obvious that the population of several frontier areas opposed their incorporation into the new states and that there were clusters of people left in neighboring countries who wanted to be incorporated but were not. As a result of competing claims, Poland got into a quarrel with Czechoslovakia over Teschen, Spis, and Orava, with the "West Ukrainian Republic" over Eastern Galicia,[40] with the "Republic of Lithuania" over Vilnius, and with the Russian Bolsheviks over most of its eastern border. Yugoslavia got embroiled in a particularly acrimonious dispute with Italy over a number of cities and districts along the eastern Adriatic coast, with the Austrian Republic over Carinthia, with Romania over Banat, and with Albania over the location of the Yugoslav–Albanian border. Additionally, Czechoslovakia bickered with Austria over the incorporation of Sudeten Germans. With the peace conference underway, the number of territorial disputes amplified. In fact, in the course of negotiations in Paris the three new states had disputes with all of their neighbors (the Yugoslavia–Greece dyad being the single exception) and several escalated into full-blown armed encounters.

In the nineteenth century the primary principle of delineating borders of new states was *de facto*; that is, borders were to define the area where the old authorities were removed and habitual obedience to the new ones could be presumed. This obedience was understood in civic-political rather than ethno-national terms: the ethnic Greeks of Thessaly and Epirus were left out of the Greek state because their general passivity in the struggle for independence was taken to indicate their unbroken loyalty to the Ottoman Empire. The *de facto* line could have been modified, but when such modifications on military-strategic, economic, or demographic grounds did take place in Europe, they were invariably minor. Beyond the emphasis on the *de facto* border principle, the balance of power politics of the Concert of Europe, be it in relation to Belgium or the Balkans, gravitated toward the lowest common denominator among the powers and this virtually assured that any alteration of the original *status quo* would be moderate. Insofar as new states were to contain people who feared or opposed their formation – and the Boundary Protocol of Poros noted as early as 1828 that no ideal line of separation existed where populations with different allegiances intermixed – their governments had to guarantee internationally equal treatment of all their citizens.

In contrast, agreement on a set of general criteria for drawing borders of the new states was not easy to discern at the Paris Peace Conference. Wilson's blanket pronouncements on self-determination encouraged a host of claims and counterclaims, but the peacemakers had difficulties devising some sort of transparent general basis for arbitrating among them.[41] The four powers with most say on European territorial issues could not reach consensus on how much weight to give to self-determination. Italy was not willing to countenance it when it conflicted with its own interests. France took a similar line when self-determination ran counter to the post-armistice balance of power. In the view of French Prime Minister Georges Clemenceau, international peace hinged not so much on the internal legitimacy of states as on the relative weakness of aggressive states. It was essential that Poland and Czechoslovakia emerge as strong as possible so that Germany could be hemmed in from both east and west. The British position oscillated somewhere between Wilson's and Clemenceau's, though it was closer to the former than the latter. Once in Paris, even Wilson realized that the principle of self-determination had its limits in determining state boundaries.

Challenges to Wilson's conception became apparent as soon as the conference got under way. One was the ethnic mixture of many disputed areas. Given the geographical scope of the settlement they were far more numerous than either in 1828 or 1878. Banat, East Galicia, Carinthia, Istria, Fiume (Rijeka), Upper Silesia, Vilnius, and plenty of others were mosaics of multifarious peoples where clean-cut divisions, if the inhabitants were to stay put, were plainly impossible. New minorities were unavoidable regardless of how one recast previous boundaries; some people were bound to end up, despite their resistance, on the wrong side. Compounding this basic difficulty were the questions of how to decide the exact area on which to solicit the wishes of the people and the means by which to do so. The town of Fiume proper had an Italian majority, but if one added its suburb of Porto Barros (Susak) and surrounding villages, then the majority was Croat. Italy wanted the entire area on the basis of Fiume's majority, Yugoslavia on the basis of Greater Fiume's one. It was not obvious which claim was *a priori* more compelling. A plebiscite was a doubtful solution to situations like this because accord on the size of the electorate was extremely improbable. A contending party was hardly keen to endorse a plebiscite if its conditions made the win implausible. A further problem was that both claimant governments and conference participants tended to impute the will of the people of a particular area by their ethnicity, buttressing the arguments by miscellaneous demographic statistics and census data. But that essentialist presumption was not necessarily correct – ethnicity did not automatically determine political loyalty. Yugoslavia claimed Carinthia because of its substantial ethnically

Slovene population, but the local Slovenes did not appear especially keen to join the new state. When a plebiscite was eventually held there, most Slovenes who cast a ballot preferred Austria. Likewise, in the Allenstein, Marienwerder, and Upper Silesia plebiscites most ethnic Poles who voted chose Germany over Poland.[42]

In contrast, the *de facto* border-making principle did not give rise to either problem as it worked backward, presuming wishes *ex post facto* from the acceptance of, or resistance to, the actual attempt to establish political authority rather than from voiced or imputed wishes. Wilson's wish-based conception of self-determination was more attractive theoretically – there was hardly anything more progressive than letting people decide what sovereignty to belong to – yet also radically more challenging in practical terms. What was apparent to many nineteenth-century foreign policymakers had eluded Wilson and his sympathizers: the normatively sound principle of the consent of the governed suggested no clear-cut international procedure for solicitation of that consent. His idea of self-determination, as Arnold Toynbee argued, proved "merely the statement of the problem and not the solution of it."[43]

However, as daunting as the competing character of demands based on the wishes of the people might have been, the new European states did not restrict themselves to land claims in this category. Like their nineteenth-century predecessors, they also claimed border territories for reasons of economic integrity, geographical unity, historic right, or strategic necessity, even when these manifestly belied the wishes of the people living there. The Prague government hurriedly occupied Sudetenland, where a comparatively large number of ethnic Germans constituted a majority, by contending that the area was a part of the historic Bohemian kingdom, that its mountainous topography was indispensable for military protection of the predominantly flat heartland, and that its industry and natural resources were pivotal for Czechoslovakia's "economic self-determination." Austria and Sudeten German deputies of the last imperial parliament protested that this violated the self-determination principle and appealed for a plebiscite that would be carried out by a neutral party, but the request fell on deaf ears. In the case of Poland, the demand for boundaries encompassing "indisputably Polish populations," as formulated in the thirteenth of Wilson's "Fourteen Points," actually conflicted with the associated demand of Poland's "free and secure" access to the sea. Poland could have obtained a shoreline only by incorporating regions inhabited by a large number of ethnic Germans. In the east, the Polish delegation demanded the frontier as it stood prior to the first partition of Poland in 1772 and, to the exasperation of nearly all, rejected the more western ethnic border known as the Curzon Line drawn by the conference.[44] Yugoslavia was resisting doggedly Italy's demands stemming from the 1915 Treaty of London, which were to give Italy sizeable Slovene- and Croat-populated areas on strategic grounds. Yet, its delegation asked for the northern Albanian port of Scutari on the very same grounds and would not so much as discuss Bulgaria's claim of Serbian Macedonia, supposedly populated by a people with pro-Bulgarian affinities, or Albania's claim of

Kosovo, predominantly ethnic Albanian but of great historical and religious significance to the Serbs. Serbia's pre-1914 territory, as that of any other Allied country, was off limits regardless of the wishes of its inhabitants,[45] despite the fact that both Kosovo and what used to be a northern part of the Ottoman province of Macedonia had been acquired by the now repudiated right of conquest as late as 1912/13.

None of this is meant to suggest that most Allied leaders and experts working in various commissions did not sincerely desire to follow the wishes of the people in prospective border areas as faithfully as possible. As the limitations of the concept itself became apparent, several devices were employed to help achieve a reasonable and equitable post-war settlement. Referenda were scheduled to take place in a number of contested areas. Danzig (Gdansk) and Fiume, the two most disputed cities at the conference, were eventually made free cities with international personality rather than put under sovereignty of either claimant. This solution resembled the status given to the contested city of Cracow in the General Act of the Congress of Vienna; though, unlike Cracow, administration of the two cities was to be the responsibility of the League of Nations and not of select great powers. In a few cases, the border was drawn so as to include a matching number of respective minorities on both sides. The new states had to pledge in the Treaties of Versailles with Germany (Czechoslovakia, Art. 86; Poland, Art. 93) and St. Germain with Austria (Yugoslavia, Art. 51; Czechoslovakia, Art. 57) that they would legally bind themselves to protect the interests of the inhabitants "who differ from the majority in race, language or religion" and subsequently each was made accede to special minority conventions. In those conventions they had to guarantee internationally, similarly to the Treaty of Berlin (1878), cultural and civil rights of minorities, though the compliance with the guarantees was now to be monitored by the League of Nations rather than a group of great powers. And, finally, there was an expectation – Wilson was its chief exponent – that whatever errors might have been committed at the peace conference, the League, as the world's instrument of peaceful change, would be procedurally and institutionally equipped to correct them.[46]

However, while these tools might have appeared as unavoidable exceptions to self-determination, the lack of any transparent hierarchy among the criteria determining territorial delimitations – that is, some *a priori* conception of how to balance self-determination with economic, geographical, historical, or strategic factors – encouraged maximal demands, discouraged compromise, and led inevitably to perceptions of inconsistencies across cases. Being on the losing side of the decisions – however sensibly they might have been justified in any particular instance – engendered widespread feelings of injustice and accusations of hypocrisy and double standards. No party appreciated when ambiguous criteria were used to its disadvantage. It might well have been that without Sudetenland Czechoslovakia could not have hoped for a robust industrial base, or adequate defense of its interior, or that without a western land "corridor" Poland would not have had the economically vital access to the Baltic Sea, but that did not persuade a lot of the five million ethnic Germans living in the two regions. They did not wish to be cogs in Czech or Polish wheels and thought that Wilson's principle of self-determination was wantonly denied to them. The wishes of the Germans in the periphery pockets of Upper Silesia, Allenstein, and Marienwerder did get hearing in plebiscites, but because of the conference's refusal to hold them in the other (and far larger) German-populated territories these did not placate either Germany or those Germans themselves.[47] Nor were the Germans who were to remain outside Germany mollified by the offer of minority rights guarantees – they did not want to be made into minorities in the first place. The German delegation in Versailles conjured up Wilson's own words to plead that it was "inadmissible that by the treaty of peace German populations and territories should be bartered about from sovereignty to sovereignty as if they were mere chattels and pawns,"[48] but this did not alter the verdict of the conference. Neither did similar pleadings of the Hungarian delegation that had to swallow the loss of three million ethnic Hungarians to Czechoslovakia, Yugoslavia, and Romania, a majority of whom resided contiguously alongside the three countries' border with the shrunken Hungary. Contrary to pre-conference expectations of many on the defeated side, interests of the new (and old) states belonging to the Entente were allowed to prevail over self-determination of peoples belonging to the states that lost the war.

However, disappointment was also palpable in the Entente ranks. The Italian delegation complained that its claims in the eastern Adriatic were not supported by its allies even though strategic and security arguments prevailed when Czechoslovakia's and Poland's borders were drawn, when Austria was deprived of the right of union with Germany without the approval of the League's Council, and when Italy received German-populated South Tyrol. The pro-Entente Ukrainians of Eastern Galicia complained bitterly of being abandoned after the quick Polish victory over the "West Ukrainian Republic." Unable to elicit Poland's acceptance of the Curzon Line and unwilling to use coercion to reverse its military occupation of the former Austrian region, the allies eventually accepted Eastern Galicia with its three million ethnic Ukrainians as a part of Poland.

Finally, the demand to accede to minority treaties as part of "confirmation" of their recognition produced bitterness among the new states themselves.[49] In the justificatory letter to the Polish delegation that accompanied the minority treaty with Poland – the first one to be completed and a model for others – Conference President Clemenceau wrote in the name of the Principal Allied and Associated Powers (France, Britain, Italy, Japan, and the United States):

> It has long been the established procedure of the public law of Europe that when a state is created, or even when large accessions of territory are made to an established state, the joint and formal recognition by the great powers should be accompanied by the requirement that such state should, in the form of a binding international convention, undertake to comply with certain principles of government.

The letter went on to provide an example of state recognition at the Congress of Berlin and cited the statements of Waddington, Bismarck, and other pleni-potentiaries from Berlin Protocol No. 8 on religious liberty as a condition of Serbia's acknowledgment. The letter then declared that the principled allied and associated powers would not depart from this established tradition, and added:

> It is to the endeavors and sacrifices of the powers in whose name I am addressing you that the Polish nation owes the recovery of its independence. It is by their decision that Polish sovereignty is being re-established over the territories in question and that the inhabitants of these territories are being incorporated into the Polish nation.

After pointing to the fact that "the obligations imposed upon new states seeking recognition have at all times varied with particular circumstances," the letter got to the heart of the matter. Poland was to receive minorities, some of which had been hostile to the Poles and to being inserted into Poland, and the knowledge of foreign guarantees of their rights would help their reconciliation to the new political reality as well as to the new majority people. The lack of internationally enforceable regulations in the area of minorities was thought to carry with it the potential of international insecurity. As Wilson put it in an earlier statement during the conference, "nothing . . . is more likely to disturb the peace of the world than the treatment which in certain circumstances may be meted out to minorities. . . . [The victorious great powers] are entitled to say: 'if we agree to these additions of territory we have the right to insist upon certain guarantees of peace.'"[50]

The objection to the treaties was that they made domestic policy of select states subject to an unprecedented degree of international supervision. Clemenceau's letter argued that minority protection under the aegis of the League would be less prone to arbitrary interferences into a state's domestic affairs than the former system of obligations to the great powers; however, the states compelled to sign the treaties complained all the same that the Principal Allied Powers would never accept such intrusions on their state authority. The most noted example of this double standard was Italy, which was not required to conclude a minority treaty despite the fact that it received large areas populated by non-Italians in the north and northeast.

To summarize up to this point, recognition of the three new states disclosed fundamental continuities with the pre-1914 practice. The Poles, Czechoslovaks, and Yugoslavs were able to lay empirical foundations of their statehood prior to the Paris Peace Conference. Akin to a number of nineteenth-century new states whose birth had been accompanied by major international crises, they had their boundaries and related issues settled by an international conference and under-stood that acceptance of the settlement was a necessary condition of their recognition. The only significant departure from the past was in border-making: The great power practice of grafting borders of new states primarily onto indige-nously generated *de facto* lines did not continue. The outcome of the boundary settlement was ironic. Soon after Wilson's utterances on self-determination had overtaken European public imagination, millions of people were relegated to the three new states against their wishes. However, the vast expectations produced by the American president made the conference decisions harder to take than would have perhaps otherwise been the case.

Recognizing States Emergent from the Russian Empire

If anything, the emphasis on previous international practice of endorsing *de facto* states was even more pronounced in regard to those claimants that had previously formed the western periphery of the Russian Empire. The enormous strains of war caused internal convulsions from which Russia did not recover until the Bolshevik consolidation of power in 1921/2. For four years, from the fall of tsardom in March 1917 and the frail provisional government that followed it, through the Bolshevik revolution in November 1917 and the subsequent civil war, the conditions in European Russia were even more turbulent and mercurial than those of the former Habsburg domains.

Various national groups reacted to Russia's weakness by claiming the right of self-determination and proclaiming their independence following the November 1917 revolution. Facing the prospect of the loss of a critical ally, the Entente was understandably loath to sanction alienation of Russian territory. It formally espoused the transfer of Russian Poland to the new Polish state, but only because the provisional government had given its express approval in March 1917.[51] Lenin's regime proclaimed itself ardently in favor of self-determination as a positive right, though given that it also hoped to set off a worldwide socialist revolution that would eventually see the end of sovereign statehood as such, it was not obvious how it would react to concrete attempts at independence from Russia or what value was to be attached to its potential acts of acknowledgment.

Ukraine, which declared independence in November 1917, was, in fact, first accorded recognition by the Central Powers. Germany, Austria-Hungary, Turkey, and Bulgaria were at the time still at war with Russia and this was a way to force the isolated Bolshevik government, which occupied parts of Ukraine, including Kiev, to negotiate its surrender and troop withdrawal. In the Treaty of Brest-Litovsk, which achieved this objective, Russia was compelled to recognize Ukraine as a sovereign country. The fortunes of Finland, the Baltic republics, and the Caucasian republics were similar: Russia was forced to renounce and vacate these territories in Brest-Litovsk too and in the course of 1918 Germany and its allies recognized them. All of them, then, fell into dependence on the Central Powers and most had German military presence on their soil. Finland and Lithuania went so far as to transform themselves into monarchies and, in acts redolent of Napoleon's satellite states, tendered their thrones to the relatives of the Hohenhollzern royal family.

This situation changed suddenly with the capitulation of the Central Powers. As a condition of armistice, they had to renounce the Treaty of Brest-Litovsk – deemed by the Allies as concluded under duress with an illegitimate Russian regime – and put their troops in the former Russian lands at the disposal of the Supreme Allied Council. With Germany out of the picture and the Peace of Brest-Litovsk in tatters, the Bolshevik government re-entered the Baltic and Caucasian republics, Russian Poland, and Ukraine with the intention of retaking as much territory as possible for the "proletarian revolution."

Recognition by the Allied countries was eventually extended to all the communities that maintained themselves *de facto* and outlasted the incursions of their neighbors. The Allied countries were, for the most part, quite guarded in their approach to the independence-minded entities of the former Romanov Empire and essentially waited for the various contests to play themselves out. Just as the Polish, Czechoslovak, and Yugoslav causes undoubtedly profited from the Entente's war on Germany and Austria-Hungary, so did some of these entities benefit from Entente's antagonism toward the new Russian regime. Though they initially concurred that while Russia was in the grip of revolutionary turmoil, disruptions to its territorial integrity, encouraged or affected from outside, should not be recognized, by the end of 1918 the Allies became fearful that the Bolsheviks, undefeated as they were by their domestic foes, might well want to fill the sudden power vacuum in the west. The Supreme Allied Council, for example, opted against the immediate withdrawal of the surrendered German troops from the eastern Baltic, so that their void would not be filled by the Soviet Red Army. This decision then in turn contributed, albeit only in a limited and temporary way, to the internal consolidation of the Baltic republics.

Finland was recognized first. Finnish envoys sought recognition of major Allies from the very beginning, but they were initially successful in only one case. Fearing that, if spurned, the republic could fall under German domination, France recognized Finland in early January 1918 without excessive concern about the usual *de facto* criteria.[52] At the moment of its proclamation, however, Finland was a fissiparous and volatile society. It had two competing armed forces, one of which, belonging to the socialist "Reds," was being furnished from abroad by the Red Army. The expedient bid to pull Finland into the orbit of the Entente rather than that of the Central Powers did not persuade other key allies of France, and in retrospect with good reason. Three weeks after France's undertaking a civil war broke out and Germany proved to be the only player in a position to interfere in it directly. When in the wake of the German military foray the Finnish parliament elected Kaiser Wilhelm's brother-in-law as king, France angrily broke its diplomatic relations with the recently recognized country. With Germany's capitulation, however, Finland and its institutions stabilized. In March 1919 it held its first general election. In May, then, the Council of Foreign Ministers at the Paris Peace Conference with the United States, Britain, Japan, and France present agreed that the first three – hitherto resisting Finnish appeals on account of deficiencies in effective statehood – would recognize Finland's independence.[53] Later that year, other allied countries did the same.

Although their governments had been treated as *de facto* authorities since late 1918,[54] Latvia, Estonia, and Lithuania were recognized as sovereign states by the Principal Allied Powers[55] only in 1921, after each had signed a peace treaty with Soviet Russia (in the case of Lithuania also with Poland). In addition, Lithuania had to pledge observance of the provisions of the Treaty of Versailles concerning the navigation of the river Niemen.[56] The United States, at this time not present in the allied council due to its failure to ratify the treaties signed at Paris, once again followed rather than led the European powers. Still, its July 1922 statement publicizing the decision provides a very instructive reading on what were taken to be the relevant principles:

> In extending to [the Baltic republics] recognition on its part, the government of the United States takes cognizance of the actual existence of these governments during a considerable period of time and of the successful maintenance within their borders of political and economic stability.
>
> The United States has consistently maintained that the disturbed condition of Russian affairs may not be made the occasion for the alienation of Russian territory, and this principle is not deemed to be infringed by the recognition of the governments of Estonia, Latvia and Lithuania which *have been set up and maintained by an indigenous population*.[57] (italics added)

Armenia was recognized in early 1920 and became a signatory of the Treaty of Sevres with Turkey as well as its own minority treaty with the allies in August of that year.[58] Georgia was acknowledged in January 1921 by the powers on the Supreme Allied Council and a number of other countries, though not the United States. But before both countries could join the League of Nations, they became internally divided and were reconquered by Soviet Russia in December 1920 and March 1921, respectively.[59] Armenia and Georgia are the only cases of extensively recognized countries whose forcible external takeovers were legally accepted, although it must be noted that their recognized status was rather brief and they never managed to become members of the organization designed to serve as a bulwark against conquest.

The "Ukrainian People's Republic," the "Republic of Azerbaijan," the "White Russian Republic," the "Kuban Republic," and the "Republic of North Caucasus" were recaptured by Soviet Russia. Having proved vitally dependent on the arrangements made at Brest-Litovsk, their *de facto* independence was short-lived. Despite their relentless pleading in individual capitals, at the Paris Peace Conference and then in the headquarters of the League of Nations in Geneva, they were never acknowledged by states other than those that had been part to that settlement.[60]

The political communities that had been previously wholly within the Russian Empire had not fully met the traditional *de facto* criteria before the start of the Paris conference. Though none was invited to take part in its proceedings, these criteria were taken to apply to these communities no less than to Poland, Czechoslovakia, and Yugoslavia. Mere wishes to change sovereigns did not suffice in the case of political communities from any former empire. In the aftermath of World War I, there was no positive right of self-determination.[61]

The Stimson Doctrine of Non-Recognition

Chapter 3 identified the single unambiguous instance in which the post-1815 recognition practice strayed away from acknowledging states other than those that were internally founded. Foreign recognition of first the North German Confederation and then the German Empire entailed acknowledgment of facts established through the application of *external* force. Germany was transformed from a conglomerate of sovereign entities into a unified state partly through Prussia's conquest and annexation of several German states as well as parts of Denmark and France, and third powers, however grudgingly, recognized this *fait accompli.* One of the main purposes of the League of Nations was to take away any stamp of legitimacy or legality from conquests and forcible annexations, including those that resulted in the creation of new states. Article 10 of its Covenant stipulated: "The members of the League undertake to respect and preserve as against external aggression the territorial integrity and existing political independence of all members of the League."

This resolve was tested by the 1932 proclamation of sovereignty of the "State of Manchukuo" in Manchuria, a Chinese province forcibly seized and occupied by Japan in 1931. Japan officially portrayed the founding of Manchukuo to be an example of a spontaneous, homegrown revolution. Claiming that while it had an obligation to respect China's territorial integrity it could not bar the peoples of China from exercising self-determination, Japan recognized the entity in September 1932.[62] The first to state its intention not to recognize the altered situation in Manchuria was the United States. In identical letters sent to China and Japan even before Manchukuo's arrival on the scene, Secretary of State Henry Stimson announced that the United States did not "intend to recognize any situation, treaty or agreement which may be brought about by means contrary to the covenants and obligations of the Pact of Paris of August 27, 1928, to which treaty both China and Japan, as well as the United States, are parties."[63] The United States was not a member of the League of Nations and thus it could not embed its argument in Art. 10 of the Covenant. It instead based its case on the Kellogg–Briand Pact, a multilateral treaty that renounced war as a legitimate instrument of change in mutual relations of its signatories and committed them to settling their disagreements by peaceful means. In a matter of weeks, the League of Nations Council adopted the American position, added a reference to Art. 10 and, going further than Stimson's note, made non-recognition a policy that all League members "ought" to follow.[64] Indicating again that it was a matter of obligation rather than discretion, the League's Assembly then passed a resolution that made the policy "incumbent" upon its members.[65] After a thorough investigation of the Japanese assault on China and ensuing developments by a specially appointed commission, the Assembly acknowledged Chinese sovereignty over Manchuria in February 1933. It likewise confirmed that Japan's recognition of Manchukuo was illegal.[66]

The Stimson Doctrine of non-recognition subsequently became a target of relentless criticism. Japan reacted to the Assembly's censure by withdrawing from the League rather than from China, and there was no will in the organization to undertake steps – probably requiring the use of force – to align the illegal *de facto* situation with the legal or *de jure* one. The League's collective security system appeared to flounder on insufficient solidarity among its members, and in this situation, the argument went, non-recognition was at best an ineffective resort to legal fictions and at worst a downright risk to peaceful relations with the castigated country.[67] This contention gained influence when the League failed to respond effectually to Italy's conquest of Ethiopia (1935) and Germany's annexation of Austria (1938), both victims being members of the organization. Since these events had exposed League members not to regard themselves earnestly obligated to fulfill their pledge to preserve the territorial integrity of fellow member states and instead to tolerate conquest, a frank recognition of *de facto* situations was preferable to a pretense that, in the eyes of international law, nothing changed.[68] Law had to follow facts on the ground or face irrelevance: there was not much point, as one critic deftly put it, in "closing the barn door after the horse has escaped."[69]

The past international legal theory and practice indeed lent support to the arguments against the policy of non-recognition. As repulsive as forcible territorial expansionism might have appeared to classical international lawyers, central to the acceptance of the right of conquest from Grotius and Vattel was the belief that it limited the duration of interstate wars and contributed to order within international society. If a military subjugation of one country's territory by another country had taken place and no third party would or could affect materially this state of affairs, then, the reasoning went: (*a*) the possibility of turning the conquest into rightful possession would provide the victor with an incentive to terminate rather than drag out the hostilities and (*b*) the title of the conquered territory obtained via a legal act would settle the matter conclusively and thus replace uncertainty, and possibly prolonged strife, by certainty and stability.[70] As seen in Chapter 3, the British and Russian response to the Prussian conquests preceding the proclamation of the German Empire in 1871 was consonant with this basic rationale. Since the two powers could not actively oppose Prussia's exploits, they regarded the reluctance to accept them yielding no real benefit.

While non-recognition cannot by itself make an effective system of collective security, it is nevertheless possible to argue that the Stimson Doctrine did signal an improvement in the international rule of law. Although vagaries of international politics make perfect identity between law and facts unlikely – because facts may well not be brought into line with law without coercive force which third parties may be, for whatever reason, reluctant to apply – if international law simply were to absorb all facts, even those established through patently illegal acts, then it would sow seeds of its own destruction as a system of law. One of the fundamental maxims of jurisprudence is *ex injuria jus non oritur*: an illegality cannot, as a rule, become a source of legal right to the wrongdoer.[71] A forcible territorial acquisition could have been turned into a legal title by the right of conquest prior to 1919,[72] but the signatories of the legally binding League of Nations Covenant and the Kellogg–Briand Pact – including Japan, Italy, and

Germany – abolished this right. As James Crawford writes, "international law risks being ineffective precisely when it does not challenge effective but unlawful situations."[73]

Even if one chooses to discount the argument about the integrity of the system of international law, it is apparent, at least in retrospect, that automatic recognition of Manchukuo or other Axis exploits would not have been a stabilizing factor in the international relations of the 1930s. In fact, having been preceded by a number of League members, Britain and France eventually veered away from non-recognition and, as an exceptional measure, each legally acknowledged Italian sovereignty over Ethiopia in 1938. Their express purpose, after the policy of non-recognition and (abortive) economic sanctions, was to keep the general peace,[74] but the act had a rather different effect. Rather than being pacified, the offender grew emboldened to embark on further conquests, invading Albania in April 1939.

Following the Italian fiasco, Britain and France returned to the policy of non-recognition. The "Slovak Republic" and the "Independent State of Croatia," created on the heels of German aggression against Czechoslovakia (1939) and Yugoslavia (1941), were recognized primarily by Axis powers and functioned as satellite states of Germany. Both Czechoslovakia and Yugoslavia as well as several other overrun countries established their respective governments-in-exile (mostly in London), and the Allies treated them as the legal representatives of their illegally occupied or fragmented countries. Important wartime documents of the Allies such as the Atlantic Charter (1941), the Declaration of the United Nations (1942), and the Yalta Declaration of Liberated Europe (1945)[75] indicated that an essential objective was to achieve their restoration. The post-war settlement accomplished this goal and Manchukuo, Slovakia, or Croatia were denied their continued existence.

By carrying with it support for the pre-existing legal rights, non-recognition makes the hold of *de facto* powers over a disputed domain continually doubtful and problematic. Such a possession is totally dependent on the holder's power. But because rightful possession hinges internationally to a great extent also on legitimacy, *de facto* possession is necessarily deficient if the objective is permanent and stable possession. A sharp decline or collapse of power behind illegitimate possession leads inevitably to its end. Generally non-recognized claims are thus far more prone to extinction than those generally recognized. Manchukuo, Slovakia, and Croatia are often referred to as "wartime states" precisely because their emergence and survival were contingent upon, and circumscribed by, war ascendancy of Japan and Germany. At the end of World War II, political circumstances did not allow the United States and Britain to reverse the 1940 annexation of the three Baltic republics by their major ally, the USSR, but they nevertheless maintained *de jure* non-recognition. As Chapter 6 will show, the restoration of Lithuanian, Latvian, and Estonian sovereignty in 1991 depended directly on the application of the Stimson Doctrine.

Conclusion

When President Wilson enunciated his strong support of self-determination at the close of World War I, there was popular elation across Europe but also apprehension in various government circles. The anxious comment of Wilson's own Secretary of State Lansing in December 1918, just prior to the opening of Paris negotiations, is perhaps the most famous:

> The more I think about the president's declaration as to the right of "self-determination," the more convinced I am of the danger of putting such ideas into the minds of certain races. It is bound to be the basis of impossible demands on the peace congress, and create trouble in many lands.
>
> The phrase is simply loaded with dynamite. It will raise hopes which can never be realized. It will, I fear, cost thousands of lives. In the end it is bound to be discredited, to be called the dream of an idealist who failed to realize the danger until too late to check those who attempt to put the principle into force. What a calamity that the phrase was ever uttered! What misery it will cause! Think of the feelings of the author when he counts the dead who died because he coined a phrase! A man who is a leader of public thought, should beware of intemperate or undigested declarations.[76]

Lansing was correct in predicting the magnitude of demands on the Paris Conference. Allied leaders were indeed swamped by "a blizzard of appeals" from peoples "they had never heard of."[77] Even Wilson himself admitted in September 1919, with regret, that "when I gave utterance to those words ['that all nations had a right to self-determination'], I said them without the knowledge that nationalities existed, which are coming to us day after day."[78]

Lansing's observation is a cautionary tale pointing to the perils of excessive idealist rhetoric. Wilson's political impact was as powerful as it was due to the absence of clear caveats in his formulations on self-determination. As Alfred Cobban writes, it is hard to come across any Wilson's public statement on the right of self-determination which was adequately qualified.[79] But he was not able to escape qualifications once he had to speak of the real world of specific places, peoples, or boundaries. He could not but go along with his secretary of state and Entente colleagues and acknowledge only political communities that had erected themselves on their own. Moreover, he could prevent his principle of self-determination neither from being often indeterminate nor from being supplanted by other principles in actual border-making.

Wilson's conception of self-determination as a positive right did not undermine the established recognition practice. However, another of Wilson's ideas, that of eliminating the right of conquest, can be said to have improved it. It provided a foundation for a lasting rule of non-recognition of states created in the aftermath of external use of force. As long as conquest had been legal, a new state could have arisen legitimately on its heels. After 1919 it could not.

Notes

1. Richard Holbrooke, "Foreword," in Margaret Macmillan, *Paris 1919: Six Months that Changed the World* (New York: Random House, 2002), p. viii.
2. France's unilateral recognition of Finland in January 1918 is, it will be seen in the second section, the only exception to this thesis.
3. Address of President Wilson to the Senate, January 22, 1917, James Brown Scott (ed.), *Official Statements of War Aims and Peace Proposals: December 1916 to November 1918* (Washington, DC: Carnegie Endowment for International Peace, 1921), p. 52. As early as May 1916 Wilson declared, "every people has a right to choose the sovereignty under which they shall live." See An Address in Washington to the League to Enforce Peace, May 27, 1916, Arthur S. Link (ed.), *The Papers of Woodrow Wilson*, Vol. 37, (Princeton, NJ: Princeton University Press, 1982), p. 115.
4. Message from President Wilson to Russia on the Occasion of the Visit of the American Mission, June 9, 1917, Scott, *Official Statements of War Aims and Peace Proposal*, p. 105.
5. Wilson made a notable link between the denial of self-determination and the break-down of international order in 1914. "This war," he maintained, "had its roots in the disregard of the rights of small nations and of nationalities which lacked the union and the force to make good their claim to determine their own allegiances and their own forms of political life."
6. Address of the President of the United States Delivered at a Joint Session of the Two Houses of Congress, February 11, 1918, FRUS, Supplement 1, Vol. 1 (1918), pp. 108–13.
7. Address in the City Auditorium in Pueblo, Colorado, September 25, 1919, Link, *The Papers of Woodrow Wilson*, Vol. 63, p. 502; On this, see also Michla Pomerance, "The United States and Self-Determination: Perspectives on the Wilsonian Conception," *The American Journal of International Law*, 70 (1977), p. 23; Derek Heater, *National Self-Determination: Woodrow Wilson and His Legacy* (Basingtoke: St. Martin's Press, 1994), p. 24; and Allen Lynch, "Woodrow Wilson and the Principle of 'National Self-Determination': A Reconsideration," *Review of International Studies*, 28 (2002), p. 424.
8. See Anthony Whelan, "Wilsonian Self-Determination and the Versailles Settlement," *The International and Comparative Law Quarterly*, 43 (1994), pp. 100, 108.
9. Perhaps the only document in which Wilson offered at least some details of how the positive right of self-determination might work is the original draft of what eventually became Art. 10 of the League of Nations Covenant. Wilson's original proposal of December 1918, which he refused to make public, guaranteed the League members their territorial integrity and political independence, but at the same time it allowed the League Assembly to make territorial changes if approved by at least three-fourths of the delegates. This suggests that the right of self-determination was to be conditional on overwhelming support among League members. The three-quarters formula encountered immediate resistance once the conference convened. It underwent several changes – in one of them the projected territorial adjustments were made dependent on the consent also of "the states from which the territory is separated or to which it is added" – but opposition remained unyielding. Neither the formula nor any reference to self-determination made it to the covenant. See Pomerance, "The United States and Self-Determination: Perspectives on the Wilsonian Conception," p. 23.

10. Address of the President of the United States Delivered at a Joint Session of the Two Houses of Congress, January 8, 1918, FRUS, Supplement 1, Vol. 1 (1918), pp. 12–17. In the December 1917 speech to the Congress advising the declaration of war on Austria-Hungary, President Wilson explicitly disavowed any intention of dismantling the country: "We do not wish in any way to impair or rearrange the Austro-Hungarian Empire. It is no affair of ours what they do with their own life, either industrially or politically." See Address of President Wilson Reviewing American War Aims and Recommending the Declaration of a State of War between the United States and the Austro-Hungarian Government, December 4, 1917, Scott, *Official Statements of War Aims and Peace Proposals*, p. 196.

11. See Erez Manela, *The Wilsonian Moment: Self-Determination and the International Origins of Anti-Colonial Nationalism* (New York: Oxford University Press, 2007), pp. 13, 62.

12. Statement of British War Aims by Prime Minister Lloyd George, January 5, 1918, Scott, *Official Statements of War Aims and Peace Proposals*, pp. 228–9.

13. Quoted in Alfred Cobban, *The Nation-State and National Self-Determination*, rev. ed. (London: Collins, 1969), p. 52.

14. This was a treaty among Britain, France, Russia, and Italy. Its main purpose was to induce Italy's entry into the war on the Entente side.

15. Proclamation of the Russian Provisional Government in Reference to its War Aims, April 10, 1917, Scott, *Official Statements of War Aims and Peace Proposals*, p. 95.

16. Lansing to Wilson, May 10, 1918, FRUS: The Lansing Papers 1914–1920, Vol. 2, p. 127.

17. Lansing to Wilson, August 19, 1918, ibid., p. 139; For the correspondence between Lansing and Department of State legal counselor on the legal aspects of potential recognition of Czechoslovaks as well as related documents, see Victor Mamatey, "The United States Recognition of the Czechoslovak National Council of Paris (September 3, 1918): Documents," *Journal of Central European Affairs*, 13 (1953), pp. 49–56.

18. An autonomous Polish army was being formed as well – in Russia and France.

19. Page to Lansing, April 12, 1918, ibid., p. 796.

20. Lansing to Page, May 29, 1918, ibid., p. 809.

21. Jusserand to Lansing, June 15, 1918, ibid., p. 813.

22. Pichon to Lansing, June 29, 1918, ibid., p. 817.

23. Lansing to Wilson, August 19, 1918, FRUS: The Lansing Papers, Vol. 2, p. 139.

24. For a discussion of foreign recognition of belligerency in civil conflicts which includes a survey of the US and British practice of recognizing *de facto* belligerency, see Lauterpacht, *Recognition in International Law*, ch. 12.

25. See Mamatey, "Documents," pp. 53–5.

26. Michailovitch to Lansing, June 14, 1918, FRUS, Supplement 1, Vol. 1 (1918), pp. 812–13.

27. Masaryk to Polk, July 20, 1918, ibid., p. 818.

28. Lansing to Michailovitch, June 24, 1918, ibid., p. 816.

29. For the very similarly phrased British recognition of Czechoslovak belligerency, see Balfour's Declaration of August 9, 1918, Smith, *Great Britain and the Law of Nations*, Vol. 1, p. 236.

30. Wilson to Lansing, September 2, 1918, FRUS: The Lansing Papers, Vol. 2, pp. 144–5; Britain's earlier recognition of Czechoslovak belligerency of August, 9, 1918 was a similar recital of facts. The decision was firmly linked to the "efforts to achieve independence," most important of which was the constitution of "a considerable army, fighting on three battlefields and attempting, in Russia and Siberia, to arrest the

Germanic invasion." See Skinner to Lansing, August 14, 1918, FRUS, Supplement 1, Vol. 1 (1918), p. 824.

31. H. W. Temperley, "Recognition of New States," in H. W. Temperley (ed.), *A History of the Peace Conference of Paris*, Vol. 5 (London: Henry Frowde and Hodder & Stoughton, 1921), p. 160.

32. The Poles received recognition of belligerency similar to the Czechoslovaks in October 1918. See FRUS, Supplement 1, Vol. 1 (1918), pp. 878–81.

33. This included Wilson's announcement on October 18 that he could no longer accept mere autonomy for the Czechoslovak and Yugoslav peoples of Austria-Hungary. Referring to the key US public statements in regard to the Czechoslovaks and Yugoslavs since the "Four Points" address, the president stated that he was "no longer at liberty to accept the mere 'autonomy' of these peoples as a basis of peace, but is obliged to insist that they, and not he, shall be the judges of what action on the part of the Austro-Hungarian government will satisfy their aspirations and their conception of rights and destiny as members of the family of nations." See Reply of President Wilson, October 18, 1918, Scott, *Official Statements of War Aims and Peace Proposals*, pp. 428–9.

34. Quoted in Derek Heater, *National Self-Determination*, p. 67.

35. The Austrian and Hungarian governments, just as the German one, continued to profess their acceptance of the core tenets of Wilson's key 1918 speeches. This acceptance was an Allied condition of armistice with the Central Powers and is evidence that the speeches were more than a mere influential statement of intention.

36. K. R. Stadler, "The Disintegration of the Austro-Hungarian Empire," *Journal of Contemporary History* 3 (1968), p. 179; see also Alfred Cobban, *The Nation-State and National Self-Determination*, pp. 55–6; Victor S. Mamatey, *The United States and East Central Europe, 1914–1918* (Princeton, NJ: Princeton University Press, 1957), pp. ix–x, 384; Though focused specifically on Yugoslavia, the same argument runs through Ivo Lederer, *Yugoslavia at the Paris Peace Conference: A Study in Frontier-making* (New Haven, CT: Yale University Press, 1963), pp. 45, 81–2, 119.

37. The Yugoslav National Committee never obtained recognition similar to that of the Czechoslovak and Polish National Councils because of Italy's opposition. In Yugoslavia Italy feared a rival to several territories promised to it by the 1915 Treaty of London. Though not in principle opposed to the "Kingdom of Serbs, Croats and Slovenes," as Yugoslavia was officially called following its proclamation on December 1, 1918, Italy sought to delay Entente recognition of the new state until it gained a favorable allocation of territory in the eastern Adriatic. The Allies did not want to act without Italy and postponed acting on the Yugoslav request for recognition. While Czechoslovakia and Poland were allowed to take their places at the peace conference without any difficulties, the Yugoslav delegation had to sit under the banner of "Serbia." Frustrated by Italian obstructionism, the United States, Britain, and France acknowledged the new kingdom without Italy during the conference. Italy's recognition is dated from the signature of the Treaty of Versailles in late June 1919. See FRUS, Vol. 2 (1919), pp. 892–900 and Lederer, *Yugoslavia at the Paris Peace Conference*, pp. 148, 204–5; there was another twist to Yugoslavia's recognition. On November 26, 1918 the Montenegrin parliament deposed King Nicholas I and resolved that Montenegro would join the new country. But Nicholas disputed the legality of these decisions and appealed personally to Wilson. The Allies left the Montenegrin dispute open without, however, letting the royal delegation participate for the whole duration of the conference. Montenegro's status was definitely settled in the aftermath of the first Yugoslav election in November 1920. As the absolute majority of deputies elected

were pro-Yugoslav, the principal powers revoked the diplomatic status of Montenegrin missions in their capitals. See R. G. D. Laffan, "The Liberation of the New Nationalities," in Temperley, *A History of the Peace Conference of Paris*, Vol. 4, pp. 201–4, and FRUS, Vol. 2 (1921), pp. 945–9.

38. The norm is conveyed perhaps most powerfully in the preambles to the minority treaties between the Principal Allied and Associated Powers and Poland, Czechoslovakia, and Yugoslavia. Each preamble recaps how the new state was created. The treaty with Czechoslovakia makes references to how "the peoples of Slovakia, have decided of their own free will to unite, *and have in fact united*, in a permanent union for the purpose of forming a single sovereign independent State under the title of the Czecho-Slovak Republic" and how "the Czecho-Slovak Republic *in fact* exercises sovereignty over the aforesaid territories." The latter formulation also found its way into the Polish treaty. The treaty with Yugoslavia, in a slight variation, talks about how "the Kingdom of the Serbs, Croats and Slovenes *has been constituted* and *has assumed sovereignty* over the territories inhabited by these peoples" (italics added). See the text of the preambles in Temperley, *A History of the Peace Conference of Paris*, Vol. 5, p. 461 (Czechoslovakia), pp. 437–8 (Poland) and pp. 446–7 (Yugoslavia).

39. The norm might have been undisputed by the governments set to assemble in Paris, but not necessarily to stateless peoples buoyed by Wilson's rhetoric on self-determination. They were inevitably disappointed. For example, during a pre-conference meeting with Irish representatives Wilson dismissed with undisguised irritation their demand for an independent Ireland.

40. With the downfall of Austria-Hungary, the Ukrainians of Eastern Galicia proclaimed a "West Ukrainian Republic" in the former Austrian province. This entity, centered in Lvov, was to be later connected with the "Ukrainian People's Republic" which emerged in Kiev in the wake of the Bolshevik revolution.

41. Which claims were to be properly considered by the conference was not clear either. Wilson's universally sounding utterances on self-determination encouraged claims from within allied or neutral countries, not just the defeated ones. The Irish, for example, were unsuccessful, but the appeal of neutral Denmark on behalf of the ethnic Danes in Schleswig led to a plebiscite and subsequent change of boundaries there. Later Wilson admitted: "It was not within the privilege of the conference of peace to act upon the right of self-determination of any peoples except those which had been included in the territories of the defeated empires." See his Address in the San Francisco Civic Auditorium, September 17, 1919, Link, *The Papers of Woodrow Wilson*, Vol. 63, p. 332; See also Pomerance, "The United States and Self-Determination: Perspectives on the Wilsonian Conception," p. 9.

42. See E.H. Carr, "The Crisis of Self-Determination," in his *Conditions of Peace* (New York: Macmillan, 1942), pp. 44–8.

43. Arnold J. Toynbee, "Self-Determination," *The Quarterly Review*, 243 (1925), p. 319. A similar critique of Wilsonian conception of self-determination is Ivor Jennings': "On the surface it seemed reasonable: let the people decide. It was in fact ridiculous because the people cannot decide until somebody decides who are the people." See Sir Ivor Jennings, *The Approach to Self-Government* (Boston: Beacon Press, 1956), p. 56.

44. The Curzon Line could not become Poland's border at the conference itself because Russia was not invited to Paris and because Poland prosecuted war against the Bolsheviks. Poland's eastern boundary was, in fact, settled directly between the two belligerents in the peace Treaty of Riga (1921), and the Allies found themselves unable to affect its change.

45. The pre-1914 German conquests were, however, treated differently. Alsace-Lorraine was returned to France as a matter of historical right and the ethnically Danish northern Schleswig was slated to have a plebiscite, denied to it in the 1860s and 1870s.
46. Wilson argued after his return from Paris that "if the desire for self-determination of any people in the world is likely to affect the peace of the world," the League would be able – through its mechanisms of conflict resolution embodied in Art. 12 – to preserve it. See his Address in the San Francisco Civic Auditorium, September 17, 1919, Link, *The Papers of Woodrow Wilson*, Vol. 63, p. 332.
47. In the case of the rejection of the demand for referendum in the province of Posen and West Prussia, the Allies admitted their partiality quite openly: "There is imposed upon the Allies a special obligation to use the victory which they have won in order to re-establish the Polish nation in the independence of which it was unjustly deprived more than a hundred years ago.... To undo this wrong is the first duty of the Allies." See Reply of the Allied and Associated Powers, June 16, 1919, Temperley, *A History of the Peace Conference of Paris*, Vol. 2, p. 284. The Austro–German union, declared by both Austrian and German parliaments, was similarly never a subject of popular vote. The Allies saw an enlarged Germany as an external threat and the Treaties of Versailles and St. Germain prohibited the two countries from seeking a union unless they had the prior consent of the League Council.
48. German Note to the Allies, May 13, 1919, quoted in Heater, *National Self-Determination*, p. 122.
49. Letter Addressed to M. Paderewski by the President of the Conference transmitting to him the Treaty to be signed between Poland under Art. 93 of the Treaty of Peace with Germany, June 24, 1919, Temperley, *A History of the Peace Conference of Paris*, Vol. 5, pp. 432–7; The Polish and Czechoslovak treaties in their preambles likewise explicitly "confirm" the recognition of the two new states by the major allies. The defeated states, on the other hand, had to recognize the new states in their borders in their respective peace treaties.
50. President Wilson's Speech, May 31, 1919, Temperley, *A History of the Peace Conference of Paris*, Vol. 5, pp. 130–1.
51. This consent was noted in the preamble to the Polish Minority Treaty. The explicit reference was presumably to dispel potential suggestions that the Allies recognized independence of a former Russian territory prematurely.
52. Malbone W. Graham, *The Diplomatic Recognition of the Border States. Part I: Finland* (Berkeley, CA: University of California Press, 1935), pp. 109–10; The first to recognize Finland was the Soviet regime on January 4, 1918. Besides France, Finland was in its first three months also recognized by Germany and Austria-Hungary as well as several neutral countries (Denmark, Sweden, Norway, Switzerland, the Netherlands, and Spain). The conduct of the neutrals was thus more in line with the position of the Central Powers than that of the Entente, which refused to treat the Bolsheviks as the legitimate Russian government and accept the validity of their decisions.
53. For the development of US and Allied positions toward recognition of Finland, see Green H. Hackworth (ed.), *Digest of International Law*, Vol. 1 (Washington, DC: Government Printing Office, 1940), pp. 209–13.
54. Article 433 of the Treaty of Versailles mentions the "provisional governments of Estonia, Latvia, and Lithuania."
55. See Notes addressed by the President of the Inter-Allied Conference at Paris to the President of the Estonian (Latvian) Delegation notifying the Decision of the Supreme

Council of the Allied Powers to recognize Estonia (Latvia) as a State *de jure*, January 26, 1921, BFSP, Vol. 114 (1921), pp. 558–9.

56. See Lauterpacht, *Recognition in International Law*, pp. 360–1 (n. 4).

57. Quoted in Hackworth, *Digest of International Law*, Vol. 1, p. 201.

58. See Secretary of State Bainbridge Colby's note of US recognition of Armenia of April 23, 1920 in *The New York Times*, April 25, 1920; and Treaty between the British Empire, France, Italy, Japan, as the Principal Allied Powers, and Armenia, August 10, 1920, BFSP, Vol. 113 (1920), pp. 458–63. Armenia, however, neither ratified the treaty nor did it become a member of the League of Nations.

59. See Malbone W. Graham, *In Quest of a Law of Recognition* (Berkeley, CA: University of California Press, 1933), pp. 31–3 (n. 27, 29).

60. Employing the same rationale as in regard to Finland, France was set to recognize Ukraine in late January 1918. However, when the Kiev government failed to take a pro-Entente stand and instead entered into peace negotiations with the Germans at Breast-Litovsk, the French quickly abandoned the idea. See Jusserand to Lansing, January 7, 1918, and Sharp to Lansing, January 22, 1918, FRUS: Russia, Vol. 2 (1918), pp. 655, 660–3; It should be noted that Azerbaijan was acknowledged by the principal allied powers in early 1920 *de facto*, but not *de jure*. The distinction between *de facto* and *de jure* recognition was a novelty. The former noted provisionally that a new entity exists in some form and allowed dealings with its authorities. It, however, suggested neither that full *de facto* independent statehood has been achieved nor acknowledged a new entity's sovereignty – only legal or *de jure* recognition did that. To the extent that such a distinction had a practical impact, the concern of this study is exclusively *de jure* recognition.

61. This conclusion is supported by two important League documents on the dispute over the Aaland Islands. When the Swedish population of the Finnish islands expressed in 1920 its aspiration to join Sweden, the Commission of Jurists of the League of Nations judged in an important advisory opinion that:

> Although the principle of self-determination of peoples plays an important part in modern political thought, especially since the Great War, it must be pointed out that there is no mention of it in the Covenant of the League of Nations. The recognition of this principle in certain number of international treaties cannot be considered as sufficient to put it on the same footing as positive rule of the law of nations.
>
> On the contrary, in the absence of express provisions in international treaties, the right of disposing of national territory is essentially an attribute of the sovereignty of every state. Positive international law does not recognize the right of national groups, as such, to separate themselves from the state of which they form a part of *by the simple expression of a wish*, any more than it recognizes the right of other states to claim such a separation.

In another League of Nations report on the matter in 1921, by the Committee of Rapporteurs, the authors contended:

> To concede to minorities, either of language or religion, or to any fraction of a population the right of withdrawing from the community to which they belong, *because it is their wish or good pleasure*, would be to destroy order and stability within states and to inaugurate anarchy in international life; it would be to uphold a theory incompatible with the very idea of the state as a territorial unit. (italics added)

See Report of Commission of Jurists, *League of Nations Official Journal: Special Supplement No. 3* (October 1920), p. 5, and Report of the Committee of Rapporteurs, April 21, 1921, League of Nations Council Doc. B/7/21/68/106, p. 28.

62. See Quincy Wright, "The Legal Background in the Far East," in Quincy Wright (ed.), *Legal Problems in the Far Eastern Conflict* (New York: Institute of Pacific Relations, 1941), p. 57, and Protocol of Recognition of Manchukuo and Japanese Statement on Protocol, January 15, 1932, John W. Wheeler-Bennett (ed.), *Documents on International Affairs 1932* (London: Oxford University Press, 1933), pp. 312–16.

63. Identical Notes from the US Secretary State to the Chinese and Japanese Governments, January 8, 1932, ibid., p. 262.

64. Note by Members of the Council of the League of Nations other than China and Japan to Japan, February 16, 1932, *The Monthly Summary of the League of Nations*, 12 (February 1932), p. 45.

65. Resolution of the Assembly of the League of Nations, March 11, 1932, *The Monthly Summary of the League of Nations*, 12 (March 1932), p. 106.

66. Extracts from the Report of the Committee of Nineteen to the Assembly of the League of Nations, February 15, 1933, and Resolutions adopted by the League Special Assembly, February 24, 1933, Wheeler-Bennett, *Documents on International Affairs 1932*, pp. 384–91.

67. See Edwin M. Borchard and Phoebe Morrison, "The Doctrine of Non-Recognition," in Quincy Wright (ed.), *Legal Problems in the Far Eastern Conflict* (New York: Institute of Pacific Relations, 1941).

68. Herbert W. Briggs, "Non-Recognition of Title by Conquest and Limitations on the Doctrine," *American Society of International Law Proceedings*, 34 (1940), pp. 79–82.

69. Ibid., p. 81

70. Korman, *The Right of Conquest*, pp. 25–6.

71. Lauterpacht, *Recognition in International Law*, p. 420. See also Robert Langer, *Seizure of Territory: The Stimson Doctrine and Related Principles in Legal Theory and Diplomatic Practice* (Princeton, NJ: Princeton University Press, 1947), p. 290.

72. To return to another example from the preceding chapter, even as British Foreign Minister Russell took vigorous moral objection to the Austro-Prussian conquest of the Danish duchies in 1865, Prime Minister Palmerston admitted that they were, strictly speaking, acquired legally. Although seized by force, the duchies were ceded by Denmark in a peace treaty. This legal act met the requirements for Austria and Prussia to obtain them by the right of conquest. See Palmerston to Russell, September 19, 1865, Gooch, *The Later Correspondence of Lord John Russell*, Vol. 2 pp. 315–16.

73. James Crawford, *Creation of States in International Law*, 2nd ed. (Oxford: Clarendon Press, 2006), p. 98.

74. See Statement by the Representative of the United Kingdom with regard to the Anglo-Italian Agreement of April 16, 1938, May 10, 1938, *The Monthly Summary of the League of Nations*, 18 (May 1938), pp. 102–3; Hersch Lauterparcht additionally writes that it was on the basis of Italy's failure to maintain that peace that Britain, in 1940, withdrew its recognition of Italian annexation and declared itself in favor of the restoration of Ethiopia's independence and its king. See ibid., p. 356.

75. The Atlantic Charter, which formed the basis of the latter major Allied documents, called for "sovereign rights and self-government restored to those who have been forcibly deprived of them." See *Declaration of Principles*, known as the Atlantic Charter, August 14, 1941, Louise W. Holborn (ed.), *War and Peace Aims of the United Nations*, Vol. 1 (Boston, MA: World Peace Foundation, 1943), p. 2; This formulation resembled the preamble of the first treaty forming the last anti-Napoleonic coalition, the 1813 Anglo–Prussian Treaty of Reichenbach, which sought to "re-establish the independence of the states oppressed by France."

76. Robert Lansing, *The Peace Negotiation: A Personal Narrative* (Boston, MA: Houghton Mifflin Company, 1921), pp. 97–8.
77. Kalevi J. Holsti, *The State, War, and the State of War* (Cambridge: Cambridge University Press, 1996), p. 53.
78. Quoted in ibid.
79. Cobban, *The Nation-State and National Self-Determination*, p. 104.

5

New States in Decolonization After 1945

The distinguishing characteristic of the new states recognized in the aftermath of World War I – and consistent with the nineteenth-century practice surveyed in Chapters 2 and 3 – was their prior *de facto* emergence. These polities shared, however, another attribute. Just like those American and European polities acknowledged between 1776 and 1914, they had previously been, in terms of constitutional law, integral components of the sovereign states they succeeded. Nevertheless, a large portion of the globe's surface, namely the non-settler European colonies in Asia, Africa, and Oceania acquired mostly in the nineteenth century, was not integrally part of any sovereign state in that period.[1] In the eyes of international law the colonies belonged to the European countries that acquired them, but in the constitutional law of those countries they were distinguished from, and made dependent on and subordinated to, the imperial metropole.

The principal justification for their exclusion from the sovereignty regime was their lack of civilization. In the course of the nineteenth century, as even numerous references to "civilized nations" in recognition decisions relating to Latin America and Europe vividly demonstrate, sovereignty presupposed civilization. The colonized peoples of non-European origin were, due to their professed backwardness, deemed incapable of self-government and, consequently, in need of tutelage from the more advanced outsiders. Though independence was understood as an option for the future, there was no question of considering it before the colonies' marked improvements in their social, political, educational, economic, and administrative conditions; before they first reached what had been habitually referred to since the mid-nineteenth century as the "standard of civilization."[2] In the post-World War I period it was still generally believed, including by President Wilson,[3] that the colonies' native inhabitants were not ready for sovereign statehood.

By the early 1960s, the beliefs that had buttressed colonial rule were fatally undermined and formal hold of overseas dependencies became internationally illegitimate. The colonial idea was thoroughly displaced by the belief, repeatedly enunciated at various global fora and most notably in United Nations General Assembly Resolution 1514 (XV), that the dependent peoples have a right to self-determination and independence (see Table 5.1). The process of decolonization, which overwhelmingly consisted of accession of territories with colonial to sovereign status, made a wholesale change to the long-standing recognition practice. Unlike the past, these territories staked their requests for foreign acknowledgment not on the basis of having attained *de facto* statehood, but on the inadmissibility of

Table 5.1 Present-day states that have arisen out of formal dependencies since 1941

Algeria	Cyprus	Kuwait	Nigeria	Swaziland
Angola	Democratic Republic of Congo	Laos	Oman	Syria
Antigua and Barbuda	Djibouti	Lebanon	Pakistan	Tanzania
Bahamas	Dominica	Lesotho	Palau	Togo
Bahrain	East Timor	Libya	Papua New Guinea	Tonga
Barbados	Equatorial Guinea	Madagascar	Philippines	Trinidad and Tobago
Belize	Fiji	Malawi	Qatar	Tunisia
Benin	Gabon	Malaysia	Rwanda	Tuvalu
Bhutan	Gambia	Maldives	Saint Kitts and Nevis	Uganda
Botswana	Ghana	Mali	Saint Lucia	United Arab Emirates
Brunei	Grenada	Malta	Saint Vincent and the Grenadines	Vanuatu
Burkina Faso	Guinea	Marshall Islands	Samoa	Vietnam
Burundi	Guinea-Bissau	Mauritania	Sao Tome and Principe	Zambia
Cambodia	Guyana	Mauritius	Senegal	Zimbabwe
Cameroon	India	Micronesia	Seychelles	
Cape Verde	Indonesia	Morocco	Sierra Leone	
Central African Republic	Israel	Mozambique	Solomon Islands	
Chad	Jamaica	Myanmar	Sudan	
Comoros	Jordan	Namibia	Somalia	
Congo	Kenya	Nauru	Sri Lanka	
Côte d'Ivoire	Kiribati	Niger	Suriname	

their second-class rank in the family of nations. By the same token, and also breaking with the past, existing states conditioned their acknowledgment neither by demanding prior evidence of *de facto* statehood nor by seeking fulfillment of conditions that might be in the general interest of international society.

Most existing countries after 1950 in fact actively minimized the weight to be given to empirical aspects of governance and statehood. The ex-colonies were being acknowledged as sovereign more or less automatically because the new global political climate could not tolerate the continuation of the institution of formal empire, and not as a result of appraisal in terms of some substantive standards. State recognition thus moved from assessing fact to evaluating right.[4] The right of decolonization was more expansive than the last doctrine of international right, that of dynastic legitimacy. Whereas the latter postulated that an entity could be acknowledged only if it had obtained consent of the discretion-holding parent sovereign, the former in effect stipulated that a dependency wishing to be independent was entitled to recognition *a priori* by virtue of its status, with the colonial power in question having no legitimate veto in the matter. Decolonization was a phenomenon without precedent: never before had non-sovereign groups reached independence as a matter of mere assertion of aspiration.

In this respect, decolonization was the triumph of Wilson's conception of self-determination as a positive right over the nineteenth-century Anglo-American one: it substituted the self-help-based mode of acquiring independence for a wish-based mode. The scope of that triumph, however, was limited precisely because the right of self-determination that involved the choice of independence became restricted to entities with a particular status. Wilson spoke of self-determination as the right of all peoples, but border-making at the Paris Peace Conference revealed that the principle of letting people express their wishes was of little help whenever different groups were after the same territory,[5] and in fact sowed seeds of discord and instability within and between countries. Already in the 1950s there were signs of an international consensus that, unless there was agreement to proceed otherwise, colonies should become independent in their existing boundaries. The evidence of the past several decades was taken to suggest that a rational and generally satisfactory method of drawing new state boundaries could not be found and it was thought that a return to the default rule of territorial delimitation employed in the course of Latin American emancipation was preferable. Indeed, by the early 1960s *uti possidetis juris* had become widely regarded as applicable to the process of decolonization.

It can be safely said that the *uti possidetis* of decolonization has not solved the dilemmas associated with Wilson's idea of self-determination. Colonial borders too often did not correspond to the actual patterns of political allegiance and many communities within and across the newly minted interstate frontiers, usually defined in ethnonational terms, claimed the right of self-determination against the countries in which they found themselves. The rate of secessionist bids, most of which descended into armed clashes of varying intensity, rose nearly as quickly as the number of post-colonial states. If one compares the aftermath of territorial settlement in 1919 and that of decolonization, it is apparent that while the solution – *uti possidetis juris* – changed, a major predicament – groups pursuing claims of unjust denial of self-determination – remained the same. The right to self-determination ushered in by decolonization might have been noticeably different from the hitherto familiar claims of the right to *national* self-determination, but the latter has not gone away.

Notwithstanding the prevalence and seriousness of secessionist conflicts, the independence claims other than those falling within the new paradigm of international legitimacy were excluded from foreign recognition. Unlike Central and South America where *uti possidetis juris* provided protection solely against *external* conquest, the *uti possidetis* of decolonization served to safeguard the new states also against *internal* fragmentation. In fact, in subsequent practice the protection of territorial integrity against internal as well as external challenges was extended to non-colonial settings as well. With the lone exception of Bangladesh, the internally driven secessionist ventures, no matter how successful empirically, have not received general foreign acknowledgment without the consent of the sovereign government. This was a significant departure from the recognition practice going all the way back to the 1820s. The nearly religious emphasis on consent of existing states has approximated more the post-1815 doctrine of dynastic legitimacy than the views of any past advocate of the right of self-determination. As a result, long-enduring *de facto* states – that is, effective states subsisting for years without foreign recognition such as a number of South American republics prior to their acknowledgment by the United States and Britain – made a comeback in world affairs. Decolonization and its aftermath thus revealed a major paradox: as self-determination was authoritatively declared to be a universal right and an unprecedented number of states entered the society of states under its banner, the chances for future emergence of new states narrowed more than ever.

Decolonization and State Recognition

For all the tumult that the idea of self-determination set off at the end of World War I, the Paris Peace Conference never seriously contemplated that it might apply to the peoples of European overseas colonies. Despite occasional qualms that President Wilson's utterances on self-determination might undercut colonial rule, the debate at the conference was framed by the fifth of Wilson's "Fourteen Points," which limited itself to the call for

> A free, open-minded, and absolutely impartial adjustment of all colonial claims, based upon a strict observance of the principle that in determining all such questions of sovereignty the interests of the populations concerned must have equal weight with the equitable claims of the government whose title is to be determined.

Although the concept of mandates, as embodied in Art. 22 of the League Covenant, was a definite innovation in the institutional history of colonialism, it was based on the paternalistic idea of trusteeship that had underpinned colonial rule in some parts of the globe for more than a century.[6] The Paris Peace Conference was scarcely a venue wanting in great controversies, but virtually everyone in attendance took for granted the article's assertion that for "peoples not yet able to stand by themselves under the strenuous conditions of the modern world there should be applied the principle that the well-being and development of such peoples form a sacred trust of civilization." It was equally uncontroversial that "the best method of giving practical effect to this principle is that the tutelage of such peoples should be entrusted to advanced nations who by reason of their resources, their experience or their geographical position can best undertake this responsibility."[7] Mandates, which covered solely the dependent territories of the defeated Central Powers, were divided into three classes according to their level of development. Apart from one nebulous exception,[8] the conference rejected immediate sovereignty even for the Arab principalities of the Middle East that fought for independence against the Ottomans and were deemed the most advanced of all the territories under consideration. Article 22 agreed that "certain communities formerly belonging to the Turkish Empire have reached a stage of development where their existence as independent nations can be provisionally recognized," but these ex-vassal jurisdictions were, in the same breath, consigned to being "subject to the rendering of administrative advice and assistance by a mandatory until such time as they are able to stand alone."

That the premium placed on the substantive "standards of civilization" was generally very high in the interwar period can be seen when one examines the only case of decolonization carried out under the auspices of the League of Nations, the termination of the Iraq mandate.[9] After Britain had asked in 1929 that its mandate come to an end and Iraq be admitted as a sovereign member of the League of Nations in 1932, the Permanent Mandates Commission – the League's agency charged with the oversight of mandates – and the League Council deliberated for months on what to do. The Commission did everything from extensive cross-examination of British officials on Iraqi preparedness for independence to devising, on the Council's request, very detailed guidelines that were to assist the principal League bodies determine whether a mandated territory was ready for emancipation. The guidelines titled *General conditions to be fulfilled before the mandate regime can be brought to an end in respect of a country placed under that regime* recommended that a candidate meet the following "*de facto* conditions:"

1. It must have a settled government and an administration capable of maintaining the regular operation of essential government services.
2. It must be capable of maintaining its territorial integrity and political independence.
3. It must be able to maintain the public peace throughout the whole territory.
4. It must have at its disposal adequate financial resources to provide regularly for normal government requirements.
5. It must possess laws and a judicial organization that will afford equal and regular justice to all.

In addition to these conditions, the Commission advised that the Council obtain from the candidate certain guarantees concerning the protection of minorities, the position of foreigners, the civil liberties of inhabitants, the vested rights acquired under the mandatory regime, and the maintenance of treaty obligations in accordance with international law.[10] The Council adopted these guidelines in September 1931 and the Commission in turn built around them its report on Iraq's readiness for independence.[11] Iraq's dependent status was finally terminated and its membership in the League approved by the Assembly after nearly three years of busy activity of multiple League bodies on the original British request. Just like the states that emerged in the aftermath of World War I, Iraq had to pledge to safeguard its relatively large (and in the cases of the Kurds and Assyrians also audibly worried) ethnic and religious minorities.

Despite notable differences, the colonial passages of the United Nations Charter contained the same general philosophy as that which had informed the text of Art. 22 and mandate practice. Only the territories that were substantively prepared could ascend to independence, and this assumption was not thought to have been diluted at the time of the Charter's adoption by the sentence in Art. 1(2) that one of the UN purposes was "to develop friendly relations among nations based on respect for the principle of equal rights and self-determination of peoples."[12]

The section concerning dependencies – the Charter was the first international document that encompassed all of them – was divided into two categories: non-self-governing (Chapter XI) and trust (Chapters XII and XIII) territories.[13] Only Chapter XII mentioned independence explicitly. Its Art. 76 (b) stipulated that a purpose of the trusteeship system was "to promote the political, economic, social, and educational advancement of the inhabitants of the trust territories, and their progressive development towards self-government or independence as may be appropriate to the particular circumstances of each territory and its peoples and the freely expressed wishes of the peoples concerned, and as may be provided by the terms of each trusteeship agreement." Chapter XI, however, also does not leave much doubt that the first order of business was wide-ranging material advancement, and that evolution toward self-government was to mirror the pace of this progress.[14]

One of the most extraordinary developments of the post-1945 period was just how speedily this long-held approach crumbled. Britain, France, and the Netherlands in the next fifteen years relinquished, sometimes rather hastily, a handful of their dependencies in Asia. The number of new states rose sharply in 1958–60 when most British, French, and Belgian colonies in Africa declared their independence. The new states promptly became members of the United Nations and in December 1960 added their voices to help pass the landmark *Declaration on the Granting of Independence to Colonial Countries and Peoples* in the form of GA Resolution 1514.[15] The contrast between this document and the 1931 Permanent Mandates Commission's guidelines on the conditions for accession of mandated territories to statehood could not be more striking.

The resolution's second paragraph revived Woodrow Wilson's vocabulary; it proclaimed: "all peoples have the right to self-determination" and "by virtue of that right they freely determine their political status and freely pursue their economic, social and cultural development."[16] In direct opposition to previous attitudes and practice, the third paragraph then postulated that "inadequacy of political, economic, social or educational preparedness should never serve as a pretext for delaying independence." The fifth paragraph conveyed the central message of the declaration. It enunciated both who the peoples entitled to independence on the basis of their wishes were, and what the responsibility of those ruling over them consists of:

> Immediate steps shall be taken, in trust and non-self-governing territories or all other territories which have not yet attained independence, to transfer all powers to the peoples of those territories, without any conditions or reservations, in accordance with their freely expressed will and desire, without any distinction as to race, creed or color, in order to enable them to enjoy complete independence and freedom.

It was not long before it became apparent that Resolution 1514 – adopted by the vote of 89 to 0, with 9 abstentions – would have far-reaching effects. It was invoked by a plethora of subsequent UN documents, among them Security Council resolutions and two principal human rights conventions. In Resolutions 183 (1963) and 218 (1965), the Security Council authoritatively "re-affirmed" the *Declaration's* key section on "the right to self-determination." Article 1(1) of the International Covenant on Civil and Political Rights (1966) and the International Covenant on Economic, Social and Cultural Rights (1966) repeated the second paragraph of the declaration and their common Art. 1(3) obligated the parties to the treaties, including those having responsibility for the administration of non-self-governing and trust territories, to promote and respect the realization of the right of self-determination. The positive obligations of states were defined even more robustly in UN GA Resolution 2625 (XV), the renowned *Declaration on Principles of International Law concerning Friendly Relations and Co-operation among States*: "Every state has the duty to promote, through joint and separate action, realization of the principle of equal rights and self-determination of peoples . . . in order . . . to bring a speedy end to colonialism."

How should one understand this watershed series of events in the history of international legitimacy? Why did colonialism lose its attractiveness as rapidly as it did? The story of decolonization, like that of other major international changes, is complex and multidimensional. Observers have pointed to several aspects, relevant, at minimum, in regard to some colonies. One was that the colonial countries faced armed revolts for independence, not unlike those faced between 1775 and 1825 by Britain and Spain in the Western Hemisphere. These occurred with varying intensity in the immediate post-war period in Indochina, Indonesia, Kenya, Malagasy, Malaya, Morocco, Palestine, and Tunisia and later in Algeria, Angola, Cameroon, Cyprus, Mozambique, Namibia, and Portuguese Guinea. While the colonial powers rarely suffered outright defeats of the kind Britain and Spain had endured in the Americas – Vietnam and Algeria would be the prime examples of such losses – the rising costs of maintaining overseas empires must have surely left them with a dwindling number of options, particularly given that the power of Britain, France, Italy, Belgium, and the Netherlands had been severely sapped during World War II. The imperial weakness argument has been extended also to the colonies, such as India, Burma, or Ceylon, that did not resist European rule with force, but that were nevertheless difficult and expensive to maintain. In the situation of waning power nothing was easier than to project weakness as a virtue – to cloak decline in the language of benevolence.

The arguments focusing on military or economic weakness do sound plausible, particularly when one considers the new states that emerged prior to 1955 or so. They sound far less plausible for the later period when most colonies actually shed their dependent status. Britain and France had by then largely recovered from the war and began to prosper.[17] What is more, even if their former stature as great powers faded, their power relative to their overseas territories did not decrease. Still, they retreated from an overwhelming majority of their colonies of their own volition, and they did so in a negotiated and orderly transfer of authority to the indigenous governments. This process was for the most part full of civility and had more than local dimensions: most administering powers actively pressed for their ex-colonies' membership in major international organizations. Britain, France, and Italy, for instance, cosponsored General Assembly resolutions recommending their former territories for membership in the United Nations during the famed 1960 session, which admitted, in a single day and by acclamation, seventeen new members.[18]

But if the diminished international standing of the main colonial powers had little bearing on the colonies themselves, it nevertheless did have an effect. Its impact was indirect in that both the Soviet Union and the United States, the countries that replaced Britain and France at the helm of global power, were critical of formal empire on ideological grounds. The Soviet Union and the communist block attacked colonialism consistently and virulently. The American position was more complicated. During their wartime meetings President Franklin Roosevelt repeatedly conveyed to Prime Minister Winston Churchill the United States' opposition to colonialism in a post-war world. But this stance became more flexible as the British and later French government opposed Roosevelt's suggestions, and the president did not want to press his Western allies too much so as not to alienate them at the time of budding discords with the Soviet Union. As one historian puts it, "the US support for decolonization was not a zero-sum game."[19] To the extent that particular anti-colonial movements were perceived as overly sympathetic to communism and the Soviet Union, the United States was inclined to join Britain or France, if they opposed immediate independence. Political considerations of the balance of power, so central in the nineteenth century but also in the French policy toward the new states in 1919, once again took on vital importance.

Ultimately, however, the two superpowers cannot be said to have played as critical a role in the admission of new states into international society as had the great powers prior to decolonization. It is true that their backing for, or at least non-opposition to, independence of a territory was of cardinal importance, but the anti-colonial sentiment grew to be a genuinely global phenomenon. In setting the parameters of international legitimacy, the United Nations General Assembly in the end overshadowed the bodies where the great powers' influence predominated as well as their foreign ministries.[20]

The anti-colonial forces assailed colonialism essentially with normative weapons. Their arguments were framed in the Western liberal idiom of human equality, dignity, and freedom that stood at the very beginning of the philosophy of self-determination.[21] The grounds on which Immanuel Kant dismissed paternal government of absolute monarchy in 1793 – that human beings cannot be treated like "immature children who cannot distinguish what is truly useful or harmful to themselves" and be "obliged to behave passively and to rely upon the judgment of the head of state as to how they ought to be happy"[22] – formed the core of the anti-colonial case among both elites within administered territories as well as a sizeable opinion within metropolitan societies of democratic colonial powers. Though one could hear plenty of grievances of European selfishness, material exploitation and neglect, this was not, on its own, a sufficient reason for abandoning colonialism. The forms and methods of colonial administration, after all, could have been reformed.[23] But the contention that "the subjection of peoples to alien subjugation, domination and exploitation represents a denial of fundamental human rights" – made by the final communiqué of the Bandung Conference of twenty-nine African and Asian countries in 1955 and then reiterated word by word in the opening paragraph of GA Resolution 1514 – was of an altogether different kind. It was a categorical rejection of alien rule *per se*. If "colonialism in all its manifestations" was "an evil," as the Bandung Conference concluded, then the only way to remedy could have been to end the institution unconditionally and without delay.[24]

As the pressure for decolonization was gaining steadily in strength, skeptical voices were raised. The questioning persons typically had extensive experience in international affairs or first-hand knowledge of dependent societies. Several of them were quite willing to acknowledge errors in colonial methods of the past, but still pressed the point that sovereignty without sufficient preparedness was very unlikely to translate into a better life for the dependent peoples. In 1953, Clyde Eagleton, a former legal advisor to the State Department and a member of the US delegation at the founding UN conference in San Francisco, bemoaned the General Assembly's "political" decisions on the independence of Libya and Italian Somaliland since they had been taken without anyone querying "whether these areas had sufficient cohesiveness or capability to stand alone."[25] He contended that "self-determination . . . cannot be allowed to any group for the sole reason that the group chooses to claim it. The United Nations must inquire whether there is enough homogeneity or unity or common desire to hold the new state together; whether it has economic resources and political capacity; how far it can defend itself against attack."[26] As late as 1956, the British constitutional lawyer and former administrator in Ceylon, Sir Ivor Jennings, argued likewise that colonies ought not to accede to independence unless they were effective economic units, had efficient administrative and security capabilities, and could rely on the loyalty of their citizens.[27] These and the like suggestions were, however, brushed aside. By the end of the 1950s, government officials of European democracies with overseas territories had not been willing to make them.[28] In 1943, Herbert Morrison, the deputy leader of the progressive British Labor Party, felt the liberty to say that giving Britain's African colonies independence would be "like giving a child of ten a latch-key, a bank account and a shot-gun."[29] A dozen years later, nobody in the high echelons of British politics would dare to say openly anything remotely comparable.

That by the end of the 1950s there had been a blanket change in the global climate toward colonies is clearly detectable in the pattern of state recognition. In the 1940s, the key question still was whether an entity claiming sovereignty actually constituted a *de facto* state. The United States, for example, delayed recognition of Syria and Lebanon for three years, even though the mandated territories acquired independence by transfer from the Free French government, an American ally, in 1941. The Roosevelt administration supported the objective of Syrian and Lebanese independence – the preparation for this goal was, after all, the stated purpose of the two Class A mandates – but it nonetheless felt that the hasty French move was designed first and foremost to elicit Arab backing for the Allied cause. The undersecretary of state concluded in September 1942 that "in the present instance . . . we are faced with the fact that neither Syria nor the Lebanon in actuality enjoys an independent status. The local governments in Beirut and Damascus have been appointed by the Fighting French, and exercise only very limited degree of sovereign independence . . . According full recognition . . . would be participating in an action . . . contrary to the facts."[30] The two countries were acknowledged only in September 1944 when it was judged that the two governments were "representative, effectively independent and in a position to fulfill their obligations and responsibilities."[31] The United States also postponed, for three years, its recognition of Transjordan's independence.[32] Although Britain, the mandatory power, recognized sovereignty of its mandate in a 1946 treaty, the United States, and most other countries were concerned that Britain's disproportionate influence over Transjordan set by that treaty, especially in the military field, in fact compromised the latter's independence.[33]

An even better example of the continued emphasis on effective statehood was the birth of Israel. Israel's declaration of independence, adopted a day before the expiration of the British mandate over Palestine on May 15, 1948, dwelt on the new state's international legitimacy at considerable length. It notes that the "national and historic right of the Jewish people" was presumed by the terms of the 1922 Palestine mandate, which, among other things, obliged Britain to facilitate the establishment of a "national home" for the Jewish people, and UN General Assembly Resolution 181 (II) of 1947, which recommended the post-mandate partition of Palestine into Jewish and Arab states.[34] Nevertheless, foreign countries focused on whether the nascent entity was a *de facto* state and with the exception of the countries under the influence of the Soviet Union did not refer in their decisions to Resolution 181 (II).[35] Whether Israel qualified as a *de facto* state was hotly disputed, and not only between countries but also within them. The Atlee government came under pointed attack from Winston Churchill, then the leader of Britain's opposition, and several key members of the Truman administration stood opposed to the president. What was not disputed was the need to assess the situation by the factual criteria as such. The character of Israel's call for recognition very much conformed to this reality: whereas Abba Eban, a representative of its provisional government, remarked at the UN Security Council that his fledgling homeland possessed "the only international birth certificate in the world of unproven virtue" and was the only country on earth to have "the advanced assurance that its origin was ordained by the community of nations," he also insisted the criterion of statehood was "effectiveness: control over a certain area, the authority of a government over its population, its readiness and capacity for defense, its willingness and ability to assume and fulfill international obligations."[36]

At the center of the controversy was the question of whether an entity that had a functioning, unified government as well as control over territory could be said to constitute a *de facto* state even if it had no settled borders and was immediately attacked by its neighbors. The United States, the Soviet Union, and more than a dozen East Central European and Latin American states took the position that Israel could be recognized and swiftly did so. Britain, on the contrary, argued that Israel did not fulfill the "basic criteria" of an independent state and announced that it would not make good on Israel's request for acknowledgment for the time being.[37] France and Commonwealth states were also reluctant to do so. While there were, as countless times before, plenty of suspicions that the powers involved had overriding instrumental motivations – the two superpowers were already locked in a global competition for spheres of influence and could not easily leave the new state to fall to the sway of the other power, and Britain was anxious to hold back its diminishing standing in the Arab world[38] – their respective public positions concentrated chiefly on the fulfillment or non-fulfillment of the conventional *de facto* criteria. This framing was of critical importance. As soon as it became plain that Israel had the ability to withstand the onslaught of the Arab armies and was there to stay, the British government was left with few options but to recognize Israel, whatever the true motivations of its earlier unwillingness to do so might have been. Britain, France, and most other non-Arab countries recognized Israel after its first general election in January 1949 and the United Nations, though it rejected Israel's membership application in 1948, voted to admit it in May 1949.

By the late 1950s, recognizing states had largely abandoned the traditional tests of effectiveness in favor of acknowledgment predicated on a particular status, namely being a colony. This policy, by no means restricted to the Soviet bloc or the already independent states of Asia and Africa, stemmed from the dominant form decolonization had acquired by this time. Most colonial powers, under combined pressure from the committees of the United Nations, various foreign capitals and, not least, influential segments of their own public, resorted to negotiation of agreements on the date of independence and hand-over of authority to their dependencies. As one author writes, "in an international atmosphere conducive to independence, granting independence became almost an industry of the metropoles, and recognition of the result politically automatic."[39] With the world opinion turning sharply against colonialism, third parties could not easily defend being unreceptive to those that cast off their dependent status.

Recognition by third parties turned into a formality regardless of how viable or unviable the new states might have appeared,[40] and this tendency was also very much reflected in the admittance of new UN members.[41] Where Greece or Finland had their admission into international society delayed because of their internal conflicts in 1830–2 and 1918–19, respectively, the Republic of Congo (today the Democratic Republic of Congo) was accorded foreign recognition in 1960 with no questions asked, even though its declaration of independence was accompanied by a descent into civil war. Third parties were deterred still less by strong indications that the military and administrative remnants of Belgium, the withdrawing administering power, might well become an active factor in that war. Likewise, no country raised objections to Rwanda's declaration of independence in 1962 despite the fact that several years of massive hostilities between Rwanda's Hutu and Tutsi populations had not ended in any real political settlement between the two groups.

The United States followed this general trend as much as other countries. Its acknowledgment of the former colonies was "instantaneous, sometimes even anticipatory."[42] As O'Brien and Goebel make clear in their exhaustive survey of the US recognition practice between 1945 and 1965, "demonstration of the capacity to exist independently [was] not usually required of new states."[43] Presidents Eisenhower and Kennedy had template letters to congratulate the ex-colonies on the proclamation of their independence[44] and the delivery of their cordial message on the day of independence went usually hand in hand with the establishment of diplomatic relations. Two senior American officials boasted toward the end of 1960 that the United States had "been and will probably continue to be the first country to be officially represented in each of the newly independent African states."[45] This statement might have been uttered primarily with an eye at the Cold War contest with the Soviet Union, but it can also be taken as one more piece of evidence of the earthquake-like breakdown of the previous conception of international legitimacy. The very fact that a superpower thought it important to make such a gesture indicated that, henceforth, the normal state of affairs was for the former dependencies to be treated as sovereign states.

That recognition of ex-colonies became an activity that forsook the *de facto* criteria and instead involved a notion of international right is also apparent from the treatment meted out to the two principal holdouts from the decolonization consensus as well as those judged to violate the self-determination principle with respect to individual territories. Portugal and South Africa, the former governed by an autocratic and the latter by an apartheid regime, consistently refused to give up their dependencies in Africa and instead sought to suppress the national liberation movements within them. Prior to decolonization, the parties to such a struggle would normally have been left to their own devices, provided that in the course of the contest rights of third parties had not been infringed. Not this time. The recalcitrant governments in Lisbon and Pretoria had to endure constant pillorying by UN organs[46] as well as other intergovernmental organizations for resisting their territories' will.

The most damaging to the two countries were the Security Council's decisions. Following the failure of several General Assembly resolutions to change Portugal's conduct, the Council in its sternly worded Resolution 180 (1963) confirmed UN GA Resolution 1514, rebuked the Lisbon government's assertion that the African territories under its administration were constitutionally parts of metropolitan Portugal rather than non-self-governing territories in the sense of the UN Charter, and called upon its government to recognize at once the right of peoples under its administration to self-determination and independence and to grant immediate independence to all those that aspired to it. With Portugal's continued refusal to comply with this and later texts, the Security Council went so far as to endorse, in Resolutions 312 and 322 (1972), the legitimacy of the struggle by the liberation movements of the four territories under its rule. In this decision, as in many others, the Council followed the path set by the General Assembly. UN GA Resolutions 2621 (XXV) and 2625 had enshrined the general principles that armed resistance to colonialism as well as foreign intervention in support thereof were legitimate. South Africa was stigmatized for not relinquishing its hold over Namibia[47] in numerous General Assembly documents, more than a dozen Security Council resolutions beginning with Resolution 245 (1968), and in the 1971 *Namibia* advisory opinion of the International Court of Justice.

These decisions, along with those adopted in regard to East Timor and Western Sahara,[48] the non-self-governing territories denied self-determination by their decolonized neighbors, had nothing to do with the substantive criteria of statehood that might or might not have been satisfied but everything to do with their *a priori* right to choose independence. In fact, once Portugal, upon its conversion to democracy in 1974–5, pulled out from its territories, Angola and Mozambique were acknowledged immediately, even as both followed the footsteps of the Congo and plunged into civil war upon their respective proclamations of independence. Guinea-Bissau, on the other hand, had been widely recognized even before its government controlled the entirety of its territory or reached an agreement with Portugal on ending the conflict. For a great majority of states, its right to independent existence counted for more than its incomplete factual existence.[49] Missing attributes of *de facto* statehood were also no obstacle to foreign acknowledgment and UN admission in the single case of French refusal to leave a colonial possession. The Comoros, a non-self-governing territory composed of four separate isles, was recognized as an independent state despite France's continued control of one of them, the disputed island of Mayotte.

By contrast, Security Council Resolution 216 (1965) scolded Southern Rhodesia's unilateral declaration of independence in November 1965 and called upon UN members not to recognize it, in spite of the fact that its government had effective control over the country. The governing regime of Southern Rhodesia excluded all except the white settler minority and this was considered to be a negation of the widespread consensus, engraved in GA Resolution 1514, that the right of self-determination pertained to all peoples of trust or non-self-governing territories "without any distinction as to race, creed or color."[50] The perceived attempt to perpetuate racial domination was also a key reason for the non-recognition of Bantustans, the first of which, Transkei, was proclaimed independent by the South African parliament in 1976.[51] But although the Bantustans were censured on the legitimacy grounds of denial of self-determination, they would not have been eligible for recognition even under the old standard of effective statehood. Established by an outside authority – a comparison to the "Kingdom of Poland" of 1916 would not be inappropriate – the Bantustans were from the very beginning dependent on that authority for their survival.

Uti Possidetis Juris as the New "Dynastic Legitimacy"

By the end of 1960, decolonization was a process governed by an identifiable set of general principles. Even if its pattern was set largely before, starting with the year 1960 we can point to authoritative pronouncements on the manner decolonization should proceed. The formulation of these rules was spearheaded in the UN General Assembly, both because of its specific competences with respect to non-self-governing and trust territories under the UN Charter and because, with the increase in the number of new members from Asia and Africa during the 1950s, it developed into the UN organ with the strongest anti-colonial voice. The requirement of GA Resolution 1514 that the majority of the population must be adequately represented in the government of each new state was already touched upon in the preceding section. Another important guideline was GA Resolution 1541 (XV) which stipulated that a non-self-governing territory's "full measure of self-government" could be realized in one of three ways depending on the will of its inhabitants: (*a*) emergence of a sovereign state; (*b*) free association with an independent state; or (*c*) integration with an independent state.[52] The document then goes on to spell out how to realize (*b*) and (*c*), though, curiously, it steered clear of outlining by what procedure to solicit the wishes for (*a*).[53]

One of the most critical passages defining the mode of decolonization was the sixth paragraph of GA Resolution 1514 dealing with territorial integrity. It postulated that "any attempt aimed at the partial or total disruption of the national unity and the territorial integrity of a country[54] is incompatible with the purposes and principles of the Charter of the United Nations." That an ex-colony cannot lose territory against its will – not just from outside, by way of conquest, but also from inside, by way of secession – was later broadened to encompass all UN member states in GA Resolution 2625. In the words of Rupert Emerson, "with its right hand [the UN] endowed all peoples with the right of self-determination, but with its left hand it denied that people embraced within the newly independent states might appeal to the right on their own behalf . . . secession from what purported to be national states was outlawed."[55]

The illegality of forcible takeover of foreign territory had already been articulated in Art. 10 of the League Covenant, the Stimson Doctrine and Art. 2(4) of the UN Charter,[56] and in this respect Resolutions 1514 and 2625 were significant additions to the global measures prohibiting conquest. Secession, however, was a radically different matter. Though ordinarily discouraged, secession as such had been neither international illegitimate nor illegal. The theory and practice of recognizing *de facto* states presupposed that the purpose of international law was to regulate states' external relations and not to immunize them internally against disloyalty of their citizens. This understanding was in no way denied even in the already cited *Aaland Islands* opinions delivered under the aegis of the League of Nations, which is by many taken to be an authoritative statement that parts of sovereign states do not have a right to secede.[57]

The strong presumption against secession among existing states could be traced to the founding conference of the United Nations.[58] The main reference point at San Francisco was the unhappy interwar history of Europe: its plenitude of peoples and minorities dissatisfied with post-1919 boundaries and revisionist and irredentist governments standing by to answer their calls for assistance.[59] Secessionism in the name of self-determination appeared in light of the Munich and other interwar crises as a major destabilizing element of world politics and the San Francisco conference was in particular ill-disposed toward the League minority rights regime, which was seen in several cases, rightly or wrongly, to have nourished belligerent separatism.[60] Of notable importance is that the concern had a distinctly *international* character: self-determination claims involving secession were looked upon as problematic because, though originating in the domestic arena, they had led to cross-border tensions, aggressive demands for revising interstate boundaries as well as interstate armed conflict.

Decolonization reinforced the negative view even more. The pool of entities eligible for independence was roughly as big as the number of already independent states and, given that their demographic composition was on average no less complicated than that of Europe in 1919, sanctioning other than reciprocally agreed upon border changes risked wreaking havoc with regional and international order. The international conflicts that followed the 1947 British partition of pre-independence India into India and Pakistan as well as the 1947 UN recommendation to divide Palestine were still unresolved and on the agenda of the United Nations. Though there were some musings in Africa that the colonial lines should be modified at the time of independence – in 1958 the All-African Peoples Conference of political parties and trade unions denounced them as arbitrary and called for their speedy adjustment or abolition and in 1960 it specifically applauded the vision of unifying all "artificially divided" ethnic Somalis in a greater Somalia[61] – at the end the absolute majority of both old and new states did not accept this option as palatable. Unless and until there was agreement of all pertinent parties to do otherwise, trust and non-self-governing territories were to accede to independence in their colonial boundaries.[62]

Besides the concern about external ramifications of not accepting former colonial borders, paragraph 6 reflected a concern about *internal* coherence of the new states. There was, in particular, a palpable fear that secessions, if successful in one place, may give encouragement to fragmentation elsewhere. Their very possibility was seen as a danger to inner stability of the former colonies. Thus conceived, however, *uti possidetis juris* went well beyond the principle that steered the concluding phase of the emancipation of Latin America. There it was an instrument intended exclusively for *external* protection. *Uti possidetis juris* was to shield all *de facto* states from actual or potential territorial encroachment by their neighbors.[63] It was not designed to shelter, nor did it actually shelter, any entity – either prior or subsequent to independence from Spain – from internal acts of separation. The territorial integrity of Mexico and Colombia was not inoculated internationally against the respective secessionist bids of Texas in 1836 and Panama in 1903. Those acts fell under the regular *de facto* recognition criteria.

What is now considered a clash between the rights of territorial integrity and self-determination did not exist in these and other pre-decolonization cases of secession, because states simply did not have their territorial integrity protected against challenges from their own population.

The objective to employ *uti possidetis juris* as a mechanism that would define the self-eligible for sovereignty and, at the same time, deny sovereignty to all the other selves that might want it had an obvious rational foundation. While the colonial boundaries in Central and South America on the whole enclosed *bona fide* national communities, those in Africa, Asia, and Oceania in numerous cases did not. A vast majority of colonial boundaries had been artificial in the sense that imperial powers had normally delineated and imposed them in disregard of pre-colonial political systems and without input from native inhabitants. Still, in Latin America these frontiers crystallized over time into lines of political demarcation. By the time of the wars of independence they had contained entities with distinct and fairly well developed national consciousness. The best evidence of this is that (*a*) all the Latin American territories overthrew their Iberian rulers and/or fended off their neighbors' designs for incorporation as Mexicans, Chileans, Brazilians, Paraguayans, etc.; and that (*b*) for all the subsequent turbulence in Central and South America's domestic governance, internal legitimacy of the new states proved impressively robust. The subcontinents experienced no unilateral state fissions beyond the secessions of Texas and Panama.[64] Territorial conflicts in post-imperial Latin America, as indicated in Chapter 2, concerned overwhelmingly the physical location of frontiers, not their legitimacy.

The situation in the colonial world after 1945 was quite different. Even if the anti-colonial sentiment across the colonial world had arguably been a mass phenomenon, there were few dependencies that disposed of colonial rule by exerting as much effort as had commonly been requisite in the past.[65] The old recognition formula had by no means been an ironclad guarantee that new states could forever or in all circumstances count on the allegiance of their citizens – aside from Texas and Panama one only has to think of the US Civil War or the centrifugal tendencies consuming interwar Yugoslavia. However, putting the threshold at the attainment of *de facto* state made the emergence of an authentic political community much more likely than unlikely. The explanation is not hard to find: it was highly improbable that people who did not see their political future together would join forces and embark on what could be expected to be an arduous and taxing quest for a common country. Indeed, a group demonstrated to the outside world that it constituted a genuine body politic most convincingly precisely via its "self-determining" efforts. However, as international society embraced the notion that non-sovereign entities are entitled to sovereignty solely because their particular status was no longer tolerable, the assumption that populations previously governed from London, Paris, Brussels, or The Hague would want to continue to live together in independent states governed from the ex-colonial capitals rested on uncertain footing.

As it happened, national identification with post-1945 colonies was often underdeveloped or altogether missing. In contrast to the Latin Americans of the 1810s and 1820s, the loyalty of most people of sub-Saharan Africa, South Asia, or the South Pacific prone to political mobilization did not surpass their ethno-national group. The widespread rejection of colonial rule did not necessarily translate into a desire to constitute new states within former colonial confines. As James Mayall contends:

> Anti-colonial nationalism was essentially reactive. The nationalist leaders more often than not mobilized diverse groups who shared a hostility to colonial rule rather than a pre-colonial group sentiment or identity of interest. In the aftermath of independence many of the new leaders faced a crisis of legitimacy: political control was now in their hands, yet they were seldom able either to redeem the broad promises they had made to bring about the rapid social and economic transformation of society, or more specifically, to satisfy all the sub-national interests whose competition for state largesse now dominated the political arena.[66]

Decolonization thus did not eliminate the problem of "alien rule" even as it dismantled the institution of formal empire.[67] Many frustrated ethno-national communities within post-colonial states became embroiled in conflicts with the group or groups they perceived as unjustly discriminating against them, and these quarrels frequently escalated into open armed clashes. The biggest challenge to the territorial integrity of new states did not derive from the source traditionally understood as internationally problematic – external claims or designs[68] – but from the many acts of secession in which ethnonational groups announced, in some instances just after the proclamation of independence, that they had a right of self-determination and were entitled to a sovereign state too. Scenes of post-colonial secessionist tensions – and in many cases large-scale violence – have included Algeria, Angola, Burma, Cameroon, Chad, the Comoros, the Democratic Republic of Congo, Cyprus, Ethiopia,[69] Ghana, Guinea, India, Indonesia, Ivory Coast, Kenya, Laos, Mali, Mozambique, Namibia, Niger, Nigeria, Oman, Pakistan, Papua New Guinea, the Philippines, Saint Kitts and Nevis, Saint Vincent and the Grenadines, Senegal, the Solomon Islands, Somalia, Sri Lanka, Sudan, Tanzania, Uganda, Vanuatu, and Zambia.[70] This reality led Kalevi Holsti to remark that "it may not be an exaggeration to claim that outside of Latin America only a minority of Third World countries are socially integrated and able to govern effectively over a unified and reasonably disciplined citizenship."[71]

Notwithstanding all these developments, there has been little willingness to alter the practice of underwriting the territorial integrity of states from not only external but also internal challenges. The tone was in many ways set in the Congo crisis that constituted the first major test of *uti possidetis juris* as conceived in paragraph 6 of UN GA Resolution 1514. The intervention of the UN Force, initially a neutral operation to calm the chaos of post-independence Congo and to see to the removal of leftover Belgian troops from its soil, changed its direction in the wake of UN SC Resolution 169 (1961). That resolution rejected "completely" Katanga's claim that it was "a sovereign independent nation" and the subsequent UN campaign involved direct hostilities with, and eventual defeat of, Katanga's gendarmerie. From the point of view of foreign authorities, each change in the international status of a territory had to be blessed by the sovereign government in question. Withholding state consent has meant almost certain non-recognition and international illegitimacy. Aside from Bangladesh in 1971, no sub-state entity has been able to create a new state or join some other state without such consent.[72] As Robert Jackson wrote, "Baluchis, Biafrans, Eritreans, Tigreans, Ewes, Gandans, Karens, Katchins, Kurds, Moros, Pathans, Sikhs, Tamils, and many other ethnonationalities are the abandoned peoples of the contemporary community of states."[73]

Some peoples in this collection managed to create *de facto* states with effective control over the area they claimed.[74] Under the old rules, the "Republic of Eritrea," the "Tamil Eelam," the "Free South Sudan," the "Republic of Bougainville," or the "Republic of Somaliland" would have at certain point of their existence likely qualified for foreign recognition, but under the new rules privileging existing states they were condemned to languish in an international legal and political limbo. Non-recognition meant that they legally remained parts of the states they had empirically broken away from, leaving them permanently exposed to reabsorption by the central government[75], as was "Tamil Eelam" in 2009. Eritrea did eventually garner recognition, but this occurred only after Ethiopia's assent to let the Eritreans choose independence in a 1993 referendum.[76] It was this consent that accomplished what the three-decades-long control of large swaths of Ethiopian territory could not.

The supreme importance given to state consent went not only against the grain of antecedent practice – of not making recognition to internally established *de facto* entities conditional on the consent of the relevant sovereign government – but also against earlier understandings of the concept of self-determination. Many notable figures in the liberal tradition thought secession could indeed be justifiable; even thinkers such as Grotius[77] and Kant who otherwise questioned the general right of revolution. This was also how the Americans, Latin Americans, Belgians, Greeks, Serbs, Czechs and Slovaks, Finns, or Latvians defended their bids for independence. As suggested in Chapters 2 and 3, the founders of American and British policy of recognizing *de facto* states also held this belief. They argued that peoples who establish their own states should not have their achievement denied or hindered by outsiders to a large extent because they believed that oppressed political communities should have outlets to alter their condition. Sovereignty was not a life sentence without parole. The authoritative determination of whether a particular government was arbitrary or abusive belonged exclusively to the people living under it, and no third party was entitled to act against a bid to break away or refuse to acknowledge its fruits. This was Woodrow Wilson's belief too, even though he went beyond it. As he defended the founding of the League of Nations and the Covenant's Art. 10, Wilson was adamant in his Pueblo address that

> Article 10 provides that every member of the League covenants to respect and preserve the territorial integrity and existing political independence of every other member of the League as against *external aggression. Not against internal disturbance.* There was not a man at that table who did not admit

the sacredness of the right of self-determination, the sacredness of the right of any body of people to say that they would not continue to live under the government they were then living under.[78] (italics added)

Adams, Canning, Palmerston, and Russell articulated this belief as they challenged the anti-revolutionary doctrine of dynastic legitimacy, which considered consent of the sitting monarch to be the only valid means to effect changes in titles to sovereignty or territory. The necessity of consent made a monarchy's dominion in principle inalienable. If a dynasty lost its land either to conquest or secession, the "right" made it recoverable in the future when the dynasty rebuilt its coercive capacity or found foreign partners disposed to intervene on its behalf. The territorial provisos of UN GA Resolutions 1514 and 2625 appear to have resurrected this past. If one substitutes "the Charter of the United Nations" for "dynastic legitimacy" in their stipulations that "any attempt aimed at the partial or total disruption of the national unity and the territorial integrity of a country is incompatible with the purposes and principles of the Charter of the United Nations," one gets a fair description of what the legitimist powers espoused as they confronted the events in Latin America, Belgium, or Italy.

The post-1960 practice has exhibited the logic of this long surmounted doctrine, even if instead of established dynasties it has strived to conserve established states and their borders. The finding of UN SC Resolution 169 (1961) that Katanga's secessionist activities against the Republic of Congo were, as such, contrary to the Congolese constitution as well as Security Council decisions[79] is clearly predicated on the assumptions that (*a*) outside authorities are entitled to determine questions of a state's internal legality; and (*b*) secession from an existing state which has not consented to it can be illegitimate internationally and not just domestically. Denied by the Anglo–American architects of recognizing *de facto* states, the two were cardinal beliefs of the Holy Alliance; for example, the Preliminary Protocol of the Congress of Troppau (1820) avowed that the three powers would "refuse to recognize any [interior] changes brought about by illegal methods."[80]

Contra this argument that post-colonial international society delegitimized unilateral secession, a number of legal commentators contend that the right of secession as a remedial right against extreme oppression is allowed under customary international law. They interpret another paragraph from UN GA Resolution 2625, later restated in the Vienna Declaration of the UN World Conference on Human Rights (1993), as evidence of this right.[81] The paragraph, after asserting once more that "nothing in the foregoing paragraphs shall be construed as authorizing or encouraging *any* action which would dismember or impair, totally or in part, the territorial integrity or political unity of sovereign and independent states," qualifies the statement by denoting these states as "conducting themselves in compliance with the principle of equal rights and self-determination of peoples as described above *and thus possessed of a government representing the whole people belonging to the territory without distinction as to race, creed or color*" (italics added). The specification – labeled the "safeguard" or "saving" clause – is taken to envisage a door for secession for a distinct group totally shut out from, or grossly abused by, a country's central government. This interpretation was also noted, though not endorsed, in the highly respected opinion of the Supreme Court of Canada in *Reference re Secession of Quebec* (1998).[82]

However, as Chapter 6 will also show, the practice of states over the last forty years does not provide convincing support for this contention. Instead, it suggests that the legitimacy of existing sovereign states and their borders has been paramount. There were large-scale massacres against the people of eastern Nigeria by the Nigerian military prior to and after the "Republic of Biafra's" declaration of independence in 1967, but Biafra's right to separate under these circumstances was acknowledged by just five states. Tanzania, Gabon, the Ivory Coast, Zambia, and Haiti did so when they recognized Biafra in 1968: each argued that the massive violations of human rights of its population dealt an irreparable blow to Nigerian unity.[83] France was the sole other power moving in that direction, but at the end it did not go publicly further than observing (more in nineteenth-century than post-1945 fashion) that "the bloodshed and suffering endured by the peoples of Biafra for more than a year show their will to affirm themselves as a people."[84] The explicit contention of the five states that there was a right of secession in extreme situations such as Biafra gained little sympathy from other countries.[85]

Far more prevalent was the British view that the attempt of the Biafrans, "*whatever their grievances*, at rebellion and secession . . . was a tragic and disastrous error and therefore the Nigerian government were right to resist it" (italics added). The British government, in fact, played an important role in the events: Despite considerable parliamentary opposition, it continued to supply weapons to the Nigerian government throughout the civil war. Prime Minister Harold Wilson defined Britain's purpose to be "to help preserve the integrity of Nigeria," so, in that context, to cut off arms supply "would have been an un-neutral act."[86]

The government provided three main justifications for this policy.[87] One was that Britain could not remain indifferent as a close Commonwealth partner and the most populous country in Africa faced an internal revolt threatening its union. The United States, which for its part suspended military sales to Nigeria, expressed understanding for this position.[88] In addition, Britain very much shared the fear of African (and many other new and old) states that Nigeria's failure to survive within its original borders could stimulate a chain reaction of secessionist attempts elsewhere,[89] with adverse repercussions for continental stability. In a keynote speech to the House of Commons on the war in the West African country, Foreign Secretary Michael Stewart described the Biafran undertaking as "evil for Nigeria and dangerous for Africa."[90] And the third argument concerned the East–West balance: the Soviets were already supplying weapons to the federal government and the continued flow of British arms was seen as necessary to prevent a crucial member of the British Commonwealth from crossing into the Soviet camp.

The Biafra episode was indicative of how even a founding country departed from the practice it had set. Nineteenth-century Britain had had for 300 years ties of alliance to Portugal and a vital interest to keep the Ottoman Empire intact, yet its leaders remained neutral with respect to the secessions of Brazil or Balkan principalities. Neither old bonds of amity nor interest in regional stability nor balance-of-power considerations – such as the deep apprehensions of the Disraeli cabinet in 1875–8 that Russia was bent on domination of Southeastern Europe and the Middle East – were valid reasons to throw their active support behind the territorial integrity of friendly states and thus deny their peoples the moral right to disconnect themselves from abusive governments, which, in the view of those peoples, in Lord Russell's words, "subvert the fundamental laws."[91]

As for principal intergovernmental organizations, the United Nations never put the conflict on its agenda, but UN Secretary-General U Thant commented against its backdrop that the organization "spent over $500 million in the Congo primarily to prevent the secession of Katanga. . . . The United Nations' attitude is unequivocal. As an international organization, the UN has never accepted and does not accept and I do not believe it will ever accept the principle of secession of a part of its member state."[92] The Organization of African Unity (OAU) did take up the crisis at its annual Assembly of Heads of State and Government. Unable to win OAU support with the oppression argument, Biafra's leader Lt. Col. Odumegwu Ojukwu tried to persuade the African organization that the principle of territorial integrity "can legitimately be invoked if one member state attempts to enlarge its territory at the expense of another member state, but certainly not in respect of the emergence of new states arising from the disintegration of a member state."[93] This was a point made by Woodrow Wilson in his Pueblo address and taken for granted by liberal constitutional states in the nineteenth and early twentieth century – the principle did not shield Mexico from the secession of Texas after a little more than a decade of its independence – but it did not carry a lot of credence in the post-colonial world.[94] Territorial integrity now *a priori* trumped self-determination claims involving independence that emanated from within sovereign states. The OAU Assembly's Resolution 51 (IV) on the situation in Nigeria expressed its "trust and confidence in the federal government of Nigeria" and "condemnation of secession in any member state."

The secession of East Pakistan in 1971 met with even less foreign approval than that of Biafra despite the fact that, unlike the Nigerian army, the Pakistani armed forces were widely condemned for their brutality in East Pakistan. India was the only country that acted toward the "People's Republic of Bangladesh" in the same way Tanzania et al. had done toward Biafra.[95] Other countries did eventually recognize Bangladesh without Pakistan's prior assent to let it go. They did so in the wake of Pakistan's defeat by India and the subsequent removal of its forces from Bangladeshi territory. Again, however, neither individual states (including those that supported India)[96] nor the UN bodies suggested that there was a *right* to secede from even extremely repressive government.[97] Despite the putative safeguard clause of one of its most significant resolution and the fact the

Bangladeshis formed a distinct people in several ways, the UN General Assembly admitted Bangladesh as a member only subsequent to its recognition by Pakistan in 1974. The treatment of the people of Iraqi Kurdistan in 1991 and Kosovo in 1998–9 – which will be considered in Chapter 6 – elicited nothing less than armed humanitarian interventions on their behalf; yet the intervening countries chose not to take notice of the peoples' wishes and with the UN Security Council affirmed that they remained a part of their respective states. One may regard the eventual recognition by more than five dozen of countries of Kosovo's unilateral declaration of independence in 2008 as casting doubt on this argument, but as will be seen, most recognizing states regarded it as a *sui generis* exception to the post-decolonization norm of territorial integrity rather than as a redefinition of this norm along the lines of the safeguard clause. Alongside the previously discussed trend of general non-recognition of *de facto* states, it is hard to shake off the conclusion that unilateral secession, whatever the rationale given by those who launched it, has become taboo in the post-colonial society of states.[98]

Conclusion

This chapter has argued that post-war decolonization brought about a radical change in recognizing new states. The practice shifted from ascertaining the fulfillment of *de facto* criteria of statehood to virtually unreserved embrace of a specific category of entities. International law no longer required statehood to be tangible but merely posited it.[99] In the parlance of Machiavelli's most famous work, where before the prince had to go after the foundations of his state, now those foundations came to him. The prince empowered by Resolution 1514 discovered that he did not have to do more than to convey, by virtually any means, the aspiration to be sovereign. State recognition thus acquired, for the first time in its history, the character of a "casual,"[100] "mechanical,"[101] and "wholesale transaction."[102]

The United Nations elevated self-determination into a positive right of all peoples, but as Rupert Emerson put it, what was stated in big print was drastically modified by the small print.[103] In practice, only the peoples of non-self-governing and trust territories as a whole could legitimately claim independence. Moreover, the right of self-determination could be exercised only once per colonial unit: as a territory was to accede to sovereign status, its territorial integrity was inoculated against both external and internal challenges. Borders constituted a crucial component of the state foundations rendered to the prince empowered by Resolution 1514. This was a striking development: never before could those seeking independence have any certainty of their territorial limits as independent states. Major nineteenth- and twentieth-century endeavors to lessen territorial conflicts – be it in Vienna, Paris, or San Francisco – looked to restrict or proscribe solely external conquest; the single concerted campaign to disallow acts of secession internationally was that of the Holy Alliance. It was no less striking that at the moment self-determination was proclaimed a right of all peoples, it became far more difficult for stateless groups to establish their own independent homelands[104] than before the phrase ever made its way into the commonplace vocabulary of international relations and law.

Notes

1. Robert Jackson, "Quasi-States, Dual Regimes, and Neoclassical Theory: International Jurisprudence and the Third World," pp. 535–6.
2. This was also the basis for admission of non-European countries, such as the Ottoman Empire, Siam, Japan, and China, with whom Europeans had had prior relations, into international society as equal sovereign states. See Gong, *The Standard of "Civilization" in International Society*, chs. 1 and 2.
3. See Manela, *The Wilsonian Moment*, ch. 1.
4. There were rare exceptions to this; for instance, when most Western countries refused to follow other UN members in recognizing Guinea-Bissau in the midst of its continuing hostilities with Portugal in 1973 or when they recognized Bangladesh in 1972 in the aftermath of India's intervention which solidified its *de facto* establishment. See Roth, *Governmental Illegitimacy in International Law*, pp. 220–2, and Janice Musson, "Britain and the Recognition of Bangladesh in 1972," *Diplomacy and Statecraft*, 19 (2008), pp. 125–44.
5. Lloyd E. Ambrosius, "Wilsonian Self-Determination," *Diplomatic History*, 16 (1992), p. 144.
6. See William Bain, *Between Anarchy and Society: Trusteeship and the Obligations of Power* (Oxford: Oxford University Press, 2003), p. 107.
7. See ibid., p. 99.
8. This exception was the Kingdom of Hedjaz, today a western portion of Saudi Arabia. The Hedjaz declared independence from the Ottoman Empire in 1916, sat at the peace conference table, and was a party to, among others, the Treaties of Versailles and Sevres. By Art. 98 of the latter treaty, Turkey was, "in accordance with the action already taken by the Allied Powers," obliged to recognize "the Hedjaz as a free and independent state." However, the kingdom never ratified any of the documents its delegation signed in Paris. Likewise, it failed to take up its membership in the League of Nations. For all intents and purposes, the Hedjaz chose to exist outside of the international legal framework. When, in 1924, it was conquered by, and annexed to, the neighboring Sultanate of Najd (also *de facto* independent but not integrated into the society of states), there was, in sharp contrast to 1931 when Japan conquered northeastern China, no international outcry.
9. The same emphasis could be seen in the proposal for a Kurdish state in the Treaty of Sevres. This scheme never materialized because the accord never entered into force, but the wording of its Art. 64 outlining the proposal is nevertheless telling. The provision gave the Kurds a choice of independence if they demonstrated to the League Council within a year of the treaty coming into force that a majority of the population of Turkish Kurdistan desired this option. In the affirmative case, the Council was then charged to consider whether the people of Turkish Kurdistan were "capable" of independence. Should it have recommended this choice – the article is clear that the Council could

have said no – the new state could have expanded to encompass Iraqi Kurdistan (the former Ottoman vilayet of Mosul) if the Kurds there wished to join it.

10. *The Monthly Summary of the League of Nations*, 11 (1931), p. 210.
11. Ibid., pp. 329–32.
12. On this point, see Rosalyn Higgins, "Self-Determination and Secession," in Julie Dahlitz (ed.), *Secession and International Law* (The Hague: T. M. C. Asser Press, 2003), pp. 23–4; The phrase "the principle of equal rights and self-determination of peoples" is also used in Art. 55 in the section on international economic and social cooperation.
13. Trust territories were to be administered under the UN supervision and include former mandates. Non-self-governing territories, on the other hand, did not fall directly under the organization's guardianship, but there was nevertheless an obligation on the part of states administering them to report regularly to the UN Secretary-General on their advancement.
14. This is also apparent from General Assembly Resolution 648 (VII) containing an annex titled *Factors Indicative of the Attainment of Independence or of Other Separate Systems of Self-Government.*
15. This document was preceded by several General Assembly resolutions lauding the right of all peoples to self-determination and demanding its realization. Among the most important are 421 (V), 545 (VI), 637 A (VII), 742 (VIII), and 1188 (XII). None of them, however, went nearly as far as Resolution 1514.
16. On the considerable influence of Wilson's conception of self-determination on anti-colonial movements, see Manela, *The Wilsonian Moment.*
17. M. E. Chamberlain, *Decolonization: The Fall of the European Empires*, 2nd ed. (Oxford: Blackwell, 1999), p. 118.
18. See the United Nations, General Assembly, Official Records, Fifteenth Session, 864th Plenary Meeting, September 20, 1960, pp. 5–16.
19. David Ryan, "By Way of Introduction: The United States, Decolonization and the World System," in David Ryan and Victor Pungong (eds.), *The United States and Decolonization* (Basingtoke: Macmillan, 2000), p. 16.
20. This influence was, however, very much maintained in other contexts when issues of statehood were involved – for instance, in relation to post-war status of Germany, Austria, Finland, and Korea.
21. See Rupert Emerson, "The New Higher Law of Anti-Colonialism," in Karl W. Deutsch and Stanley Hoffmann (eds.), *The Relevance of International Law: Essays in Honor of Leo Gross* (Cambridge, MA: Schenkman Publishing, 1968), p. 157. For studies emphasizing the normative aspect of decolonization, see Robert Jackson, "The Weight of Ideas in Decolonization: Normative Change in International Relations," in Judith Goldstein and Robert Keohane (eds.), *Ideas and Foreign Policy: Beliefs, Institutions and Political Change* (Ithaca, NY: Cornell University Press, 1993); Daniel Philpott, *Revolutions in Sovereignty: How Ideas Shaped Modern International Relations* (Princeton, NJ: Princeton University Press, 2001), chs. 8–12; and Neta C. Crawford, *Argument and Change in World Politics: Ethics, Decolonization, and Humanitarian Intervention* (Cambridge: Cambridge University Press, 2002), chs. 7 and 8.
22. Immanuel Kant, "On the Common Saying: This May be True in Theory, but it does not Apply in Practice," in Kant, *Political Writings*, p. 74.
23. Bain, *Between Anarchy and Society*, p. 133.
24. Final Communiqué of the Bandung Conference, April 24, 1955, N. Frankland (ed.), *Documents on International Affairs 1955* (Oxford: Oxford University Press, 1958), p. 433.

25. Clyde Eagleton, "Self-Determination in the United Nations," *The American Journal of International Law*, 47 (1953), p. 89.

26. Clyde Eagleton, "Excesses of Self-Determination," *Foreign Affairs*, 31 (1953), p. 602.

27. Jennings, *The Approach to Self-Government*, pp. 47–55.

28. See Adam Watson, *The Limits of Independence: Relations between States in the Modern World* (London: Routledge, 1997), p. 58.

29. Quoted in Wm. Roger Louis, *Imperialism at Bay: The United States and the Decolonization of the British Empire, 1941–1945* (New York: Oxford University Press, 1978), p. 14.

30. Welles to Roosevelt, September 1, 1942, Marjorie Whiteman (ed.), *Digest of International Law*, Vol. 2 (Washington, DC: US Government Printing Office, 1963), p. 193.

31. Woadsworth to Takla, September 7, 1944, ibid., p. 196. See also Crawford, *Creation of States in International Law*, 2nd ed., p. 84.

32. See Whiteman, *Digest of International Law*, Vol. 2, p. 172.

33. See W. Keith Pattison, "The Delayed British Recognition of Israel," *The Middle East Journal* 37 (1983), pp. 418–19.

34. Declaration of the Establishment of the State of Israel, May 14, 1948, Blaustein, Sigler, Beede, *Independence Documents of the World*, Vol. 1, pp. 366–9.

35. See James Crawford, "Israel (1948–1949) and Palestine (1998–1999): Two Studies in the Creation of States," in Guy S. Goodwin-Gill and Stefan Talmon (eds.), *The Reality of International Law: Essays in Honour of Ian Brownlie* (Oxford Clarendon Press, 1999), p. 109–10. A host of Arab and Muslim states, of course, did refuse to recognize Israel by denying that it had a right to exist. Although this opposition has had very profound political and military repercussions for Israel, this was the position of only a minority of states worldwide. Despite the persistence of the Arab–Israeli conflict, this group has lost membership since 1948, most notably Egypt and Jordan.

36. United Nations, Security Council, Official Records, 340th Meeting, July 27, 1948, pp. 29–30.

37. See Philip Marshall Brown, "The Recognition of Israel," *The American Journal of International Law*, 42 (1948), p. 620.

38. For a detailed discussion of the British policy and motives, see Pattison, "The Delayed British Recognition of Israel," pp. 412–28.

39. Denys Myers, "Contemporary Practice of the United States Relating to International Law," *The American Journal of International Law*, 55 (1961), pp. 706–7.

40. See Malcolm Shaw, *Title to Territory in Africa: International Legal Issues* (Oxford: Clarendon Press, 1986), pp. 157–8; and Gerard Kreijen, *State Failure, Sovereignty and Effectiveness: Legal Lessons from the Decolonization of Sub-Saharan Africa* (Leiden, The Netherlands: Martinus Nijhoff, 2004), chs. 3 and 4.

41. Article 4 (1) of the Charter specified, and the *Conditions of Admission of a State to Membership in the United Nations* advisory opinion of the International Court of Justice (1948) confirmed, that applicants had to be peace-loving states that were willing and able to carry out the obligations contained in the Charter. A detailed study of UN procedures in regard to this article nevertheless concludes that

> the admission of states which had gained their independence in the course of decolonization took place as a rule without even mentioning the criteria referred to in Art. 4 (1). The admission of new member states thus became a mere procedural formality, permitting the automatic admission of even micro-states . . . the practical relevance of Art. 4 of the Charter had become more or less reduced to solving special cases and problems.

See Konrad Ginther, "Article 4," in Bruno Simma (ed.), *The Charter of the United Nations: A Commentary*, 2nd ed. (Oxford: Oxford University Press, 2002), p. 180.

42. Myers, "Contemporary Practice of the United States Relating to International Law," p. 706.

43. O'Brien and Goebel, "United States Recognition Policy toward the New Nations," p. 212. They write (p. 209) that "in forty of fifty-nine cases, recognition was granted at once without any possibility of making an independent determination on whether the new nation did in fact possess the physical attributes of a sovereign state."

44. See "The Recognition of States," in Whiteman, *Digest of International Law*, Vol. 2, pp. 133–242.

45. Myers, "Contemporary Practice of the United States Relating to International Law," p. 718.

46. In addition to the General Assembly and Security Council, an important role was played by the International Court of Justice. In its *Namibia* (1971) and *Western Sahara* (1975) advisory opinions, the ICJ made clear that the right to self-determination was an international legal right. See ICJ Reports 1971, pp. 16, 31, and ICJ Reports 1975, pp. 12, 31–3.

47. It is worth noting that up to 1968 the UN bodies referred to the old mandate name "South West Africa," but following GA Resolution 2372 (XXII) they switched to the territory's African name "Namibia." This was, of course, done without South Africa's say in the matter and reflected the worldwide consensus that the territory should belong to its people.

48. UN SC Resolution 384 (1975) confirmed the right of the people of East Timor to self-determination in accordance with UN GA Resolution 1514 (XV) and urged Indonesia to withdraw its troops from the territory without delay. UN SC Resolution 377 (1975) as well as the *Western Sahara* (1975) advisory opinion of the ICJ reaffirmed this right for Western Sahara, which was invaded by Morocco and Mauritania. Dozens of Security Council and General Assembly resolutions dealing with the two conflicts later stipulated that any solution to them must be based on the respect for this right.

49. See Bunyan Bryant, "Recognition of Guinea (Bissau)," *Harvard Journal of International Law*, 15 (1974), pp. 491–2, and Wilson, *International Law and the Use of Force by National Liberation Movements*, pp. 111–13.

50. Prior to November 1965, Britain, the administering power in Southern Rhodesia, was asked in SC Resolution 202 (1965) to "promote the country's attainment of independence by a democratic system of government in accordance with the aspirations of the majority of the population."

51. The other "independent" Bantustans – there were also six non-independent ones and four on Namibia's soil – were Bophuthatswana, Venda, and Ciskei. Transkei's new status was at once pronounced invalid by General Assembly Resolution 31/6/A. Deprecating South Africa's act in the strongest terms, the text implored UN members not to recognize the "so-called independent Transkei" and to refrain from having any dealings with its authorities. The UN Security Council endorsed this decision in Resolutions 402 (1976) and 407 (1977), which reprimanded South Africa for its activities designed to compel neighboring Lesotho into recognition of Transkei and praised Lesotho for resisting the cross-border threats and complying with the international policy of non-recognition. The General Assembly also condemned the plans of independent Bophuthatswana in Resolution 32/105/N in 1977 and the Security Council repulsed the purported emancipation of Venda and Ciskei in statements by the

president of the body in 1979 and 1981, respectively. See "Statement, September 21, 1979" and "Statement, December 15, 1981," Karel Wellens (ed.), *Resolutions and Statements of the United Nations Security Council (1946–1989): A Thematic Guide* (Dordrecht, the Netherlands: Martinus Nijhoff, 1990), pp. 190–2.

52. This formula was broadened somewhat in GA Resolution 2625 (XXV) where, in addition to the three options, "the emergence into any other political status freely determined by a people" was also said to constitute a mode of "implementing the right of self-determination by that people."

53. See Roth, *Governmental Illegitimacy in International Law*, p. 226. The lack of such a procedure made possible both not doing any assessments of popular will at all, as when Eritrea was attached to Ethiopia in 1960, and endorsing highly questionable popular consultations, as when West Irian was appended to Indonesia in communal caucuses rather than in a referendum based on the principle one person – one vote.

54. The term "country" was used in GA resolutions dealing with decolonization to mean both existing states and states-to-be.

55. Emerson, "The New Higher Law of Anti-Colonialism," p. 173. See also Marc Weller, "The Self-Determination Trap," *Ethnopolitics*, 4 (2005), pp. 4, 10.

56. Article 2(4) reads: "All members shall refrain in their international relations from the threat or use of force against the territorial integrity or political independence of any state, or in any other manner inconsistent with the purposes of the United Nations."

57. The Commission of Jurists of the League of Nations concluded in the 1920 advisory opinion that "positive international law does not recognize the right of national groups, as such, to separate themselves from the state of which they form a part of by the simple expression of a *wish*" (italics added). The commission did not put forward the far more restrictive proposition that any separatist *attempt* is against the principles or purposes of the League of Nations Covenant. While it clearly refuted the existence of any positive international right to secede, the commission did not deny that there was a negative international right to secede, that is, that entities that actually separated themselves from their parent states are entitled to foreign recognition.

58. See *Documents of the United Nations Conference on International Organization* (London: United Nations Information Organization, 1945–1955), Vol. 6, p. 296, and Vol. 17, pp. 142, 143, and 381. See also Michla Pomerance, *Self-Determination in Law and Practice: The New Doctrine in the United Nations* (The Hague: Martinus Nijhoff, 1982), pp. 28, 38, 101–2.

59. See Antonio Cassese, *Self-Determination of Peoples: A Legal Reappraisal* (Cambridge: Cambridge University Press, 1995), pp. 38–42. There were persisting disputes between Germany and Czechoslovakia, Germany and Poland, Germany and Lithuania, Hungary and Czechoslovakia, Hungary and Romania, Hungary and Yugoslavia, Yugoslavia and Italy, Czechoslovakia and Poland, Poland and Lithuania, Yugoslavia and Albania, Yugoslavia and Bulgaria, Bulgaria and Greece, Greece and Albania, and Greece and Turkey. The German claims of Sudetenland justified by "the right of all Germans to self-determination" led to the most significant crisis of the interwar period.

60. See Jennifer Jackson Preece, "Ethnocultural Diversity and Security after 9/11," in William Bain (ed.), *The Empire of Security and the Safety of the People* (London: Routledge, 2006), pp. 147–8.

61. See Resolutions adopted by the All-African Peoples Conference, December 5–13, 1958 and Resolutions adopted by the All-African Peoples Conference, January 25–30, 1960, Colin Legum, *Pan-Africanism: A Short Political Guide* (London: Pall Mall Press, 1962),

pp. 231, 246; Besides Somalia, there were ethnic Somalis in neighboring Kenya, Ethiopia, and Djibouti.

62. There were, as indicated, a handful of exceptions to this. They were the British-administered trust territory of Cameroons, the Belgian trust territory of Ruanda-Urundi and the British colony of the Gilbert and Ellice Islands. Cameroons was divided into two provinces, one of which, Northern Cameroons, was administered, according to the terms of the mandate and trusteeship agreements with Britain, as part of the adjoining British colony of Nigeria. At decolonization the UN General Assembly gave Northern Cameroons a choice to join the independent Federation of Nigeria. A plebiscite was held and the area voted for the merger. As for Ruanda-Urundi, the UN General Assembly recommended its independence as one unit. But after a period of large-scale violence between the Hutus and Tutsis, the decision was made to split the two units, previously administered as separate kingdoms, into the sovereign states of Rwanda and Burundi. In the case of the Gilbert and Ellice Islands, the British heeded the pre-independence calls for referendum on separation of the ethnically Polynesian Ellice Islanders from the ethnically Micronesian Gilbert Islands. The Gilbert Islands acceded to sovereignty as the Republic of Kiribati and the Ellice Islands as Tuvalu.

63. See Malcolm Shaw, "The Heritage of States: The Principle of *Uti Possidetis Juris* Today," *British Year Book of International Law 1996* (Oxford: Clarendon Press, 1997), pp. 98–9, 104.

64. To reinforce the point made in the previous paragraph, the United States, which was first to recognize both countries, was accused by Mexico and Colombia of premature recognition. The US government denied it in both cases. All participants in the debate, however, based their arguments on the same *de facto* criteria. The controversy was exclusively over whether these criteria had been met.

65. See Rupert Emerson, "The Problem of Identity, Selfhood and Image in New Nations: The Situation in Africa," *Comparative Politics*, 1 (1969), p. 306.

66. Mayall, *Nationalism and International Society*, p. 49. Analogous points are made in Robert Jackson, "Negative Sovereignty in Sub-Saharan Africa," pp. 250–1, and K. J. Holsti, *The State, War and the State of War* (Cambridge: Cambridge University Press, 1996), ch. 4.

67. See Pomerance, *Self-Determination in Law and Practice*, p. 37–38, and Yehuda Z. Blum, "Reflections on the Changing Concept of Self-Determination," *Israel Law Review*, 10 (1975), p. 513.

68. In Africa, for example, only Morocco and Somalia refused to accept *uti possidetis juris* as they claimed several neighboring territories.

69. Ethiopia itself was never colonized. It is included into this category because in 1952 it was joined by Eritrea, a British trust. The Eritreans began their rebellion against Ethiopian rule in 1961.

70. Internal legitimacy was also questioned in cases where secession was not an issue – places with different populations living non-contiguously – but where significant conflict among diverse peoples nevertheless occurred. This category includes Bhutan, Burundi, Djibouti, Fiji, Ghana, Guyana, India, Indonesia, Lebanon, Malaysia, Nigeria, and Rwanda.

71. K. J. Holsti, "International Theory and War in the Third World," in Brian Job (ed.), *The Insecurity Dilemma: National Security of Third World States* (Boulder, CO: Lynne Rienner Publishers, 1992), p. 55. In 1974 Onyerono Kamanu wrote with respect to independent countries in sub-Saharan Africa that "perhaps more Africans have lost their lives in the past ten years fighting against tribal or ethnic domination than against European

domination during the previous half century. A basic fact of life in Africa is that those outside one's cultural group are regarded as foreigners." See Onyeonoro S. Kamanu, "Secession and the Right to Self-Determination: An OAU Dilemma," *The Journal of Modern African Studies*, 12 (1974), p. 358, n. 1. Since then, several authors have argued that artificial borders are one of the main reasons for state failure in Africa. See, among others, Makau wa Mutua, "Why Redraw the Map of Africa: A Moral and Legal Inquiry," *Michigan Journal of International Law*, 16 (1994–1995), p. 1150, and Jeffrey Herbst, *State Power in Africa: Comparative Lessons in Authority and Control* (Princeton, NJ: Princeton University Press, 2000), pp. 266, 269.

72. As in the past, such consent was extremely hard to come by. Between 1945 and 1993 Singapore was the only sub-state unit of a post-colonial country that managed to obtain it when it left Malaysia in 1965 on the initiative of the federal government in Kuala Lumpur.

73. Jackson, *Quasi-States*, p. 41.

74. See Scott Pegg, *International Society and the De Facto State* (Aldershot, UK: Ashgate, 1998), chs. 3 and 4. It is clear that Pegg understands the term *de facto* state in the same way as the nineteenth-century Anglo-American doctrine: "A *de facto* state exists where there is an organized political leadership which has risen to power through some degree of indigenous capability; receives popular support; and has achieved sufficient capacity to provide governmental services to a given population in a defined territorial area, over which effective control is maintained for an extended period of time" (p. 26).

75. On the other hand, the "Turkish Republic of Northern Cyprus," which is commonly inserted into the category of recent *de facto* states, would not qualify for recognition under the old rules, because it came into being as a product of external use of force, Turkey's invasion of Cyprus in 1974. Its birth thus contravened the Stimson Doctrine. SC Resolutions 541 (1983) and 550 (1984) that avowed the illegality of Northern Cyprus' independence and called on UN members not to recognize this entity fall, therefore, into the same class as the 1932 League of Nations Assembly resolution with respect to the "State of Manchukuo."

76. The members of the European Community, for instance, were urging as late as February 1991 that a just solution to the Eritrea–Ethiopia conflict can only be achieved on the basis of "the territorial integrity and unity of Ethiopia." See Renaud Dehousse, "The International Practice of the European Communities: Current Survey," *European Journal of International Law*, 4 (1993), p. 153.

77. See Hugo Grotius, *The Rights of War and Peace*, ed. by Richard Tuck (Indianapolis, IN: Liberty Fund, 2005), ch. 6, para. 5.

78. Address in the City Auditorium in Pueblo, Colorado, September 25, 1919, Link, *The Papers of Woodrow Wilson*, Vol. 63, p. 506. Of course, as argued in the previous chapter, the Wilson's administration recognized groups as states based on what they *did* rather than what they said.

79. Paragraph 8 of UN SC Resolution 169 (1961) declared "that all secessionist activities against the Republic of Congo are contrary to *Loi fondamentale* [Congo's constitution] and Security Council decisions" and specifically demanded "that such activities which are now taking place in Katanga shall cease forthwith."

80. Quoted in Webster, *The Foreign Policy of Castlereagh*, p. 295.

81. For examples, see Lee C. Buchheit, *Secession: The Legitimacy of Self-Determination* (New Haven, CT: Yale University Press, 1978), pp. 221–2; James Crawford, *Creation of States in International Law* (Oxford: Clarendon Press, 1979), p. 101; Cassese, *Self-*

Determination of Peoples, pp. 109–25; Thomas D. Musgrave, *Self-Determination and National Minorities* (Oxford: Clarendon Press, 1997), ch. 8; Karl Doehring, "Self-Determination," in Simma (ed.), *The Charter of the United Nations*, p. 58; Ved P. Nanda, "Self-Determination outside the Colonial Context: The Birth of Bangladesh in Retrospect," in Yonah Alexander and Robert A. Friedlander (eds.), *Self-Determination: National, Regional, and Global Dimensions* (Boulder, CO: Westview Press, 1980), pp. 200–1; and John Dugard and David Raič, "The Role of Recognition in the Law and Practice of Secession," in Marcelo G. Kohen (ed.), *Secession: International Law Perspectives* (Cambridge: Cambridge University Press, 2006).

82. See Crawford, *Creation of States in International Law*, 2nd ed., p. 120.

83. See David A. Ijalaye, "Was 'Biafra' at Any Time a State in International Law?," *The American Journal of International Law*, 65 (1971), pp. 553–4; Tanzania's statement justifying the recognition of Biafra is a particularly noteworthy document. It contains several passages that are remarkably close to the ideas found in the *US Declaration of Independence*. The government of President Julius Nyerere underlined its acceptance of the boundaries inherited from colonialism, but insisted that that was not the only relevant principle in the situation in which a government's actions led to the killing of tens of thousands of its citizens and about two million displaced persons:

> States are made to serve people; governments are established to protect the citizen of a state against external enemies and internal wrongdoers. It is on these grounds that people surrender their right and power of self-defense to the government of the state in which they live. But when the machinery of the state, and the powers of the government, are turned against a whole group of the society on the grounds of racial, tribal or religious prejudice, then the victims have the right to take back the powers they have surrendered, and to defend themselves.
>
> For while people have a duty to defend the integrity of their state, and even to die in its defense this duty stems from the fact that it is theirs, and that it is important to their well-being and to the future of their children. When the state ceases to stand for the honor, the protection, and the well-being of all its citizens, then it is no longer the instrument of those it has rejected. In such a case the people have the right to create another instrument for their protection – in other words, to create another state.
>
> This right cannot be abrogated by constitution, nor by outsiders. The basis of statehood, and of unity can only be general acceptance by the participants.

See Statement by the Government of Tanzania, April 13, 1968, A. H. M. Kirk-Greene (ed.), *Crisis and Conflict in Nigeria: A Documentary Sourcebook 1966–1970*, Vol. 2 (London: Oxford University Press, 1971), pp. 209–10.

84. Statement by France's Council of Ministers, July 31, 1968, ibid., p. 245.

85. Nor did other countries, importantly, resort to *de facto* practice-based criticism that recognitions of Biafra, coming when they did, were legally premature as the breakaway territory still battled the central government. There were some legal scholars, however, who did. See Iyalaye, "Was 'Biafra' at Any Time a State in International Law?," p. 559.

86. Interview by Prime Minister summarizing Britain's stand on Nigeria, March 25, 1969, Kirk-Greene, *Crisis and Conflict in Nigeria*, p. 368.

87. The three arguments are well summarized in ibid. and Speech made by Foreign Secretary to the House of Commons, March 13, 1969, ibid., pp. 360–6.

88. A State Department official said of the British course of action: "I do not really see how they could have made any other choice.... If they had stopped sales they could, in fact, be helping to support the dismemberment of a fellow Commonwealth country with

which they have had a special relationship since independence." Quoted in Buchheit, *Secession*, p. 172.

89. See Charles R. Nixon, "Self-Determination: The Nigeria/Biafra Case," *World Politics*, 24 (1972), p. 493. On the domino effect fears in Africa, see Kamanu, "Secession and the Right to Self-Determination: An OAU Dilemma," pp. 366–70.
90. Speech made by Foreign Secretary to the House of Commons, March 13, 1969, Kirk-Greene, *Crisis and Conflict in Nigeria*.
91. Russell to the Queen, January 12, 1860, Gooch, *The Later Correspondence of Lord John Russell*, Vol. 2, p. 255.
92. Secretary-General's Press Conference in Dakar, Senegal, January 4, 1970, *UN Monthly Chronicle*, 7 (February 1970), p. 36. On another occasion, U. Thant was emphatic that "self-determination of peoples does not imply self-determination of a section of population of a particular member state." See Secretary-General's Press Conference in Accra, Ghana, January 9, 1970, *UN Monthly Chronicle*, 7 (February 1970), p. 39.
93. Quoted in Eisuke Suzuki, "Self-Determination and World Public Order: Community Response to Territorial Separation," *Virginia Journal of International Law*, 16 (1976), p. 802.
94. The early OAU documents did not contain any formulation that could be construed as prohibiting secession. Article 3(3) of the OAU Charter (1963) mirrored Art. 2(4) of the UN Charter. The association's members affirmed in it "respect for the sovereignty and territorial integrity of each state and for its inalienable right to independent existence." In another key document, Resolution 16 (I), better known as the Cairo Resolution (1964), OAU heads of state and government, acting in response to a number of interstate boundary disputes, pronounced the borders of African states existing on the day of their independence a "tangible reality" and pledged to respect them. OAU practice, however, emulated paragraph 6 of Resolution 1514 faithfully. See Kamanu, "Secession and the Right to Self-Determination: An OAU Dilemma," p. 355.
95. See Indian Recognition of Bangladesh: Text of Prime Minister's Statement in the Parliament, December 6, 1971, *International Legal Materials*, 11 (1972), pp. 121–2.
96. India defended its intervention in East Pakistan in terms of the right of self-defense – the right to stop the destabilizing cross-border flow of refugees that reached in December 1971 approximately ten million people. It was on this basis that it received support from the Soviet bloc and a handful of other countries. Though the Indian government had initially evoked also humanitarian reasons, these were hurriedly de-emphasized as India's armed foray came under heavy criticism in the United Nations.
97. See John F. Murphy, "Self-Determination: United States Perspectives," in Alexander and Friedlander, *Self-Determination: National, Regional, and Global Dimensions*, p. 49; Nicholas J. Wheeler, *Saving Strangers: Humanitarian Intervention and International Society* (Oxford: Oxford University Press, 2000), pp. 62–3, 67.
98. Interestingly, Crawford's position on the admissibility of secession had shifted by the end of the 1990s. While he admits that in his 1979 book he argued "tentatively" that "in extreme cases of oppression international law allows remedial secession to discrete peoples within a state, and that the 'safeguard clauses' in the Friendly Relations Declaration and the Vienna Declaration recognize this, even if indirectly," in his 1999 paper he writes that "if the 1970/1993 proviso is taken to mean that unilateral secession is constituted on a discriminatory basis, it is doubtful whether the proviso reflects international practice." See James Crawford, "The Right of Self-Determination

in International Law: Its Development and Future," in Philip Alston (ed.), *Peoples'*
Rights (Oxford: Oxford University Press, 2001), p. 57; and James Crawford, "State
Practice and International Law in Relation to Secession," *British Year Book of Inter-*
national Law 1998 (Oxford: Clarendon Press, 1999), p. 117.

99. Kreijen, *State Failure, Sovereignty and Effectiveness*, p. 141.
100. Ibid., pp. 143–4.
101. Nicholas Tsagourias, "International Community, Recognition of States, and Political
     Cloning," in Colin Warbrick and Stephen Tierney (eds.), *Towards an "International*
     Legal Community?" (London: British Institute of International and Comparative
     Law, 2006), p. 234.
102. Myers, "Contemporary Practice of the United States Relating to International Law,"
     p. 717.
103. Rupert Emerson, "Self-Determination," *The American Journal of International Law*
     65 (1971), p. 459.
104. Except, of course, those fitting the decolonization paradigm.

6

New States in the Post-Cold War Period

The introduction to this study began with a brief discussion of the demands of statehood since the end of the Cold War. According to a number of observers, this landmark moment in the twentieth century led to the opening up of long-suppressed self-determination claims in Central and Eastern Europe and modifications to state recognition practice as more than twenty countries were fully admitted into international society in the non-colonial context.[1] In particular, some have argued that the society of states has moved toward acceptance,[2] even toward a qualified right,[3] of unilateral secession from sovereign states.

This chapter, on the contrary, contends that the developments of the last twenty years have solidified the norms of international legitimacy settled in the 1960s and early 1970s in the wake of the largest wave of post-1945 decolonization. Rather than transforming the previously established recognition practice, the end of the Cold War in fact extended it beyond the ex-colonial world. That practice has continued to inhibit secession without consent of the sovereign government in question as a legitimate way of acquiring statehood. The breakup of the Soviet Union and of Czechoslovakia might have commenced as separatist bids by some of their constituent units, but foreign recognition of the successor states came only once the respective federal governments had agreed to the dissolution of the unions.[4] Western and other countries sought prior agreement of the central government even in the case of the Baltic republics, despite the fact that most considered them to be under illegal occupation by a foreign power rather than an integral part of the USSR.

Unilateral separatist drives from the newly independent states, whether it was the "Nagorno-Karabakh Republic" (Azerbaijan), the "Republic of Abkhazia," the "Republic of South Ossetia" (both Georgia), the "Transdnester Republic," the "Republic of Gagauzia" (both Moldova), the "Republic of Crimea" (Ukraine), or the "Republic of Chechnya" (Russia), met with general foreign non-recognition. The first four on this list in fact succeeded in creating long-surviving *de facto* entities, but they merely swelled the ranks of the non-recognized entities of the post-colonial world. Thus again, the principle of *uti possidetis juris* was not limited to the external challenges to the newly heralded international boundaries – as in the case of Armenia's involvement on behalf of the ethnic Armenians of Nagorno-Karabakh. It also encompassed the internal ones.

The foreign response to the claims arising out of the complex and tragic breakup of the Socialist Federal Republic of Yugoslavia (SFRY) was consistent with this "neo-decolonization territorial approach."[5] During the initial phase of the Yugoslav collapse, which also started as a series of secessionist undertakings by its constituent republics, foreign authorities came out in support of the territorial integrity of the SFRY. That position changed only after a majority of Yugoslav republics had ceased to be represented in the highest federal institution under contentious circumstances. The withdrawal of the majority of the population and territory from a federal state was a historically unprecedented occurrence, but one to which third parties as well as relevant international organizations found a speedy and generally uncontroversial solution: they came to regard what was occurring in the SFRY as a case of dissolution legally equivalent to the consensual dissolutions of the USSR or Czechoslovakia. Only after this judgment did the individual republics become eligible for recognition.

As during decolonization, the successor states became safeguarded, as a matter of international right, against external territorial designs as well as against unilateral secessions even prior to recognition. This was made evident in non-recognition policies toward those who challenged the territorial integrity of Croatia, Bosnia and Herzegovina, and later the Federal Republic of Yugoslavia (FRY). The 1991/2 independence claims of the "Republic of Serbian Krajina," the "Croat Community of Herzeg-Bosna," the "Republika Srpska," and the "Republic of Kosova" were rebuffed internationally. In Bosnia in 1995 and the FRY in 1999, the main actors went so far as to insist on interim international administration within their territories rather than to sanction separation of their respective secessionist entities. The major Western powers and a number of other countries eventually recognized Kosovo's second unilateral declaration of independence in 2008, but most recognizing countries went to extraordinary lengths to justify their move as a special, no-precedent-creating exception to, rather than as a qualification or abandonment of, the post-decolonization norm of territorial integrity. Even so, recognition of Kosovo's independence has not met with general international support and the subsequent Russian recognition of Georgia's two breakaway republics, also defended as an exception to the norm, elicited virtually no global backing. There can be few doubts that territorial integrity has continued: (*a*) to be protected normatively against disruptions from inside as well as outside; and (*b*) to prevail over self-determination of peoples as the idea was reflected in the practice of recognition of new states prior to decolonization.

Recognition of new states of the last twenty years has curiously blended two elements of past practice. First, as can be deduced from the earlier paragraphs, the recognizing states have persisted in depreciation of the effectiveness criteria that began with decolonization. The recent admission of new states into international society outside of the colonial context has not suggested a departure from understanding self-determination as a positive right and a throwback to the pre-decolonization tests of *de facto* statehood. At the time of their foreign acknowledgment, Azerbaijan, Moldova, Georgia, Croatia, and, most conspicuously, Bosnia did not possess effective control over considerable segments of their territory. As well, whatever the future settlement of international disputes over the status of Kosovo, Abkhazia, and South Ossetia will be, at the moment of their recognition each was effectively dominated by foreigners rather than actually functioning independently, with Kosovo's authorities having no control at all over the northern parts populated by most of the remaining Kosovo Serbs. On the other hand, *de facto* states within the territory of the former USSR and SFRY that had not previously had the status of a constituent republic failed to garner international recognition.

Second, the practice returned to placing conditions upon entities seeking recognition. As in the past, they were devised by great and regional powers and their purpose was to eliminate perceived dangers to international security emanating from new states, to make new states conform to important international standards, and to curb sources of their actual or potential internal conflicts which could have external ramifications. The accent on these conditions varied from place to place and from issue to issue, but it is crucial to keep in mind that the international oversight of their post-recognition implementation generated difficulties in the past also. Such conditions had always been secondary discretionary devices that followed the fulfillment of primary norms specifying when an entity can be considered for recognition as a new state. The successor states of the USSR, SFRY, and Czechoslovakia became recognized first and foremost because these federations were deemed to have dissolved. It was up to the recognizing states to decide what, if any, conditions to submit to the emerging states – the Baltic countries, the Czech Republic, or Slovakia were presented with none[6] – but they could not submit anything to, say, the "Nagorno-Karabakh Republic" because it was not eligible for recognition to begin with.

None of this is meant to suggest that the secondary political and discretionary aspects of recognition were somehow unimportant. Not only the conditions but also the timing of recognition impacted subsequent developments within and between new states. In fact, it is these aspects that have attracted most attention and controversy, especially in the case of the Yugoslav republics. Still, the last part of this chapter suggests that the key question concerns the justification of the primary customary norm that upholds the territorial integrity of former jurisdictions even at the expense of the wishes of peoples who might choose different arrangements.

Recognition and Non-Recognition in the Former Soviet Union

The democratizing changes that the government of Mikhail Gorbachev had been making since 1985 emboldened various constituencies within the country. The Union of the Soviet Socialist Republics was composed of fifteen republics and a number of those were further sub-divided into a patchwork of jurisdictions with lower-level constitutional standing, including thirty-eight ethnically defined sub-republican autonomous units.[7] As the 1980s drew to a close, a growing number of republics and other jurisdictions expressed dissatisfaction with their status within the Soviet state. Just as in the final days of the Russian Empire at the end of World

War I, the strongest demands for independence emanated from the western fringes of the country: the Baltics, the Ukraine, and the Caucasus.

The first full-fledged challenge to the integrity of the Soviet Union took place in Lithuania four months after the fall of the Berlin Wall. In March 1990, the freshly elected republican parliament proclaimed nearly unanimously the restoration of Lithuanian sovereignty from 1918–40. Though Art. 72 of the 1977 Soviet constitution gave the republics "the right freely to secede from the USSR,"[8] the Lithuanian legislature was careful to portray its act as a case of reinstatement of statehood in continuous legal existence rather than secession from the USSR.[9] This step found backing in other parts of the Soviet Union with similar aspirations – the other two Baltic republics adopted more circumspect legislation announcing merely "transition" to independence – but the federal authorities in Moscow rejected it as an anti-constitutional act of unilateral secession.[10]

Foreign states, including most Western countries that had refused to grant *de jure* recognition to the Soviet conquest of the Baltic republics in 1940 as contrary to the Stimson Doctrine, treaded cautiously in response to Lithuania's move. The United States noted that it had never recognized forcible incorporation of the three states into the USSR and urged the Soviet Union to respect the will of the Lithuanian citizens. Still, the administration of President George H. W. Bush made it known that it supported "the Baltic peoples' inalienable right to *peaceful* self-determination" (italics added) and that the issue of Lithuanian statehood had to be resolved via constructive negotiations between Moscow and Vilnius.[11] The European Community (EC), which in the aftermath of the Cold War emerged as a pivotal player in European international relations, only conveyed collectively the need for negotiations between the two sides. Nevertheless, several EC countries, among them Britain, individually took a stand similar to that of the United States.[12]

There were two major reasons for this guarded approach, and they are a very good illustration of how even a rather straightforward case of justice can clash with other vital considerations in the actual practice of international relations. First, albeit weakened, the Soviet Union was still a considerable military power. It possessed massive stockpiles of military hardware, most portentously tens of thousands of nuclear warheads, and any act that could potentially trigger an uncontrollable chain reaction of disintegration had to be avoided. International security could not but figure as a major issue for the outsiders deliberating on how to handle the self-determination claims emanating from within the USSR. Second, Western states were quite sympathetic to the democratic reforms undertaken by Gorbachev's government and there was little willingness to undermine the Soviet leader already under relentless attack from various quarters at home. Especially acute was the concern that the hard-liners in the Communist Party Politburo opposed to Gorbachev could try to stage a political comeback.

The approach underlining negotiations and mutual agreement, which, of course, presumed consent of the federal government, was applied consistently for almost a year and half through various crises of Soviet unity. These included the energy embargo against recalcitrant Lithuania in April 1990, the unsuccessful but vocal insistence by the Baltic republics to take part in the first post-Cold War summit of the Conference for Security and Co-operation in Europe (CSCE) in Paris in November 1990 as well as to be parties to the Conventional Forces in Europe Treaty (CFE),[13] the use of force by the federal troops against civilians in Vilnius and Riga in January 1991, the referenda on independence in each Baltic republic in February and March 1991, and the refusal of the Baltic republics as well as Armenia, Moldova, and Georgia in March 1991 to partake in a Soviet-wide referendum on a new union treaty.

These EC and US policies were criticized both by the Baltic leaders, especially those of Lithuania, and by various domestic groups supporting recognition of those Soviet republics wishing independence. Lithuania's President Vytautas Landsbergis was indignant when instead of congratulations on his homeland's reversion to sovereignty, France and Germany, backed by the United States, presented him, in late April 1990, with a plan for a "suspension" of the declaration of independence so as to enhance the chances for a negotiated settlement with Moscow.[14] Landsbergis' reproach of American and French timidity was reminiscent of the criticism of the United States and France leveled by his country's founders seventy years earlier. But the objectives sought by the two powers in 1990/1 diverged from those of 1918–22. Whereas at the end of World War I recognition was to be preceded by conclusive establishment of effective statehood, they now put the accent on concurrence of the central government.

An important debate about proper approach toward those desiring independence was also sparked by the address delivered by President Bush to the Ukrainian Supreme Soviet on August 1, 1991. Many commentators saw the speech – instantly dubbed the "Chicken Kiev" speech – as a conscious attempt to discourage the drive for independence by republics and reinforce the support for President Gorbachev.[15] The administration denied this and stressed that its policy was not to advocate any specific outcome, but to support good faith negotiations and dialogue between the center and the federal (including the Baltic) republics.[16]

The decisive event leading to the dissolution of the USSR was the *coup d'état* attempt against President Gorbachev between August 19 and 21, 1991. Though quickly quashed, the coup had an instant and substantial impact on the internal reality of the USSR. In its first day, the plotters set in motion a major military offensive against the Baltic republics. In response to the president's overthrow, Latvia and Estonia declared the restoration of their independence. Russia, whose president, Boris Yeltsin, played a key role in bringing shaken Gorbachev back to his office, gained in stature vis-à-vis the emaciated federal government and on August 24 it "recognized" the two republics (it had already "recognized" Lithuania in July). On August 25, President Gorbachev urged in the USSR Supreme Soviet the immediate resumption of the process of signing a new union treaty (the signing was originally scheduled for August 20), but he crucially stressed that "those republics which are not going to sign . . . must be given the right to make an independent choice."[17] This was perhaps the most authoritative statement to date that each republic was free to determine its future and that none would be forced to remain in the USSR against its will. On August 26, the Soviet acknowledgment of Baltic independence was put on the agenda of the hastily convened extraordinary session of the principal legislative body, the USSR Congress of People's Deputies.[18]

In the days following, foreign states moved to establish diplomatic relations with the Baltic states. The twelve members of the EC did so on August 27 and the United States on September 2. Though the official extension of recognition by the Soviet government was not announced until September 6, the Bush administration did coordinate its decision with the Soviet leadership.[19] In its statement the EC welcomed "the restoration of the sovereignty and independence of the Baltic States which they lost in 1940" and said that "it is now time, after more than fifty years, that these states resume their rightful place among the nations of Europe."[20] At the same time, both EC countries and the United States announced they would set up diplomatic relations with the three states and assist them in joining key international organizations.[21] The latter was also pledged by the USSR in its statement.[22]

The coup accelerated the disintegration of the Soviet Union. Between August 22 and the end of September all but two republics declared, in one form or another, their intention to become independent. At the same time, most opted for continuous engagement and talks with the flagging center on a treaty that would define future relations among republics. Outsiders made it clear that they drew a distinction between the Baltic and other republics of the USSR. Estonia, Latvia, and Lithuania were neither treated as new states in need of recognition nor were they deemed to be successor states to the USSR. Secretary of State James Baker pointed out that for the United States the Baltic republics had "never been Soviet republics but, instead, separate states for whom we helped keep alive the promise and diplomatic symbols of independence." Not all countries could identify with the second part of the statement, but none now disputed the first part.[23] The issue of how to approach other claims still had to be confronted.

It was not the EC, by now absorbed deeply by the Yugoslav conflict, but rather the United States that took the initiative. On September 4, 1991, Secretary Baker announced five principles that would guide his administration vis-à-vis "the changes that are taking place in centre–republic relations." These were not conditions of recognition, for no republic declared yet with finality constitutional independence from the Soviet Union, but they nevertheless were an indication of American preferences. The United States appealed to the leaders at all levels of government to:

1. Determine their future peacefully and in conformity with democratic values and practices and the principles of the Helsinki Final Act. In this process, there can be no legitimate place for threats, intimidation, coercion, or violence.

2. Respect existing borders, both internal and external. Any change of borders should occur only legitimately by peaceful and consensual means consistent with CSCE principles.[24]

3. Support the rule of law and democratic processes. Peaceful change ought to be effected only through orderly, democratic processes, especially the processes of elections.

4. Safeguard human rights, including equal treatment of minorities.

5. Respect international law and obligations, especially the provisions of the Helsinki Final Act and the Charter of Paris.[25]

After the Ukrainian referendum on independence on December 1, the United States called upon the second largest Soviet republic, in addition, to:

1. Ensure safe, responsible, and reliable control of nuclear weapons; to prevent proliferation of dangerous military-related technology; and to support implementation of relevant international agreements including Strategic Arms Reduction Treaty, the Conventional Armed Forces in Europe Treaty, the Non-Proliferation Treaty, and the Biological Weapons Convention.

2. Demonstrate its commitment to economic policies aimed at facilitating free markets and fair trade both with other republics and with the international community more generally.

3. Take responsibility for its share of the Soviet Union's debt.[26]

These provisos were transformed into conditions for the republics only after the Soviet Union had officially dissolved. Though there were strong domestic pressures in the United States and the EC to recognize Ukraine after its referendum, both opted to delay it.[27] The EC, on the one hand, welcomed "the democratic manner in which the Ukrainian people declared their wish for their republic to attain full sovereignty," but, on the other, stressed that "as the transformation of the Soviet Union enters this crucial phase it is incumbent upon the representatives of Ukraine, of the Union and of the other republics to take matters forward in a peaceful, democratic and orderly way."[28] The United States issued an analogous call.[29] Democratic choice for sovereignty in one or more republics thus clearly did not remove the requirement to achieve it by mutual agreement. On December 21, 1991, eleven republics met in Alma Ata and created a Commonwealth of Independent States (CIS). They concomitantly declared the end of the USSR.[30] Having been previously unable to generate a new union treaty, the federal government accepted the Alma Ata decision.

Upon the resignation of President Gorbachev on December 25, the United States granted recognition to all the former Soviet republics, but established diplomatic ties with only six that made specific commitments to the Bush administration.[31] The EC countries proceeded in a like manner, except that they attached conditions to recognition, not diplomatic relations. On December 23, they welcomed the formation of the CIS as well as the agreement that Russia should continue to exercise the international rights and obligations of the former USSR, including those under the UN Charter. At the same time, they announced that they were prepared to recognize the other republics constituting the CIS as soon as the dissolution entered into force and as they received assurances from those republics that they were ready to fulfill the requirements contained in the *Guidelines on the Recognition of New States in Eastern Europe and in the Soviet Union.*[32]

The guidelines, adopted on December 16 and prompted no less by contemporaneous Yugoslav events, represented the first written set of conditions for admission into international society since the Permanent Mandate Commission guidelines of 1931. The document noted the attachment of the EC members to the principle of self-determination and then affirmed, in a slightly convoluted fashion, "their readiness to recognize, subject to normal standards of international practice and the political realities in each case, those new states which, following the historic changes in the region, have constituted themselves on a democratic basis, have accepted the appropriate international obligations and have committed themselves in good faith to a peaceful process and negotiations." The document specifically required:

- respect for the provisions of the UN Charter and the commitments subscribed to in the Helsinki Final Act and in the Charter of Paris, especially with regard to the rule of law, democracy, and human rights;

- guarantees for the rights of ethnic and national groups and minorities in accordance with the commitments subscribed to in the framework of the CSCE;

- respect for the inviolability of all frontiers which can only be changed by peaceful means and by common agreement;

- acceptance of all relevant commitments with regard to disarmament and nuclear non-proliferation as well as to security and regional stability; and

- commitment to settle by agreement, including where appropriate by recourse to arbitration, all questions concerning state succession and regional disputes.[33]

All these stipulations were contained or implied in the American policy statements of September 4 and December 2, 1991. The EC decision of December 23 also specified that the Community expected to receive assurances that the non-Russian republics would fulfill the international obligations ensuing for them from treaties and agreements concluded by the Soviet Union, including the ratification and full implementation of the CFE Treaty by the republics to which that agreement applies, and that they would ensure single control over nuclear weapons and their non-proliferation. On December 31, with the dissolution of the USSR in effect, the EC recognized the eight republics that pledged to comply with the requirements contained in the *Guidelines.*[34] The announcement spelled out that recognition of the republics that station nuclear weapons would be extended on the understanding that they would adhere to the Nuclear Non-Proliferation Treaty as non-nuclear weapon states. On January 15, 1992, they recognized two more republics[35] and on March 23, the last one, Georgia.

Recognition of the constituent republics of the USSR clearly indicates a return to conditionality that had been a recurrent component of the practice from the 1820s until World War II. Sharing the concerns of the recognizing states of the past, the United States and the EC countries did not want to see the emergence of countries whose policies would be the source of regional or international insecurity, or contravene international rules and agreements. Implicit in their conditions was also the belief that there is a strong link between the nature of internal rule and the conduct of external relations, though there can be no question that the United States and the EC were more immediately concerned to receive, say, Belarus' or Kazakhstan's commitment to nuclear non-proliferation than to scrutinize their professed transformation to democracy. Still, following the footsteps of the great powers that had spearhead the recognition of Greece, Romania, or Czechoslovakia, the United States and the EC thought that the best way to prevent the new states from being wayward members of international society was for the latter to convert into the image of the former. Secretary Baker suggested as much on December 12, 1991, when, in a major speech on the events in the USSR, he contended that in face of uncertainty about the disposition of new authorities "the West should stick to fundamentals and support those who put into practice our principles and values."[36]

In contrast to 1991, however, past recognition conditions were presented to actually established and factually independent states. The latter preceded and presupposed the former. Brazil was asked to terminate the slave trade, Romania obligated to institute religious equality, and Poland compelled to conclude a treaty on protection of minorities, but these conditions were presented to the three only after they had been established *de facto*. Effective independent statehood, on the other hand, was not a decisive criterion for the United States and the EC as they led the acknowledgment of the former Soviet republics. Azerbaijan had not had effective possession over the "Nagorno-Karabakh Republic" since 1988. During 1991, Moldova's government lost control of territories that proclaimed to form independent "Trans-Dnester Republic" and "Republic of Gaugazia." What's more, these "republics" became supported, in a situation reminiscent of Katanga's secession from the Congo, by some remnants of the Soviet government and army.[37] Georgia faced an active secession from the "Republic of South Ossetia," internal convulsions in Abkhazia, and a *coup d'état* attempt against its president on December 21, 1991. Although the Bush administration took a dim view of the developments in that republic,[38] it recognized Georgia along with the other eleven republics on December 25, 1991, postponing only the setting up of diplomatic relations. The EC did delay its acknowledgment until the resolution of the coup in March 1992, but its statement announcing the recognition made it seem as if the EC had merely waited for Georgia's assurances to fulfill the *Guidelines*. It made no mention whatsoever of the prior lack of a government exercising effective control.[39]

Nevertheless, however deficient the new states might have been in meeting the pre-decolonization effectiveness criteria, once recognized, they became legitimate actors on the world stage entitled to the same protection as other sovereign states.

As in the case of the former non-self-governing and trust territories, their territorial integrity became, at least in terms of international right, unassailable without their government's consent, even prior to their independence. Although the USSR was not a colonial situation, the second principle of the statement of US policy toward the fragmenting Soviet Union of September 4, 1991, and the third condition of the EC recognition guidelines of December 16, 1991, were entirely consistent with the territorial integrity provision of UN GA resolutions 1514 and 2625 analyzed in Chapter 5. Moreover, as with the former post-1945 colonies and unlike Latin America of the 1820s, *uti possidetis juris* was applied *a priori* to units with a particular juridical status rather than *ex post facto* to bounded entities that attained effective control over a territory. Where the claims by the government in Buenos Aires to all the territories governed by it prior to independence had not been recognized because the absence of effective control over them had been taken as the absence of the consent of the governed, the similar claims by the governments in Tbilisi, Baku, or Kisinev (or, as will be seen below, those in Zagreb or Sarajevo) were acknowledged without much hesitation. The USSR was a union of federal republics and, consequently, it was never admitted that the country could fragment along any other lines, no matter how artificial or historically unjust they might have appeared to the peoples separated by, or enclosed within, them.

The sovereignty or border claims emerging from and across several republics bore a resemblance to the claims that had arisen in the wake of decolonization. The grievances involved ethnonational minority groups who cited a past record of maltreatment by the majority population (Chechnya), forced jurisdictional or territorial transfers (Nagorno-Karabakh, Crimea, Trans-Dnestria, and South Ossetia), denial of a particular constitutional status (Abkhazia), or some combination thereof. Regardless of the justification or means by which they were pursued, none of the claims were recognized since they involved alteration of republican borders against the will of the respective republican government.

The successful empirical achievement of a claim made no difference. In 1992, the Abkhaz and South Ossetian authorities of Georgia followed ethnic Russian groups of Moldova and ethnic Armenian groups of Azerbaijan in carving out *de facto* independent entities. By 1996 the Chechen authorities accomplished the same in relation to Russia. The fact that none of these entities has been considered legitimate candidates for statehood is discernible from numerous CSCE/OSCE, EC/EU,[40] and UN texts. The CSCE took the lead in trying to resolve these conflicts, but the EC also played an important, if on the whole, secondary role. Beginning in 1993, the UN became the principal international agency involved in the Abkhaz conflict. In the same year, it also addressed the war over Nagorno-Karabakh. The primary OSCE texts confirming the sovereignty and territorial integrity of Azerbaijan, Georgia, Moldova, and Russia are the 1994 Budapest Summit Decisions (Moldova and Georgia), the 1996 Lisbon Summit Document (Azerbaijan), and the 1999 Istanbul Summit Declaration (Moldova, Georgia, and Russia). The EU's foreign policy arm also has formally endorsed the sovereignty and territorial integrity of Azerbaijan, Moldova, Russia, and Georgia on multiple occasions.[41]

The UN Security Council took up the issue of Nagorno-Karabakh in Resolutions 822 (1993), 853 (1993), 874 (1993), and 884 (1993). All of them reaffirmed the sovereignty and territorial integrity of all states in the region, including the Republic of Azerbaijan. In addition, each underscored "the inviolability of international borders and the inadmissibility of the use of force for the acquisition of territory." Beginning with Resolution 876 (1993), the Security Council has affirmed the sovereignty and territorial integrity of the Republic of Georgia within its internationally recognized borders at least twice every year for fifteen years. Resolutions 1582 and 1615 (2005), reiterate the formulation found in a number of texts on other conflicts as they avow "the necessity to define the status of Abkhazia within the State of Georgia in strict accordance with these principles."[42] The same documents express deep regrets that the Abkhaz side has refused discussions on the latest international proposals for solving the dispute between the two sides and declares that "the purpose of these documents is to facilitate meaningful negotiations between the parties . . . on the status of Abkhazia within the State of Georgia . . . is not an attempt to impose or dictate any specific solution to the parties," oddly glossing over that it was precisely the status *within* Georgia that the Abkhaz side felt had been forced on it. Russia departed from the international consensus on the status of Abkhazia and South Ossetia by recognizing the two republics following its military occupation of their territories in the armed intervention against Georgia in August 2008. But this dramatic step was roundly condemned by many individual countries as well as the EU, OSCE, G8, and NATO as violating Georgia's territorial integrity, and, at the time of this writing, has been emulated only by Nicaragua and Venezuela.

Recognition and Non-Recognition in the Former SFRY

As challenging internationally as the breakup of the USSR might have been, it was, in hindsight at least, rather orderly. Whatever the initial fears about loss of control over the vast stockpiles of nuclear weapons and other military assets or the restoration of the hard-line communist regime – and they were considerable – the USSR in the end splintered by mutual agreement of the constituent republics and the center. Notwithstanding the armed conflicts discussed earlier, the end of the USSR was relatively peaceful. The same cannot be said of the end of the SFRY, where the confrontation over who had the right to govern whom, where, and in what form cost tens of thousands of lives. Still, the norms informing recognition of new states were no less operational in the SFRY than in the USSR.

At the beginning of the 1990s Yugoslavia was in the midst of a full-blown constitutional impasse. The crisis was sparked by Serbia's campaign to centralize the country and to give the ethnic Serbs – wherever in the SFRY they might have lived – more say in the affairs of the state. This campaign was perceived as heavy-handed by all other republics except Montenegro, most vocally by Slovenia and Croatia, both of which actually proposed further decentralization of the country. The principal tension revolved around the meaning and mutual relation of two sets of constitutional rights which came into conflict – the rights of Yugoslavia's six constituent ethnonations and the rights of Yugoslavia's six republics.[43] An additional and related source of discord was the constitutional relationship of the Republic of Serbia and its two autonomous provinces, in particular the alleged abuses by the ethnic Albanian majority of the rights of Serbs in Kosovo. All key actors urged modifications to the 1974 federal basic law, the complexity of which was perhaps even more bewildering than that of the USSR, but no accord could be found on either the procedure or substance of such changes.

The events came to a head on June 25, 1991, when Slovenia and Croatia, following abortive talks on renewing the federation and their respective referenda on independence in December 1990 and May 1991, "disassociated" themselves from the SFRY, invoking their inherent right of self-determination, including the right to secession under the federal constitution.[44] The right of self-determination, which was used to justify the creation of Yugoslavia in 1918, was thus now employed to defend its breakdown. On the same day, the federal cabinet denounced the declarations as "illegal and illegitimate" and added that "all the effects of those acts are null and void."[45] The actions of Slovenia and Croatia were nevertheless followed by (*a*) the Macedonian referendum on independence on September 8 and the subsequent declaration thereof on September 17, 1991; (*b*) the referendum, declared illegal by Serbia, on the independence of the "Republic of Kosova" on September 26–30, 1991, and the ensuing proclamation thereof on October 19, 1991; and (*c*) the Bosnian memorandum on sovereignty on October 14, 1991, which asserted that Bosnia would not remain in the SFRY without the two northwestern republics.

Serbia did not object to the secession of the republics *per se* nor did it dispute the right of Slovenes, Croats, Macedonians, or Bosnian Muslims to self-determination. But it objected to the unilateral character of these secessions, which in Serbia's view violated Art. 5 of the 1974 constitution prohibiting a modification of the external SFRY boundaries without the consent of all republics and autonomous provinces (this was also the position of the federal government), and, even more emphatically, with the departure of Croatia and Bosnia and Herzegovina with their borders intact.[46]

As with the arguments of the four republics, the Serb counterarguments were predicated on the right of self-determination. The core disagreement, as has so often been the case historically, was about who bore this right. The government of Serbia and later the government of the diminished Yugoslavia (Serbia and Montenegro) argued that, according to the federal constitution, the right to self-determination belonged to the constituent ethnonations of Yugoslavia, and not, as the four republican governments claimed, to the federal republics in their inherited borders.[47] The boundaries between republics, the Serbs argued, were administrative rather than political. The Croatian and Bosnian Serbs were in the view of Serbia and the political representatives of those Serbs entitled to the right of self-determination as members of the constituent Serb nation.[48] They could not be just taken against their will out of Yugoslavia, a country to which they remained loyal, be cut off from their fellow Serbs, and relegated to the status of ethnic minority in the states to the independence of which they did not consent. Kosovo, according to Serbia, was an altogether different case. However one chose to read the 1974 constitution, neither the jurisdiction of Kosovo nor the Kosovo Albanians had a right of self-determination: Kosovo was not a republic of Yugoslavia but a province of one of its republics, and the Kosovo Albanians were not a constituent nation but a nationality.[49]

International society opposed independence of Slovenia and Croatia when these republics announced their intention to declare it unilaterally. The CSCE Council of Foreign Ministers adopted during its meeting on June 19–20, 1991, a statement which expressed support for the territorial integrity of Yugoslavia.[50] During his visit to Belgrade on June 21, the US Secretary of State James Baker was categorical that "neither the US nor any other country will recognize unilateral secession" of Slovenia and Croatia.[51] He did not deny that the Yugoslav republics had a right of self-determination. Rather, as in the Soviet case, he insisted that "self-determination cannot be unilateral and must be pursued by dialogue and peaceful means" and that, in this respect, "borders must not be changed except by consent."[52] The USSR and the EC voiced identical sentiments; the EC by way of a statement of its foreign ministers a mere two days before June 25.[53] After his return from Belgrade, Baker suggested to President Bush that the United States should "work with the Europeans to maintain a collective non-recognition policy against any republic that unilaterally declared independence."[54]

After the fighting had begun, the EC, with the support of the United States, the USSR, CSCE, and the UN, took a lead in the attempts to resolve the Yugoslav conflicts. Its activities helped terminate the ten-day confrontation between the federal Yugoslav People's Army (JNA) and Slovenia. The Brioni Accord of July 7 also included a three-month suspension of the implementation of the Slovenian and Croatian declarations of independence modeled after the April 1990 Franco-German scheme aimed at Lithuania. However, the EC's efforts to mediate the bloodshed in Croatia, where the Croatian Serb paramilitaries and the JNA began to resist the republican forces in order to forestall the departure of Serb-inhabited territories from Yugoslavia,[55] were abortive.

The *Brussels Declaration* of August 27 was the first major EC statement on the mounting violence in Croatia. It censured the Serbian irregulars for trying to solve problems of "a new constitutional order through military means" and condemned the JNA's active support of the Serbian side, adding:

> [The Community and its member states] remind those responsible for the violence of their determination never to recognize changes of frontiers which have not been brought about by peaceful means and by agreement.... The Community and its member states will never accept a policy of *fait accompli*. They are determined not to recognize changes of borders by force and will encourage others not to do so either. Territorial conquests, not recognized by the international community, will never produce the kind of legitimate protection sought by all in the new Yugoslavia.[56]

With the consent of all parties the EC convened a permanent conference on Yugoslavia, headed by Peter Carrington. The forum was to help mediate a settlement of the conflict and, more broadly, assist in negotiations on the future of the Yugoslav state. As part of the conference, the EC set up an *ad hoc* arbitration panel of jurists, led by President of the French Constitutional Court Robert Badinter. Its mandate was to render non-binding advisory opinions that would clarify legal norms in contentious claims.

The dangerously escalating confrontation in Croatia might have been hard to curb, but the international legal personality of the SFRY remained unaffected either by the fighting or by additional referenda on, or declarations of, sovereignty. Soon, however, that legal standing began to look increasingly tenuous. On October 3, 1991, the representatives of Montenegro, Serbia, and Serbia's two provinces[57] on the SFRY presidency met in the absence of, and against protests from, the members from the other four republics, including the SFRY president Croat Stipe Mesic, who claimed that the JNA had deliberately prevented them from traveling to Belgrade to attend the meeting.[58] The representatives of Montenegro, Serbia, and Serbia's two provinces determined that the country was in the condition of "an immediate threat of war" and, on that constitutional ground, decided to conduct the affairs of the SFRY henceforth by only "the majority of votes of the presidency members present and voting."[59] On October 5, the EC foreign ministers rejected "the seizure of the presidency by Montenegro and Serbia, which has already been condemned by other republics of Yugoslavia," and stated that they were "not prepared to acknowledge any decisions taken by a body which can no longer pretend to speak for the whole of Yugoslavia."[60] On October 28, the EC went further and called the October 3 decision a *"coup d'état."*[61] In his October 25 report, the Security Council UN Secretary-General Javier Perez de Cuellar described the SFRY presidency as "rump" and observed, "JNA no longer has political direction from a civilian authority that enjoys the support of all the republics and all communities of the federation."[62]

On October 11, the "rump" presidency, conforming with the positions of Serbia and Montenegro, rejected accusations of seizure and warned that every attempt to recognize unilateral secessionist acts would be flagrant interference into the SFRY's internal affairs and "an act directed against its international subjectivity and territorial integrity."[63] Still, at the October 4 Hague meeting, which included Presidents Milosevic and Tudjman, Serbia agreed that what was needed was "a political solution on the basis of the perspective of recognition of the independence of those republics wishing it, at the end of a negotiating process conducted in good faith." This process was to involve "all parties concerned" and recognition was to be granted as part of "the framework of a general settlement" which would permit "no unilateral changes in borders."[64] Later, on November 8, the EC repeated that "the prospect of recognition of the independence of those republics wishing it can only be envisaged in the framework of an overall settlement."[65]

The negotiations at the EC peace conference toward a general settlement, however, bore no fruit. Two issues in particular were plaguing the talks: one was the legal description of events in Yugoslavia and the other the status of Serbs outside Serbia. On the first issue, Serbia and Montenegro contended that the four republics sought to secede from Yugoslavia and that the SFRY continued to exist. In contrast, the other four republics maintained that Yugoslavia had been breaking up as a result of concurring exercise of the right to self-determination by the majority of republics. The question was not one of secessions and, therefore, the republics were to be considered equal successors to the SFRY, without any of them being able to claim its continuation. On November 20, Carrington asked the Badinter Commission to give its opinion on the dispute.

The Commission issued its judgment as Opinion No. 1. After noting that four republics expressed their desire for independence, the justices observed that "the composition and workings of the essential organs of the federation . . . no longer met the criteria of participation and representativeness inherent in a federal state."[66] Their conclusion was that "the Socialist Federal Republic of Yugoslavia is in the process of dissolution" and that "it is incumbent upon the republics to settle such problems of state succession as may arise from this process in keeping with the principles and rules of international law."[67] James Crawford believes that the underlying rationale for Opinion No. 1 was that "in the absence of a reconstituted federal government which represented the population of Yugoslavia as a whole, there was no government which had the authority to seek to prevent the separation of the constituent republics, and that such separation would lead inevitably to the disappearance of the Socialist Federal Republic itself."[68] Be that as it may, the only parties disagreeing with the opinion were the "rump" presidency and the two republics sitting on it.[69] The rest of the world identified as the cause of the SFRY break-up "a non-functional government rather than the secession of several republics."[70] Foreign countries and intergovernmental organizations declined to treat the federal authority composed of only Serbia and Montenegro as a government legitimately representing the SFRY. This implied that any decision on recognition could be made, at least as far as international law was concerned, without seeking consent of this body.[71]

A no less critical item that had to be agreed upon in any overall settlement was that of the Serbian population in Croatia and Bosnia and Herzegovina and, by extension, the boundaries of those republics. Serbia argued at the EC peace talks on October 8 that "it was essential for all Serbs to live in one state, not in number of independent republics bound by little more than interstate relations."[72] In the wake of Muslim-Croat vote for sovereignty in the Sarajevo parliament, the Bosnian Serbs formed a separate "Assembly of the Serbian People in Bosnia and

Herzegovina" on October 25 and then held a referendum in Serb-inhabited regions to remain in Yugoslavia on November 9–10. And the Croatian Serbs, who having boycotted Croatia's referendum on independence held the all-Serb referendum on remaining in Yugoslavia on May 12,[73] were already engaged in a rebellion against the Croatian government.

The question of rights of the Croatian and Bosnian Serbs was thus of utmost urgency. On November 20, as he inquired into the status of the SFRY, Carrington also requested the Badinter Commission to provide an opinion on Serbia's question: "Does the Serbian population in Croatia and Bosnia and Herzegovina, as one of the constituent peoples of Yugoslavia, have the right to self-determination?" All republics with the exception of Serbia and Montenegro responded in the negative: that right belonged to the republics and all citizens within their boundaries. The "rump" SFRY presidency put forward this position:

> The right of self-determination can only be exercised by a people in the sense of the nation and not in the sense of "demos." This means that a decision based on the said right cannot be made by a vote of all citizens of a particular region, republic or state, except if they are populated by only one people, i.e. nation. Otherwise, the said right would be transformed into self-determination of citizens, instead of the people in the sense of a nation. Neither can this decision be made by the republican assembly (parliament) because it is also an assembly of citizens, rather than a one-nation assembly.

The presidency maintained that the right of self-determination applied to *ethnos* (i.e., the ethno-nation) as opposed to *demos* (i.e., all citizens of a particular republic or the civic nation), that the Serbs of Croatia and Bosnia had the right of self-determination as a constituent nation of Yugoslavia and of those republics, and that they had to be, as a result, consulted on their wishes in separate Serbian, not all-republican, referenda.[74]

The Commission asserted in Opinion No. 2 that "it is well-established that, whatever the circumstances, the right to self-determination must not involve changes of existing frontiers at the time of independence (*uti possidetis juris*) except where the states concerned agree otherwise." In the absence of such agreement, it contended, the Serbs in the two republics were only entitled "to all the rights accorded to minorities and ethnic groups under international law."[75] In Opinion No. 3, released on the same day as a response to Serbia's query whether its internal borders with Croatia and Bosnia can be regarded as frontiers in terms of public international law, the Commission maintained that "except where otherwise agreed, the former boundaries become frontiers protected by international law." It then elaborated on the principle of *uti possidetis* by underlining its global character:

> *Uti possidetis*, though initially applied in settling decolonization issues in America and Africa, is today recognized as a general principle, as stated by the International Court of Justice in its Judgment of 22 December 1986 in the case between Burkina Faso and Mali (*Frontier Dispute* (1986) ICJ Reports 554 at 565): "Nevertheless the principle is not a special rule which pertains solely to one specific system of international law. It is a general principle,

which is logically connected with the phenomenon of the obtaining of independence, wherever it occurs. Its obvious purpose is to prevent the independence and stability of new states being endangered by fratricidal struggles."

The Commission also noted that "the principle applies all the more readily to the republics since . . . Article 5 of the Constitution of the SFRY stipulated that the republics' territories and boundaries could not be altered without their consent" and underscored that "according to a well-established principle of international law the alteration of existing frontiers or boundaries by force is not capable of producing any legal effect."[76] The verdicts that the territorial integrity of existing republican jurisdictions overrides the right of *national* self-determination and in effect demotes it to the right of minorities enraged Serb politicians in all three republics. Offers of recognition of Bosnian and Croatian sovereignty without some sort of prior settlement with the Serbs of both republics and Serbia, which pleaded their case, were thus bound to create, especially in the still-peaceful Bosnia where Serbs constituted the second-largest group, a highly explosive environment. However, this is exactly what transpired in the end. Barely a month after its November 8 position, and with no settlement on the future of Yugoslav republics, the EC opted for a radical change in its policy. On December 16, 1991, the EC proposed in its *Declaration on Yugoslavia* to recognize on January 15, 1992, independence of all republics wishing it, provided that they commit themselves to the *Guidelines on the Recognition of New States in Eastern Europe and in the Soviet Union,* accept the provisions of the draft convention on settling the conflict in Yugoslavia (especially those on human and minority rights), continue to support efforts of the UN and the continuation of the Conference on Yugoslavia, and guarantee that they have no territorial claims toward a neighboring Community state, including the use of denomination which implies territorial claims.[77] The last condition reflected the fears of Greece that "Macedonia" in the official name of one of the republics expected to ask for recognition might lead to that republic's irredentist claim to the northern Greek province of the same name. The *Declaration* also conveyed the EC's attachment to the early deployment of UN peacekeeping force between the belligerents in Croatia as outlined in UN SC Resolution 724 (1991).

The main driving force behind the shift in EC policy was Germany. Despite the fact that no international borders had been crossed, its government became strongly convinced that the fighting in Yugoslavia was a consequence of "Serbian aggression." It contended that "preventive recognition" would have a constitutive effect and provide legal grounds for declaring the presence of the JNA in Croatia an unsolicited intervention against a *foreign* country. International law allows in such a case counterintervention, including all forms of foreign military assistance, against the intervening state.[78] Germany's foreign minister of the day, Hans-Dietrich Genscher, writes that his government worked on the assumption that "delaying recognition would lead to further escalation of violence by Yugoslavia's People's Army, since the troops would necessarily regard our refusal to recognize the republics as an encouragement for their policy of conquest toward Croatia."[79] German officials claimed that they pressed for a speedy recognition respecting the EC framework – the two-month deadline given on October 10 by Dutch foreign minister Hans van der Broek (the Netherlands at the time held the EC presidency) for an overall settlement to be reached as envisaged in the October 4 Hague agreement. However, this deadline was never formally agreed upon and other EC members do not appear to have taken it as binding, even if a handful of them sympathized with Germany's substantive position.[80]

The German initiative within the EC was resisted most strongly by the United States and the UN. While not rejecting recognition of Yugoslav republics in principle, UN Secretary-General Javier Perez de Cuellar in his letter to Van der Broek of December 10 expressed apprehension that premature recognition of some of them without an overall settlement could be a "potential time bomb."[81] He added:

> Let me be clear: I am not in any way calling into question the principle of self-determination which is enshrined in the Charter of the United Nations. However, I am deeply worried that any early, selective recognition could widen the present conflict and fuel the explosive situation especially in Bosnia and Herzegovina and also Macedonia; indeed serious consequences could ensue for the entire Balkan region. I believe, therefore, that uncoordinated actions should be avoided.

On December 2, Carrington, opposing the planned decision of his own organization, wrote to van der Broek that premature recognition of Croatia by the EC "might well be the spark that sets Bosnia and Herzegovina alight."[82] Cyrus Vance, the UN envoy for Yugoslavia, assessed the situation in a December 5 conversation with US ambassador Warren Zimmermann in these terms: "My friend Genscher is out of control on this. What he is doing is madness."[83] Carrington and Vance wanted recognition to be withheld until the Yugoslav republics had all agreed on their mutual relationships. To do it before meant, in their view, that the situation was being prejudged in favor of some and at the expense of others. And that promised further inflammation of the already extreme tensions between various parties. Prophetically, Zimmermann himself cabled to Washington on December 20 that "let nobody believe that the ten thousand or so who have died so far [in Croatia] mean that violence has reached its peak. A war in Bosnia could increase that number tenfold."[84]

These cautionary voices did not prevail. Croatia (and, much less controversially, Slovenia) was recognized first by Germany on December 23 and then by the EC member states collectively on January 15, 1992. Most EC states, and principally Britain and France, were very uneasy about the action, but, following Germany's December 5 notification that it was prepared to recognize Croatia unilaterally,[85] they concurred. Fresh from a major undertaking to integrate the conduct of EC external relations, they were anxious to showcase cohesion and effectiveness of European foreign policy.[86] Not only did recognition of Croatia occur in the absence of any settlement, but also at odds with the EC's own agreed procedure for assessing the individual applications for recognition. According to the *Declaration on Yugoslavia*, the Badinter Commission was to issue an advisory opinion for the EC foreign ministers on each submission, but the German government recognized Croatia without waiting for the Commission's view. When Opinion No. 5, released on January 11, actually suggested that Croatia's constitution did not provide sufficient guarantees for protection of minorities, the EC extended recognition to that country on the set day anyway. Preempted by Germany, the EC settled for Croatia's acceptance rather than fulfillment of one of its key conditions. On the other hand, in Opinion No. 6 of the same day, the Commission took the view that Macedonia satisfied the *Guidelines*, but the EC member states did not recognize the republic because of Greece's vehement objections to its official name. The wish to display a unified front made the other members go along with Germany's recognition of Croatia; now, despite misgivings about the sagacity of the Greek position, they went along with the non-recognition of Macedonia. Instead of acting on the recommendation of the Badinter Commission, Macedonia was presented with a brand new condition: to adopt "a name that can be accepted by all parties concerned."[87] That name, it was specified afterward, was "not to include the term Macedonia."[88] If by "the normal standards of international practice" the *Guidelines* meant the classical effectiveness criteria of statehood, nowhere in the Badinter opinions or EC recognition statements (just as in those pertaining to the former Soviet republics) is there any reference to them. Recognized Slovenia and unrecognized Macedonia did satisfy them, recognized Croatia did not.

Anticipating recognition of Croatia, the Croatian Serb leadership declared the "Republic of Serbian Krajina" on December 19 and also applied for EC recognition. Not being a federal republic, its application, along with that of the "Republic of Kosova," was never as much as passed on to the Badinter Commission. A cease-fire agreement was signed in Croatia on January 2, 1992, but this was achieved only as a condition for the arrival of UN peacekeepers who were to police the areas of Croatia where Serbs formed either an outright majority or a substantial minority. Croatia began its life as an internationally recognized country without control of about one-third of its territory, but given that its government made no secret of its intention to retake it – after all, the EC recognition for all intents and purposes determined that the territories inhabited by the Croatian Serbs were rightfully part of Croatia – the truce promised to be precarious.

The prospect of Bosnian recognition radicalized the Bosnian Serb community and also encouraged those Bosnian Croats who had no commitment to a unified Bosnia and wished to attach Croat-inhabited areas to Croatia. On December 21, the day after Bosnia submitted its request to be recognized by the EC, the "Assembly of the Serbian People" created a separate Bosnian Serb republic within the Yugoslav state. The independence of the "Serbian Republic of Bosnia and Herzegovina" (more commonly known by its Serbian name "Republika Srpska") from Bosnia was then proclaimed on January 9, 1992. Also in January, the new leader of what was in effect a Bosnian branch of Tudjman's ruling party affirmed the intention of Bosnian Croats to establish in parts of Herzegovina a separate "Croat Community of Herzeg-Bosna."[89]

The EC did heed the advice of the Badinter Commission's Opinion No. 4, handed down on January 11, 1992, that Bosnia should not be recognized since "the will of the peoples of Bosnia and Herzegovina" to constitute a "sovereign and independent state cannot be held to have been fully established."[90] The Commission recommended soliciting the views of the people "possibly by means of a referendum of all the citizens of [Bosnia and Herzegovina] without distinction," that is an exercise akin to those that had taken place earlier in Slovenia and Croatia. Although the wording of this counsel suggested that there was more than one way of ascertaining the wishes of Bosnia's populace, the EC and the United States urged the vote predicated on the simple majority of all citizens without considering other options.

The difficulty with such a plebiscite was that the Bosnian Serbs, as one of three constituent nations of Bosnia, rejected simple majoritarianism as contrary to the republican constitution. Bosnia, they insisted, had a consociational system in which two peoples could not impose a constitutional change on the third one. Ambassador Zimmermann's admonition of the Bosnian Serb leader Radovan Karadzic – "why do not you participate in the referendum on independence and come to terms with the fact that with thirty percent of the population Serbs cannot be expected to dictate the outcome?"[91] – was grounded in a principle that, of course, frequently serves as a procedural benchmark of the consent of the governed, but given Bosnia's constitutional realities, it was fundamentally misguided. Stipe Mesic, for example, warned in a February 15 speech that holding a referendum on which there was no consensus among the three Bosnian peoples would lead to war.[92] Predictably, the February 29–March 1, 1992, referendum endorsed independence and, also predictably, nearly all Bosnian Serbs boycotted it. The Bosnian Croats (around 17% of the republic's total population) did partake in the exercise, but it was by no means evident that the motivation of most of them was a genuine wish to reside in an independent Bosnia rather than a calculation that Bosnia's independence from what remained of the SFRY was an indispensable intermediate step on the path to amalgamation of ethnically Croat areas with Croatia.[93]

Even though it scolded Germany for rupturing the collective non-recognition consensus, the Bush administration abandoned the earlier guarded approach toward the Baltic republics, the rest of the USSR as well as the initial phase of Yugoslav crisis and virtually replicated the strategic thinking behind the German course of action. In March 1992, the Bush administration pressed the EC for speedy recognition of Bosnia similar to the way Germany pressured it with respect to the two northeastern republics in late 1991. Ambassador Zimmermann, echoing Genscher's reasoning, wrote that "our view was that we might be able to head off a Serbian power grab by internationalizing the problem,"[94] adding:

The Community's action had changed the whole political landscape. Now the Europeans had recognized Croatia and Slovenia, and Izetbegovic's Bosnia was threatened with isolation in a Milosevic-dominated "Serbo-slavia." To keep Bosnia in international limbo would increase that isolation and assist Serbian designs. . . . I believed that early Western recognition, right after the expected referendum majority with independence, might present Milosevic and Karadzic with a *fait accompli* difficult for them to overturn.[95]

The Bosnian parliament declared independence on March 3, 1992. The Bosnian Serb leaders, absent from the Sarajevo parliament for half a year now, foretold disaster if Bosnia were to be recognized internationally. The EC did attempt to find a consensual political settlement prior to recognition in the form of the Cutileiro Plan,[96] but this initiative was subsequently, despite the initial agreement of all three parties, repudiated by the Bosnian Muslim side.[97] Nevertheless, the EC and the United States then, in a coordinated move, recognized the country on April 7. The US statement announcing the decision referred to Bosnia and Herzegovina as having met "the requisite criteria for recognition" and to "the peaceful and democratic expression of the will of [its] citizens for sovereignty."[98] If the former denoted the traditional effectiveness tests of independence, then Bosnia was far less of a *de facto* state than even Croatia. Its government did not control vast swaths of the republic's territory that were in the hands of parallel Bosnian Serb and Bosnian Croat authorities. In addition, as of April 7, two outside armies with undefined status – the JNA and the Croatian Army – operated in the republic. Their intentions were at best uncertain, yet it was evident that the Sarajevo government did not have any direct influence over them. As for the latter justification, the wish of the citizens to live together in an independent country was no less dubious now than some three months earlier when the Badinter Commission delivered its Opinion No. 4. No past referendum or plebiscite carried out without the agreement of all concerned parties led to the resolution of the underlying question that the exercise was supposed to answer, and the Bosnian independence referendum was no exception. It is nothing short of astonishing that the Bush administration found fitting to defer the acknowledgment of Macedonia until that country's resolution of the "outstanding issues" with Greece, but that the serious unresolved matters in relation to Bosnia – the last of which, as Chapter 3 notes, precluded its independence from being considered at all in 1875–8 – did not merit the same kind of postponement.

The American and European conjecture that recognition would deter the Serbs from fighting tragically failed. As Steven Burg and Paul Shoup contend, no matter how hard it might have been to reach, "only a negotiated solution agreed by all three nationalist parties could avert the mounting crisis."[99] General hostilities in Bosnia began concurrently with the EC–US decision. The fight of secessionist Bosnian Serbs, supported by the JNA, took place alongside the Bosnian Croat campaign to merge parts of Bosnia with Croatia. The Bosnian Croats were backed by Croatia and its nascent armed forces, even though the Zagreb government denied this very demand to its Serbian population and insisted on the inviolability of Croatia's borders. Rightly or wrongly, the Serbs outside Serbia as well as the Bosnian Croats, both understanding their nationhood and political loyalty in ethnic rather than civic terms, wanted to be attached to their fellow Serbs and Croats, just as they had been in Yugoslavia for over seventy years. They considered recognition to be partial to the claim of Bosnia's Muslim population and the subsequent conflict as their struggle for self-determination.

As indicated in the previous chapters, international recognition had been used as a political and strategic tool on frequent occasions. Even when primary customary norms on when and how a new state can be acknowledged are followed – and this book has endeavored to show that countries have in general sought to conform to them – existing countries still have discretion to determine when and in what overall package to extend recognition. This endows them with an opportunity to influence a particular situation. Delaying, accelerating, or putting conditions on recognition can effect conflict resolution, avert hostilities, or achieve other goals deemed important for the wider society of states. The Badinter Commission clarified what the international norms in the circumstances of a country's dissolution were, and besides Serbia and Montenegro, no state or intergovernmental organization disagreed with its findings. The panel implied that those Yugoslav republics wishing independence could be recognized in their previous borders without the assent of the "rump" SFRY government. However, while no foreign government suggested that recognition of individual republics might be premature legally, there were major disagreements, especially prior to the acknowledgment of Croatia, over whether recognition would not be premature politically. The EC and other governments had to make a choice on whether to go the "Genscher" or "Vance–Carrington–Perez de Cuellar" route. In the view of numerous participants and observers, the former course, which prevailed, was the less prudent one: it came about in the midst of dangerously unsettled conditions on the ground and without any commitment on the part of recognizing countries to intervene should the situation subsequently deteriorate.[100] But that does not change anything on the fact that norms related to acquisition of statehood that solidified in the aftermath of the main wave of decolonization – principally the prerequisite of consent by the sovereign parent government prior to recognition of a new state by third parties and the new *uti possidetis juris* – affected also the recognition of new countries in Southeastern Europe.

Whatever one's views of the timing of Croatian or Bosnian recognition, the constitutive and prescriptive effects, visible right away, became irreversible. Once broadly recognized, the new states could seek membership in international organizations, which they did, and rather successfully. Most importantly, on May 22, Bosnia and Croatia, together with Slovenia, became members of the UN. Each thus could appeal for protection of the UN Charter, including its Art. 2(4). Even prior to this date, UN SC Resolution 752 (1992) of May 15 demanded that all units of the JNA and the Croatian Army "now in Bosnia and Herzegovina must either be withdrawn, or be subject to the authority of the government of Bosnia and Herzegovina, or be disbanded and disarmed." It classified their presence in Bosnia as "interference from outside" – international recognition transformed what had been a civil war into a mix of civil war and illegitimate foreign intervention.

Resolution 757 (1992) then stated, "no territorial gains or changes brought about by violence are acceptable... and the borders of Bosnia and Herzegovina are inviolable."[101] Given that the Council had not even reacted to the plea of Slovenian President Milan Kucan on June 28, 1991, to take action against the JNA "invasion and foreign occupation," on the ground that the armed clashes in Slovenia constituted an internal Yugoslav matter,[102] the content of these resolutions was a reflection of the swift change in the political/juridical map of the Balkans.

In contrast, non-recognition left Macedonia in international limbo for months. Although in the course of 1992 it was, despite Greek protests that the "Republic of Skopje" represented a potential threat, recognized by a few states, the acknowledgment by the United States, the EC, and many other countries following their lead, was not forthcoming. In April 1993, Macedonia was admitted to the UN with the proviso that, for UN purposes, its name would provisionally be the "Former Yugoslav Republic of Macedonia" (FYROM) until differences over its name were settled. This settlement, however, was not in the offing because Macedonia rejected the EC demands of name change as an affront to its dignity. Finally, in December 1993, six EC states simply broke away from the EC position – a step threatened by Germany, and feared by the rest, in relation to Croatia – and recognized Macedonia under its UN name. The United States followed in February 1994, even though it still talked about "outstanding differences" with Greece[103] – the very differences that had been declared to be the barrier to its recognition in April 1992. Isolated on the issue, Greece first imposed crippling economic sanctions on Macedonia in February 1994, but after the European Commission had taken it to the European Court of Justice for the unilateral move, it recognized the new state under its UN name in 1995.[104] The core disagreement has not been resolved, however, and the Republic of Macedonia continues to be a unique case of a country that for most international purposes exists under a denomination different from its constitutional name.[105]

The Federal Republic of Yugoslavia, jointly proclaimed by Serbia and Montenegro on April 27, 1992, was also a casualty of uncertain legal status. It claimed that it was the continuing state of the SFRY, but this was not accepted abroad. In the views of the EC, the United States, other countries, and international organizations the SFRY, having dissolved, ceased to exist and thus the FRY was a new state.[106] As such, it had to ask for the same recognition as the other four republics, and it had to apply for membership in international organizations. The FRY refused to do either.[107] Non-recognition of its claim, however, had a smaller practical impact than had been common in the past. The dual federation was crucial to any peace settlement and the severing of diplomatic relations with the Belgrade authorities (most states continued to maintain their embassies in Belgrade, but without accreditation to the FRY), exclusion from diplomatic activities on Bosnia or complete non-participation of the FRY in the UN was thought to have been counterproductive.[108]

As in the case of other former Yugoslav republics, the EC displayed inconsistency in relation to the recognition of the FRY. On July 4, 1992, the Badinter Commission in its Opinion No. 10 advised that the FRY, being a new state, was subject to EC recognition in accordance with the *Guidelines* and *Declaration on Yugoslavia*. Although the FRY, given its position that the FRY was the continuation of the SFRY, never asked for recognition, the EC did offer one, but not under the terms suggested by the Commission. In April 1996, the EU declared that the way is open "to recognition by member states . . . of the Federal Republic of Yugoslavia as one of the successor states to the Socialist Federal Republic of Yugoslavia," but it referred to its appreciation of a bilateral treaty that normalized relations between the FRY and FYROM, not to the texts of December 16, 1991.[109] Rather than insisting on the commitment to the preconditions as in the case of the other former Yugoslav republics – particularly with respect to Kosovo, which has raised international concerns ever since it was for all practical purposes stripped of its autonomy within Serbia in 1989–90 – the EU appeared to reward the FRY for a string of commendable foreign policy acts. Besides the treaty with FYROM, it was the accession to the Dayton Peace Agreement in November 1995.

Throughout the Bosnian war the Serb entities in Croatia and Bosnia and the Croat entity in Bosnia were denied international recognition. UN SC Resolution 787 (1992) affirmed that "any entities unilaterally declared or arrangements imposed in contravention [of Bosnia and Herzegovina's territorial integrity] will not be accepted." None emerged from the war as independent states. The "Croat Community of Herzeg-Bosna" was set for extinction when the Bosnia Croat and Muslim representatives signed an agreement creating a Croat-Muslim federation within Bosnia and Herzegovina under American pressure in Washington in March 1994. The "Republic of Serbian Krajina" ceased to exist in two stages. In May and August 1995, the Croatian Army bypassed the UN peace-keepers' lines and took over Serb-held regions in three out of four UN Protected Areas.[110] Krajina's fate was sealed in November 1995 when, during the Dayton negotiations, the Serb representatives from the remaining area not yet under the Zagreb government's control, desiring to avoid the fate of their fellow Croatian Serbs, signed an agreement on the gradual transfer of the area to the Croatian government.[111] The "Republika Srpska" did survive as an entity, though not outside but within Bosnia and Herzegovina. In January 1992, the entity declared its intent to join what remained of Yugoslavia, but the Dayton Peace Agreement, including the attached new Bosnian constitution, denied it this option.

With the exception of Albania, the independence of the "Republic of Kosova" declared in October 1991 was not recognized either. In fact, outside actors did not seem to take note that it had been proclaimed, even though the United States, the EC, and others monitored the developments in Kosovo closely and the "republic" applied for EC recognition in December 1991.[112] In June 1992, the EC plainly misconstrued the Kosovo Albanian aims when it declared in the *Lisbon Declaration*:

> The Community and its member states recall that frontiers can only be changed by peaceful means and remind the inhabitants of Kosovo that their legitimate quest for autonomy should be dealt with in the framework

of the EC Peace Conference. They also call upon Albanian government to exercise restraint and act constructively.[113]

The formulation of the passage, however, was yet another piece of evidence that decolonization's conflation of non-consensual border changes from inside with the ones from outside persisted and that acts of unilateral secession, prior to 1945 internationally legitimate, continued to be viewed as internationally illegitimate.

During the crisis of 1998/9, every international attempt to deal with the violent developments stressed that Kosovo was part of the FRY and that the territorial integrity of Yugoslavia was guaranteed. UN SC Resolution 1160 (1998) affirmed "the commitment of all member states to the sovereignty and territorial integrity of the Federal Republic of Yugoslavia" and added that a solution of the Kosovo problem should be based on it. At variance with the aspirations of Kosovo Albanians, the Security Council, akin to the EC's *Lisbon Declaration*, expressed sympathy for no more than "an enhanced status for Kosovo which would include a substantially greater degree of autonomy and meaningful self-administration;" that is, roughly the status Kosovo enjoyed under the 1974 SFRY constitution. These objectives did not change with the worsening situation in Kosovo and the NATO threat of force against the FRY: in Resolutions 1199 and 1203 (1998) the Council repeated them in language identical to that of Resolution 1160. They were also reiterated in the "non-negotiable principles/basic elements" for a settlement at the Rambouillet conference.[114]

During and after the NATO military humanitarian intervention of 1999 – which otherwise generated a considerable international controversy and a split between major Western powers and Russia – the FRY was confronted with no text that would permit change in Kosovo's status without the consent of its government and the intervening countries emphasized their opposition to an independent Kosovo. Resolution 1244 (1999) that authorized a UN military and civilian presence in the province once again re-affirmed the commitment to the FRY's sovereignty and territorial integrity. The civilian component of the UN presence was "to provide an interim administration for Kosovo under which the people of Kosovo can enjoy substantial autonomy within the Federal Republic of Yugoslavia."

After almost eight years of UN administration and a year of abortive talks between Serbia and the Kosovo Albanian authorities on the final settlement of the conflict, the UN Special Envoy overseeing the negotiations, Martti Ahtisaari, recommended to the UN Security Council that UN administration Kosovo end and the province gain "independence, supervised by the international community."[115] This proposal was supported by the Kosovo Albanians and Western powers as the only viable future option for Kosovo, but rejected by Serbia and Russia as a breach of Serbia's right of territorial integrity and Resolution 1244. After several more months of fruitless talks co-mediated by the EU, the United States, and Russia, the Kosovo Albanian authorities declared unilateral independence for the second time in February 2008. Despite resistance from Serbia, Russia, China, India, and other powers, this time the Kosovo Albanians gained recognition from all the major Western powers and dozens of other countries. Still, at the time of this writing Kosovo has not been acknowledged by almost three-quarters of UN members and the United States and European powers went to great lengths to emphasize that Kosovo's recognition constitutes a *sui generis* exception to, rather than any kind of departure from, the norm of territorial integrity. The US Secretary of State's recognition statement, for example, included the following proviso:

> The unusual combination of factors found in the Kosovo situation – including the context of Yugoslavia's breakup, the history of ethnic cleansing and crimes against civilians in Kosovo, and the extended period of UN administration – are not found elsewhere and therefore make Kosovo a special case. Kosovo cannot be seen as a precedent for any other situation in the world today.[116]

Justifying Territorial Integrity and Self-Determination of Peoples

It is apparent from the foregoing account that the recognition practice of the post-Cold War period has preserved the supremacy of the principle of territorial integrity as understood since decolonization over self-determination of peoples as disclosed in the state recognition practice prior to decolonization. The two principles did not necessarily stand in opposition to each other – for example, in Slovenia or the former Czechoslovakia – but where they did, the former prevailed. Still, given the heavy human toll exerted by their clash, especially in the former Yugoslavia, the questions over the relationship between the two are bound to persist.

As seen in both this and preceding chapters, the prime justification for the presumptive rule of *uti possidetis juris* has been to foil internal, regional, and international instability. It could hardly be objected to that borders prior to independence should be presumptively protected against external military attack. Conquest has now stood outside international law for ninety years (twice as long in the Americas) and it would be inconsistent with this reality to let established jurisdictions acceding to independence, such as Western Sahara or East Timor, fall by the wayside simply on account of outside armed takeover. However, the really vexing issue is how to treat the groups that clearly refuse to be part of those jurisdictions as they become independent, and particularly when these groups object to being separated from their ethno-national group with whom they hitherto shared a country and constitutional ties. The post-colonial experience has shown that the retention of historical and colonial boundaries, which fails to take account of the actual political loyalties on the ground, can lead to failed states or continuing civil conflicts.[117]

Uti possidetis juris allows change of borders by agreement and this option was mentioned in a host of documents related to the disintegration of the USSR and the SFRY. However, international diplomacy never seriously explored it in any contentious cases prior to recognition of new states. David Owen, the co-chairman of the Steering Committee of the successor to the EC Conference on Yugoslavia established in August 1992, complained:

> My view has always been that to have stuck unyieldingly to the internal boundaries of the six republics within the former Yugoslavia ... before there was any question of recognition of these republics, as being boundaries for independent states, was a folly far greater than that of premature recognition itself. The refusal to make these borders negotiable greatly hampered the EC's attempt at crisis management in July and August 1991 and subsequently put all peacemaking from September 1991 onward within a straitjacket that greatly inhibited compromises between the parties in dispute.[118]

If the exploration of all possible consensual outcomes, including change of borders, could have possibly maintained stability and avoided fratricidal struggles – the two reasons for *uti possidetis juris*, according to the ICJ *Frontier Dispute* judgment[119] – then a question is why this has not been done. Owen contends that there were three reasons for this rigid EC stance in the Yugoslav case: (*a*) fear of opening a Pandora's box of competing claims; (*b*) conviction that drawing borders along ethnic lines is outdated; and (*c*) concern that such redrawing would have necessarily created new minorities because of many areas had intermingled rather than contiguous ethnic populations.[120] These are, in fact, typical international concerns with respect to other secessionist conflicts.[121]

Part of the rationale in the SFRY indeed seems to have been the potential negative consequences of a boundary alteration for the order and stability in other contemporary and prospective self-determination disputes, particularly on the territory of the concomitantly crumbling USSR. The fear that a precedent of border change achieved in the wake of violence or a threat of violence, could encourage other groups to use similar tactics in other places echoed the domino theory that had developed during decolonization. Whatever the worth of such mechanistic conjectures, they cannot provide automatic guidance to particular situations, especially those where the conversion of internal borders into international ones would itself produce new unwilling minorities and create conflict, as it did in both the SFRY and the USSR.[122] Would not a territorial compromise prior to recognition of Bosnia, if the Bosnian Muslim leadership could have been persuaded by international diplomacy to think in that direction, have been better than war, particularly when this war was anticipated so widely and no foreign country volunteered to fight those within Bosnia who resisted the ex-Yugoslav republic's independence in its previous borders? Would not a bargain which could have given each group something – and if not making all of them happy at least making each more or less equally unhappy – have been preferable to ignoring the claims of some even at the risk of worsening the conflict?

A major reason why this has never been suggested is almost certainly normative antagonism toward claims based on ethnic or racial exclusivity. This hostility goes back to the end of World War II and goes beyond the concerns for order and stability. Despite the Cold War and the very sharp ideological divisions among states, virtually all governments extolled, at least verbally, virtues of civic nationhood. Their motivations were diverse, but their views were unmistakable in a case such as Bantustans in apartheid South Africa. During the negotiations leading to the adoption of the UN Covenant on Civil and Political Rights in the 1960s as well as UN GA Resolution 2625 and the Helsinki Final Act in the 1970s, all of which dealt with self-determination of peoples, Western states in effect argued that groups living in a democratic society whose human and minority rights were respected had no reason to strive for change of international borders.[123] They appeared to have come to believe that given the right constellation of democracy and a variety of rights, diverse people could coexist, or learn to coexist, within any given jurisdiction.[124] The solution to the problem of external self-determination in the post-colonial and non-colonial context lay in extensive internal self-determination. That was the initial reaction to the centrifugal forces within the SFRY. When it was clear that the USSR and SFRY were on their way to dissolution, this belief was reflected in the conditions given to the successor republics. It was also very much mirrored in the proposed solutions by intergovernmental organizations to conflicts involving attempted secessions from these republics.[125]

But as this conception undoubtedly prevailed both with respect to the former USSR and SFRY, and as multi-ethnic democracy has been set as a goal by Western states in Bosnia and Kosovo,[126] it is not clear how much has been left of the original understanding of the idea of self-determination. Though the three peoples did agree in the Dayton Peace Agreement to preserve Bosnia as an independent state, this only materialized by applying extreme pressure from without, including the use of force against one party to the civil war.[127] Revealingly, the preamble of Bosnia's Dayton constitution noted no more than the commitment of its three peoples to "the sovereignty, territorial integrity, and political independence of Bosnia and Herzegovina in accordance with international law."[128] The preamble did not even feign that the people of Bosnia and Herzegovina united to constitute an independent state despite the fact such proclamations have been a staple of constitutional texts all around the world since the *US Declaration of Independence*.

The country had to be placed under international administration and the protection of foreign troops to have any chance of internal survival. Coming to possess nearly unlimited authority, its head, the high representative, can, *inter alia*, overrule any decision by any domestic authority or dismiss any public official, elected no less than appointed, without any chance of appeal by, and without being accountable to, the citizens of Bosnia and Herzegovina.[129] Whether or not one finds the comparison of the high representative to colonial rule of the British Raj in India[130] apt or thinks that the international venture in post-Dayton Bosnia is a case of "neo-imperialism,"[131] it is indisputable that the ideas of self-determination and sovereignty were always the opposite of government by foreigners. The Berlin Congress (1878) also opted for international administration of Bosnia, but the whole premise of that decision was the denial of sovereignty to it because of the lack of demonstrable will of Bosnia's inhabitants to form a common independent state. That outsiders should guarantee sovereign countries against internal breakup on account of their international legitimacy was, at any rate, a doctrine of Ferdinand VII and Metternich, not liberal-minded governments. Indeed, the Anglo-American practice of recognizing *de facto* statehood, embedded as it was in the belief in the consent of the governed, emerged through opposition to this legitimist creed.

Similar questions arose with respect to Kosovo, which, though a part of a sovereign country, was too placed under international administration with final *de facto* authority.[132] The FRY consented to this arrangement but only after NATO's military intervention, unauthorized by the UN Security Council, had long been in progress. Bent on independence for more than a decade, the Kosovo Albanians were even more encouraged by the intervention to pursue this ambition; yet Kosovo was consistently proclaimed to be an integral part of the FRY and its government was adamant that it would not assent to such an option under any circumstances. After 1999, the future of Kosovo within Serbia without international administration was even more difficult to imagine than the future of Bosnia and Herzegovina without one. The major Western powers' way out of this self-made conundrum was to abandon eventually their opposition to Kosovo's unilateral independence while insisting on their continued general support for the post-decolonization norm of territorial integrity: they came to declare Kosovo to be an outside-of-the-norm situation and to support its independence on account of its unique circumstances. As indicated, this argument did not convince most countries[133] and it left the indignant Russians feeling entitled to consider Abkhazia and South Ossetia to be exceptional situations and to acknowledge them on account of their special circumstances,[134] thus seemingly perpetuating disarray in state recognition.

Regardless of how these unsettled cases may evolve, should territorial integrity, as a general matter, continue to have decisive normative superiority over self-determination, either for the sake of stability or multi-ethnic democracy, or human rights, or some other externally identified goal? It is clear that Bosnia and Kosovo have raised this question in a way that *de facto* states in the post-colonial world or the former USSR have not. The conclusion of this study will attempt to answer this question in light of previous recognition practice.

Notes

1. Aside from Eritrea, considered in the previous chapter, they are: Armenia, Azerbaijan, Belarus, Bosnia and Herzegovina, Croatia, the Czech Republic, Estonia, Georgia, Kazakhstan, Kyrgyzstan, Macedonia, Moldova, Latvia, Lithuania, Russia, Serbia, Montenegro (from 1992 to 2003, Serbia and Montenegro formed the Federal Republic of

Yugoslavia; then from 2003 to 2006 the Union of Serbia and Montenegro), Slovakia, Slovenia, Tajikistan, Turkmenistan, Ukraine, and Uzbekistan.

2. See, among others, Lawrence S. Eastwood Jr., "Secession: State Practice and International Law After the Dissolution of the Soviet Union and Yugoslavia," *Duke Journal of Contemporary and International Law,* 3 (1992), pp. 299–349; John Dugard, "Is the Case of Yugoslavia a Precedent for Africa?," *African Journal of International and Comparative Law,* 5 (1993), pp. 163–75; Fawn and Mayall, "Recognition, Self-Determination and Secession in Post-Cold War International Society"; Gerry J. Simpson, "The Diffusion of Sovereignty: Self-Determination in the Post-Colonial Age," *Stanford Journal of International Law* 26 (1993), pp. 255–86; Allen Buchanan, "Democracy and Secession," in Margaret Moore (ed.), *National Self-Determination and Secession* (Oxford: Oxford University Press, 1998); Donald Horowitz, "Self-Determination: Politics, Philosophy and Law," in Margaret Moore (ed.), *National Self-Determination and Secession* (Oxford: Oxford University Press, 1998); and Peter Radan, *The Break-up of Yugoslavia and International Law* (London: Routledge, 2002).

3. See David Raič, *Statehood and the Law of Self-Determination* (The Hague: Kluwer Law International, 2002).

4. The 2006 dissolution of the Union of Serbia and Montenegro also falls into this category.

5. Hurst Hannum, "Rethinking Self-Determination," *Virginia Journal of International Law,* 34 (1993), p. 38.

6. The same is true for Eritrea, which split from Ethiopia after the Addis Ababa government had assented to, and lost, an independence referendum in Eritrea.

7. See Edward W. Walker, *Dissolution: Sovereignty and the Breakup of the Soviet Union* (Lanham, MD: Rowman & Littlefield, 2003), p. 2.

8. Constitution of the USSR, October 7, 1977, William B. Simons (ed.), *The Constitutions of the Communist World* (Alphen aan den Rijn, the Netherlands: Sijthoff & Noordhoff, 1980), p. 369.

9. Supreme Council of the Republic of Lithuania on the Restoration of the Lithuanian State, March 11, 1990, Charles F. Furtado Jr. and Andrea Chandler (eds.), *Perestroika in the Soviet Republics: Documents on the National Question* (Boulder, CO: Westview Press, 1992), p. 182.

10. Resolution by the Extraordinary Session of the Third Congress of People's Deputies of the USSR on the Decisions of March 10–12, 1990 by the Supreme Soviet of the Lithuanian SSR, March 15, 1990, ibid., pp. 183–4.

11. Statement by Press Secretary Fitzwater on the Restoration of Lithuanian Independence, March 11, 1990, *Public Papers of the Presidents of the United States: George Bush, 1990,* Vol. 1 (Washington, DC: Government Printing Office, 1991), p. 348. See also Nikolas K. Gvosdev, "The Formulation of an American Response to Lithuanian Independence, 1990," *East European Quarterly,* 29 (1995), p. 33.

12. See United Kingdom Materials on International Law, *The British Year Book of International Law 1991* (Oxford: Clarendon Press, 1992), p. 565.

13. See Appeal to the Parties to the Treaty on Conventional Armed Forces in Europe and to the Member States of the Conference on Security and Cooperation in Europe, November 9, 1990, at http://www.letton.ch/lvx_ap14.htm

14. Lithuania did do so, for the period of 100 days, on June 29, 1990. See Christine Gray, "Self-Determination and the Break-up of the Soviet Union," in *Yearbook of European Law 1992* (Oxford: Clarendon Press, 1993), p. 481.

15. Remarks to the Supreme Soviet of the Republic of the Ukraine in Kiev, Soviet Union, August 1, 1991, *Public Papers of the Presidents of the United States: George Bush, 1991*, Vol. 2, pp. 1005–8; The passage that drew most fire read: "Americans will not support those who seek independence in order to replace a far-off tyranny with a local despotism. They will not aid those who promote suicidal nationalism and ethnic hatred."

16. Brent Scowcroft, "Bush Got It Right in the Soviet Union," *The New York Times*, August 18, 1991.

17. "Demise of the Soviet Union: Chronology, 1991," Background Brief, UK Foreign & Commonwealth Office, March 1992, p. 13.

18. Rafal Rohozinski, "The August Coup: A Thirty Day Chronology, 18 August – 17 September 1991," in J. L. Black (ed.), *USSR Document Annual 1991*, Vol. 2 (Gulf Breeze, FL: Academic International Press, 1993), p. 103.

19. See George Bush and Brent Scowcroft, *A World Transformed* (New York: Vintage Books, 1998), pp. 538–9.

20. Statement by an extraordinary EPC Ministerial Meeting concerning the Baltic States, August 27, 1991, *European Foreign Policy Bulletin* (henceforth EFPB), Document 91/251.

21. See ibid.; and "US to Establish Diplomatic Relations with Baltic States," September 2, 1991, *US Department of State Dispatch*, Vol. 2, 35 (1991).

22. See Décision du Conseil d'état de l'URSS sur la Reconnaissance de l'Indépendance de la République de Lettonie, September 6, 1991, at http://www.letton.ch/lvrurss. htm#URSS The Baltic republics joined the CSCE on September 10 and the UN on September 17.

23. The UN General Assembly, for example, spoke in Resolution 47/21 of November 1992, of "particular satisfaction that independence was restored in Estonia, Latvia and Lithuania."

24. While the Helsinki Final Act, like the OAU Charter, affirms the principles of inviolability of frontiers and territorial integrity of states only in the context of *interstate* relations, the Charter of Paris extends it to *intrastate* relations as well. The signatories of the document reaffirmed "the equal rights of peoples and their right to self-determination in conformity with the Charter of the United Nations and with the relevant norms of international law, including those relating to territorial integrity of states." The 1990 CSCE Copenhagen Document contains even stronger language in this regard: it stipulates that persons belonging to national minorities do not have "any right to engage in any activity or perform any action in contravention of . . . the principle of territorial integrity of states."

25. "US Approach to Changes in the Soviet Union," September 4, 1991, *US Department of State Dispatch*, Vol. 2, 36 (1991).

26. "Ukrainians Vote for Independence," December 2, 1991, *US Department of State Dispatch*, Vol. 2, 49 (1991).

27. James Baker, III with Thomas DeFrank, *The Politics of Diplomacy: Revolution, War and Peace 1989–1992* (New York: G.P. Putnam's Sons, 1995), pp. 560–2.

28. Statement by an EPC Ministerial Meeting concerning Ukraine, December 2, 1991, EFPB, Document 91/427.

29. "Ukrainians Vote for Independence," *US Department of State Dispatch*.

30. All the Soviet republics except Georgia (it joined the CIS in late 1993) proclaimed that "with the establishment of the Commonwealth of Independent States, the Union of

Soviet Socialist Republics ceases to exist." See Alma Ata Declaration, December 21, 1991, *International Legal Materials*, 31 (1992), p. 149.

31. The six republics were Russia, Ukraine, Armenia, Kazakhstan, Belarus, and Kyrgyzstan. Diplomatic ties with the rest were delayed until "they have made commitments to responsible security policies and democratic principles, as have the other states." See Address to the Nation on the Commonwealth of Independent States, December 25, 1991, *Public Papers of the Presidents of the United States: George Bush, 1991*, Vol. 2, p. 1654.

32. Statement concerning the Future Status of Russia and other Former Soviet Republics, December 23, 1991, EFPB, Document 91/469.

33. Statement by an Extraordinary EPC Ministerial Meeting concerning the "Guidelines on the Recognition of New States in Eastern Europe and in the Soviet Union," December 16, 1991, EFPB, Document 91/464.

34. They were Armenia, Azerbaijan, Belarus, Kazakhstan, Moldova, Turkmenistan, Ukraine, and Uzbekistan. See Statement concerning the Recognition of Former Soviet Republics, December 31, 1991, EFPB, Document 91/472.

35. They were Kyrgyzstan and Tajikistan. See Statement on the Recognition of the Republics of the Commonwealth of Independent States, January 15, 1992, EFPB, Document 92/008; In this statement the EC also summarized the key commitments of the recognized states: the acceptance by the republics concerned of the commitments contained in the CFE Treaty and in the other arms reduction agreements; their acceptance of other international obligations, and of the commitments outlined by the Helsinki Final Act, the Charter of Paris, and all other CSCE documents; their acceptance of obligations related to economic questions in general and the question of foreign debts of the former USSR in particular; their commitment to solve in a peaceful manner and through the appropriate international mechanisms and procedures their differences in conformity with the UN Charter and the CSCE; and their adherence to the Non-Proliferation Treaty as non-nuclear weapon states.

36. "America and the Collapse of the Soviet Empire: What Has to Be Done," December 12, 1991, *US Department of State Dispatch*, Vol. 2, 50 (1991).

37. This pattern would repeat itself later in Georgia in 1992/3 after the republic had been recognized despite the presence of Russian troops on its territory.

38. See "America and the Collapse of the Soviet Empire: What Has to Be Done."

39. See Statement on the Recognition of the Republic of Georgia, March 23, 1992, EFPB, Document 92/111.

40. The EC transformed into a "European Union" on January 1, 1993. The Conference for Security and Co-operation in Europe was renamed "Organization for Security and Co-operation in Europe" on January 1, 1994.

41. As for sovereignty disputes which did not result in civil war, the EU endorsed the sovereignty and territorial integrity of Ukraine in the context of Crimea's bid to secede. See Statement on the Situation in Crimea, May 25, 1994, Document 94/179.

42. The EU declaration on the Trans-Dnester conflict in Moldova of December 4, 2002, for instance, underlined that "a solution to the conflict must be found which fully respects the territorial integrity of the Moldovan state." A document of the OSCE's 1996 Lisbon Summit, to give another example, endorsed "legal status of Nagorno-Karabakh defined in an agreement based on self-determination which confers on Nagorno-Karabakh the highest degree of self-rule within Azerbaijan." See Statement of the OSCE Chairman-In-Office, December 3, 1996, Annex 1 to the Lisbon Summit Document.

43. There were six "constituent nations" in Yugoslavia according to the 1974 constitution: the Serbs, the Croats, the Montenegrins, the Bosnian Muslims, the Slovenes, and the Macedonians. Their territorial units were the six republics: Serbia, Croatia, Montenegro, Bosnia and Herzegovina, Slovenia, and Macedonia.

44. See Republic of Slovenia Assembly Declaration of Independence and Constitutional Decision on the Sovereignty and Independence of the Republic of Croatia, June 25, 1991, Trifunovska, *Yugoslavia Through Documents*, pp. 286–90 and 299–301. The "right to secession" was mentioned only in the preamble. The constitution spelled out no procedure for its operationalization.

45. Statement by the Federal Executive Council, June 25, 1991, *Review of International Affairs* (Belgrade), 42 (June 20, 1991), p. 25.

46. It is crucial to note that neither Slovenia nor Macedonia had any substantial Serb population (Slovenia is almost completely ethnically Slovene) and that both republics left the federation without a full-scale war.

47. The Serbs drew their arguments from the constitution's preamble that stated that the country was formed by "the nations of Yugoslavia, proceeding from the right of every nation to self-determination, including the right to secession" and from Art. 1 that Yugoslavia was a community of "voluntarily united nations and their socialist republics." The support for the territorial-republican as opposed to ethnonational interpretation of the right of self-determination could be found in Arts. 2 and 3 (Art. 3 characterized the republics as "states") and Art. 5 which postulated that "the territory of the Socialist Federal Republic of Yugoslavia is a single unified whole and consists of the territories of the socialist republics." According to Art. 5, the borders between republics could only be altered by agreement between the republics concerned. See Constitution of the Socialist Federal Republic of Yugoslavia, February 21, 1974, Simons (ed.), *The Constitutions of the Communist World*, pp. 428, 444–5.

48. In addition to being a "constituent nation" of the SFRY, those Serbs living in Croatia and Bosnia had constituent nation status in the two republics, according to the 1974 Croatian and Bosnian republican constitutions. In the same fashion, the Bosnian Croats were a "constituent nation" of Bosnia, and not merely a part of the larger Croat people, a "constituent nation" of the SFRY.

49. By "nationality" the constitution understood an ethno-national minority whose ethnic kin formed a nation-state outside the SFRY. In the case of the Kosovo Albanians this was Albania.

50. Statement on the Situation in Yugoslavia, June 20, 1991.

51. Baker, *The Politics of Diplomacy*, p. 482.

52. Ibid., pp. 482–3, 480. The United States declared already in May it "will not encourage or reward secession; it will respect any framework, federal, confederal, or other, on which the people of Yugoslavia peacefully and democratically decide. We firmly believe that Yugoslavia's external or internal borders should not be changed unless by peaceful consensual means." See "US Policy Towards Yugoslavia," May 24, 1991, *US Department of State Dispatch*, Vol. 2, 22 (1991).

53. See Peter Radan, "The Badinter Arbitration Commission and the Partition of Yugoslavia," *Nationalities Papers*, 25 (1997), p. 543, and Richard Caplan, "The European Community's Recognition of New States in Yugoslavia: The Strategic Implication," *The Journal of Strategic Studies* 21 (1998), p. 25. Earlier, the EC declared that "a united and democratic Yugoslavia stands the best chance to integrate itself into the new Europe." See Informal Ministerial Meeting on Yugoslavia, March 26, 1991, EFPB, Document 91/35.

54. Baker, *The Politics of Diplomacy*, p. 483.

55. Most Croatian Serbs boycotted the republican referendum on independence and instead voted in a May 1991 counter-referendum, unauthorized by the Zagreb government, on remaining in Yugoslavia. After its affirmative outcome, the leadership of Croatian Serbs declared Krajina's "union" with Serbia.
56. Statement by an Extraordinary EPC Ministerial Meeting concerning Yugoslavia, August 27, 1991, EFPB, Document 91/252; On September 3, 1991 participants at a CSCE meeting declared that territorial gains within Yugoslavia brought about by violence are unacceptable; this statement became explicitly noted in UN SC Resolution 713 (1991), the first UN resolution on the Balkan wars.
57. Since the abrogation of autonomous powers of Vojvodina and Kosovo in 1989–90 presidency members representing the two Serbian provinces had been chosen by the Serbian government in Belgrade.
58. Stipe Mesic, *The Demise of Yugoslavia: A Political Memoir* (Budapest: Central European University Press, 2004), p. 359.
59. Public Statement, October 3, 1991, *Review of International Affairs* (Belgrade), 42 (October 5 – November 5, 1991), p. 11.
60. Statement by an Informal Meeting of Ministers of Foreign Affairs concerning Yugoslavia, October 5, 1991, EFPB, Document 91/295.
61. Statement concerning the Situation in Yugoslavia, October 28, 1991, ibid., Document 91/328.
62. See paras. 21 and 31, UN Document S/23169, October 25, 1991; The Secretary-General makes clear in his memoirs that the UN did not consider the SFRY presidency legitimate after its "hijacking" by Serbia and Montenegro. One practical consequence of the "de-recognition" he mentions was that the letter of vice president of the rump presidency was not allowed to circulate as an official document in the Security Council. See Javier Perez de Cuellar, *Pilgrimage for Peace: A Secretary-General's Memoir* (New York: St. Martin's Press, 1997), pp. 482, 487–8.
63. Assessments and Positions of the SFRY Presidency concerning the Proclamation of the Independence of the Republic of Croatia and Slovenia, October 11, 1991, Trifunovska, *Yugoslavia Through Documents*, p. 354.
64. See UN Document S/23169, Annex II.
65. Declaration by an extraordinary EPC Ministerial Meeting on Yugoslavia, November 8, 1991, EFPB, Document 91/349.
66. Opinion No. 1 of the Arbitration Commission of the Peace Conference on Yugoslavia, November 29, 1991, Trifunovska, *Yugoslavia Through Documents*, p. 417; Opinion No. 8 further explained that "the existence of a federal state, which is made up of a number of separate entities, is seriously compromised when a majority of these entities, embracing a greater part of the territory and population, constitute themselves as sovereign states with the result that federal authority may no longer be effectively exercised." See Opinion No. 8 of the Arbitration Commission of the Peace Conference on Yugoslavia, July 4, 1992, ibid., p. 635.
67. Opinion No. 1 also stated, in contrast to the argument here, that "the existence or disappearance of the State is a question of fact" and that "the effects of recognition by other states are purely declaratory." However, this assertion is in tension with Opinion No. 8 which says that "while recognition of a state by other states has only declarative value, such recognition, along with membership of international organizations, bears witness to these states' conviction that the political entity is a reality and confers on it certain rights and obligations under international law." If recognition indeed *confers* international rights and obligations, then its effects can be described as "purely

declaratory" only with considerable difficulty. See Steve Terrett, *The Dissolution of Yugoslavia and the Badinter Arbitration Commission* (Aldershot, UK: Ashgate, 2000), pp. 278, 282–3.

68. Crawford, "State Practice and International Law in Relation to Secession," p. 100.
69. Both the reasoning and conclusion of this and other Commission opinions have been met with trenchant critique by academic international lawyers. While I share many of the criticisms offered, these accounts have so far failed to grapple with the fact that no foreign state reached conclusions on the issues of self-determination, sovereignty, or borders that deviated from those of the Badinter Commission. For critical assessments of the Commission's work see, among others, Radan, *The Break-up of Yugoslavia and International Law,* ch. 7; Terrett, *The Dissolution of Yugoslavia and the Badinter Arbitration Commission;* Hurst Hannum, "Self-Determination, Yugoslavia, and Europe: Old Wine in New Bottles?," *Transnational Law and Contemporary Problems,* 57 (1993), pp. 57–69; Marc Weller, "International Law and Chaos," *Cambridge Law Journal,* 52 (1993), pp. 6–9; Matthew Craven, "The European Community Arbitration Commission on Yugoslavia," *The British Year Book of International Law 1995* (Oxford: Clarendon Press, 1996); and Michla Pomerance, "The Badinter Commission: The Use and Misuse of the International Court of Justice's Jurisprudence," *Michigan Journal of International Law,* 20 (1998), pp. 31–58.
70. Paul Szasz, "Discussion on the Fragmentation of Yugoslavia," *American Society of International Law Proceedings,* 88 (1994), p. 47.
71. See Craven, "The European Community Arbitration Commission on Yugoslavia," p. 367.
72. Quoted in Laura Silber and Alan Little, *The Death of Yugoslavia,* revised ed. (London: Penguin, 1996), p. 192.
73. This exercise, just as the later referenda by Bosnian Serbs and Kosovo Albanians, was declared illegal by the republican government.
74. Position of the SFRY Presidency, December 18, 1991, Trifunovska, *Yugoslavia Through Documents,* pp. 478–9.
75. Opinion No. 2 of the Arbitration Commission of the Peace Conference on Yugoslavia, January 11, 1992, ibid., pp. 474–5.
76. Opinion No. 3 of the Arbitration Commission of the Peace Conference on Yugoslavia, January 11, 1992, ibid., p. 480.
77. Statement by an Extraordinary EPC Ministerial Meeting concerning Yugoslavia, December 16, 1991, EFPB, Document 91/465.
78. Germany, of course, neither planned to fight the JNA nor did it believe that the United States or the other EC states, many of which actually opposed recognition of republics prior to the overall settlement, would. Helmut Kohl's government hoped that recognition would have, above all, a deterring effect on the Serbs. Even one of the staunchest defenders of Germany's policy toward Yugoslavia in 1991 admits that "the essential flaw in German policy was ... that Germany herself could not really contribute to the policies that logically followed from her own attitude; namely, to the protection, by military means if necessary, of the smaller Yugoslav republics and nations against Serb aggression." See Michael Libal, *Limits of Persuasion: Germany and the Yugoslav Crisis, 1991–1992* (Wesport, CT: Praeger, 1997), p. 163.
79. Hans-Dietrich Genscher, *Building a House Divided: A Memoir by the Architect of Germany's Reunification,* transl. by Thomas Thornton (New York: Broadway Books, 1998), p. 489.

80. See Norbert Both, *From Indifference to Entrapment: The Netherlands and the Yugoslav Crisis, 1990–1995* (Amsterdam: Amsterdam University Press, 2000), pp. 125, 132–3 and Caplan, *Europe and the Recognition of New States in Yugoslavia*, pp. 20–2.
81. See UN Document S/23280, Annex IV, December 11, 1991.
82. Quoted in Susan L. Woodward, *Balkan Tragedy: Chaos and Dissolution After the Cold War* (Washington, DC: Brookings Institution, 1995), p. 184.
83. Warren Zimmermann, *Origins of a Catastrophe: Yugoslavia and its Destroyers* (New York: Times Books, 1996), p. 177.
84. Ibid., p. 178.
85. Statement of Minister of State for Foreign Affairs, Seiler-Albring, December 5, 1991, Klabbers, Koskenniemi, Ribbelink, and Zimmermann, *State Practice Regarding State Succession and Issues of Recognition: The Pilot Project of the Council of Europe*, pp. 227–8.
86. The question of imminent German recognition surfaced right in the wake of the Maastricht Treaty and the EC members did not want to be publicly seen as marring the prospects of the newly instituted Common Foreign and Security Policy. But privately grave misgivings remained. French President Francois Mitterand asked in an early December newspaper interview whether states that were pressing for immediate recognition planned to dispatch troops to support the fact of Croat and Slovene statehood. Roland Dumas, his foreign minister, later went as far as to say that by recognizing Croatia German diplomacy fueled the war in Bosnia. See, respectively, Grant, *The Recognition of States*, p. 175, and Michael Thumann, "Between Ambition and Paralysis – Germany's Policy Toward Yugoslavia 1991–3," *Nationalities Papers*, 25 (1997), p. 581.
87. Statement on the Former Yugoslav Republic of Macedonia, May 4, 1992, EFPB, Document 92/164.
88. Declaration on the Former Yugoslavia, June 27, 1992, ibid., Document 92/254.
89. Woodward, *Balkan Tragedy*, pp. 194, 472 (n. 139); Mate Boban, Tudjman's protégé, and a hand-picked choice to lead the main Bosnian Croat party, formally proclaimed the independence of "Herzeg-Bosna" on July 3, 1992. In his conversations with foreign officials the Croatian president did not hide his preference to divide Bosnia between Croatia and Serbia. Tudjman discussed the division of Bosnia with Milosevic several times, at one point even while the JNA bombarded towns and villages in Croatia. What Tudjman did not want Serbia to have in Croatia he was apparently willing to seek in Bosnia. For more details, see Zimmermann, *Origins of a Catastrophe*, pp. 181–6, and Perez de Cuellar, *Pilgrimage for Peace*, p. 483.
90. Opinions No. 4 on International Recognition of the Socialist Republic of Bosnia and Herzegovina by the European Community and its Member States, January 11, 1992, Trifunovska, *Yugoslavia Through Documents*, p. 486.
91. Zimmermann, *Origins of a Catastrophe*, p. 187.
92. Steven L. Burg and Paul S. Shoup, *The War in Bosnia-Herzegovina: Ethnic Conflict and International Intervention* (Armonk, NY: M.E. Sharpe, 1999), p. 108.
93. Croatia and those Bosnian Croats who wanted to amalgamate with Croatia thought that this goal would be easier to accomplish in a Bosnia already separated from Yugoslavia. I agree with Burg and Shoup who argue, "in the end the Croat vote for the Bosnian government's version of the referendum must be understood in the light of Zagréb's desire to see Bosnia separated from Yugoslavia." See ibid., p. 107.
94. Quoted in Emil Nagengast, "German and U.S. Intervention Against Yugoslav Sovereignty," in Andrew Valls (ed.), *Ethics in International Affairs* (Lanham, MD: Rowman and Littlefield, 2000), p. 160.

95. Zimmermann, *Origins of a Catastrophe*, pp. 191–2.

96. Statement of Principles for New Constitutional Arrangements for Bosnia and Herzegovina, March 18, 1992, B. S. Ramcharan (ed.), *The International Conference on the Former Yugoslavia*, Vol. 1 (The Hague: Kluwer Law International, 1997), pp. 24–7.

97. See Jose Cutileiro, "Letter to the Editor," *The Economist*, December 9, 1995.

98. The United States on this occasion recognized also Slovenia and Croatia, but, following the EC consensus, not Macedonia.

99. Burg and Shoup, *The War in Bosnia-Herzegovina*, p. 105.

100. Besides the already mentioned names, Martti Koskenniemi judged "the use of recognition as pressure . . . a tragic mistake." David Owen called the Bosnian recognition, as it was carried out, "foolhardy in the extreme" and Robert Badinter "a large error." See, respectively, Martti Koskenniemi, "National Self-Determination Today: Problems of Legal Theory and Practice," *International and Comparative Law Quarterly*, 43 (1994), p. 208; David Owen, *Balkan Odyssey*, updated ed. (San Diego, CA: Harcourt Brace and Company, 1997), p. 377; and Robert M. Hayden, "Reply," *Slavic Review*, 55 (1996), p. 768.

101. Later, literally dozens of UN SC resolutions would repeat the commitment of UN member states to "the sovereignty, territorial integrity and political independence of the Republic of Bosnia and Herzegovina and the responsibility of the Security Council in this regard" and "preserving the territorial integrity of all the States [in the Balkan region] within their *internationally recognized borders*" (italics added).

102. See Perez de Cuellar, *Pilgrimage for Peace*, p. 477; Silber and Little, *The Death of Yugoslavia*, p. 156; and James Steinberg, "International Involvement in the Yugoslav Conflict," in Lori Damrosch (ed.), *Enforcing Restraint: Collective Intervention in Internal Conflicts* (New York: Council on Foreign Relations, 1993), p. 38.

103. Statement released by the White House on US Recognition of the Former Yugoslav Republic of Macedonia, February 9, 1994, *US Department of State Dispatch*, Vol. 5, No. 8 (1994).

104. See Petros Sioussiouras, "The Process of Recognition of the Newly Independent States of Former Yugoslavia by the European Community: The Case of the Former Socialist Republic of Macedonia," *The Journal of Political and Military Sociology*, 32 (2004), p. 15.

105. On November 4, 2004, however, the United States, without coordinating with Greece or the EU, decided to accept Macedonia's constitutional name. See US Department of State Daily Press Briefing, November 4, 2004, at http://2001–2009.state.gov/r/pa/prs/dpb/2004/37819.htm The unilateral move, which generated Greek protests, appeared to be designed to sway Macedonian voters not to reject a key US–EU-mediated constitutional accord giving more rights to the ethnic Albanian minority in a referendum scheduled three days later.

106. UN SC Resolution 757 (1992) referred to "the former Socialist Federal Republic of Yugoslavia" and noted that the claim by the FRY "to continue automatically the membership of the former Socialist Federal Republic of Yugoslavia in the United Nations has not been generally accepted." In Resolution 777 (1992) the Security Council, "considering that the state formerly known as the Socialist Federal Republic of Yugoslavia has ceased to exist," recommended "to the General Assembly that it decide that the Federal Republic of Yugoslavia (Serbia and Montenegro) should apply for membership in the United Nations" as a new state. The General Assembly did just that in its Resolution 47/1.

107. The question of the FRY's status was resolved only with the fall of the Milosevic government in October 2000, after which the new government abandoned the claim of legal continuity with the SFRY and, as one of the successor states, applied for, and was admitted to, membership in the UN, OSCE, International Monetary Fund, World Trade Organization, and other international organizations.
108. The FRY was excluded from the work of the General Assembly and the Economic and Social Council, but as the SFRY's UN membership was never formally suspended or terminated, the FRY delegation was not excluded from the UN altogether.
109. Statement on Recognition by EU Member States of the Federal Republic of Yugoslavia, April 6, 1996, EFPB, Document 96/103.
110. Though the Croatian operations involved scenes reminiscent of earlier scenes of ethnic cleansing undertaken by the Bosnian Serb army against the Muslim population, international protests were tepid partly because the Croatian government was "re-integrating" its own, that is, internationally recognized, territory. The term "re-integration" was, for instance, used in the UN Secretary-General's report on Croatia to the Security Council. See para. 32, UN Document S/1995/730, August 23, 1995.
111. See Basic Agreement on the Region of Eastern Slavonia, Baranja, and Western Sirmium, November 12, 1995, *International Legal Materials*, 35 (1996), pp. 186–7; UN SC Resolution 1025 (1995) welcomed the agreement, affirmed that "the territories of Eastern Slavonia, Baranja, and Western Sirmium, known as Sector East, are integral parts of the Republic of Croatia" and decided to end UN peacekeeping presence in Croatia by January 15, 1996. On this day the Council in its Resolution 1037 established an eleven-month-long United Nations Transitional Administration for Eastern Slavonia, Baranja, and Western Sirmium to oversee the implementation of the November 12, 1995, agreement. By January 1997, the unrecognized "Republic of Serbian Krajina" had been wiped off the map completely and the entire Croatian territory had fallen under direct control of the Zagreb government. Even before this date, the FRY and Croatia formally affirmed that they recognize each other's boundaries in a bilateral Agreement on Normalization of Relations of August 23, 1996. For this agreement, see *International Legal Materials*, 35 (1996), pp. 1220–2.
112. See Letter of the Chairman of the Assembly of the Republic of Kosova addressed to the Extraordinary EPC Meeting held in Brussels on December 16, 1991, December 21, 1991, Snezana Trifunovska (ed.), *Former Yugoslavia Through Documents: From its Dissolution to the Peace Settlement* (The Hague: Martinus Nijhoff, 1999), pp. 767–9.
113. Statement on the Situation in Yugoslavia, June 15, 1992, EFPB, Document 92/226.
114. Quoted in Marc Weller, "The Rambouillet Conference on Kosovo," *International Affairs*, 75 (1999), pp. 225. The second draft of the Rambouillet document, which Russia claimed its envoy had been excluded from seeing before it was presented to the two parties and which Yugoslavia claimed had not been negotiated at all but rather imposed, provided for an international conference on Kosovo's ultimate status in three years. Its Art. 1(3) contained an ambiguous reference to "the will of the people" as forming a basis of the final settlement and, as Marc Weller writes, "the delegation of Kosovo obtained certain assurances that this formula actually establishes a legal right to hold a referendum of the people of Kosovo (as opposed, say, to the people of the FRY or the Serb Republic)." Being suspicious that this was what was in reality meant by the reference, the joint Yugoslav–Serb delegation rejected Art. 1 and, objecting to other provisions of the package, also the entire Rambouillet proposal.
115. UN Document S/2007/168, March 26, 2007.

116. "U.S. Recognizes Kosovo as Independent State," February 18, 2008, at http://2001–2009.state.gov/secretary/rm/2008/02/100973.htm. For the same basic position of the EU, which was reflected in the recognition decisions of those EU members who have recognized Kosovo, see Presidency Conclusions, Council of the European Union, December 14, 2007, para. 69 at http://www.consilium.europa.eu/ueDocs/cms_Data/docs/pressData/en/ec/97669.pdf

117. See John Dugard, "A Legal Basis for Secession – Relevant Principles and Rules," in Julie Dahlitz (ed.), *Secession and International Law* (The Hague: T. M. C. Asser Press, 2003), p. 95.

118. Owen, *Balkan Odyssey*, p. 34. A similar point is made in Kamal S. Shehadi, *Ethnic Self Determination and the Break-up of States*, Adelphi Paper No. 283 (London: The International Institute for Strategic Studies, 1993), pp. 28–30; Owen discusses in some detail (pp. 32–5) what in retrospect was a very unique proposal of the Dutch government – at the time in charge of the EC presidency – that the option of boundary changes should be looked at. The Netherlands suggested in the July 13, 1991 telegram "a voluntary redrawing of internal borders as a possible solution" and pointed out that "if the aim is to reduce the number of national minorities in every republic, better borders than the present ones could be devised." If the republics were to become independent, the proposal stressed, "the first principle of Helsinki should be applied, which means that the frontiers of Yugoslavia's constituent republics can only be changed 'in accordance with international law, by peaceful means and by agreement.'" One can only speculate what course would the events have taken had the Dutch proposition, introduced less than three weeks after the first shots in Slovenia, not been so promptly rejected by the other EC members on July 29, 1991. On the Dutch proposal, see also Both, *From Indifference to Entrapment: The Netherlands and the Yugoslav Crisis*, pp. 107–9.

119. Of course, the purpose of *uti possidetis juris* in Latin America was not to obviate civil conflicts, if that is what the ICJ meant by "fratricidal struggles," but only interstate conflicts. The requirement of *de facto* statehood presupposed that a new state's population consented, if only tacitly, to its independence.

120. Owen, *Balkan Odyssey*, p. 34.

121. Not infrequently, there are also concerns about economic viability of secessionist/parent entities. See Gertrude E. Schroeder, "On the Economic Viability of New Nation States," *Journal of International Affairs*, 45 (1992), pp. 549–74.

122. See Steven Ratner, "Drawing a Better Line: *Uti Possidetis* and the Borders of New States," in Robert J. Beck and Thomas Ambrosio (eds.), *International Law and the Challenge of Ethnic Groups: The State System and the Challenge of Ethnic Groups* (New York: Chatham House, 2002), p. 252.

123. See Cassese, *Self-Determination of Peoples*, pp. 277–96 and 302–12.

124. See Pomerance, *Self-Determination in Law and Practice*, p. 38, and Ratner, "Drawing a Better Line," pp. 251, 273–4. On the seminal importance of democracy for the maintenance of existing states, especially in the post-Cold War period, see Amitai Etzioni, "The Evils of Self-Determination," *Foreign Policy*, 89 (Winter 1993), pp. 21–35; Strobe Talbott, "Self-Determination in an Interdependent World," *Foreign Policy*, 118 (Spring 2000), pp. 152–62; and Philip Alston, "'Peoples' Rights: Their Rise and Fall'," in Philip Alston (ed.), *Peoples' Rights* (Oxford: Oxford University Press, 2001), pp. 270–1.

125. This was no less the premise of UN SC 688 (1991), which served as a basis for the establishment of a no-fly zone to protect the Iraqi Kurds. It called for the Iraqi

government to support and respect human and political rights of the Kurds, but, at the same time, declared the UN members' support for the territorial integrity of Iraq.

126. For example, in a speech during the Dayton negotiations, US Secretary of State Warren Christopher said that the United States and the EU "share the conviction that Europe's post-Cold War peace must be based on the principle of multiethnic democracy." See Warren Christopher, *In the Stream of History: Shaping Foreign Policy for a New Era* (Stanford, CA: Stanford University Press, 1998), p. 364.

127. Authorized by UN Resolution 836 (1993) on the protection of the "safe areas," NATO conducted massive air strikes against the Bosnian Serb army in August and September 1995 around the Sarajevo safe area and many other parts of Serb-held territories. The intervention had the effect of reinforcing the Croat-Muslim offensive against the Bosnian Serbs and contributed to major territorial losses of the "Republika Srpska" prior to the pre-Dayton cease-fire.

128. Constitution of Bosnia and Herzegovina, Annex 4 to the General Framework Agreement for Peace in Bosnia and Herzegovina, December 14, 1995.

129. The extent of the high representative's authority was set in Annex 10 to the General Framework Agreement for Peace in Bosnia and Herzegovina. It was then greatly expanded by the subsequent decisions of the Peace Implementation Council (PIC), which in December 1995 subsumed the International Conference for the Former Yugoslavia (ICFY) and to which the high representative is accountable. See, in particular, Chapter XI of the Bonn Conclusions, December 10, 1997; *Declaration of the Peace Implementation Council*, May 24, 2000; and High Representative Decisions at www.ohr.int

130. See Gerald Knaus and Felix Martin, "Travails of the European Raj," *Journal of Democracy*, 14 (2003), pp. 60–74.

131. Richard K. Betts, "The Lesser Evil: The Best Way out of the Balkans," *The National Interest*, 64 (Sumer 2001), p. 54.

132. Section 1(1) of United Nations Interim Administration Mission in Kosovo Regulation on the Authority of the Interim Administration Mission in Kosovo reads: "All legislative and executive authority with respect to Kosovo, including the administration of the judiciary, is vested in UNMIK and is exercised by the Special Representative of the Secretary-General." See UN document UNMIK/REG/1999/1, July 25, 1999.

133. Additional evidence of this skepticism is the passing of UN General Assembly Resolution A/RES/63/3 in October 2008 by which the majority of UN members voting on the resolution supported Serbia's request to submit the question of the legality of Kosovo's unilateral declaration of independence to the International Court of Justice.

134. See, for example, Interview of President Medvedev with BBC Television, August 26, 2008 at http://www.kremlin.ru/eng/speeches/2008/08/26/2131_type82915type82916_205790. shtml

Conclusion

Statehood remains the golden chalice from which all wish to drink.[1]

In their endorsement of human rights, democratic countries, including the entire UN, are not sufficiently prepared for the present historical wave of creating national states. They have not found a satisfactory answer to the question of how to ensure the realization of every nation's natural right to self-determination.

(Croatia's President Franjo Tudjman in 1991[2])

This book opened with the observation that claims of statehood continue to arise in, and provide a variety of serious challenges to, contemporary international society. The process of decolonization did not put a stop to demands of independence; they have arisen in both post-colonial and non-colonial settings. There is widespread acknowledgment that the idea of self-determination has not exhausted itself.[3] But while there is continuing general agreement that self-determination cannot be made into a universal positive right – aptly captured by former UN Secretary-General Boutros Boutros-Ghali's statement that "if every ethnic, religious or linguistic group claimed statehood, there would be no limit to fragmentation"[4] – there is no comparable consensus on who should qualify for international recognition. What is more, scholarly reflection on this topic has been scant in recent years.

The purpose of this concluding chapter, in view of what has been written so far, is to cast doubt on the view that nineteenth-century Anglo-American thought on self-determination and state recognition has been superseded by subsequent ideas. *De facto* statehood has proved to be the only viable international standard when there is no agreement among relevant parties on who, and by what self-determination procedure, can become a state – which has been the case for the majority of time in the last 200 years. Even decolonization, where a near-universal global consensus did develop on this question, did not pass without subsequent denial of statehood to those who felt trapped in the new states against their will.

It would be erroneous to pretend that the *de facto* standard has been or can be without difficulties when applied to particular situations. First, there have been occasions where states could not concur whether a particular entity was or was not a *de facto* state. Britain refused to recognize Chile in 1824 because the small archipelago of Chiloe claimed by the Santiago government was still under Spanish control, yet this fact had been no obstacle to the US acknowledgment in 1822. Colombia accused the United States of premature recognition of Panama in 1903. The United States and Britain had diametrically opposed views on whether Israel was a *de facto* state when it declared independence in 1948. Second, the *de facto* recognition doctrine was premised on the absence of coercive, non-neutral intervention into civil conflicts, but occasionally such interventions not only occurred, but they were also decisive for the outcomes of those conflicts. It is quite possible that Montenegro or Serbia would have been defeated by, rather than liberated from, the Ottoman Empire in 1878 had it not been for Russia's threat and use of force against the Ottomans.

Third, the standard was not able to preclude the incorporation of pockets of peoples into new states against their will, for example, in the cases of Greece and Montenegro in the nineteenth century. It could provide no easy answer on how to draw boundaries of new states where diverse but intermingled populations held different political allegiances, and had to be supplemented from the very beginning by the condition that the new states treat all their citizens equally. And fourth, as it was predicated on the assumption that in the course of contests over sovereignty inhabitants stay where they are, the standard could provide no guidance in case massive involuntary population transfers did occur.

Yet it is unlikely that all these difficulties are different from those encountered in application of other international norms or principles. For one, international relations constantly generate unprecedented as well as highly complex situations. Various normative imperatives can work against each other and original assumptions informing the advent of a norm can be missing in later contexts. The emergence of Israel did not have, in several respects, any close historical parallel. The British might have urged Russian non-intervention during the Great Eastern Crisis, but once the intervention did take place they could not wish it or its consequences away. In addition, international society, being an anarchical association, is not able to assure common judgments or positions. States, even the closest allies, may in good faith interpret the same reality differently because what the "facts" are may not be plainly obvious.[5] The Americans did not regard Spanish possession of Chiloe as really affecting the overall picture of Chile's independence. The British perhaps did not either, but they had more to risk by appearing to trample upon their own declared principles in the eyes of the fellow members of the Quintuple Alliance.

Furthermore, there is scarcely an international rule or principle that cannot be stretched or misused. If suspect cases of recognition of *de facto* statehood occurred and were left to stand, then so did dubious cases of self-defense, treaty denunciation, proclamation of an exclusive economic zone, and so on. Still, admitting that respect for international norms is not perfect does not mean that they matter little: even the most powerful countries have had to worry about facing negative consequences in case justifications for their actions were found generally unconvincing. Finally, norms can never operate as a complete foreign policy blueprint. As moral and/or legal standards of proper conduct, norms constrain and shape foreign policy choices, but they do not fully determine these choices. That an entity ought not to be recognized unless it is a *de facto* state does not tell us how outsiders may help should the emergence of that entity be occurring under contentious circumstances, what, if any, conditions to attach to recognition, or how to time it. The exercise of discretionary, political judgment in these matters is both inescapable and of paramount importance – it can, as seen, make a difference between peace and war.

The principal virtue of *de facto* statehood as the recognition standard is that it demonstrates to outsiders, better than anything else devised so far, a political community's sanction of independent existence. The Grotian–Jeffersonian notion of habitual obedience of a new authority is an observable phenomenon. Though it may not be without ambiguities in particular instances, its lengthy track record of working reasonably well makes it as compelling a proof of a population's will as may be obtained in an international system that lacks the authority to ensure an agreed upon procedure for assessing it in individual cases.[6] The concept is certainly a far more reliable test and prescriptive guide of a population's wishes than is non-consensual referendum. Not a single independence referendum took place in Latin America, yet all the states that had emerged in Central and South America by the late 1830s still exist 180 years later. The same is true of Haiti, Greece, Belgium, Liberia, Romania, Panama, Bulgaria, Finland, Poland, Estonia, Syria, Israel, and Jordan. Croatia and Bosnia did hold it, only to implode in appalling violence weeks later. Even if the concept of *de facto* statehood was not razor sharp, each time it was put into practice it was clear what it was *not*: a substantial section of a claimant's population actively opposed to independence as evidenced by the claimant's lack of effective control over the claimed territory. That Croatia and Bosnia did not enjoy habitual obedience of their populace in December 1991 – January 1992 and April 1992, respectively, was unambiguous.

But even if one is persuaded that foreign recognition ought not to occur in the absence of *de facto* statehood, a more general question remains: how should outsiders respond to civil contests over sovereignty? There is probably no better general answer than that disclosed by the nineteenth-century British approach set forth during the contests in Spanish and Portuguese America. That approach sought first of all to discourage changes to the existing distribution of sovereignty by proposing reforms through non-coercive diplomatic techniques such as persuasion, good offices, mediation, and conciliation. Indeed, this is the starting point for external involvement today as well. At present these proposals contain suggestions of changes in the area of autonomy, minority, indigenous, human, civil, cultural, economic, and other relevant rights.[7] Recent external mediation efforts have not been without success, whether in achieving the autonomy of Gagauzia within Moldova (1994), Crimea within the Ukraine (1998), Northern Ireland within the United Kingdom (1998), and Aceh within Indonesia (2005), or in achieving provisional constitutional settlements containing procedures for future settling of independence claims, as in the cases of Bougainville (2001), Southern Sudan (2002/5), and Montenegro (2003). However, the really thorny problem has been what to do if some or all parties to a contest reject foreign proposals, such as when four Yugoslav republics persisted in their claims of independence in the fall of 1991 and a considerable segment of the population of two of those republics, with no less determination, rejected them. There is, and can be, no simple prescription, particularly in case the contest acquires direct external or massive humanitarian dimensions. But in general, the Castlereagh–Canning dictum ought to apply: siding with neither existing states nor challengers of their territorial integrity, foreign authorities should encourage parties to find any consensual solution grounded in the *de facto* state(s) and, if their intervention does become necessary, they should abstain from direct coercive involvement in the substance of the contest.

Leaving everything on the table means that measures such as voluntary population exchanges[8] and partition[9] ought not to be *a priori* ruled out as part of the settlement.[10] Although they are deplorable and offensive to contemporary Western sensibilities, the alternatives, the events of last twenty years have shown, are no less problematic: either practical acquiescence to, if not formal acceptance of, their actual forcible occurrence or coercive intervention to undo them. Involuntary movements of populations are generally very difficult to reverse and outside intervention may perpetuate rather than cease them. NATO interventions to stop the ethnic cleansing perpetrated by Serbs first in Bosnia and then in Kosovo inadvertently contributed to the exodus of Croatian and Kosovo Serbs. While many Croatian Serbs have returned to their homes, the majority has not, and most Kosovo Serbs remain outside Kosovo despite the presence of foreign troops there.

As for practical acquiescence to, or outside reversal of, partitions, neither option allows for normal self-government associated with the concept of statehood in international law. From 1993 until the Russian military intervention of 2008, the UN Security Council ritualistically proclaimed Abkhazia to be an integral part of Georgia. It did so even though Abkhazia was never effectively controlled by independent Georgia and was a relatively compact, indigenously governed entity since 1994. Neither could the Georgian government exercise its sovereignty over what were legally its citizens, nor could the Abkhazian government actually governing them, act as their sovereign authority internationally. Somaliland has existed *de facto* since 1991, yet the entity has been blocked from assuming normal relations with the outside world. Despite being the only area of post-colonial Somalia with consistently functional government, Somaliland's governance as well as social and economic development have suffered from the inability of its authorities to receive foreign aid and loans, to enter into trade and other cooperative agreements, and to participate in regional and global organizations. On the other end of the scale, Bosnia and Herzegovina has been held together only thanks to the robust international administration that in fact, if not in law, is the real sovereign authority.

International order is a social order and it is natural that countries would want to help others mitigate and settle their internal conflicts. It is no less natural that they would want to promote, either individually or collectively, their domestic values abroad. Britain, as shown, engaged in both kinds of activities already in the first half of the nineteenth century. That the United States or the European Union (EU) today encourage human rights and peaceful coexistence of all regardless of their ethnic background around the globe is both legitimate and laudable. Yet the post-colonial world is also one of equal sovereignty: a state's political authority, its right to govern, does not extend beyond its boundaries. Countries may offer amicable assistance in resolving foreign intrastate conflicts, but that facilitative role does not bring with it a *prima facie* entitlement to impose a settlement on unwilling parties to the conflict. Although powerful governments are occasionally tempted to behave as if they had such an entitlement, they do not exhibit similar willingness to assume the obligation to underwrite the settlement against internal disruptions or to be accountable for their conduct to the people who have to live with the settlement. No less than in the past, these governments seek to prevent their responsibilities toward others from being too costly and protracted and from colliding with their national interests, priorities, and obligations. At most they have displayed a "limited liability approach."[11] Even in post-1995 Bosnia and post-1999 Kosovo they showed reluctance to apply all-out measures to stem the flight of local minorities or to protect them against vengeful local majorities.[12] They have certainly not parted with their right to withdraw from foreign missions at their own discretion. But besides the twin issue of rights and obligations vis-à-vis foreign sovereignty contests, there is another matter, at least for Western countries: compelling people who demonstrate beyond any reasonable doubt that they do not want to be together to coexist despite that goes against international liberal thought and practice of the pre-decolonization past. That tradition admitted only one conceivable reason that would justify international society to guarantee, either in law or in fact, the territorial integrity of its members against their citizens: the prevention of direct harm to third parties, as when the Treaties of Versailles and St. Germain barred Germany and Austria from uniting in the absence of the League of Nations consent.

Furthermore, an instrumental argument can be made that important objectives such as human rights, democracy, interethnic tolerance, and regional stability would fare better under the *de facto* self-determination/recognition regime than under the contemporary self-determination/recognition regime, which privileges existing states irrespective of their internal reality. *De facto* states may be asked to fulfill various conditions prior to their recognition. Their very legitimization would make them amenable to external influence to a degree that their illegitimate standing cannot. Such legitimization would also counter the very instability and problems that are inherent in politically unsettled circumstances, especially if these are the legacy of armed conflict.[13] From 1994 to 2008, Abkhazia was separated from Georgia only by a cease-fire. While this freezing of the conflict might have, from afar, seemed stable and at any rate preferable to hard choices on the contested question of statehood, tens of thousands of civilians displaced by the 1992–4 war were unable to return home or to begin life in new homes, persisting economic embargoes stunted growth and contributed to the rise of criminal and smuggling networks, and regional tensions continued to fester, re-igniting military confrontation in the wake of armed clashes between Georgian troops and Russian peacekeepers in South Ossetia. On the other hand, the present robustness of international norms against forcible territorial revisionism across international boundaries would likely discourage – in dramatic contrast to the pre-1945 world – coercive irredentism by or against recognized *de facto* states.[14]

Perhaps most importantly, the internal coherence of *de facto* states' body politic would greatly reduce the likelihood of state failure and violence with external or humanitarian repercussions. That cannot be assumed with, say, Bosnia: given that the country descended into the 1992–5 inferno because its peoples were unable to agree on constituting a common independent state, it may be unduly optimistic to expect them to do so once foreign military and administrative presence end. Although this hope may, of course, materialize, the historical record of foreign social and constitutional engineering – whether short- or long-term, whether attempted by the United States in the Caribbean and Central America in the first three decades of the twentieth century or by the European empires in their "uncivilized" overseas colonies or by the United States in Afghanistan and Iraq after 2001 – is rather sobering. According to one prolific scholar of post-war Bosnia as well as international state-building, after more than a decade since Dayton, "the Bosnian state still lacks a secure basis in Bosnian society and commands little social and political legitimacy."[15]

Even if all this is accepted, objections may be raised that a departure from the upholding of the territorial integrity of states in some places may open a Pandora's box of sovereignty claims – and bring additional instability – all around the globe. In the last forty-five years, the dread of the domino effect, so reminiscent of the trepidation of the Holy Allies first in Latin America and then in Europe, penetrated the psyche of statespersons far beyond the post-colonial world. Britain used it as a justification for its weapon sales to Nigeria as its key African partner was engaged in a brutal fight against Biafra's secession. The members of the European Community referred to it as they dismissed the Dutch Foreign Ministry mediation proposal for border change in the initial days of the Yugoslav conflict.

Keeping in mind the potential precedent-setting impact of foreign policy decisions is undoubtedly a prudent approach. Russia's recognition of Abkhazia and South Ossetia in the aftermath of Western recognition of Kosovo demonstrated that even precedent-sensitive foreign policy justifications may not achieve their desired effect if they are not accepted by major powers. However, international relations are not an arena in which one thing leads to another in an easily predictable, mechanical fashion. Events do not just happen: human beings make choices. In thinking about, and planning for, secession from the parent country, they respond to local conditions at least as much as – and likely more than – the external environment.[16] Furthermore, the external environment may itself offer contradictory messages and lessons. Aside from reacting to the Nigerian army massacres of 1966, the Biafrans were likely more inspired by UN GA Resolution 1514's Wilsonian paragraph 2 proclaiming the right of all peoples to self-determination than its paragraph 6 that pronounced the territorial integrity of countries to be sacrosanct. The Biafrans could also have been dissuaded by the lesson of the UN-backed defeat of Katanga in 1963, but they were not. The defeat of Biafra in 1970 then could have deterred the Bangladeshis in 1971, but it did not. More recently, the Isaaqs of Somaliland, the Bosnian Serbs and Croats, the Karabakh Armenians, the Chechens, the Abkhazians, or the Kosovo Albanians all made bids for independence in circumstances when they could have reckoned that their respective chances for eventual foreign recognition were quite poor. None was restrained by the post-decolonization territorial integrity norm.

To the extent that the conduct of parties to intrastate conflict is influenced by the external environment, one may take issue with a departure from the current self-determination/recognition regime for an additional reason. It may be contended that even if this regime has not led to a reduction in violence, the *de facto* regime would positively encourage it by placing a premium on the attainment of territorial control. This book does not offer easy answers on the problem of violence. If its historical survey is any guide, then violence is unlikely to be extirpated from conflicts over statehood – there will probably always be those who will see no other means left to respond to what they regard as intolerable injustice or rebellion. However, there are reasons to believe that a non-interventionist regime in which only *de facto* independent states are recognized would discourage violence at least somewhat. For a secessionist group that can expect no coercive help from others, a *de facto* independent state is exceedingly hard to achieve against the opposition from the parent state. Resorting to violence is at minimum very risky because the secessionists may loose against what typically are the more powerful parent governments. On the other hand, if the parent state can expect the neutrality of, and no coercive help from, third parties, it may seek a peaceful compromise with prospective secessionists. Calculations are different in a regime that, as a matter of preexisting doctrine, favors certain types of claims over others. Such a regime has given incentives to resort to violence both to those feeling normatively protected, such as the governments of Nigeria (1968–70), Pakistan (1971), Croatia (1995), the FRY (1998–9), and Sri Lanka (2008–9), as well as to those normatively disadvantaged who conclude their basic interests are in peril, such as the Bosnian Serbs and Croats and the Kosovo Albanians after the acknowledgment of Bosnia and Herzegovina and the FRY in their existing borders.

It is doubtful that any system of international legitimacy will inoculate groups that are deeply dissatisfied with the states in which they presently find themselves against seeking their salvation in independence. We can conclude this not only from all the post-decolonization cases mentioned in this book, but also when we appreciate that even such democratic and prosperous countries as Canada, Spain, France, Belgium, and Britain have for years had to contend with their own separatist movements. The architects of nineteenth-century British and American foreign policy grasped this reality almost 200 years ago, and they thought that those feeling discontented or oppressed had a right to change their condition by becoming independent. At the same time they believed that judging the justice of foreign peoples' causes was fraught with immense difficulties; that there were normative and practical limits to what outsiders could do on their behalf; and that the primary responsibility of third parties was to prevent or assuage harm to themselves and their citizens. New claimants could be welcomed into the fold of sovereign states only on the basis of indigenously established *de facto* statehood. It is unlikely that contemporary international society has outgrown the need for that wisdom.

Notes

1. Dominic McGoldrick, "Yugoslavia – The Responses of the International Community and of International Law," in M. Freeman and R. Hanson (eds.), *Current Legal Problems: Collected Papers*, Part 2 (Oxford: Oxford University Press, 1996), p. 386.
2. Address Delivered by the President of the Republic of Croatia Franjo Tudjman to the Croatian Assembly, May 30, 1991, *Review of International Affairs* (Belgrade) 42 (June 20, 1991), p. 16.
3. See, among others, Alexis Heraclides, "Secession, Self-Determination and Non-Intervention: In Quest of Normative Symbiosis," *Journal of International Affairs*, 45 (1992), pp. 399–420; Robert McCorquodale, "Self-Determination Beyond the Colonial Context and its Potential Impact on Africa," *African Journal of International and Comparative Law*, 4 (1992), pp. 592–608; Simpson, "The Diffusion of Sovereignty: Self-Determination in the Post-Colonial Age"; Hurst Hannum, "The Specter of Secession: Responding to Claims for Ethnic Self-Determination," *Foreign Affairs*, 77 (March/April 1998), pp. 13–18; Adam Roberts, "Beyond the Flawed Principle of National Self-Determination," in Edward Mortimer (ed.), *People, Nation and State: The Meaning of Ethnicity and Nationalism* (London: I. B. Tauris, 1999); and Martin Griffiths, "Self-Determination, International Society and World Order," *Macquarie Law Journal*, 3 (2003), pp. 29–49.
4. B. Boutros-Ghali, *An Agenda for Peace* (New York: United Nations, 1992), p. 9.
5. See Brownlie, "Recognition in Theory and Practice," p. 633 and Warbrick, "States and Recognition in International Law," p. 259.
6. For an argument that popular sovereignty is impossible to capture institutionally without considerable ambiguities, even in the domestic setting of mature democracies, see Margaret Canovan, *The People* (Cambridge: Polity, 2005), pp. 88–121.
7. This arena of "internal self-determination" is today where most scholarly interest in self-determination lies. See, for instance, chapters on this topic by Patrick Thornberry, Allan Rosas, and Jean Salmon in Christian Tomuschat (ed.), *Modern Law of Self-Determination* (Dordrecht, the Netherlands: Martinus Nijhoff, 1993); Cassese, *Self-Determination of Peoples*, pp. 346–59; Hurst Hannum, *Autonomy, Sovereignty, and Self-Determination: The Accommodation of Conflicting Rights*, rev. ed. (Philadelphia, PA: University of Pennsylvania Press, 1996); and Ruth Lapidoth, *Autonomy: Flexible Solutions to Ethnic Conflict* (Washington, DC: US Institute of Peace Press, 1997).
8. See, among others, Maynard Glitman, "US Policy in Bosnia: Rethinking a Flawed Approach," *Survival*, 38 (1997), pp. 71–2; David Miller, "Secession and the Principle of Nationality," in Margaret Moore (ed.), *National Self-Determination and Secession* (Oxford: Oxford University Press, 1998), p. 72; and Adam Roberts, "Communal Conflict as a Challenge to International Organization: The Case of the Former Yugoslavia," in Olara A. Otunu and Michael W. Doyle (eds.), *Peacemaking and Peacekeeping for the New Century* (Lanham, MD: Rowman & Littlefield, 1998), p. 41.
9. See, for example, Robert W. Tucker and David C. Hendrickson, "America and Bosnia," *The National Interest*, 33 (Fall 1993), p. 26; Chaim Kaufmann, "Possible

and Impossible Solutions to Ethnic Civil Wars," *International Security*, 20 (1996), pp. 136–75; Kaufmann, "When All Else Fails: Separation as a Remedy for Ethnic Conflicts, Ethnic Partitions and Population Transfers in the Twentieth Century," *International Security*, 23 (1998), pp. 120–56; Hannum, "The Specter of Secession," pp. 17–18; Betts, "The Lesser Evil," pp. 58–65; Lalonde, *Determining Boundaries in a Conflicted World*, pp. 232–40; and Ratner, "Drawing a Better Line."

10. The partition option was explicitly considered in the 2007 Kosovo status talks co-mediated by the EU, the United States, and Russia, but under circumstances biased against it. Serbia continued to appeal to its right of territorial integrity and the Kosovo Albanians believed at that stage – having seen the endorsement by Western powers of the Ahtisaari proposal recommending Kosovo's independence in its existing borders – that they could get independence in the entire territory of Kosovo. See Marc Weller, "Kosovo's Final Status," *International Affairs*, 84 (2008), p. 1226.

11. James Mayall, "The Limits of Progress: Normative Reasoning in the English School," in Cornelia Navari (ed.), *Theorizing International Society: English School Methods* (Basingstoke, UK: Palgrave Macmillan, 2009), p. 225.

12. See Susan L. Woodward, "Bosnia and Herzegovina: How Not to End Civil War," in Barbara F. Walter and Jack Snyder (eds.), *Civil War, Insecurity and Intervention* (New York: Columbia University Press, 1999), pp. 99–102 and Julie A. Mertus, "Operation Allied Force: Handmaiden of Independent Kosovo," *International Affairs*, 85 (2009), p. 472.

13. On the instability associated with unrecognized *de facto* situations, see Barry Bartmann, "Political Realities and Legal Anomalies: Revisiting the Politics of International Recognition," in Tozun Bahceli, Barry Bartmann, and Henry Srebrnik (eds.), *De Facto States: The Quest for Sovereignty* (London: Routledge, 2004), p. 14, and Dov Lynch, *Engaging Eurasia's Separatist States: Unresolved Conflicts and De Facto States* (Washington, DC: United States Institute for Peace, 2004), p. 127.

14. See Robert Jackson and Mark W. Zacher, *The Territorial Covenant: International Society and the Stabilization of Boundaries*, Working Paper No. 15 (Vancouver, Canada: Institute of International Relations, 1997) and Mark W. Zacher, "The Territorial Integrity Norm: International Boundaries and the Use of Force," *International Organization*, 55 (2001), pp. 215–50; this is evident even from post-1990 recognition cases. Despite preferences of Armenia, Serbia, and Croatia to unite with their co-ethnic secessionists across what became international boundaries, international society opposed their aspirations in word and in deed.

15. David Chandler, *Empire in Denial: The Politics of State-Building* (London: Pluto Press, 2006), p. 69.

16. See Stephen M. Saideman, "Is Pandora's Box Half Empty or Half Full? The Limited Virulence of Secessionism and the Domestic Sources of Disintegration," in David A. Lake and Donald Rothchild (eds.), *The International Spread of Ethnic Conflict: Fear, Diffusion, and Escalation* (Princeton, NJ: Princeton University Press, 1998).

Bibliography

Collections of Primary Sources

Annual Register. London: J. Dodsley, 1779–80.

British and Foreign State Papers. Multiple Vols. London: H.M. Stationery Office, 1814–.

"Demise of the Soviet Union: Chronology, 1991." Background Brief. UK Foreign & Commonwealth Office, March 1992.

Documents of Herbert Hoover, Representing the United States and Dr. Rudolf Holsti, Representing Finland: 1918–1920. Stanford, CA: Hoover War Library, 1938.

Documents of the United Nations Conference on International Organization. Multiple Vols. London: United Nations Information Organization, 1945–55.

European Foreign Policy Bulletin. Multiple Vols.

The House of Commons Parliamentary Papers 1801–1900. Multiple Vols. Cambridge: Chadwyck-Healey Microform Publishing Services, 1980–.

International Legal Materials. Multiple Vols.

League of Nations Official Journal: Special Supplement No. 3 (October 1920).

The Monthly Summary of the League of Nations. Multiple Vols.

Papers Relating to the Foreign Relations of the United States. Multiple Vols. Washington, DC: Government Printing Office, 1861–.

Public Papers of the Presidents of the United States: George Bush. Multiple Vols. Washington, DC: Government Printing Office, 1989–93.

Review of International Affairs (Belgrade). Multiple Vols.

United Kingdom Materials on International Law, in *The British Year Book of International Law 1991.* Oxford: Clarendon Press, 1992.

US Department of State Dispatch. Multiple Vols.

USSR Document Annual 1991. Vol. 2. Gulf Breeze, FL: Academic International Press, 1993.

Anderson, Frank Malloy, ed. *The Constitutions and Other Select Documents Illustrative of the History of France, 1789–1901.* Minneapolis, MN: The H. W. Wilson Company, 1904.

Anderson, M. S., ed. *Documents of Modern History: The Great Powers and the Near East 1774–1923.* London: Edward Arnold, 1970.

Bashkina, Nina N. et al., eds. *The United States and Russia: The Beginning of Relations, 1765–1815.* Washington, DC: Government Printing Office, 1980.

Basler, Roy P., ed. *Collected Works of Abraham Lincoln.* Vol. 5. New Brunswick, NJ: Rutgers University Press, 1953.

Benson, Arthur and Viscount Esher, ed. *The Letters of Queen Victoria*, Vol. 3. London: John Murray, 1907.

Blaustein, Albert P., Jay Sigler, and Benjamin R. Beede, eds. *Independence Documents of the World.* 2 Vols. Dobbs Ferry, NY: Oceana Publications, 1977.

Boutros-Ghali, B. *An Agenda for Peace.* New York: United Nations, 1992.

Ford, Worthington, ed. *Writings of John Quincy Adams.* Vol. 6. New York: Macmillan, 1916.

Fortescue, Sir John, ed. *The Correspondence of King George the Third.* Vol. 5. London: Macmillan and Co., 1928.

Frankland, N., ed. *Documents on International Affairs 1955.* Oxford: Oxford University Press, 1958.

Freitag, Sabine and Peter Wende, eds. *British Envoys to Germany, 1816–1866*. Vol. 1. Cambridge: Cambridge University Press, 2000.

Furtado Jr., Charles F. and Andrea Chandler, eds. *Perestroika in the Soviet Republics: Documents on the National Question*. Boulder, CO: Westview Press, 1992.

Giunta, Mary A., ed. *The Emerging Nation: A Documentary History of the Foreign Relations of the United States under the Articles of Confederation, 1780–1789. Volume 1: Recognition of Independence*. Washington, DC: National Historical and Records Commission, 1996.

—— *Documents on the Emerging Nation: US Foreign Relations 1775–1789*. Wilmington, DE: Scholarly Resources, 1998.

Gooch, G. P., ed. *The Later Correspondence of Lord John Russell, 1840–1878*. Vol. 2. London: Longmans, 1925.

Grewe, Wilhelm G., ed. *Sources Relating to the History of the Law of Nations*. Band 2, Vol. 2. Berlin: Walter de Gruyter, 1988.

Hackworth, Green H., ed. *Digest of International Law*. Vol. 1. Washington, DC: Government Printing Office, 1940.

Hertslet, Edward, ed. *The Map of Europe by Treaty*. 4 Vols. London: Harrison and Sons, 1875.

Holborn, Louise W., ed. *War and Peace Aims of the United Nations*. Vol. 1. Boston, MA: World Peace Foundation, 1943.

Holland, Thomas Erskine, ed. *The European Concert in the Eastern Question: A Collection of Treaties and Other Public Acts*. Oxford: Clarendon Press, 1885.

Hopkins, James F., ed. *The Papers of Henry Clay*. Vol. 3. Lexington, KY: University of Kentucky Press, 1963.

Israel, Fred, ed. *Major Peace Treaties of Modern History, 1648–1967*. Vol. 1. New York: Chelsea House Publishers, 1967.

Kirk-Greene, A. H. M., ed. *Crisis and Conflict in Nigeria: A Documentary Sourcebook 1966–1970*. Vol. 2. London: Oxford University Press, 1971.

Kossmann, E. H. and A. F. Mellink, eds. *Texts Concerning the Revolt of the Netherlands*. London: Cambridge University Press, 1974.

LaFeber, Walter, ed. *John Quincy Adams and American Continental Empire*. Chicago, IL: Quadrangle Books, 1965.

Link, Arthur S., ed. *The Papers of Woodrow Wilson*. Vols. 37 and 63. Princeton, NJ: Princeton University Press, 1980–2.

Makarov, A. N. and Ernst Schmitz, eds. *Digest of the Diplomatic Correspondence of the European States 1856–1871*. Vol. 1. Berlin: Carl Heymanns Verlag, 1932.

Mamatey, Victor. The United States Recognition of the Czechoslovak National Council of Paris (September 3, 1918): Documents. *Journal of Central European Affairs* 13 (1953): 49–56.

Manning, William R., ed. *Diplomatic Correspondence of the United States Concerning the Independence of the Latin American Nations*. 3 Vols. New York: Oxford University Press, 1925.

Moore, John B., ed. *A Digest of International Law*. Vol. 1. Washington, DC: Government Printing Office, 1906.

Parry, Clive, ed. *The Consolidated Treaty Series*. Vol. 63. Dobbs Ferry, NY: Oceana Publications, 1969.

Pribram, Alfred, ed. *The Secret Treaties of Austria-Hungary*. Vol. 2. Cambridge, MA: Harvard University Press, 1921.

Ramcharan, B. S., ed. *The International Conference on the Former Yugoslavia*. Vol. 1. The Hague: Kluwer Law International, 1997.

Scott, James Brown, ed. *Official Statements of War Aims and Peace Proposals: December 1916 to November 1918*. Washington, DC: Carnegie Endowment for International Peace, 1921.

Simons, William B., ed. *The Constitutions of the Communist World*. Alphen aan den Rijn, the Netherlands: Sijthoff & Noordhoff, 1980.

Smith, Herbert A., ed. *Great Britain and the Law of Nations*. Vol. 1. London: P. S. King & Son, 1932.

Stewart, John Hall, ed. *A Documentary Survey of the French Revolution*. New York: Macmillan, 1951.

Temperley, Harold and Lillian M. Penson, eds. *Foundations of British Foreign Policy: From Pitt (1792) to Salisbury (1902)*. New York: Barnes & Noble, 1966.

Therry, R., ed. *The Speeches of the Honourable George Canning with a Memoir of His Life*. Vol. 5. 3rd ed. London: James Ridgway and Sons, 1836.

Trifunovska, Snezana, ed. *Yugoslavia Through Documents: From Its Creation to Its Dissolution*. Dordrecht, the Netherlands: Martinus Nijhoff, 1994.

—— *Former Yugoslavia through Documents: From Its Dissolution to the Peace Settlement*. The Hague: Martinus Nijhoff, 1999.

Walker, Mack, ed. *Metternich's Europe*. New York: Walker and Company, 1968.

Webster, Charles K., ed. *Britain and the Independence of Latin America*. 2 Vols. London: Oxford University Press, 1938.

—— *British Diplomacy 1813–1815: Select Documents Dealing with the Reconstruction of Europe*. London: G. Bell and Sons, 1921.

Wellens, Karel, ed. *Resolutions and Statements of the United Nations Security Council (1946–1989): A Thematic Guide*. Dordrecht, the Netherlands: Martinus Nijhoff, 1990.

Wharton, Francis, ed. *A Digest of the International Law of the United States*. Vol. 1. Washington, DC: Government Printing Office, 1887.

—— *Revolutionary Diplomatic Correspondence of the United States*. 6 Vols. Washington, DC: Government Printing Office, 1889.

Wheeler-Bennett, John W. ed. *Documents on International Affairs 1932*. London: Oxford University Press, 1933.

Whiteman, Marjorie, ed. *Digest of International Law*. Vol. 2. Washington, DC: US Government Printing Office, 1963.

Books and articles

Alderson, Kai and Andrew Hurrell, eds. *Hedley Bull on International Society*. London: Macmillan Press, 2000.

Alexandrowicz, C.H. "The Theory of Recognition In Fieri." In *The British Year Book of International Law 1958*. London: Oxford University Press, 1959.

Almeida, João Marques de. "Challenging Realism by Returning to History: The British Committee's Contribution to IR 40 years On." *International Relations* 17 (2003): 273–302.

Alston, Philip. "Peoples' Rights: Their Rise and Fall." In Philip Alston, ed. *Peoples' Rights*. Oxford: Oxford University Press, 2001.

Ambrosius, Lloyd E. "Wilsonian Self-Determination." *Diplomatic History* 16 (1992): 141–8.

Anderson, Benedict. *Imagined Communities: Reflections on the Origins and Spread of Nationalism*. Revised ed. London: Verso, 1991.

Arend, Anthony Clark. *Legal Rules and International Society.* New York: Oxford University Press, 1999.

Armitage, David. *The Declaration of Independence: A Global History.* Cambridge, MA: Harvard University Press, 2007.

Armstrong, David. *Revolution and World Order: The Revolutionary State in International Society.* Oxford: Clarendon Press, 1993.

Bain, William. *Between Anarchy and Society: Trusteeship and the Obligations of Power.* Oxford: Oxford University Press, 2003.

Baker, III, James and Thomas DeFrank. *The Politics of Diplomacy: Revolution, War and Peace 1989–1992.* New York: G. P. Putnam's Sons, 1995.

Bartmann, Barry. "Political Realities and Legal Anomalies: Revisiting the Politics of International Recognition." In Tozun Bahceli, Barry Bartmann, and Henry Srebrnik, eds. *De Facto States: The Quest for Sovereignty.* London: Routledge, 2004.

Berlin, Isaiah. *The Sense of Reality: Studies in Ideas and Their History.* Ed. by Henry Hardy. London: Pimlico, 1996.

—— "Two Concepts of Liberty." In *Four Essays on Liberty.* Oxford: Oxford University Press, 1969.

Bernárdez, Santiago Torres. "The *Uti Possidetis Juris* Principle in Historical Perspective." In Konrad Ginther et al. *Völkerrecht zwischen Normativen Anspruch und Politischer Realität.* Berlin: Duncker & Humblot, 1994.

Betley, J. A. *Belgium and Poland in International Relations 1830–1831.* The Hague: Mouton & Co., 1960.

Betts, Richard K. "The Lesser Evil: The Best Way Out of the Balkans." *The National Interest* 64 (Summer 2001): 53–65.

Biersteker, Thomas J. and Cynthia Weber, eds. *State Sovereignty as Social Construct.* Cambridge: Cambridge University Press, 1996.

Blum, Yehuda Z. "Reflections on the Changing Concept of Self-Determination." *Israel Law Review,* 10 (1975): 509–14.

Bolkhovitinov, Nikolai N. *Russia and the American Revolution.* Transl. and ed. by C. Jay Smith. Tallhassee, FL: The Diplomatic Press, 1976.

Borchard, Edwin M. and Phoebe Morrison, "The Doctrine of Non-Recognition." In Quincy Wright, ed. *Legal Problems in the Far Eastern Conflict.* New York: Institute of Pacific Relations, 1941.

Both, Norbert. *From Indifference to Entrapment: The Netherlands and the Yugoslav Crisis, 1990–1995.* Amsterdam: Amsterdam University Press, 2000.

Briggs, Herbert W. "Non-Recognition of Title by Conquest and Limitations on the Doctrine." *American Society of International Law Proceedings,* 34 (1940): 72–82.

Brown, Philip Marshall. "The Recognition of Israel." *The American Journal of International Law,* 42 (1948): 620–7.

Brownlie, Ian. "Recognition in Theory and Practice." In R. Macdonald and Douglas Johnston, eds. *The Structure and Process of International Law: Essays in Legal Philosophy, Doctrine and Theory.* Dordrecht, the Netherlands: Martinus Nijhoff, 1983.

Bryant, Bunyan. "Recognition of Guinea (Bissau)." *Harvard Journal of International Law,* 15 (1974): 482–95.

Buchanan, Allen. "Democracy and Secession." In Margaret Moore, ed. *National Self-Determination and Secession.* Oxford: Oxford University Press, 1998.

Buchheit, Lee C. *Secession: The Legitimacy of Self-Determination.* New Haven, CT: Yale University Press, 1978.

Bull, Hedley. "International Theory: The Case for a Classical Approach." In Klaus Knorr and James N. Rosenau, eds. *Contending Approaches to International Politics*. Princeton, NJ: Princeton University Press, 1969.

—— *The Anarchical Society: A Study of Order in World Politics*. 2nd ed. New York: Columbia University Press, 1995.

—— "The European International Order." In Kai Alderson and Andrew Hurrell, eds. *Hedley Bull on International Society*. London: Macmillan Press, 2000.

—— "The State's Positive Role in World Affairs." In Kai Alderson and Andrew Hurrell, eds. *Hedley Bull on International Society*. London: Macmillan Press, 2000.

—— and Adam Watson, eds. *The Expansion of International Society*. Oxford: Clarendon Press, 1984.

Burg, Steven L. and Paul S. Shoup. *The War in Bosnia-Herzegovina: Ethnic Conflict and International Intervention*. Armonk, NY: M. E. Sharpe, 1999.

Bush, George and Brent Scowcroft. *A World Transformed*. New York: Vintage Books, 1998.

Byers, Michael, ed. *The Role of Law in International Politics: Essays in International Relations and International Law*. Oxford: Oxford University Press, 2000.

Canovan, Margaret. *The People*. Cambridge: Polity, 2005.

Caplan, Richard. "The European Community's Recognition of New States in Yugoslavia: The Strategic Implication." *The Journal of Strategic Studies*, 21 (1998): 24–45.

—— *Europe and the Recognition of New States in Yugoslavia*. Cambridge: Cambridge University Press, 2005.

Carr, E. H. "The Crisis of Self-Determination." In *Conditions of Peace*. New York: Macmillan, 1942.

Cassese, Antonio. *Self-Determination of Peoples: A Legal Reappraisal*. Cambridge: Cambridge University Press, 1995.

Chamberlain, M. E. *Decolonization: The Fall of the European Empires*. 2nd ed. Oxford: Blackwell, 1999.

Chandler, David. *Empire in Denial: The Politics of State-Building*. London: Pluto Press, 2006.

Christopher, Warren. *In the Stream of History: Shaping Foreign Policy for a New Era*. Stanford, CA: Stanford University Press, 1998.

Clark, Ian. *Legitimacy in International Society*. Oxford: Oxford University Press, 2005.

Cobban, Alfred. *The Nation-State and National Self-Determination*. Revised ed. London: Collins, 1969.

Craven, Matthew. "The European Community Arbitration Commission on Yugoslavia." In *The British Year Book of International Law 1995*. Oxford: Clarendon Press, 1996.

Crawford, Beverly. "Explaining Defection from International Cooperation: Germany's Unilateral Recognition of Croatia." *World Politics*, 48 (1996): 482–521.

Crawford, James. *Creation of States in International Law*. Oxford: Oxford Clarendon Press, 1979.

—— "State Practice and International Law in Relation to Secession." In *The British Year Book of International Law 1998*. Oxford: Clarendon Press, 1999.

—— "Israel (1948–1949) and Palestine (1998–1999): Two Studies in the Creation of States." In Guy S. Goodwin-Gill and Stefan Talmon, eds. *The Reality of International Law: Essays in Honour of Ian Brownlie*. Oxford: Clarendon Press, 1999.

—— "The Right of Self-Determination in International Law: Its Development and Future." In Philip Alston, ed. *Peoples' Rights*. Oxford: Oxford University Press, 2001.

—— *Creation of States in International Law*. 2nd ed. Oxford: Oxford Clarendon Press, 2006.

Crawford, Neta C. *Argument and Change in World Politics: Ethics, Decolonization, and Humanitarian Intervention.* Cambridge: Cambridge University Press, 2002.

Cuellar, Javier Perez de. *Pilgrimage for Peace: A Secretary-General's Memoir.* New York: St. Martin's Press, 1997.

Cutileiro, Jose. "Letter to the Editor." *The Economist,* December 9, 1995.

Dehousse, Renaud. "The International Practice of the European Communities: Current Survey." *European Journal of International Law,* 4 (1993): 141–56.

Doehring, Karl. "Self-Determination." In Bruno Simma, ed. *The Charter of the United Nations: A Commentary.* 2nd ed. Oxford: Oxford University Press, 2002.

Dugard, John. "Is the Case of Yugoslavia a Precedent for Africa?" *African Journal of International and Comparative Law,* 5 (1993): 163–75.

—— and David Raič. "The Role of Recognition in the Law and Practice of Secession." In Marcelo G. Kohen, ed. *Secession: International Law Perspectives.* Cambridge: Cambridge University Press, 2006.

Dull, Jonathan. *A Diplomatic History of the Revolution.* New Haven, CT: Yale University Press, 1985.

Dumbauld, Edward. "Independence under International Law." *American Journal of International Law,* 70 (1976): 425–31.

Eagleton, Clyde. "Self-Determination in the United Nations." *The American Journal of International Law,* 47 (1953): 88–93.

—— "Excesses of Self-Determination." *Foreign Affairs,* 31 (1953): 592–604.

Eastwood Jr., Lawrence S. "Secession: State Practice and International Law After the Dissolution of the Soviet Union and Yugoslavia." *Duke Journal of Contemporary and International Law,* 3 (1992): 299–349.

Echard, William E. "Louis Napoleon and the French Decision to Intervene At Rome in 1849: A New Appraisal." *Canadian Journal of History,* 9 (1974): 263–74.

Emerson, Rupert. "The New Higher Law of Anti-Colonialism." In Karl W. Deutsch and Stanley Hoffmann, eds. *The Relevance of International Law: Essays in Honor of Leo Gross.* Cambridge, MA: Schenkman Publishing, 1968.

—— "The Problem of Identity, Selfhood and Image in New Nations: The Situation in Africa." *Comparative Politics,* 1 (1969): 297–312.

—— "Self-Determination." *The American Journal of International Law,* 65 (1971): 459–75.

Etzioni, Amitai. "The Evils of Self-Determination." *Foreign Policy,* 89 (Winter 1993): 21–35.

Fabry, Mikulas. "International Norms of Territorial Integrity and the Balkan Wars of the 1990s." *Global Society,* 16 (2002): 145–74.

—— "Secession and State Recognition in International Relations and Law." In Aleksandar Pavkovic and Peter Radan, eds. *On the Way to Statehood: Secession and Globalization.* Aldershot, UK: Ashgate Publishers, 2008.

Fawn, Rick and James Mayall. "Recognition, Self-Determination and Secession in Post-Cold War International Society." In Rick Fawn and Jeremy Larkins, eds. *International Society After the Cold War: Anarchy and Order Reconsidered.* London: Macmillan Press, 1996.

Fidler, David P. and Jennifer M. Welsh, eds. *Empire and Community: Edmund Burke's Writings and Speeches on International Relations.* Boulder, CO: Westview Press, 1999.

Fishman, J. S. *Diplomacy and Revolution: The London Conference of 1830 and the Belgian Revolt.* Amsterdam: CHEV, 1988.

Frowein, Jochen A. "Transfer or Recognition of Sovereignty – Some Early Problems in Connection with Dependent Territories." *The American Journal of International Law,* 65 (1971): 568–71.

Genscher, Hans-Dietrich. *Building a House Divided: A Memoir by the Architect of Germany's Reunification.* Transl. by Thomas Thornton. New York: Broadway Books, 1998.

Ginther, Konrad. "Article 4." In Bruno Simma, ed. *The Charter of the United Nations: A Commentary.* 2nd ed. Oxford: Oxford University Press, 2002.

Glenny, Misha. *The Balkans 1804–1999: Nationalism, War and the Great Powers.* London: Granta Books, 1999.

Glitman, Maynard. "US Policy in Bosnia: Rethinking a Flawed Approach." *Survival* 38 (1997): 66–83.

Goebel, Julius. *The Recognition Policy of the United States.* New York: Longmans, Green & Co., 1915.

Gong, Gerrit W. *The Standard of "Civilization" and International Society.* Oxford: Clarendon Press, 1984.

Graham, Malbone W. *In Quest of a Law of Recognition.* Berkeley, CA: University of California Press, 1933.

—— *The Diplomatic Recognition of the Border States. Part I: Finland.* Berkeley, CA: University of California Press, 1935.

Grant, Thomas. *The Recognition of States: Law and Practice in Debate and Evolution.* Westport, CT: Praeger, 1999.

—— "Defining Statehood: The Montevideo Convention and its Discontents." *Columbia Journal of Transnational Law,* 37 (1999): 403–57.

Gray, Christine. "Self-Determination and the Break-up of the Soviet Union." In *Yearbook of European Law 1992.* Oxford: Clarendon Press, 1993.

Grewe, Wilhelm G. *The Epochs of International Law.* Transl. and rev. by Michael Byers. Berlin: Walter de Gruyter, 2000.

Griffiths, Martin. "Self-Determination, International Society and World Order." *Macquarie Law Journal,* 3 (2003): 29–49.

Grotius, Hugo. *The Rights of War and Peace.* Ed. by Richard Tuck. Indianapolis, IN: Liberty Fund, 2005.

Gvosdev, Nikolas K. "The Formulation of an American Response to Lithuanian Independence, 1990." *East European Quarterly,* 29 (1995): 17–41.

Hannum, Hurst. "Rethinking Self-Determination." *Virginia Journal of International Law,* 34 (1993*a*): 1–69.

—— "Self-Determination, Yugoslavia, and Europe: Old Wine in New Bottles?" *Transnational Law and Contemporary Problems,* 57 (1993*b*): 57–69.

—— *Autonomy, Sovereignty, and Self-Determination: The Accommodation of Conflicting Rights.* Rev. ed. Philadelphia: University of Pennsylvania Press, 1996.

—— "The Specter of Secession: Responding to Claims for Ethnic Self-Determination." *Foreign Affairs,* 77 (March/April 1998): 13–18.

Hayden, Robert M. "Reply." *Slavic Review,* 55 (1996): 767–78.

Heater, Derek. *National Self-Determination: Woodrow Wilson and His Legacy.* Basingstoke, UK: St. Martin's Press, 1994.

Hegel, Georg F. W. *Philosophy of Right.* Transl. by T. M. Knox. Oxford: Clarendon Press, 1952.

Heraclides, Alexis. "Secession, Self-Determination and Non-Intervention: In Quest of Normative Symbiosis." *Journal of International Affairs,* 45 (1992): 399–420.

Herbst, Jeffrey. *State Power in Africa: Comparative Lessons in Authority and Control.* Princeton, NJ: Princeton University Press, 2000.

Higgins, Rosalyn. "Self-Determination and Secession." In Julie Dahlitz, ed. *Secession and International Law.* The Hague: T. M. C. Asser Press, 2003.

Hillgruber, Christian. "The Admission of New States to the International Community." *European Journal of International Law*, 9 (1998): 491–509.

Hinsley, F. H. *Power and the Pursuit of Peace: Theory and Practice in the History of Relations Between States*. Cambridge: Cambridge University Press, 1963.

Hoffmann, Stanley and David Fidler, eds. *Rousseau on International Relations*. Oxford: Clarendon Press, 1991.

Holsti, K. J. "International Theory and War in the Third World." In Brian Job, ed. *The Insecurity Dilemma: National Security of Third World States*. Boulder, CO: Lynne Rienner Publishers, 1992.

—— *The State, War, and the State of War*. Cambridge: Cambridge University Press, 1996.

—— *Taming the Sovereigns: Institutional Change in International Politics*. Cambridge: Cambridge University Press, 2004.

Horowitz, Donald. "Self-Determination: Politics, Philosophy and Law." In Margaret Moore, ed. *National Self-Determination and Secession*. Oxford: Oxford University Press, 1998.

Hutson, James H. *John Adams and the Diplomacy of the American Revolution*. Lexington, KY: The University Press of Kentucky, 1980.

Ijalaye, David A. "Was 'Biafra' at Any Time a State in International Law?" *The American Journal of International Law*, 65 (1971): 551–9.

Jackson, Robert. "Negative Sovereignty in Sub-Saharan Africa." *Review of International Studies*, 12 (1986): 247–64.

—— "Quasi-States, Dual Regimes, and Neoclassical Theory: International Jurisprudence and the Third World." *International Organization*, 41 (1987): 519–49.

—— *Quasi-States: Sovereignty, International Relations and the Third World*. Cambridge: Cambridge University Press, 1990.

—— "Juridical Statehood in Sub-Saharan Africa." *Journal of International Affairs*, 46 (1992): 1–16.

—— "The Weight of Ideas in Decolonization: Normative Change in International Relations." In Judith Goldstein and Robert Keohane, eds. *Ideas and Foreign Policy: Beliefs, Institutions and Political Change*. Ithaca, NY: Cornell University Press, 1993.

—— "Boundaries and International Society." In B. A. Roberson, ed. *International Society and the Development of International Relations Theory*. London: Pinter, 1998.

—— *The Global Covenant: Human Conduct in the World of States*. Oxford: Oxford University Press, 2000.

—— *Sovereignty*. Cambridge: Polity, 2007.

Jackson, Robert and Carl Rosberg. "Why Africa's Weak States Persist: The Empirical and Juridical in Statehood." *World Politics*, 35 (1982): 1–24.

—— and Mark W. Zacher. *The Territorial Covenant: International Society and the Stabilization of Boundaries*. Working Paper No. 15. Vancouver, Canada: Institute of International Relations, 1997.

Jackson Preece, Jennifer. "Ethnocultural Diversity and Security After 9/11." In William Bain, ed. *The Empire of Security and the Safety of the People*. London: Routledge, 2006.

James, Alan. *Sovereign Statehood: Basis of International Society*. London: Allen & Unwin, 1986.

—— "Diplomatic Relations and Contacts." In *The British Year Book of International Law 1991*. Oxford: Clarendon Press, 1992.

—— "The Practice of Sovereign Statehood in Contemporary International Society." *Political Studies*, 47 (1999): 457–73.

—— "States and Sovereignty." In Trevor Salmon, ed. *Issues in International Relations.* London: Routledge, 2000.

Jefferson, Thomas. *Selected Writings.* Ed. by Harvey C. Mansfield. Wheeling, IL: Harlan Davidson, 1979.

Jelavich, Barbara. *A Century of Russian Foreign Policy, 1814–1914.* Philadelphia, PA: Lippincott, 1964.

—— "Diplomatic Problems of an Autonomous State: Romanian Decisions on War and Independence." *Southeastern Europe,* 5 (1978): 26–35.

Jennings, Sir Ivor. *The Approach to Self-Government.* Boston, MA: Beacon Press, 1956.

Jennings, Robert Y. "General Course on Principles of International Law." *Recueil des Cours: Collected Courses of The Hague Academy of International Law,* 121 (1967-II): 323–605.

Kamanu, Onyeonoro S. "Secession and the Right to Self-Determination: An OAU Dilemma." *The Journal of Modern African Studies,* 12 (1974): 355–76.

Kant, Immanuel. *Political Writings.* Ed. by Hans Reiss and transl. by H. B. Nisbet. 2nd enlarged ed. Cambridge: Cambridge University Press, 1991.

Kaufmann, Chaim. "Possible and Impossible Solutions to Ethnic Civil Wars." *International Security,* 20 (1996): 136–75.

—— "When All Else Fails: Separation as a Remedy for Ethnic Conflicts, Ethnic Partitions and Population Transfers in the Twentieth Century." *International Security,* 23 (1998): 120–56.

Kent, James. *Commentary on International Law.* Ed. by J. T. Abdy. 2nd ed. Cambridge: Deighton, Bell & Co., 1878.

Klabbers, Jan, Martti Koskenniemi, Olivier Ribbelink, and Andreas Zimmermann, eds. *State Practice Regarding State Succession and Issues of Recognition: The Pilot Project of the Council of Europe.* The Hague: Kluwer Law International, 1999.

Knaus, Gerald and Felix Martin. "Travails of the European Raj." *Journal of Democracy,* 14 (2003): 60–74.

Korman, Sharon. *The Right of Conquest: The Acquisition of Territory by Force in International Law and Practice.* Oxford: Clarendon Press, 1996.

Koskenniemi, Martti. "National Self-Determination Today: Problems of Legal Theory and Practice." *International and Comparative Law Quarterly,* 43 (1994): 242–69.

Krasner, Stephen. "Westphalia and All That." In Judith Goldstein and Robert Keohane, eds. *Ideas and Foreign Policy: Beliefs, Institutions and Political Change.* Ithaca, NY: Cornell University Press, 1993.

—— *Sovereignty: Organized Hypocrisy.* Princeton, NJ: Princeton University Press, 1999.

Kreijen, Gerard. *State Failure, Sovereignty and Effectiveness: Legal Lessons from the Decolonization of Sub-Saharan Africa.* Leiden, the Netherlands: Martinus Nijhoff, 2004.

Laffan, R. G. D. "The Liberation of the New Nationalities." In Temperley, H.W, ed. *A History of the Peace Conference of Paris.* Vol. 5. London: Henry Frowde and Hodder & Stoughton, 1921.

Lalonde, Suzanne. *Determining Boundaries in a Conflicted World: The Role of Uti Possidetis.* Montreal, Canada: McGill-Queen's University Press, 2002.

Langer, Robert. *Seizure of Territory: The Stimson Doctrine and Related Principles in Legal Theory and Diplomatic Practice.* Princeton, NJ: Princeton University Press, 1947.

Lansing, Robert. *The Peace Negotiation: A Personal Narrative.* Boston, MA: Houghton Mifflin Company, 1921.

Lapidoth, Ruth. *Autonomy: Flexible Solutions to Ethnic Conflict.* Washington, DC: US Institute of Peace Press, 1997.

Laponce, Jean. "National Self-Determination and Referendums: The Case for Territorial Revisionism." *Nationalism and Ethnic Politics*, 7 (2001): 33–56.

Lauterpacht, H. *Recognition in International Law*. Cambridge: Cambridge University Press, 1947.

Lederer, Ivo. *Yugoslavia at the Paris Peace Conference: A Study in Frontiermaking*. New Haven, CT: Yale University Press, 1963.

Legum, Colin. *Pan-Africanism: A Short Political Guide*. London: Pall Mall Press, 1962.

Libal, Michael. *Limits of Persuasion: Germany and the Yugoslav Crisis, 1991–1992*. Westport, CT: Praeger, 1997.

Linklater, Andrew and Hidemi Suganami. *The English School of International Relations: A Contemporary Reassessment*. Cambridge: Cambridge University Press, 2006.

Locke, John. *Two Treatises of Government*. Ed. by Peter Laslett. Cambridge: Cambridge University Press, 1988.

Louis, Wm. Roger. *Imperialism at Bay: The United States and the Decolonization of the British Empire, 1941–1945*. New York: Oxford University Press, 1978.

Lynch, Allen. "Woodrow Wilson and the Principle of 'National Self-Determination': A Reconsideration." *Review of International Studies*, 28 (2002): 419–36.

Lynch, Dov. *Engaging Eurasia's Separatist States: Unresolved Conflicts and De Facto States*. Washington, DC: United States Institute for Peace, 2004.

Lyon, Peter. "New States and International Order." In Alan James, ed. *The Bases of International Order: Essays in Honour of C. A. W. Manning*. London: Oxford University Press, 1973.

Macfie, A. L. *The Eastern Question 1774–1923*. Revised ed. London: Longman, 1996.

Machiavelli, Niccolo. *The Prince*. Transl. by Harvey C. Mansfield. 2nd ed. Chicago, IL: The University of Chicago Press, 1998.

Macmillan, Margaret. *Paris 1919: Six Months that Changed the World*. New York: Random House, 2002.

Mamatey, Victor S. *The United States and East Central Europe, 1914–1918*. Princeton, NJ: Princeton University Press, 1957.

Manchester, Alan K. "The Recognition of Brazilian Independence." *The Hispanic American Historical Review*, 31 (1951): 80–96.

Manela, Erez. *The Wilsonian Moment: Self-Determination and the International Origins of Anti-Colonial Nationalism*. New York: Oxford University Press, 2007.

Manning, C. A. W. "The Legal Framework in the World of Change." In Brian Porter, ed. *The Aberystwyth Papers: International Politics 1919–1969*. London: Oxford University Press, 1972.

Marinescu, Beatrice. "Great Britain and the Recognition of Romania's State Independence." *Revue Roumaine d'Histoire*, 15 (1976): 71–9.

Matthewson, Tim. "Jefferson and the Non-Recognition of Haiti." *Proceedings of the American Philosophical Society*, 140 (1996): 22–48.

Mayall, James. *Nationalism and International Society*. Cambridge: Cambridge University Press, 1990.

—— "The Limits of Progress: Normative Reasoning in the English School." In Cornelia Navari, ed. *Theorizing International Society: English School Methods*. Basingstoke, UK: Palgrave Macmillan, 2009.

McCorquodale, Robert. "Self-Determination Beyond the Colonial Context and Its Potential Impact on Africa." *African Journal of International and Comparative Law*, 4 (1992): 592–608.

McGoldrick, Dominic. "Yugoslavia – The Responses of the International Community and of International Law." In M. Freeman and R. Hanson, eds. *Current Legal Problems: Collected Papers*. Part 2. Oxford: Oxford University Press, 1996.

McMahon, Matthew M. *Conquest and Modern International Law: The Legal Limitations on the Acquisition of Territory by Conquest*. Washington, DC: Catholic University of America Press, 1940.

Medlicott, W. N. "The Recognition of Romanian Independence, 1878–1880." Parts I and II. *The Slavonic and East European Review*, 11 (1933): 354–72 and 572–89.

—— *The Congress of Berlin and After: A Diplomatic History of the Near Eastern Settlement 1878–1880*. Hamden, CT: Archon Books, 1963.

Mertus, Julie A. "Operation Allied Force: Handmaiden of Independent Kosovo." *International Affairs*, 85 (2009): 461–76.

Mesic, Stipe. *The Demise of Yugoslavia: A Political Memoir*. Budapest: Central European University Press, 2004.

Mill, John Stuart. "A Few Words on Non-Intervention." In Gertrude Himmelfarb, ed. *John Stuart Mill: Essays on Politics and Culture*. Garden City, NY: Doubleday and Company, 1962.

Miller, David. "Secession and the Principle of Nationality." In Margaret Moore, ed. *National Self-Determination and Secession*. Oxford: Oxford University Press, 1998.

Morris, Richard B. *The Peacemakers: The Great Powers and American Independence*. New York: Harper & Row, 1965.

Mosse, Werner. *The European Powers and the German Question, 1848–71*. Cambridge: Cambridge University Press, 1958.

Murphy, John F. "Self-Determination: United States Perspectives." In Yonah Alexander and Robert A. Friedlander, eds. *Self-Determination: National, Regional, and Global Dimensions*. Boulder, CO: Westview Press, 1980.

Musgrave, Thomas D. *Self-Determination and National Minorities*. Oxford: Clarendon Press, 1997.

Musson, Janice. "Britain and the Recognition of Bangladesh in 1972." *Diplomacy and Statecraft*, 19 (2008): 125–44.

Mutua, Makau Wa. "Why Redraw the Map of Africa: A Moral and Legal Inquiry." *Michigan Journal of International Law*, 16 (1994–5): 1113–76.

Myers, Denys. "Contemporary Practice of the United States Relating to International Law." *The American Journal of International Law*, 55 (1961): 697–733.

Nagengast, Emil. "German and U.S. Intervention Against Yugoslav Sovereignty." In Andrew Valls, ed. *Ethics in International Affairs*. Lanham, MD: Rowman and Littlefield, 2000.

Nanda, Ved P. "Self-Determination outside the Colonial Context: The Birth of Bangladesh in Retrospect." In Yonah Alexander and Robert A. Friedlander, eds. *Self-Determination: National, Regional, and Global Dimensions*. Boulder, CO: Westview Press, 1980.

Nardin, Terry. "International Ethics and International Law." *Review of International Studies*, 18 (1992): 19–30.

Nixon, Charles R. "Self-Determination: The Nigeria/Biafra Case." *World Politics*, 24 (1972): 473–97.

Nordholt, Jan. *The Dutch Republic and American Independence*. Transl. by Herbert H. Rowen. Chapel Hill, NC: The University of North Carolina Press, 1982.

O'Brien, William V. and Ulf H. Goebel. "United States Recognition Policy Toward the New Nations." In William V. O'Brien, ed. *The New Nations in International Law and Diplomacy*. New York: Frederick A. Prager, 1965.

Oppenheim, Lassa. *International Law.* Vol. 1. 2nd ed. New York: Longmans, 1912.

Osiander, Andreas. "Sovereignty, International Relations, and the Westphalian Myth." *International Organization,* 55 (2001): 251–87.

Østerud, Oyvind. "The Narrow Gate: Entry to the Club of Sovereign States." *Review of International Studies,* 23 (1997): 167–84.

Owen, David. *Balkan Odyssey.* Updated ed. San Diego, CA: Harcourt Brace and Company, 1997.

Pattison, W. Keith. "The Delayed British Recognition of Israel." *The Middle East Journal,* 37 (1983): 412–28.

Pegg, Scott. *International Society and the De Facto State.* Aldershot, UK: Ashgate, 1998.

Perkins, Dexter. *A History of the Monroe Doctrine.* Boston, MA: Little, Brown and Company, 1955.

Peterson, M. J. *Recognition of Governments: Legal Doctrine and State Practice, 1815–1995.* New York: St. Martin's Press, 1997.

Philpott, Daniel. *Revolutions in Sovereignty: How Ideas Shaped Modern International Relations.* Princeton, NJ: Princeton University Press, 2001.

Pomerance, Michla. "The United States and Self-Determination: Perspectives on the Wilsonian Conception." *American Journal of International Law,* 70 (1977): 1–27.

—— *Self-Determination in Law and Practice: The New Doctrine in the United Nations.* The Hague: Martinus Nijhoff, 1982.

—— "The Badinter Commission: The Use and Misuse of the International Court of Justice's Jurisprudence." *Michigan Journal of International Law,* 20 (1998): 31–58.

Pufendorf, Samuel. *De Jure Naturae et Gentium Libri Octo.* Vol. 2. Transl. by C. H. and W. A. Oldfather. Oxford: Clarendon Press, 1934.

Quinn, David. "Self-Determination Movements and Their Outcomes." In Hewitt, J. Joseph, Jonathan Wilkenfeld, and Ted Robert Gurr, eds. *Peace and Conflict 2008.* Boulder, CO: Paradigm Publishers, 2008.

Radan, Peter. "The Badinter Arbitration Commission and the Partition of Yugoslavia." *Nationalities Papers,* 25 (1997): 537–57.

—— *The Break-up of Yugoslavia and International Law.* London: Routledge, 2002.

Raič, David. *Statehood and the Law of Self-Determination.* The Hague: Kluwer Law International, 2002.

Ratner, Steven. "Drawing a Better Line: *Uti Possidetis* and the Borders of New States." In Robert J. Beck and Thomas Ambrosio, eds. *International Law and the Challenge of Ethnic Groups: The State System and the Challenge of Ethnic Groups.* New York: Chatham House, 2002.

Reus-Smit, Christian, ed. *The Politics of International Law.* Cambridge: Cambridge University Press, 2004.

Rich, Roland. "Recognition of States: The Collapse of Yugoslavia and the Soviet Union." *European Journal of International Law,* 4 (1993): 36–65.

Roberts, Adam. "Communal Conflict as a Challenge to International Organization: The Case of the Former Yugoslavia." In Olara A. Otunu and Michael W. Doyle, eds. *Peacemaking and Peacekeeping for the New Century.* Lanham, MD: Rowman & Littlefield, 1998.

—— "Beyond the Flawed Principle of National Self-Determination." In Edward Mortimer, ed. *People, Nation and State: The Meaning of Ethnicity and Nationalism.* London: I. B. Tauris, 1999.

Roberts, Geoffrey. "History, Theory and the Narrative Turn in IR." *Review of International Studies,* 32 (2006): 703–14.

Robertson, William S. "South America and the Monroe Doctrine, 1824–1828." *Political Science Quarterly*, 30 (1915): 82–105.

—— "The Recognition of the Spanish Colonies by the Motherland." *The Hispanic American Historical Review*, 1 (1918): 70–91.

—— "The Recognition of the Hispanic American Nations by the United States." *The Hispanic American Historical Review*, 1 (1918): 239–69.

—— "Metternich's Attitude Toward Revolutions in Latin America." *The Hispanic American Historical Review*, 21 (1941): 538–58.

—— *France and Latin American Independence.* New York: Octagon Books, 1967.

Rodriguez, Jaime E. *The Independence of Spanish America.* Cambridge: Cambridge University Press, 1998.

Roth, Brad R. *Governmental Legitimacy in International Law.* Oxford: Oxford University Press, 1999.

Russell, Greg. "John Quincy Adams and the Ethics of America's National Interest." *Review of International Studies*, 19 (1993): 23–38.

Russell, John Earl. *Recollections and Suggestions, 1813–1873.* Boston, MA: Roberts Brothers, 1875.

Ryan, David. "By Way of Introduction: The United States, Decolonization and the World System." In David Ryan and Victor Pungong, eds. *The United States and Decolonization.* Basingstoke, UK: Macmillan, 2000.

Saideman, Stephen M. "Is Pandora's Box Half Empty or Hall Full? The Limited Virulence of Secessionism and the Domestic Sources of Disintegration." In David A. Lake and Donald Rothchild, eds. *The International Spread of Ethnic Conflict: Fear, Diffusion, and Escalation.* Princeton, NJ: Princeton University Press, 1998.

Schroeder, Gertrude E. "On the Economic Viability of New Nation States." *Journal of International Affairs*, 45 (1992): 549–74.

Schroeder, Paul W. "Austria as an Obstacle to Italian Unification and Freedom, 1814–1861." *Austrian History Newsletter*, 3 (1962): 1–32.

Scott, H. M. *British Foreign Policy in the Age of the American Revolution.* Oxford: Clarendon Press, 1990.

Scowcroft, Brent. "Bush Got It Right in the Soviet Union." *The New York Times.* August 18, 1991.

Seton-Watson, Richard. *Disraeli, Gladstone and the Eastern Question.* London: Frank Cass, 1971.

Shaw, Malcolm. *Title to Territory in Africa: International Legal Issues.* Oxford: Clarendon Press, 1986.

—— "The Heritage of States: The Principle of *Uti Possidetis Juris* Today." In *The British Year Book of International Law 1996.* Oxford: Clarendon Press, 1997.

Shehadi, Kamal S. *Ethnic Self-Determination and the Break-up of States.* Adelphi Paper No. 283. London: The International Institute for Strategic Studies, 1993.

Silber, Laura and Alan Little. *The Death of Yugoslavia.* Revised ed. London: Penguin, 1996.

Simpson, Gerry J. "The Diffusion of Sovereignty: Self-Determination in the Post-Colonial Age." *Stanford Journal of International Law*, 26 (1993): 255–86.

Sioussiouras, Petros. "The Process of Recognition of the Newly Independent States of Former Yugoslavia by the European Community: The Case of the Former Socialist Republic of Macedonia." *The Journal of Political and Military Sociology*, 32 (2004): 1–18.

Slaughter, Anne-Marie, Andrew S. Tulumello, and Stepan Wood. "International Law and International Relations Theory: A New Generation of Interdisciplinary Scholarship." *The American Journal of International Law*, 92 (1998): 367–97.

Sofer, Sasson. "The Prominence of Historical Demarcations: Westphalia and the New World Order." *Diplomacy & Statecraft*, 20 (2009): 1–19.

Stadler, K. R. "The Disintegration of the Austro-Hungarian Empire." *Journal of Contemporary History*, 3 (1968): 177–90.

Steinberg, James. "International Involvement in the Yugoslav Conflict." In Lori Damrosch, ed. *Enforcing Restraint: Collective Intervention in Internal Conflicts*. New York: Council on Foreign Relations, 1993.

Stivachtis, Yannis. *The Enlargement of International Society: Culture Versus Anarchy and Greece's Entry into International Society*. Basingstoke, UK: Macmillan, 1998.

Suzuki, Eisuke. "Self-Determination and World Public Order: Community Response to Territorial Separation." *Virginia Journal of International Law*, 16 (1976): 779–862.

Szasz, Paul. "Discussion on the Fragmentation of Yugoslavia." *American Society of International Law Proceedings*, 88 (1994): 46–8.

Talbott, Strobe. "Self-Determination in an Interdependent World." *Foreign Policy*, 118 (Spring 2000): 152–62.

Temperley, H.W., ed. *A History of the Peace Conference of Paris*. 6 Vols. London: Henry Frowde and Hodder & Stoughton, 1921.

—— "Recognition of New States." In Temperley, H. W., ed. *A History of the Peace Conference of Paris*. Vol. 5. London: Henry Frowde and Hodder & Stoughton, 1921.

Terrett, Steve. *The Dissolution of Yugoslavia and the Badinter Arbitration Commission*. Aldershot, UK: Ashgate, 2000.

Teschke, Benno. *The Myth of 1648: Class, Geopolitics, and the Making of Modern International Relations*. London: Verso, 2003.

Thumann, Michael. "Between Ambition and Paralysis – Germany's Policy Toward Yugoslavia 1991–3." *Nationalities Papers*, 25 (1997): 575–85.

Tomuschat, Christian, ed. *Modern Law of Self-Determination*. Dordrecht, the Netherlands: Martinus Nijhoff, 1993.

Toynbee, Arnold J. "Self-Determination." *The Quarterly Review*, 243 (1925): 317–38.

Tsagourias, Nicholas. "International Community, Recognition of States, and Political Cloning." In Colin Warbrick and Stephen Tierney, eds. *Towards an "International Legal Community?"* London: British Institute of International and Comparative Law, 2006.

Tucker Robert W. and David C. Hendrickson. "America and Bosnia." *The National Interest*, 33 (Fall 1993): 14–27.

Vattel, Emmerich de. *The Law of Nations or The Principles of Natural Law: Applied to the Conduct and to the Affairs of Nations and of Sovereigns*. Transl. by Charles G. Fenwick. Washington, DC: The Carnegie Institution, 1916.

Vincent, R. J. *Human Rights and International Relations*. Cambridge: Cambridge University Press, 1986.

Wæver, Ole. "International Society – Theoretical Promises Unfulfilled?" *Cooperation and Conflict*, 27 (1992): 97–128.

Walker, Edward W. *Dissolution: Sovereignty and the Breakup of the Soviet Union*. Lanham, MD: Rowman & Littlefield, 2003.

Walzer, Michael. *Just and Unjust Wars*. 4th ed. New York: Basic Books, 2006.

Warbrick, Colin "States and Recognition in International Law." In Malcolm D. Evans, ed. *International Law*. 2nd ed. Oxford: Oxford University Press, 2006.

Watson, Adam. "New States in the Americas." In Hedley Bull and Adam Watson, eds. *The Expansion of International Society*. Oxford: Clarendon Press, 1984.

—— *The Limits of Independence: Relations Between States in the Modern World*. London: Routledge, 1997.

Webster, Charles K. *The Foreign Policy of Castlereagh, 1815–1822: Britain and the European Alliance*. London: G. Bell and Sons, 1925.

—— *The Congress of Vienna, 1814–1815*. New York: Barnes & Noble, 1969.

Weintraub, Stanley. *Disraeli: A Biography*. New York: Truman Talley Books/Dutton, 1993.

Weller, Marc. "International Law and Chaos." *Cambridge Law Journal*, 52 (1993): 6–9.

—— "The Rambouillet Conference on Kosovo." *International Affairs*, 75 (1999): 211–51.

—— "The Self-Determination Trap." *Ethnopolitics*, 4 (2005): 3–28.

—— "Kosovo's Final Status." *International Affairs*, 84 (2008): 1223–43.

Wendt, Alexander. *Social Theory of International Politics*. Cambridge: Cambridge University Press, 1999.

Wesley, Charles H. "The Struggle for the Recognition of Haiti and Liberia as Independent Republics." *The Journal of Negro History*, 2 (1917): 369–83.

Wheaton, Henry. *History of the Law of Nations in Europe and America from the Earliest Times to the Treaty of Washington, 1842*. New York: Gould, Banks & Co., 1845.

Wheeler, Nicholas J. *Saving Strangers: Humanitarian Intervention and International Society*. Oxford: Oxford University Press, 2000.

Whelan, Anthony. "Wilsonian Self-Determination and the Versailles Settlement." *The International and Comparative Law Quarterly*, 43 (1994): 99–115.

Whitaker, Arthur P. *The United States and the Independence of Latin America, 1800–1830*. Baltimore, MD: The John Hopkins Press, 1941.

Wight, Martin. "International Legitimacy." *International Relations*, 4 (1972): 1–28.

—— *Systems of States*. Ed. by Hedley Bull. Leicester: Leicester University Press, 1977.

Wilson, Heather A. *International Law and the Use of Force by National Liberation Movements*. Oxford: Clarendon Press, 1988.

Woodward, Susan L. *Balkan Tragedy: Chaos and Dissolution After the Cold War*. Washington, DC: Brookings Institution, 1995.

—— "Bosnia and Herzegovina: How Not to End Civil War." In Barbara F. Walter and Jack Snyder, eds. *Civil War, Insecurity and Intervention*. New York: Columbia University Press, 1999.

Wright, Quincy. "The Legal Background in the Far East." In Quincy Wright, ed. *Legal Problems in the Far Eastern Conflict*. New York: Institute of Pacific Relations, 1941.

—— "Recognition and Self-Determination." *American Society of International Law Proceedings*, 48 (1954): 23–37.

Zacher, Mark W. "The Territorial Integrity Norm: International Boundaries and the Use of Force." *International Organization*, 55 (2001): 215–50.

Zhang, Yongjin. "China's Entry into International Society." *Review of International Studies*, 17 (1991): 3–16.

Zimmermann, Warren. *Origins of a Catastrophe: Yugoslavia and Its Destroyers*. New York: Times Books, 1996.

Index